THE ABINGDON
PREACHING
ANNUAL
2000

THE ABINGDON PREACHING ANNUAL 2000

ABINGDON PRESS
Nashville

CONTENTS

CONTENTS

CONTENTS

Empowered by the Spirit (1 John 5:1-6)
Dance Within the Heart (John 15:9-17)

JUNE

JULY

CONTENTS

DECEMBER

THE ABINGDON
PREACHING
ANNUAL
2000

INTRODUCTION

I was privileged to have Fred Craddock, acclaimed preacher and New Testament scholar, as my faculty adviser at the Candler School of Theology. In a conversation about preaching and creativity, he shared his frustration with the notion that "talent" is needed above all other ingredients for a powerful sermon. With a hand waving in the air, punctuating every word, Craddock declared that hard work and perseverance, *not* talent, are the most critical characteristics of any preacher. Let's not forget that this assertion comes from the person named as one of the five best preachers of our day.

For me, and maybe for you too, Fred Craddock's perspective is hopeful. As preachers, we have been called by Christ Jesus to proclaim God's Word, a task that seems somewhat daunting, wouldn't you agree? If I thought that my talent was the vital linchpin of homiletics, I would never step into a pulpit. On the other hand, if God wants my sweat and calluses, I am ready to announce with Isaiah, "Here am I; send me."

Every sermon, good or bad, occurs at the meeting place of three factors: the sacred Scriptures, the preacher's life story, and the congregation (as a body and as individuals). To find this meeting place and to preach with integrity, we must bring our hard work every week to a fresh exploration of all these factors. And *The Abingdon Preaching Annual* is a tool to aid in transforming your sweat into the proclamation of the Lord.

We have recruited some of the church's finest preachers to reflect on the scriptures offered to us by the *Revised Common Lectionary*, a three-year cycle encompassing the bulk of our holy book. Their work cannot replace your work, but it can provide fresh insights to help shape a sermon in progress. Likewise, some will find their exegesis useful in breaking through "preacher's block," that widely shared desert experience of not knowing even where to begin. In addition to a weekly examination of Scripture, the *Annual* provides a worship theme and pastoral prayer gleaned from these same biblical texts, and a "Call to Worship" taken from the lectionary psalm.

The Scriptures initiate the question, What am *I* supposed to preach to *them*? But careful exegesis is only one component of preaching. We also must heighten our wisdom about the "I" and "them" of our sermons. Only in prayer, meditation, devotional study, and the other spiritual disciplines can we come to know the "I." Our lives as pastors are frantic. We wear many hats. Too often an awareness of our own story, our own spiritual condition, is diminished, even lost all together.

This book cannot serve as your singular resource for personal spiritual growth, but we have included a monthly devotional designed specifically for preachers. For all of us who must haul our souls into a pulpit every week and presume to articulate the very mind of God, Donna Schaper brings great refreshment. Schaper, a well-known writer, spiritual guide, and preacher, offers genuine guidance for us pastors because she travels our same path.

The last factor to consider in this holy enterprise of preaching is our congregations. As pastors, we are invited to share the most intense moments of human existence. We can know the dreams and nightmares, the hope and despair, and the faith and doubt of our congregations, if we have the time. *The Abingdon Preaching Annual* cannot create more time, but it can provide you with the time and energy to be the pastor who God has called you to be.

May your eyes be opened to the Christ who goes with you to the pulpit and beyond. And may you know his peace.

Thomas Gildermeister

SERMONS FOR SPECIAL DAYS

THE GOD WHO IS ABOUT TO CREATE

ISAIAH 65:17-25

This is a surprising text, isn't it? We thought God had already finished the creation. We read about it in the book of Genesis—how God made a world out of the void that was there, and separated the seas from the land, and set the sun to rule the heavens by day, and the moon by night, and fashioned the animals and birds and fishes, and in a flourishing finale shaped a man from the dust and a woman from his rib, and then rested from all the exertion. As one little boy blurted out to his Sunday school teacher, "My daddy says he is just like God after God made the world—he has been tired ever since he made me!"

And then this text comes along and says God is about to create new heavens and a new earth—as if God hadn't retired from creating after all but is still very much in the business! This is a very important piece of information to have as we enter a new century and a new millennium, isn't it? It means that everything is still in the workshop. The world and the universe are still being shaped. God is still actively involved in what is happening in history. God still cares about how everything turns out. And God will not abandon us before all God's promises for a kinder, juster, gentler world have been fulfilled, before there are "new heavens and a new earth."

William L. Renfro, founder of the National Millennium Foundation, said in an article in *The Futurist* magazine: "Consider all we have accomplished during this millennium: We established governments based on the consent of the governed. We discovered science, developed medicine, and then created the universities. We proved the earth was round, and discovered new worlds beyond our horizons. We split the atom and tapped the power of stars. We mastered flight, moved toward the stars, and reached the edge of time and the universe with our minds" (William L. Renfro, "A World Future Celebration," *The Futurist*, vol. 29, March-April 1995, p. 28).

The last century alone has been a whirlwind of creativity and discovery. In a special edition, *Newsweek* devoted article after article to the explosion of discoveries that changed forever the way we human beings live our lives on earth (*Newsweek Extra*, Winter 1997-1998). The first airplane flight was in 1903; blood transfusions began in 1905; the modern assembly line appeared in 1913; the zipper in 1914; the electric mixer in 1918; frozen foods in 1924; talking movies in 1926; Scotch tape in 1930; color television in 1940; nuclear fission in 1945; the credit card in 1950; and heart transplants in 1967. We put astronauts on the moon in 1969, produced the personal computer in 1975, and developed fiber-optic communications in 1977. We had the World Wide Web in 1990, the Pentium processor in 1993, and the cloning of an adult mammal in 1997.

Many of us have lived through an extravaganza of inventions and discoveries. It is as if the world were a gigantic science fair and important new developments were popping up around us all the time. But William L. Renfro concludes the list of our great achievements of the last thousand years by asking, "If this past be prologue, what dreams can the Third Millennium hold?" ("A World Future Celebration," *The Futurist*). What dreams indeed await realization in the century ahead, not to mention an entire millennium?

I don't know how you feel about it, but it appears to me that God is already very much at work creating a new heaven and a new earth. It is occurring all around us all the time. Unfortunately, we don't always give God credit for it. In fact, quite the opposite usually occurs. The more we discover, the more we congratulate ourselves for being clever and ingenious, and the less we think about God. Philosophers of science say this is a natural tendency. We have always conceived of God as presiding over the great mysteries of existence, and whenever we have discovered how things work, we have removed them from God's territorial supervision and placed them under our own. Thus thunder and lightning once compelled people to bow down in terror before the Almighty, and now that we understand what produces thunder and lightning, we merely avoid standing under a tree during a storm. So God is left being a mere "God of the gaps," as Michael Polanyi expressed it, and the gap is constantly being reduced as we learn more about the universe.

The truth is, we don't really make or create anything on our own. All we do, for all our knowledge and inventiveness, is discover what God has already created and is continuing to create. What were the initials Johann Sebastian Bach inscribed in the corner of his manuscripts when he had just completed another masterpiece? S. D. G.—for *Soli deo gloria*, "To God alone be the glory!" Bach understood. We are not the makers or creators of anything. We, like little children at an Easter-egg hunt, only discover the surprises God has enfolded in the universe. God is the Creator, the only real creator, of everything that is, and our cleverest scientists are only adept at unraveling the clues to divine mysteries.

Entering a new millennium, we are like climbers who can stand at the brow of the mountain and gaze in two directions— back to the way the human race has come in the last few thousand years, and forward to the way it will be going. It is a wonderful opportunity to embrace a new spirituality for the new age, to bow down before the God who makes everything and to confess our great amazement. If we don't, then we enter the new era with blindness and arrogance, claiming for humanity the glory that really belongs to the Creator.

But let's go back to our text for a minute and remember what Isaiah's representation of the voice of God was saying about the new creation. The crux of God's creative attention, the real center of the divine interest, is not finally in what we know as the wonders of nature, which are constantly being discovered and harnessed for our physical welfare. It is in people. It is in human beings. It is in us. "Jerusalem as a joy, and its people as a delight" (v. 18).

Does this suggest that we, not the world around us, not all of the marvels and intricacies of nature, are God's greatest challenge as a creator? We do appear to have given God the most trouble, haven't we? We are the ones who claim the territories that really belong to the Creator and fight over them, aren't we? We are the ones who despoil the earth, paving its surface and polluting its air and streams and soil in the vanity that we are somehow enriched by doing so. We are the ones who choose up sides and threaten to destroy everything on the basis of skin pigmentation and religious beliefs and cultural traditions. We are the ones who think our inventions are really ours and bravely posture as if we would take the place of God.

God's promise in Isaiah is that God is not only working on the world, but God is also working on us, so that the people inhabiting the world will be different. God says there won't be any sound of weeping in the new Jerusalem, and there won't be any children born to live only a few days. People will live to be more than a century in age, and their houses and lands won't be overrun by others. They will enjoy the work of their hands and take pleasure in their families. They will perceive God's answers even before they call upon the divine. The wolf and the lamb and the lion and the ox will feed together in peace. Only the serpent, the symbol of evil and wickedness in the world, will find life difficult, feeding upon the dust of the earth. "They shall not hurt or destroy on all my holy mountain, says the LORD" (v. 25).

Ah, you say, all of that language is very nice, but isn't it about the heavenly Jerusalem, the one described in the book of Revelation as the final resting place of the saints? It isn't really about life on this earth. Isn't it? That isn't made clear in the book of Isaiah. In Isaiah, God is speaking as if the promise will be a reality in this world, as if all of these wonderful things will come to pass here and not in some existence yet to come.

Is it beyond all dreaming? We've spoken of the wonderful inventions and discoveries that have been made in the physical world of the last millennium. But what of all the discoveries in the personal or spiritual worlds? Think of the great insights of the mystics in the Middle Ages. Think of the humanists and reformers, and the birth of the university system. Think of the origin of hospitals and psychiatric wards and rehabilitation centers, of charitable organizations and Alcoholics Anonymous, and other helping groups too numerous to mention. Think of the League of Nations and the United Nations and the growing efforts to bring peace and prosperity to the entire world. Think of great personality models such as Francis of Assisi and Clara Barton and Gandhi and Schweitzer and Mother Teresa, and of the power of television to broadcast their lives and messages into homes around the world. Think of the great hunger we have seen in recent years for a new spirituality, one that transcends not only materialism and escapism but also former religious and ideological boundaries as well.

Evil is deeply entrenched in the world, and often expresses itself in terrible ways. In this century alone we have witnessed devastating world wars, the great Holocaust of the Jews, and shocking forms of terrorism. But that shouldn't blind us to the great strides in humanitarianism that have been achieved, and to the democratization of the great ideals of love and acceptance and generosity deriving from our religious heritage. The world may be getting worse and worse, as the power to do wicked things is increased, but it may also be getting better and better, through the love and good will and commitment of those who truly care about the rule of God in human affairs.

We don't know what another millennium will bring in the development of science and technology—surely marvels beyond our imagining. Nor can we begin to predict what it will mean in terms of the developing psyche and spirit of humankind—perhaps advances in personal understanding and world government that will make the text in Isaiah seem entirely realizable here on earth.

But whatever it brings, we know it can only enhance our sense of appreciation for the enormous might and intelligence of our Creator. And we know we would all do well to live through the coming years with the letters *S. D. G.* engraved on our foreheads, reminding us every day that we live, *Soli deo gloria*—"To God alone be the glory!" (John Killinger)

JESUS CHRIST: THE SAME YESTERDAY, TODAY, AND FOREVER?

HEBREWS 13:7-17

It actually happened in church, during the children's sermon. The minister was young and confident. "Now children," he exclaimed with enthusiasm, "we're going to do something a little different today. I want five of you to line up here, and I'm going to show you something." He whispered into the ear of the first child, then said aloud, "Now whisper the same thing into the ear of the person next to you." He had each child whisper to the next, passing along the message.

"Now," he declared, "I'm going to show the congregation what I whispered to the first one of you." He held a poster aloft bearing the message: "Jimmy kissed Brenda under the willow tree." "What I want to teach you today," he continued, "is the way gossip gets distorted as we pass it from one person to another. Then we'll talk about telling the gospel to others, and how important it is to do that instead of gossiping."

"Billy," he said to the fifth child in line, "I want you to tell us what this young lady next to you whispered in your ear." Billy looked frightened and stupefied.

"That's okay, Billy," the minister said in a loud voice, "I was a little scared the first time I spoke in public, too. I'm going to ask your friend to tell you again, and this time you remember it and repeat it for the rest of us, okay? And we'll see how gossip gets twisted around when it is passed from person to person."

The little girl next to him leaned over and whispered into his ear again. Billy looked at the minister and, in a voice clearly audible throughout the sanctuary, repeated the message exactly as it was printed on the poster.

I actually felt sorry for the young minister. He had been too confident of how his little experiment would turn out. Although he was flushed and embarrassed, he didn't let that stop him from drawing the conclusion he had planned from the beginning. "All right," he said, "gossip usually gets all changed as it is passed

24

from one person to another, although you are an extremely clever group of children. What I want you to remember is that we ought never to gossip. Instead, as Christians, we should tell people the gospel. Can you remember that? Don't gossip, but tell the gospel."

I don't know if anyone else in the sanctuary was thinking what I was thinking, but to me that innocent and ill-fated little exchange with the children raised a far more profound question than the young minister had intended to raise. That was, What about the gospel itself and how it has become distorted as it has been told and retold through the ages? If gossip gets distorted, doesn't the gospel get distorted, too?

Surely it does. Otherwise there wouldn't be so many kinds of Christianity around today, each insisting on its particular view of faith. There are, for example, the sacramentalists and the conversionists. Sacramentalists believe that God is mediated to us in many forms and that we must remain open to these various ways, which range from receiving the bread and cup in church to seeing God in art and nature and everywhere else. Conversionists, on the other hand, insist that the Christian community has been given specific instructions about what we must do to be saved and that we must follow these to the letter or be lost.

What is the truth? How much of what we hear about the gospel is a distortion passed down through the ages? Leslie Weatherhead wrote in *The Christian Agnostic* (Nashville: Abingdon Press, 1990) that what has happened to the Christian message reminds him of a legend about a shepherd's pipe that was supposed once to have belonged to Moses, the great Hebrew leader. Sometime after Moses' death, it was decided that the pipe was altogether too plain and unattractive to have been Moses', and so it was embellished with gold. A few centuries later, some enthusiastic Jews decided to make it even more attractive, and overlaid the gold with further "improvements" in gold and silver. Thus the pipe became extremely handsome and impressive, but it had lost its wonderfully pure and simple musical note and could no longer be played.

We're nearly ready to enter a new millennium of the earth's history. How many distorted understandings of the gospel will we carry along with us when we do? I don't know about you, but I'd like to move into the new millennium clean. I'd like to leave behind as many superstitions and distortions as I can, and not have them cluttering my mental and moral landscape.

Jesus, according to Scripture, is always the same. He was the same yesterday, he is the same today, and he will be the same tomorrow. Jesus doesn't change. Or does he?

Maybe it is the same with Jesus as with Moses' pipe, and the gospel. Who is he really? We tend to see him from different angles, depending on our own backgrounds and experiences. What does the Bible mean when it says he is "the same yesterday and today and forever"?

To understand what the writer of the letter to the Hebrews was saying, it is important to survey the letter itself. Otherwise we will merely read into the phrase whatever we want to, depending on our individual experiences. The overall thrust of the book of Hebrews is that it is an appeal to Jewish Christians not to desert their new faith because of persecution or difficulty. Jesus, it says, is both the perfect sacrifice for our sins and the true high priest. Had the author been addressing a non-Jewish group, he might have chosen a different emphasis. But he knew that Jews would understand the allusions to the sacrificial system in the Jewish faith, and to the importance of the high priest in that system. And then, having painted this portrait of Jesus as both sacrifice and priest, the author talks a great deal about the urgency of having faith, of trusting the things that can't be seen and verified at this point, and gives a list of examples of those who took God's promises on faith. The list includes almost everyone of significance in the history of the Jewish faith.

This, then, is the context for understanding what the writer meant by "Jesus Christ is the same yesterday and today and forever" (v. 8). What can anyone do to us? asks the writer. "Remember your leaders"—those who led you into the Christian understanding. "Consider the outcome of their way of life" (v. 7). That is, couldn't you bear whatever happened to them? Were they cowardly in the face of persecution and discomfort? "Imitate their faith." Behave as they did.

Then comes the statement, "Jesus Christ is the same yesterday and today and forever." He was not one Christ to them and another to you. If he was important enough to demand their loyalty, to call them out of their old faith into the new one, then he is important enough to demand yours as well. He does not alter from one year to the next. He will always be the Christ who commands our devotion and faithfulness.

Ah, that's a little different, isn't it? It doesn't mean that Christ doesn't change in the eyes of those who perceive him from generation to generation. It simply means that he is big enough and important enough—he is the same Christ who commanded the original apostles to risk their lives in the propagation of the faith—to be the Lord of your faith as well, in whatever time you live.

You say, that doesn't really solve any problems about the nature of Jesus, does it? You're right, it doesn't. It isn't a theological commentary on the nature of Christ's person, whether he was an exemplary leader or "very God of very God," as those who hold to a high Christology like to say. It doesn't tell us whether we ought to handle snakes or speak in tongues. It simply says, "Christ is our leader, as he has always been, and he is worth following—even worth dying for, if it comes to that. So don't give up on the faith."

But maybe that is a message we need to hear as we enter the new millennium. Maybe we need to be reminded that Jesus is still the One through whom God has been revealed to us, and that therefore we should be following him, whatever our theological and moral understandings of him. Maybe it even means that we Christians ought to be more accepting and tolerant of one another, regardless of how we see Jesus and his nature and work, for he is after all our Lord, the One before whom we all bow down in humility and devotion.

The next millennium will put Christians all over the globe to the test in many ways. In some places there will be persecutions for the faith. In others, like our own country today, there will be such laxity that people simply fall away from the faith out of boredom and inattentiveness to what they believe. But the message of this ancient book will still be important: "Jesus Christ is the same yesterday and today and forever." We ought to stand up and be counted as his followers. We ought to be faithful, for that is part of what it means to have faith. He will always be our leader, whatever the century or millennium, for he is the same yesterday (in the time of the great apostles) and today (when you and I are thinking about him and how we should be committing ourselves to him) and forever (even in the new millennium and beyond); for he is the Christ of God and the Savior of the world. (John Killinger)

DOORS AND WINDOWS

Introduction to the Monthly Meditations

It is no accident that Jesus healed many who were blind. How did he help them heal? By changing the way they saw. Many of us are as good as blind when it comes to the next century. We peer through doors. We look through windows. We think we see. And maybe we do, and maybe we don't.

Clergy bear special responsibility for sight, since we also help people to see. We relieve their blindness. We move folk to the doors and the windows—and there say, "Open your eyes, look and see."

Before we dare speak these words, of course, we must claim to see ourselves. We must have done our time at the door, the window, and the gate.

Painters love to paint doors and windows. They like to make openings in reality, much the same way that Bill Gates couldn't help himself in developing Windows 95, so soon outdated and so soon to be replaced with more windows upon windows upon windows. The Hebrew people also worked assiduously on the doors and gates of the Tabernacle. They built beautiful screens, entrances within entrances within entrances. They knew the importance of both what was within and what was beyond.

When we look at the next century, we are standing at the gate. We have many screens to get through. Many apertures. Many openings that don't quite take us where we need to go. In some instances, we will think we have arrived at the threshold of the new and the renewed, only to find that we have farther to go.

Scientists and artists love windows, and so do regular people. Whenever I go into someone's house, I go to their windows and look out so that I can see what they see. My city friends can't see much farther than their neighbor's windows. But they can look out: They can assume the posture of the spiritual adventurer, one who is looking out over the horizon, looking to see what God has in mind next.

Georgia O'Keefe, in her painting *Bell, Cross, Ranchos Church, New Mexico* (1930), put the window and door right smack in the middle of the painting. We have to look *at* not through them when we look at this painting. She is saying that these openings, these screens, these windows are essential and not just a small part of reality. According to Barbara Rose, an art historian and critic, O'Keefe in this painting tried to change the way we see.

What dare we hope for as the century turns? We may dare to hope to see the way God sees. To see the world as God sees it and not as we see it. To see how much God has planned for us. How much God hopes for.

We may be spiritual adventurers who stand tip-toed at the window, looking, watching, waiting, and hoping. There we join the artists and the scientists and the regular people of the world; there we try to see as far and as deeply as we can. We try to change the way we see.

The songs, prayers, and meditations that follow are little keys for the preacher. In order for a pastor to get ready to preach, he or she has to open up all of himself or herself to the gospel. Each part must be open—the one that is in Scripture, the one that is in people and their anguish and their little victories over their anguish, as well as the one that is deep inside. Preachers are also people who open doors to the gospel, first for themselves and then for others. These monthly meditations help pastors preach by unlocking doors. They simply open things up to the "many mansions" promised by Jesus, if we could but see. Let those who have eyes see! Let those who can open, open! Use these keys to unlock doors and windows in yourself first, and then in your people. (Donna Schaper)

DOORS AND WINDOWS

JANUARY

Reflection Verse: "Remember the sabbath day, and keep it holy" (Ex. 20:8).

The Discipline:

How would I know if I had kept the Sabbath holy? By actually keeping it. By not working on my day off. By not working when I lead worship. By not working at God or life, but playing at God and life. Work is whatever we have to do; play is whatever we want to do. We can play at work.

My calendar is a holy thing. My daily agenda is a holy thing. At some point this month, on a date certain, during an appointment I make and keep with myself, I will order my calendar. I will make and keep clear spaces clear. If I have a funeral, a crisis, or something to do that I couldn't have known to schedule, I will schedule comp time. I will find my way back to Sabbath when the crisis is over. I will practice a physical discipline of my choice; I will honor my body the way God honors it, as a holy temple. I will pray instead of eat, if that is what it takes. I will also pray when I eat. I will quietly let people know that God is in charge of my time, not them, or even me. And I will do my work with gladness.

I will put my calendar in a special place, and when I look at it, I will love it and not fear it. It will be the gift of God to me in this new century—open time, time of my own, time that I freely give away, and time that I freely enjoy.

I will "jubilee" my time—the way the people of Israel tried to let the soil go fallow every seventh year and tried to forgive debt on the "seven times seven," or forty-ninth year. I will treat this new century with respect and gratitude: It is open. It is free; it is new, and it is mine with God.

The Meditation:

Define *Sabbath*. If it is not Sunday, it is not Sunday. If it is, it is. How do you know what Sabbath is for you? By keeping a certain amount of time holy, or by "altaring" it, in the words of theologian Heather Murray Elkins.

Sabbath used to mean Sunday for Christians, and Saturday for Jews. It was the day taken off from work for religion—for the rest that religion brought to those people who regularly took Sabbaths. It was a different kind of rest than the kind we imagine we need now. It was not television and its dramatic replacement of our story with someone else's story. It was not "blitzing out." It was not hiking, with its grand viewpoints, heavy breathing, and body-changing, feel-good potential. Nor was Sabbath a time to do errands or get caught up at our desk, or pay our bills, or visit our relatives. (Clergy, like everyone else, need two days off per week—one for catching up and the other for catching God. If you can't get two days in a row, take them in units.)

Sabbath is a larger and deeper relief. It is more the kind of vacation people mean when they say, "I'm so tired that even a month's vacation won't do." Sabbath is religious rest. It is time for God, taken from time dedicated for work. Going deeper into time, for God's time, is its point.

We can even allow time its holiness at work. Religious writer Eugene Petersen says that people ask him often for a list of "spiritual reading." Instead of a reading list, Petersen offers the notion that people should do all their reading spiritually. Sabbath is a way of managing all time, including work time, spiritually. Sabbath is a way to read or a way to live but not a thing to have or a list to complete.

Not keeping Sabbath is a little like receiving a beautiful, expensive gift and forgetting to say "thank you." It is like being offered a full fellowship to a grand university and deciding not to take it, or like losing the phone number of the person you need to call to find out about the gift. Keeping Sabbath is good manners. It is the humble receiving of the gift of something as large as a fellowship.

Keeping Sabbath is knowing what Sabbath is and honoring what we know about God, time, eternity, and our giftedness. Keeping Sabbath is centering ourselves on what we know about God and giftedness. We live out from a core goodness and a core gift. We don't live "in," checking off other obligations and eventually arriving at a little free space and time. We don't keep Sabbath by living spiritually on Sunday or Saturday; we live Sabbath by living life wholly and holy every day, at work or rest.

The Song:
Create in me a new heart, O God.
Restore unto me the joy of thy salvation.
Cast me not away from your presence,
And take not your Holy Spirit from me.
                    (adapted from Psalm 51)

The Prayer:
   Where we are all locked up, O God, open us. Help us jump over our fences and find you and each other. Open us—and let a fresh breeze blow. Amen. (Donna Schaper)

JANUARY 2, 2000

Epiphany of the Lord

Worship Theme: Epiphany is the time for commitment to the experience of Christ in strange and unlikely ways, and for carrying the good news in word and deed to people who may seem unlikely recipients to us.

Readings: Isaiah 60:1-6; Ephesians 3:1-12; Matthew 2:1-12

Call to Worship (Psalm 72:1-7):

Leader:	Give the king your justice, O God,
People:	**and your righteousness to the royal son!**
Leader:	May he judge your people with righteousness,
People:	**and your poor with justice!**
Leader:	Let the mountains bear prosperity for the people, and the hills, in righteousness!
People:	**May he defend the cause of the poor of the people, give deliverance to the needy, and crush the oppressor!**
Leader:	May he live while the sun endures, and as long as the moon, throughout all generations!
People:	**May he be like rain that falls on the mown grass, like showers that water the earth!**
Leader:	In his days may righteousness flourish, and peace abound, till the moon be no more!

Pastoral Prayer:

Holy and surprising God, how wondrous to know that in the dead of winter you are alive and with us. You are here, offering promises of life now and life forever. By your grace, please give to us eyes to see and ears to hear your presence in the predictable places and people—as well as in those people and places unexpected. Forgive us for all of our self-serving resolutions at the beginning of this new year. May we all resolve to seek you and love you, so that we might seek out our brothers and sisters and, through our words and actions, offer them some good news. We ask you to provide healing and peace to your children who drag their burdens into this new year, burdens that threaten to diminish their life and their hope. And, precious Lord, ever remind us that we are not alone as we journey out into the world. Amen. (Thomas Gildermeister)

SERMON BRIEFS

COME TOWARD THE LIGHT

ISAIAH 60:1-6

The first strophe of this salvation poem summarizes the rest of the poem. Take note of the repetition of the word *come* throughout the passage. The central word is "glory" (*kabhod*). In verse 1, "Arise, shine" is an invitation to Israel to bask in God's glory. Israel had known darkness. Now God's glory "shines" and Israel is invited to respond to this manifestation by rising from its despair. The light itself is a gift of God, a chance for Jerusalem to glow for all to see. The light is also God *come* and Israel's only source of hope. Verse 2 expresses the contrast between "light" and "darkness," the difference between Jerusalem filled with God's glory, and the rest of the world. Verse 3 tells how all nations will *come* to the light. It may be summarized by Isaiah 40:5: "The glory of the Lord shall be revealed, and all people shall see it together . . ." (NRSV).

I. Come to the Light

In the second stanza, the poet uses words to create a picture of what is taking place if Israel will only look. Others will see Jerusalem reflecting the glory and will come. They are drawn by the light. Sons and daughters of Israel will return, those who have been scattered away from home long after the official homecoming. They will return with wealth from other nations and bring it to the altar (v. 7). When Israel *sees*, emotions will change from despair to joy, like a mother who has not seen her children in years. There is a thrill that comes with the glorious return.

II. Come to Worship

Verse 6 tells of others who are coming and bringing exotic gifts such as gold and frankincense. This shows that the nations too are coming to submit themselves to God's new future. All go before the altar to behold God's glory. God's presence gives the gift of life to Jerusalem and all the nations.

I write this during my son Andrew's first Christmas. We brought Andrew into the living room to see the Christmas tree for the first time, and he was amazed as we plugged in the lights for the tree. Ever since, he has been drawn by the light to come and investigate the tree. In the eyes of this young child, I see the wonder, curiosity, and joy that the light on the tree brings him.

We all sometimes need to be reminded that we are God's children who need to come to the "light" as well. Just as Jerusalem was to be the light on a hill for all nations to see God's glory, we need to come toward this "light" so that we too may be transformed by life in God's presence. This life in the presence of God should be one of wonder, curiosity, and joy, like that of a young child. By acknowledging and being transformed by the "light," we too can participate in God's kingdom. The essence of the passage is reflected in the hymn "Arise, Your Light Is Come" by Ruth Duck: "Show forth the glory of your God / Which shines on you today." (Marcia T. Thompson)

SHARE THE SECRET

EPHESIANS 3:1-12

The Ron Mason family enjoyed the best this life had to offer. Ron had done well. There was nothing they wanted that they didn't get.

The Don Mason family lacked all but the essentials. Don had been ill most of his adult life, and his only attempt at running a business had failed.

Although they were brothers, Ron and Don, along with their families, lived in different worlds. The Ron Mason cousins had always felt, talked, and acted superior to their Don Mason cousins. They wore their privileged status conspicuously, until the attorney's letter arrived from London with unexpected news.

Neither family had known of their very distant and wealthy English relative. This unknown uncle had recently died, leaving so large an inheritance that both the Ron Mason and the Don Mason families became equally wealthy.

The Don Masons celebrated the good news that had been secret all these years. The Ron Masons resented the secret news that practically eliminated them from their former superior position.

I. The Secret Is Out: The Gentiles Have Equal Standing Before God (vv. 1-6)

Not everybody wants a secret to be told. It was because Paul was telling the secret, God's divine mystery, that he had been imprisoned in Rome (v. 1). The faithful apostle had fulfilled his divine commission to share the secret (vv. 2-5). Paul called his message a "mystery." However, because he had shared this particular secret, the "establishment" was not happy.

What was the secret? That the Gentiles were

— equal heirs of the riches of God;
— equal members of the Body of Christ;
— equal sharers of the promises of God;
— right up there alongside the people of Israel (v. 6).

That was the problem. The apostles were the first to know of God's plan to make salvation universally available. And Paul couldn't keep this secret. When God broke the news that Gentiles could share equally in God's rich blessings, some Jewish elitists were not pleased. They didn't like the news, and they didn't like anybody who spread it. It made everybody too equal, too blessed. They had lost their superior position. That's why Paul was in jail. He had dared to "read the will" of God to the world.

36

II. Go Tell the Secret: God's Riches Are Available to All People (vv. 7-12)

Although Paul was nobody special (v. 8), he was made a steward of the news that the blessings of God have been made available to all people (vv. 7-10). According to the owner's will, the steward parcels out the owner's wealth and resources to those the owner directs. The great apostle was merely the "reader of the will," the steward of the good news that God's blessings are for all people.

This had always been God's ultimate plan. Salvation was not going to be limited to the Jews. Access to God was for all people who come to God through faith in Christ Jesus (vv. 11-12).

The privilege and responsibility of stewarding the secret mystery of God's universal offer of blessings have been passed down to all who inherit these blessings by faith in Christ. Those who know the secret pass it on to others, not only to their own but to all people everywhere.

I would enjoy being the reader and the steward of the will to the Mason families. I would love to see the look on the faces of the Don Masons when they realize they now possess every possible material and financial resource. I would also love to see the look on the faces of the Ron Masons when it dawns on them that their cousins are now their equals. What a shock. What a surprise. What a secret. (Timothy Warren)

RESTORING THE MASS IN CHRISTMAS

MATTHEW 2:1-12

I have never been one to become too upset by the word *Xmas*. I've sat through enough Greek New Testament classes in college and seminary to remember that *Xmas* is really a simple abbreviation for Christmas. The letter "X" (*chi*) is the first letter of the title "Christ" in Greek. Therefore, anytime I see the word *Xmas*, I don't see the word *Xmas* but the full word—*Christmas*.

Unfortunately, many of us are far more concerned about Christ being taken out of Christmas than we are about the Mass being removed from Christmas. However, when the Mass is removed from Christmas, Christmas becomes just another holiday instead of a holy day. Christmas is a compound word: *Christ* + *Mass* = *Christmas*. Christ is not Jesus' last name but his title. It originates from the word *messiah*, which literally means "anointed one." *Mass* is a Roman Catholic word that means "communion." During the season of Christmas, we celebrate our communion with God made possible through the gift of God's Son, Jesus Christ. The story of the wise men invites you and me to restore the Mass in Christmas. We can do this whenever we do the following:

I. Follow the Star

God used a star to lead the wise men to Bethlehem, the birthplace of Jesus (vv. 1-2, 9).

Contrary to the popular Christmas carol "We Three Kings," the wise men were not three kings from the Orient. More than likely they were astrologers. Astrologers were highly esteemed but highly suspect. They were also Gentiles, demonstrating that the good news comes to all people who are open and receptive to the grace of God.

We restore the Mass in Christmas whenever we follow the star that leads to Bethlehem.

> O star of wonder, star of night,
> Star with royal beauty bright,
> Westward leading, still proceeding,
> Guide us to thy perfect light.
> ("We Three Kings")

II. Focus on the Savior

The star that the wise men followed stopped over the place where the Child was. When they saw the star had stopped, they were overwhelmed with joy. Upon entering the house, the wise men saw the Child with his mother.

They were overwhelmed with joy because the baby was not just any baby. The Child was the Son of God who came not only to live on earth but also to die so that people on earth might live. They called him "Jesus" because he would save his people from their sins.

We restore the Mass in Christmas whenever we focus on the Savior of the world.

III. Fall on Our Knees

When the wise men found the Savior, they fell on their knees and worshiped the King of kings and Lord of lords. While the newborn lay in sharp contrast to Herod, the mighty and earthly king of Rome, the Magi offered the meek and heavenly King nothing short of their very best, gifts fit only for the King of kings. While all three gifts were royal gifts, there is a common symbolic interpretation for each of them—*gold* for the king, *incense* for the God, and *myrrh* for him who is to die.

We restore the Mass in Christmas whenever we fall on our knees, worship the King of kings, and offer him our best in worship.

Why not start the New Year off right by restoring the Mass in Christmas? (Bob Buchanan)

JANUARY 9, 2000

Baptism of the Lord

Worship Theme: The source of all life and any opportunity for renewed life is the Spirit of God.

Readings: Genesis 1:1-5; Acts 19:1-7; Mark 1:4-11

Call to Worship (Psalm 29:1-4):

Leader: Ascribe to the LORD, O heavenly beings, ascribe to the LORD glory and strength.

People: **Ascribe to the LORD the glory of his name; worship the LORD in holy splendor.**

Leader: The voice of the LORD is upon the waters; the God of glory thunders, the LORD, upon many waters.

People: **The voice of the LORD is powerful, the voice of the LORD is full of majesty.**

Pastoral Prayer:

Our Creator, Redeemer, Sustainer, what words can we find to thank you for the gift of your Holy Spirit? You speak, and all of the cosmos comes to life. You speak your Word into flesh, into Jesus, and all of creation is offered new life—offered a path from our broken-down lives to your perfect life and love. We confess that we turn from the gift and flee, unwilling to release our deathly grasp on these shabby, false lives we lead. O God, may your mercy always exceed your judgment. We pray for your children for whom new life seems impossible. Assure them that anything is possible in your everlasting love. Amen. (Thomas Gildermeister)

SERMON BRIEFS

LIGHT AND LIFE

GENESIS 1:1-5

When the earth was a formless void and covered by darkness, God brought light to exist with the darkness. God spoke forth light into darkness and then separated them. It has always been interesting to me that God could have given the day total and complete rule for all time. The day could have dominated and existed singularly in its entirety. Likewise, the night could have continued as the lone attribute to the formless void. God could have achieved God's purposes with either day or night existing all alone. However, it was God's design, God's divine plan, God's foreknowledge to introduce light into darkness for the purpose of which God alone knew. Only God knew what was ahead and yet to be created. Therefore, for the good of God's divine purposes and plan, God made day and night, light and darkness, each having its own distinct time under God.

God alone knew we would need the day and the night. Day and night help us to keep life in perspective. The night helps us to appreciate the day and to make good use of it to the glory of God. Jesus told the disciples on one occasion, "We must work the works of him who sent me while it is day; night is coming when no one can work" (John 9:4). The day helps us appreciate the night for what it's worth. The night is a time to rest, reflect, and to allow God to speak to us.

When darkness again covered the world due to sin, and people's lives became a formless void, God's spirit still hovered over God's creation. God again spoke of light through his prophets, promising a deliverer, a Son, a Savior who would turn people's hearts away from darkness, and toward him. We all have suffered darkness due to sin in our lives. Indeed, we were born into a dark world of sin and shame. However, the darkness shows us our need for the light. That light is Jesus Christ. Life without the "light of life" is a formless void. However, Jesus said, "I am the light of the world. Whoever follows me will never walk in darkness but will have the light of life" (John 8:12). Jesus also said, "I came that they may have life, and have it abundantly" (John 10:10).

41

Although we are in the world, we are not of the world. Paul tells us, "Do not be conformed to this world, but be transformed by the renewing of your minds" (Rom. 12:2). Jesus Christ, who calls us "out of darkness into his marvelous light" enables us to be in the world but not of the world (1 Pet. 2:9). Choose light and life that you may be able to live through the darkness. Choose life in Jesus Christ. (Harold L. Martin)

AN IMPERFECT FAITH

ACTS 19:1-7

Who has a perfect faith? Some long-dead saint? A local bishop? What about you? If we are honest with ourselves, we realize that none of us has what might be called a perfect faith.

Today's text introduces us to a group of early Christians who had great faith but did not know all the fine points of theology. They knew Christ as their Savior but did not know about the Holy Spirit.

I. Faith Need Not Be Perfect to Save

The dozen men mentioned in this text are Gentiles. They have little in the way of Jewish theological understanding. They have responded to the call of John the Baptist to repent and be baptized. However, Paul's question catches them off guard. Not only have they not received the Holy Spirit, but they also have never even heard of the Spirit.

Apollos had taught these men about Jesus, but apparently Apollos did not know the full story about Jesus. Maybe he did not understand the death/resurrection experience that is symbolized in baptism. In any case, their understanding of Christian doctrine at that point is faulty. But it was full enough to bring salvation in Christ.

Today, people do not need correct doctrine in order to enter a relationship with Christ. The relationship comes first, and the doctrine comes later. This is important to remember. Sometimes we act as if people need to know everything about Christianity before they can have faith. The fact is that they do not. They learn theology after getting to know the risen Christ, just as these men from Ephesus did.

II. Imperfect Faith Needs to Stay Open to Growth

When Paul explains who the Holy Spirit is, the dozen men want to complete their experience by being baptized in Jesus' name. Baptism, you recall, is a picture enacting what happened to Jesus. He was crucified, died, was buried, and then raised from the dead by the power of God. In baptism we are buried with him and raised to walk in newness of life, according to Romans 6.

The men do not know that baptism. They know only the baptism of John the Baptist, the baptism of repentance. When they learn more, they are willing to change, grow, and follow through on their faith. That is not always easy. Faith does not always give us comfort. Sometimes it gives us discomfort.

Flannery O'Connor, the late novelist from Georgia, was a devout Christian who never gave up her faith, even though she had an incurable illness; she died at a fairly early age. She once wrote to one of her readers, giving advice that I have found full of wisdom: "What people don't realize is how much religion costs. They think faith is a big electric blanket, when, of course, it is the cross. It is much harder to believe than not to believe; you must at least do this: keep an open mind. Keep it open toward faith, keep wanting it, keep asking for it, and leave the rest to God" (Flannery O'Connor, *The Habit of Being*, quoted by Paul W. Nisly, "Faith Is Not an Electric Blanket," in *Christianity Today*, May 17, 1985, p. 24).

No, faith does not need to be perfect—thank goodness! But it does need to keep growing, and, if necessary, make changes. Let us let these twelve unnamed early Christians teach us these facts. Amen. (Don Aycock)

A NEW SIGN OF GOD'S FAITHFULNESS

MARK 1:4-11

This passage from Mark's Gospel helps set the tone for the entire book. Perhaps the most noticeable element here is simply the stark weirdness of Jesus' epiphany. The swift, angular transitions from scene to scene in the text combined with cosmic elements lend this passage (and, indeed, the whole Gospel) an almost sci-fi quality. In fact, Mark reads like a screenplay. Only the barest essentials are present. The reader is left to fill the gaps with imagination.

Since today's text is being used during the season of Epiphany, we should pay close attention to the elements of the passage which deal with Mark's *how*'s and *why*'s of the revelation of "the good news of Jesus Christ, the Son of God" (v. 1). In other words, what is at stake for Mark in the way he inaugurates Jesus' ministry? Additionally, since this text relates the baptism of the Lord, let's seek out what is unique in Mark's portrayal of this event.

New Creation, New People, New Covenant

Before the reader even begins the fourth verse, the reader is struck by what is not present in Mark's telling. There are no infancy narratives about Jesus or John. The only clues we get as to John's identity are Mark's references to Malachi and Isaiah. What we know about Jesus is that there is good news to tell and that he is the "Christ, the Son of God" (v. 1). Still, what this means in Mark's terms is not yet fully explained. Can we somehow achieve a mind-set that appreciates Mark's uniqueness without reference to the other Synoptic accounts?

When we first meet John, portrayed as the fulfillment of Isaiah's prophecy (vv. 2-3), Mark calls him "the baptizer." So, within three words of John's entrance, the reader is cued to link God's "good news of Jesus" with baptism. The succeeding verses quickly fill the concept of baptism with meaning. John's baptism concerns "repentance for the forgiveness of sins" (v. 5), the public confession of those sins, and it takes place in the Jordan River. The fact that "all the people" from Judea and Jerusalem are said to have gone out gives us clues as to John's intention—the creation of a renewed people, a renewed Judea, a renewed Jerusalem, a renewed covenant. The Old Testament water crossings are performed again with the whole people present. John's intention in baptism is a reformation of the whole people, a renewal of commitment to the law and the Mosaic Covenant. That Jesus participates in this renewal by his own baptism suggests that his intention somehow includes this perspective.

However, Mark also makes the reader aware that Jesus' mission has to do not only with water, but also with the Spirit. When Jesus emerges from the chilly Jordan, new images, those of the Spirit, abound. The heavens are torn open as they were for forty days and nights (Gen. 7:11-12). Just as the dove was a sign to Noah that the waters of the flood were receding and that a completely new covenant by God with all humankind could be struck (Genesis 8–9), so, perhaps, this Spirit-dove signals to the reader that God in Jesus is going to do something new in relationship to all humankind, not only to repentant Judeans. To confirm God's covenant with Noah, God set a bow in the clouds (Genesis 9). This time a Galilean coming for John's baptism is directly addressed by God, and God binds God's own self to this One, the Beloved, a Son more powerful than John. Jesus renews not only the Mosaic Covenant but also a universal covenant, and becomes himself the new sign of God's faithfulness and love.

In my area of the country, debates over the meaning of Christian baptism flourish. In this passage, baptism takes different meanings. Is there a difference between John's baptism, Jesus' baptism, and Christian baptism? How are they consistent (or not) with God's saving work through Israel? How does this text help or hinder your understanding? (Sam Parkes)

JANUARY 16, 2000

Second Sunday After Epiphany

Worship Theme: God is omnipresent, knowing each one of us by name and calling each one of us to follow Christ Jesus.

Readings: 1 Samuel 3:1-10 (11-20); 1 Corinthians 6:12-20; John 1:43-51

Call to Worship (Psalm 139:1-6):

Leader: O LORD, you have searched me and known me!

People: You know when I sit down and when I rise up; you discern my thoughts from afar.

Leader: You search out my path and my lying down, and are acquainted with all my ways.

People: Even before a word is on my tongue, O LORD, you know it altogether.

Leader: You pursue me behind and before, and lay your hand upon me.

People: Such knowledge is too wonderful for me; it is high, I cannot attain it.

Pastoral Prayer:
Lord of the universe, and still, precious Friend, we praise you for creating all that was, is, and ever will be. And we stand amazed that you know our name and our every coming and going. Your call continues even when we deny it. O God, thank you for a love without limits. We claim your presence in our lives. Help us to experience you more richly and fully. By your grace

bring healing, comfort, and peace for people in great need. Sustain us through these dreary weeks of winter. In the name of your Son, Jesus Christ, we ask you to relight the fire of Emmanuel in all our hearts. Amen. (Thomas Gildermeister)

SERMON BRIEFS

THE CALL

1 SAMUEL 3:1-10 (11-20)

Each of our lives has a calling. This calling is important because it is part of who we are, and it is the reason each of us is unique. It is a facet of what grips and holds us in our faith. Our calling speaks to those feelings deep within that urge us to look beyond the daily grind and give our routines a reason for being. Our calling speaks to our feelings that we are somehow "wanted to be here and answerable to our innate image," for want of a better term, our being reflections of God (James Hillman, *The Soul's Code* [New York: Random House, 1996], p. 3).

It is this sense of calling that I want us to consider. Our calling, whether it be as an elder in a church, an accountant, a funeral director, an attorney, a minister or priest, an insurance salesperson, or whatever, is often lost in so many people's lives. Each of us is called in some way, and it is for this reason that we are alive. If somewhere along the line we have somehow lost this sense of calling, then we need to recover it, restore it to its rightful place in our lives, and celebrate it.

There's a wonderful story about jazz legend Ella Fitzgerald. It was amateur night at the Harlem Opera House (now the Apollo Theater) in New York. A skinny sixteen-year-old girl timidly walked onto the stage. The emcee bellowed, "And now, ladies and gentlemen, our next contestant is Miss Ella Fitzgerald, who is going to dance for us . . . Hold it, hold it. Now what's your problem, honey? . . . Correction, folks. Miss Fitzgerald's changed her mind. She's not gonna dance; she's gonna sing!"

Ella Fitzgerald gave three encores and won first prize. Initially, though, she had intended to dance (Sid Collins, *The Life and Times of Ella Fitzgerald* [London: Elm Tree Books, 1986], p. 2). The call is a sense of realizing, "Hey, this is what I must do, this is what I've got to have. This is who I am."

I listened to a delightful interview on National Public Radio's *Performance Today* during the show's tenth anniversary special. Host Martin Goldsmith spoke with singer Todd Duncan, who was the first to sing the role of Porgy in George Gershwin's opera *Porgy and Bess* seventy years ago.

What struck me was Duncan's strong conviction of being called to sing. He knew that God had a hand in it. This was certainly the feeling Duncan had about his role as Porgy. Apparently Gershwin had heard Duncan in recital, and Gershwin was determined to have Duncan sing some of his music. Duncan said he was a singer of serious music. To him Gershwin's music was Tin Pan Alley; it was beneath him. When Gershwin approached him about singing the role of Porgy in his new opera, Duncan wouldn't hear of it. However, Gershwin prevailed, and even paid for Duncan to ride to his house to hear the score.

When the first few notes sounded, Duncan knew he had been right. This was not serious music. But when Gershwin began playing "Summertime," Duncan said a tear came to his eye, and he knew then and there that he had to sing the role of Porgy.

Sometimes we go along with the flow of life, doing what we think is right and best for ourselves. We drift along with the current, and all of a sudden we find ourselves exactly where we want to be. If we retrace our steps, we discover that all along we were being led to this point at this time, and we recognize God's hand in it. (Eric Killinger)

THE SERIOUSNESS OF SEXUAL SINS

1 CORINTHIANS 6:12-20

We live in an age when many do not take sexual sins seriously. The Corinthians lived in a city that also did not take sexual sins seriously. Sexual sins were common in Corinth, and they are common today. But that has nothing at all to do with the nature of such sins. God takes them very seriously, and so must we.

I. They Are Sins Against Creation (vv. 12-14)

Paul lists two quotations from the Corinthians, who were using both of these sayings to justify what they were doing. The apostle says that God created the body to serve God. We were not created to use our bodies any way we choose. As our Creator, God has first claim on us. God had something in mind when creating every part of us, including both our digestive systems and our reproductive systems. It is up to God to say how they shall be used—and how they shall not be used.

II. They Are Sins Against Self (v. 18)

There is an old song called "Doing What Comes Naturally." It was not about doing good. Many people think that there is something natural about sexual sins, when in fact the opposite is the case. They are unnatural. They are destructive of the self. Sometimes that destruction is seen in the body itself—in disease. Sometimes it is seen in death. Sometimes it is seen in the mind. Preoccupation with sex is the hallmark of our generation—and a deadly one. Sometimes it is seen in the heart. Emotions become twisted, warped, and perverted. Eventually one cannot experience true love at all.

III. They Are Sins Against Christ (vv. 14-15)

We belong to Christ. Our minds belong to him. Our hearts belong to him. Our bodies belong to him. It is monstrous to think that we take members that belong to Christ and join them to a harlot. It is monstrous to think that we take that which belongs to Christ and use it carelessly, thoughtlessly, indiscriminately.

IV. They Are Sins Against the Holy Spirit (v. 19)

The city of Corinth had two magnificent temples. There was a temple devoted to Apollo, the sun god, and a temple dedicated to Aphrodite, the goddess of love. Much of the immorality of the city was attached to the temple of Aphrodite.

Christians have a temple, too. It is the human body. What marvelous architecture; what amazing engineering! In that temple dwells the Holy Spirit of God. We dare not use our bodies in a way that would embarrass or hinder the work of the Holy Spirit.

V. They Are Sins Against Calvary (v. 20)

Slaves were a familiar part of the scene at Corinth. Sometimes they were purchased and then set free. Likewise, we were slaves to sin. Christ redeemed us with his precious blood (1 Pet. 1:18-19). He bought us and we belong to him. We cannot call our time our own. We cannot call our energy our own. We cannot call our minds our own. We cannot call our bodies our own.

There is a wider application to this principle. We must do nothing with our bodies that would bring shame to God. We must make certain that our bodies bring honor to God. This means that we must honor God with our hands, with our feet, with our mouths, with our faces, with our eyes, with our ears, with our lips. While so many say, "Give your heart to Jesus," the apostle Paul says, "Give him your body, too." (Robert Shannon)

COME AND SEE

JOHN 1:43-51

Although most scholars refer to John 1:1-18 as the Prologue to the Gospel, the entire first chapter serves as a kind of prologue for the rest of John's narrative. It is in many ways the preparatory story that builds with a great crescendo to Jesus' first miracle in chapter 2. In this first chapter, Jesus is baptized and assembles his disciples so that all the pieces are in place for the account of his outward ministry.

The chapter begins with the words "in the beginning" and is organized, much like the creation story, by days. Almost every paragraph begins with "the next day." The Gospel writer is perhaps intentionally echoing the creation story so that the readers will recognize the cosmic significance of Jesus' entry into ministry.

On one of these cosmically resounding days, Jesus receives Philip and Nathanael as his disciples (1:43-51). John does not recount the details of how each disciple was called, but he obviously wanted to spotlight Nathanael. One of the keys, then, to this passage is the focus on Nathanael and his response to Jesus.

It would be easy to get bogged down in questions about why Nathanael appears only in the Gospel of John. Many scholars have come to equate Nathanael with Bartholomew of the Synoptic Gospels, which certainly is one way to answer the question. However, such questions are less relevant to the preaching of this passage than are questions about Nathanael's character and how we might learn from him.

When Philip tells Nathanael that they have found the Messiah, who is "Jesus son of Joseph from Nazareth," Nathanael responds with, "Can anything good come out of Nazareth?" He is not impressed. He obviously thinks that Philip has deluded himself. Nathanael is not expecting to see the Messiah in his own lifetime or in his own midst. Surely the Messiah would not be accessible to *him*. Things that are cosmically significant just don't happen to him. How often do we or people we know react to the good news of hope and redemption with jaded skepticism and sardonic humor? How often in our culture do we respond with the same "Yeah, whatever" attitude that Nathanael shows here?

But Philip isn't deterred from his purpose. He invites Nathanael to "come and see." At this point in the story, it would be easy to draw a parallel between Philip and the church today. Philip sets an example for us by inviting his jaded, skeptical friend to come and see Jesus for himself. Like Philip, we who believe ought to be inviting others—even the skeptics—to come and see the work that Jesus Christ is doing in our midst.

And when Nathanael does meet Jesus for himself, he is indeed changed. Jesus reveals to Nathanael that he saw him before Philip even called him. In other words, Jesus shows Nathanael that he knew him already. Nathanael witnesses Jesus' prophetic powers and is able to declare, "Rabbi, you are the Son of God! You are the King of Israel!"

In the same way, when we invite people to "come and see," they just might discover that Jesus has called them by name. They just might find that they were known and loved long before they were ever invited to "come and see." Our role in the church is not to coerce people into believing. The response of belief comes only from an encounter with Christ. Rather, our role is to do what Philip did—to invite others simply to "come and see." (Carol Cavin)

JANUARY 23, 2000

Third Sunday After Epiphany

Worship Theme: To follow Christ in this world, we must turn from the bad news (the values of this world) and embrace the good news (the values of God).

Readings: Jonah 3:1-5, 10; 1 Corinthians 7:29-31; Mark 1:14-20

Call to Worship (Psalm 62:5-8):

> *Leader*:   For God alone my soul waits in silence,
>
> ***People:*** **for my hope is from God, who alone is my rock and my salvation, my fortress; I shall not be shaken.**
>
> *Leader*:   On God rests my deliverance and my honor; my mighty rock, my refuge is God.
>
> ***People:*** **Trust in God at all times, O people; pour out your heart before God who is a refuge for us.**

Pastoral Prayer:

Most sacred God, how assuring to believe in our hearts that your good news in Christ will be the final word. In a world of sadness upon sadness, horror upon horror, we praise you that this mountain of bad news is only a word and never the last word. Not only do we ask for your grace so that we can turn away from the darkness and toward the light of the Son, but we ask that you help us to be a powerful vehicle to carry your good news into this world of sorrows. Help us to use our gifts—some with words, others with actions—as a beacon that lure your children home. Amen. (Thomas Gildermeister)

SERMON BRIEFS

AN IMPORTANT QUESTION

JONAH 3:1-5, 10

People sometimes ask me about an account in Scripture, "Do you really believe that?" No story in the Bible generates this question more than the story of Jonah. Whenever there is a discussion about the historical accuracy of the Bible, Jonah will come up. This seems to be the fish story people find hard to swallow. To be honest, I find the fish part much more believable than the part of the story in today's text.

I. What Is at Stake?

You are probably familiar with the basic plot of Jonah. God calls a prophet by that name to go to Nineveh, which happens to be the capital of the Assyrian empire—Assyrians being the most hated and feared enemies of Israel in the eighth century B.C. The reluctant Jonah arrives in the city, by way of fish, and cheerfully spreads his message of gloom and doom that God is going to destroy the city.

In response to his message, the city repents, from the greatest to the least. Now that's a miracle! What happens next is more remarkable still: God pardons the city! Verse 10 is the punch line for the entire book of Jonah: "When God saw what they did, how they turned from their evil ways, God changed his mind about the calamity that he had said he would bring upon them; and he did not do it."

This is unexpected, and here we find a word for us. It surprises everyone because no one familiar with the Assyrian empire would expect God to let Nineveh off so easily. Ancient empires, not entirely unlike empires of our day, were cruel and dehumanizing. Assyria, the worst of the worst, had a reputation for evil rarely matched in the annals of history. Naturally the people of Nineveh, especially the royal court, lived the good life by exploiting and oppressing other people. Their armies would march to a city, and if the inhabitants did not submit quietly, the Assyrians would commit acts of butchery not to be described in the presence of children. And when the subjects rebelled, the Assyrians just deported them to another part of the empire. This was the fate of Israel, and Judah paid heavily to avoid a similar fate.

No wonder Nahum calls Nineveh a "city of bloodshed, utterly deceitful, and full of booty" (3:1). No wonder he celebrates its fall. Why would God let such people off the hook? Genuine repentance. God forgives. Certainly this forgiveness is a gracious gift. Even genuine repentance does not obligate God to forgive. Nevertheless, the possibility of forgiveness is opened. If God can forgive Nineveh, God can forgive me.

This story is bad news for those who, like the Pharisee in Jesus' parable, seek to justify themselves. But it is good news for those who, like the tax collector, cry, "Lord, have mercy on me, a sinner!" Reading Jonah, we marvel at the love and mercy of God, and hopefully we reach for that ourselves.

II. Can You Believe?

So do not ask me if Jonah could have survived in a fish, or what kind of fish it was. I am ready enough to believe the fish story if anything were at stake. However, I remain skeptical about the wholesale repentance in today's text. Yet even that is only important if you happen to be a citizen of ancient Nineveh. What we are asked to believe is that God forgives those who repent. Through this story our tradition of faith makes a claim. And if we listen, then behind the witness of Scripture we might hear the Word of God saying, "I will forgive." (David Mauldin)

PRIORITIES

1 CORINTHIANS 7:29-31

Paul criticizes the placement of the priorities that fill our lives. Families, emotional connections, belongings, and even our vocational calls are placed squarely in the realm of the world-that-is, which, in Paul's mind, misdirects our priorities from the world-to-be. "For the present form of this world is passing away" (v. 31).

I. Not Our Family

In Luke 14:26, Jesus says, "Whoever comes to me and does not hate father and mother, wife and children, brothers and sisters, yes, and even life itself, cannot be my disciple." Paul tells those with wives to live "as though they had none" (v. 29). This is not about ignoring one another or leaving one's spouse. Paul very clearly states in 1 Corinthians 7:10 that "the wife should not separate from her husband." This is about placing God first and foremost in our lives.

II. Not the Way We Feel

We are an emotional people who care deeply about many things. And Paul does not say do not mourn. Paul does not say do not rejoice. Paul simply implies that we should not mourn as before. We should not rejoice as before. Christ has brought to us a new way of viewing the world, and a new set of priorities to influence the way we relate to God's new order.

III. Not Our Material Possessions

Jesus says, "Do not worry about your life, what you will eat or what you will drink, or about your body, what you will wear. . . . But strive first for the kingdom of God and his righteousness, and all these things will be given to you as well" (Matt. 6:25, 33). Our material possessions have a place in our lives, but that place takes a back seat to the priority of God's coming kingdom.

IV. Not Our Jobs

As already mentioned, Paul does not want to suggest we give up working. However, Paul does suggest we give up working for our own interests and purposes. Work as if the circumstance of this world were ending, and work as if a new world order were on the horizon.

V. God and God Realized

This is not so much a passage about whether or not to be married or single as much as it is a concerned statement about where we are placing our priorities in our married or single states. There is a clear distinction in Paul's mind about what is and what will be, and he wants to make sure the church understands that the questions they are asking belong in the realm of what is. His concern is that they learn how to focus on God and that God's will be actualized, "for the present form of this world is passing away." (Mark D. Haines)

THE TRUE MEANING OF PEOPLE-FISHING

MARK 1:14-20

Jesus has been baptized, commissioned by God, and tempted in the wilderness. The author has told the reader that Jesus is the Christ, the Son of God, that he is more powerful than John and will baptize with the Spirit, and that he is the Beloved and very pleasing to God. Mark has brought us a long way in thirteen short verses. Still, what do these functions and titles mean for mission?

For Mark, they mean good news is nearby; the time is right for a new kingdom. Above all, Jesus' presence, as the sign and promise of that kingdom, means response from those who hear the message—repentance and belief. So, Mark gives us a portrait of the way disciples responded to Jesus' message and mission. In verses 16-18, Jesus calls to Simon and Andrew, fishers who immediately drop their nets and go with him. In verses 19-20, Jesus calls James and John, fishers who leave not only nets but also Zebedee, their father, as well.

The manifestation of God's kingdom through Jesus brings good news. But it also brings certain tensions—leaving prior vocations and family relationships. It seems that this is what being a disciple has always entailed. (Read 1 Kings 19:19-21.)

I. People-fishing

These four respond not only to Jesus' power and charisma but also to the promise that if they follow, Jesus will retrain them for the people business, for the formation of new relationships. Oh, but what people they will find! I think that this is about the best understanding of discipleship one can glean from Mark—retraining for new relationships. So often we think of discipleship as "learning," which in our culture is a little more head-based than what Jesus seems to intend.

I once conducted a training seminar for youth workers in our church. Of the ten or so who started the training, only four finished. It wasn't because the skills were hard to acquire. It was because the relationships they had to forge with the youth were threatening, and some could not handle it.

What does people-fishing mean to you? What would happen if everyone in your congregation threw their people-fishing lines into the sea of your local community?

II. Decisions by the Sea

How quickly these four respond to the kingdom call of Jesus! Mark uses them consistently through his Gospel as types; they represent the typical disciple in action and reaction. Often they will be the only ones present with Jesus at critical points in the action—the raising of Jairus' daughter, the Transfiguration, Jesus' teaching on the end-times, and Gethsemane. Here they are models of repentance and belief, acting immediately, leaving behind vocation and family. What good boys! Well, you and I know the rest of the story—how Simon (Peter), Andrew, James, and John, in Marcan terms, will often be the last to really understand Jesus' mission. Repentance, belief, and people-fishing will mean more than they bargained for in that fateful moment of decision beside the sea.

I have preached too many sermons on this text which focus on the disciples' faithful, immediate responses to Jesus. I have lauded them as icons of action, being able to quickly count the cost of discipleship and follow. I repent!

In the context of the whole Gospel, their response seems naïve and uninformed. They know not what they do. I mean, having read the whole thing, wouldn't you ask for a little clarification from Jesus if you were Andrew? "Ummmm, can you define 'fishing for people' a little more clearly, Lord?"

This is, of course, no reason to blame these four. How were they to know? Nevertheless, we who sit and interpret two thousand years later know what we are in for, don't we? Or do we? These four had to learn what people-fishing meant gradually, by walking the long road from the sea to the city, from Galilee to Golgotha, from Zebedee to Pilate. They had to learn as they went, dropping their assumptions behind them like they once had dropped so many dead fish.

Do you think they would do it again, knowing what they know by chapter 16? Would you? (Sam Parkes)

JANUARY 30, 2000

Fourth Sunday After Epiphany

Worship Theme: God's power and love have conquered death, and they surely can conquer the "demons" that haunt and pursue our lives.

Readings: Deuteronomy 18:15-20; 1 Corinthians 8:1-13; Mark 1:21-28

Call to Worship (Psalm 111:6-10):

> *Leader:* The LORD has shown his people the power of his works by giving them the heritage of the nations.

> *People:* **The works of the LORD's hands are faithful and just; the precepts of the LORD are trustworthy; they are established for ever and ever, to be performed with faithfulness and uprightness.**

> *Leader:* The LORD sent redemption to his people and has commanded his covenant for ever. Holy and wondrous is God's name!

> *People:* **The fear of the LORD is the beginning of wisdom; all those who practice it have a good understanding. The praise of the LORD endures for ever.**

Pastoral Prayer:

Loving God, we praise you for your power. We are stunned by your miracles of healing. By now we should know better than to credit science and technology entirely with the marvels and majesty of your holy presence in our lives. But we do. Forgive us,

Lord, for our forgetfulness. Forgive us for being lulled into the phony notion that human potential is limitless. Apart from you, we can do nothing. Help us all to understand that you have called us to be more concerned with compassion than with being right, and that we are measured not by what we know but by how much we love. Guide us through this day. Heal us of our hurt. In the name of the one true guide and healer, Jesus Christ. Amen. (Thomas Gildermeister)

SERMON BRIEFS

MOSES' FAREWELL

DEUTERONOMY 18:15-20

In examining this portion of Moses' "farewell address" before the people finally cross over the Jordan into the promised land, several different tracks could be pursued.

One approach would be to compare this time of transition (from wilderness wandering to promised-land living) to our life as Christians for whom the final victory has already been won. We are equipped to live in the promised land, which is "already and not yet."

Though one would not use the terminology "paradigm shift," it is exactly that which is taking place for the Israelites. They have lived forty years in the framework of lostness, frustration, utter dependence on Moses, and often regret at ever having left Egypt (it is not good, but it is familiar). Now Moses is telling them they are shifting to a framework of destination arrival (good news), but without him (frightening news).

God is promising them a leader, as God has provided leadership in Moses. They will have to follow that leader and move on and make the shift to promised-land living. It will not be easy. They are accustomed to recognizing the Word from the Lord through Moses; how can they be sure of how to live when the instructions they get may *not* be from the Lord? Doubt and fear can certainly prevent them from leaving the wilderness paradigm, even if they are physically on the promised land side of the Jordan.

Why do we continue to live as if we are victims when we have already been rescued? Why do we persist in addictive behavior even though we are in recovery? Why do we respond defensively when we are so totally loved? Why do we let the enemies of God shape our life in the church when the church has already proclaimed the Body of Christ the winning side? The shift to trusting God's leading us to live in the promised land (called the "kingdom of God" by Jesus) is a prevalent mark of unfaithfulness in our day. Let's be clear that the experience of entering the promised land is not equal to entering the kingdom of God; Jesus *is* necessary for our faith. However, the reluctance to move on is the connecting point.

A second approach would be to examine the difference in "revelation" knowledge and discovery, or educated knowledge. God cannot be known by our "finding" God, and cannot be captured by human-designed labels and doctrines and rituals. God is beyond our knowing, except that God is willing to *let* us know God. The people in this passage know God because God speaks and reveals God's self through the prophet.

The frequent absence of awe and wonder in our worship experiences points toward this presumptuous attitude that God is there for us to "click on" whenever we desire. Contrast the sense of awe in the Israelites that leads them to tremble in fear of dying if they presume to see God on their own terms.

A third approach would be to explore the meaning of being a prophet, and the call of all baptized persons to be prophetic. Dismantle the notion that prophecy is foreseeing and foretelling the future. Certainly if Moses were that kind of prophet, the trip to the promised land would have been a direct route, with exact provisions packed for the journey, and the arrival date preset. One would develop a lack of dependence on God if such were the way of prophecy. Also, the dire consequences of power and authority resting in the prophet rather than in the One who informs the prophet could be delineated. Examples would be TV evangelists who start out proclaiming a faithful message and become ensnared with the need to raise money and then to *have* money and then to lose their prophetic voice.

Prophecy as revealing the presence of God and the message of God's will for this day is the key. Prophecy as connecting people with God, and not just telling *about* God, is also important. The boldness of Moses to speak the unpopular Word, and the re-forming power of that prophecy on the Israelites is comparable to the difference it makes when a believer speaks and *lives* a faithful life against the norm. (Kay Gray)

MY NEIGHBOR

1 CORINTHIANS 8:1-13

The church in Corinth had questions for Paul regarding the rightness or wrongness of eating meat that had been offered to an idol. Some people evidently felt that eating the meat was an acknowledgment of the idol and therefore wrong, while others felt that if the idol was not acknowledged, the meat was accept-able. Paul suggests that they turn their attention away from the question of whether or not meat should be eaten and instead explore the question of how they can best be in a Christlike rela-tionship with one another.

I. We Have Knowledge

Paul is careful not to disagree with the statements being made concerning the rightness or wrongness of eating meat offered to idols. As a matter of fact, he in effect says, "Yes, you are correct, but to what end?" Having or not having knowledge is not as important to Paul as whether or not one is using that knowledge on God's behalf. Knowledge that is not used for developing a more positive relationship with God is not useful at all. "Knowl-edge puffs up, but love builds up" (v. 1). "If I . . . understand all mysteries and all knowledge, . . . but do not have love, I gain nothing" (1 Cor. 13:2-3).

II. Not All Possess This Knowledge

Knowledge therefore can be a positive thing, *if* directed toward the good of the community or toward furthering God's kingdom. Or, it can be a negative thing. Knowledge by itself is neither a good nor bad thing until it is used in either a good or bad way. Paul therefore agrees that knowledge about meat being offered to idols has potential for good. "It is not everyone, however, who has this knowledge" (v. 7), which means, according to Paul, that this knowledge also has potential for bad.

III. Do Not Allow Others to Falter Because of Knowledge They Do Not Have

Looking from a single perspective at the question of meat being offered to idols, without taking into account the full Body of Christ (even if the perspective is a correct one), did not do full justice to the importance that Paul placed on relating to one another in love as the communal Body of Christ. In fact, without the perspective of the whole body, great harm was being done. "By your knowledge," Paul writes, "those weak believers for whom Christ died are destroyed" (v. 11). The question of how this meat affected each individual relationship with God was only a small part of a much bigger issue. Of equal importance was the question of how this meat affected our neighbor's relationship with God.

Determining the rightness or wrongness of any given action based solely on "my knowledge about me" is a good first step. But it is only a single step in a process that needs to include a much wider understanding of what we call community. (Mark D. Haines)

JESUS' AUTHORITY

MARK 1:21-28

From the beginning, Mark's world is surreal. John the Baptist dresses in camel's hair and a leather belt, and eats locusts and honey. At Jesus' baptism are weird, supernatural occurrences: The heavens are torn open and a Spirit-dove descends on him. The Spirit drives Jesus into the wilderness to be with wild beasts and the tempter. As Jesus ministers, demon-possessed persons recognize him and shout his identity as God's Son.

The lines between the natural and the supernatural worlds seem to blur. A world of Spirit, Satan, angels, and demons is breaking into a world of crowds, disciples, and Jewish leaders. Jesus stands astride the threshold of these two worlds. Today's passage provides us with this Gospel's first encounter of both Jesus the rabbi, and Jesus the exorcist.

I. Teaching in Word and Deed

Jesus is often given the title "teacher" in Mark's Gospel. Yet the odd thing is that Mark recounts so little of Jesus' actual teaching. There is no Sermon on the Mount or Plain, as in the other Synoptics. Here we find Jesus teaching in the synagogue at Capernaum. The crowd reaction is very positive: "They were astounded . . . for he taught them as one having authority, and not as the scribes" (v. 22). What was it that he said? Mark does not say. Note that conflict with religious authority is being set up before a single scribe or Pharisee appears.

What Mark does tell us is that Jesus' teaching incites a response from the Spirit world, from a man with an unclean spirit. Jesus handles the situation with power and authority, casting out the demon. The crowd's reaction to the exorcism is noteworthy: "What is this? A new teaching—with authority!"

Perhaps Mark is trying to tell us that he is not interested in the content of Jesus' teaching as much as the action of Jesus' saving work. Jesus' authority, in Marcan terms, does not so much rest in what Jesus says, but in what he is willing to do for another. The crowds recognize both the words and the works of Jesus as authoritative, even more so than that day's religious scholars.

In our time the authority of the church, the pastor, and the Bible are all in deep question. The relevance of all three are challenged in a culture that is often cynical about religious dogma. Perhaps we would best take a lesson in authority from Jesus— talk less and act more. Do your works match your words? Do your deeds match your declarations? If we are to teach in the way that Jesus taught, then we must have both. In some ways things today may not be so different from those in Jesus' day. Folks are still cynical about "scribal" authority, which only speaks and does not act in saving, compassionate, and reconciling ways.

II. An Exorcise in Authority

The possessed man in the synagogue had an "unclean" spirit, which is a spirit of separation. To be unclean meant to be alienated and isolated (see Mark 5). If you were unclean, then you were contaminated and were not fit to be touched. Though he was inside the synagogue, though he was in physical proximity to the gathered community, this man was spiritually detached from them.

Is any sister or brother ever so "possessed," so isolated, as to be outside the scope of Jesus' authority? Is anyone so detached as to be outside the compassionate ministry and mercy of Jesus? I would say no. (Sam Parkes)

DOORS AND WINDOWS

FEBRUARY

Reflection Verse: "Then the LORD answered me and said: Write the vision; make it plain on tablets . . ." (Hab. 2:2).

The Discipline:

Write to open the doors on your experience. Write as a way of really seeing what you see. Set aside a time early in the month to write down what you really see, think, and feel. Later in the month, read what you wrote. Did you really mean what you wrote?

Many of us paint pictures of our lives that aren't true. We glamorize. We romanticize. And we refuse to acknowledge or accept the beauty of the real. Write something real this month, just a paragraph or a page. Talk to your reality. Make it your friend.

"A good story," someone wise said, "is one that has the little goblins in it." What are your little goblins? Are they a part of your story? (*Don't* share your story with anyone.)

The Meditation:

In an article in the February 26, 1996, issue of *The New Yorker* magazine, William Maxwell described Katharine White this way: "It's funny. . . . As an editor, she was maternal; and as a mother, she was editorial." The author, Nancy Franklin, did not miss the conundrum of the comment: "Men tend to see their lives, regardless of the balance of the various parts, as a unified whole, but the prevailing metaphor for women . . . has failure built into it: We are said to "juggle" the various parts of our lives, and the only possible outcome if we concentrate on one ball in particular is that we drop the others. But this is not how Katharine White saw her life—partly because she could afford not to, by hiring people to juggle for her, but mainly because she just didn't think that way. When I started looking at her life as she looked at it—and as she lived it—it suddenly seemed all of a piece."

Our goal as pastors is to enjoy the incredible androgyny of our lives. If we are men, people sometimes think we are effeminate; if we are women, people may believe we are too aggressive. Isn't the confusion grand? Let's be both, and even more. Let's find the right metaphor for our life and then go out and live it. A good goal is not simply to live my own life, but to see my own life the way I see it. Not the way "they" see it (whoever they are).

Louise Bogan, in her biography *Journey Around My Room* (New York: Viking Press, 1980), says: "The certain method of stilling poetic talent is to substitute an outer battle for an inner one. A poet emerges from a spiritual crisis strengthened and refreshed only if [she or he] has been strong enough to fight it through at all levels, and at the deepest first. One refusal to take up the gage thrown down by his [sic] own nature leaves the artist confused and maimed. . . ."

When we think about this new century, and time becoming new, we need to make sure we are seeing our doors and our struggles and our time. Not what we are supposed to see. Not juggling other people's realities so much as the relationship between those realities and our reality. We are not really free to battle the outer only or the inner only—we must battle them both simultaneously.

Carl Jung assured us that we "smuggle" our biography into everything we say or do. Knowing this, as pastors, how can we not make every effort to really know ourselves? We are free by the grace of God to see what we see, now and in the time that is coming.

Maurya Simon, in the poem "Pride," writes about the benefit of even shame. In the poem, Simon confronts her foreignness in the person of a rickshaw driver she knows is cheating her. By doing so, she upsets the balance of things—that foreigners are supposed to be ripped off by the local cabbies—with assertiveness: "I won't be robbed blind." She threatens the cabbie's power as an insider, a position Simon had earlier supported out of guilt. "Suddenly the rickshaw driver whirls around and / throws my money on the ground, spits on it, then / zooms away, leaving me richer in my shame."

What does she mean by "richer in my shame"? How can shame make us rich? By making us talk to our own truth, that's how.

The Song:
Just as I am, without one plea,
But that your blood was shed for me,
And that you called inviting me,
O Lamb of God,
I come, I come.

Just as I am, though tossed about
With many a conflict, many a doubt,
Fightings and fears within, without,
O Lamb of God,
I come, I come.

The Prayer:
Fill us with the power we need to be your people, O God. Use us to open the closed, expand the limited, and enliven the dull. And open, expand, and enliven us, too. In the name of Jesus, the animator. Amen. (Donna Schaper)

FEBRUARY 6, 2000

Fifth Sunday After Epiphany

Worship Theme: God is infinite and almighty, and gives to God's children genuine assurance and freedom upon which we can rely.

Readings: Isaiah 40:21-31; 1 Corinthians 9:16-23; Mark 1:29-39

Call to Worship (Psalm 147:7-11):

Leader:	Sing to the LORD with thanksgiving;
People:	**make melody upon the lyre to our God**
Leader:	who covers the heavens with clouds, prepares rain for the earth, makes grass grow upon the hills.
People:	**The LORD gives to the beasts their food, and to the young ravens that cry.**
Leader:	The LORD takes no delight in the might of a horse nor pleasure in the strength of a runner,
People:	**but the Lord takes pleasure in the faithful, in those who hope in the LORD's steadfast love.**

Pastoral Prayer:

O Lord, our God, we smile to consider that you are moved not by grand displays of religion but by simple acts of faith. We praise you for your faithfulness. The sun may cease to rise, yet your love will be ever present. Our lives may seem dry and barren, but you still abide with us. Give us the endurance to spread a message of freedom. Unsettle us so that we never grow too comfortable in our neat and tidy worlds but that we always remain true to your call to share Christ in new and strange places. Bind us one to another in the love of Jesus Christ. Amen. (Thomas Gildermeister)

SERMON BRIEFS

FAITH IN THE RIGHT-SIZED GOD

ISAIAH 40:21-31

There are times when we feel as if we are simply living from day to day, driven by the wind of fate. Or worse, we feel as if our lives are controlled by evil people. Although we are able to sing boldly about an omnipotent God in the worship of our congregations, life is not lived behind stained glass. In our homes or workplaces, our faith is challenged by the circumstances of the mundane. We must ask if our faith and perspective of God is large enough to carry us through the mundane.

I. Believing Atheists (vv. 21-24)

The times our faith is tested by the mundane routines of life are when we begin to question if there is any purpose to our lives. If we question the purpose of our lives, we also are questioning the one who gave us life. The prophet here asks the rhetorical questions of the believing readers: "Have you not heard about the power of God?" He knows that the readers obviously have heard of the power and strength of God, but that they were caught up in the activities of their difficulties and must have forgotten that Yahweh is still the sovereign Lord.

The prophet begins to describe this awesome God who seems to be too easily forgotten. He is viewed as enthroned with all people, who are like grasshoppers. This reminds the readers that even their greatest enemy is still under the domain of the Almighty God. Nature also is under God's divine sovereignty. Rulers are placed in and taken out of positions not by their sole ability or fate but by God. The issue at stake here is to determine what issue causing anxiety is larger than God? We should view God's lordship in comparison to the triviality of our "giants" of anxiety. We must not proclaim God as Lord in praise on Sunday, only to let that proclamation pale in light of adversity on Tuesday. God is the Lord on Tuesday as well as Sunday.

II. Appropriating Faith in the Sovereign God (vv. 25-31)

In verse 25, the voice of the Lord is heard asking, "Who is comparable or equal to me?" God is a jealous God who desires all the worship of God's followers, and is not willing to share any of that worship with any object or idea. The prophet joins in to argue that, in observing creation, one sees the power and strength of God. In fact, the prophet is urging the readers to look in a different direction, to view God in a different light.

Apparently the problem rests with the words and the complaints of the people who feel that God has abandoned them (v. 27). But again they are reminded that the Lord does not grow weary or tired, and is in actuality the giver of strength and power. Those who learn to trust in the Almighty God will find their strength renewed. During the mundane, when our language betrays our faith, we should take another look at the sovereign God and replace our faltering hope. The natural result will be refreshing and renewing of our strength for the day. (Joseph Byrd)

WHY ARE WE IN MINISTRY?

1 CORINTHIANS 9:16-23

A friend once told a story about a young woman who was preparing to leave her place of employment for another work opportunity. Her coworkers gathered together at the end of her last day to celebrate the time they had worked together. As they shared stories of their time together, the young woman asked them to tell about what they would be doing if they could pursue any career at all. One said she would be training whales at a water-world facility. Another said she would be running her own floral shop. Still another said she would be rocking babies all day long.

So many people in our communities today work because of priorities that have been established by the secular world. We work to pay bills. We work to obtain health insurance. We work to achieve status in the community. We work for material gain and its effect on our lives. And we are sometimes granted status because of the visibility of our work.

This was true in Paul's time as well. The church in Corinth had questions about Paul's authority in part because of Paul's unwillingness to make claims concerning the physical results of his work as an apostle of Jesus Christ. Because he was not claiming the rights and privileges that some other leaders were claiming, people questioned the legitimacy of his status as a church leader.

As he has done so often in his communications with the early church, Paul turns their questions upside down as he redirects the focus of their concerns from the secular to the spiritual. Paul claims that he could have the same rights and privileges due him because of his role in the church, which brings with it the implied authority that is being questioned, but to do so would miss the point of who he is and why he does what he does.

Paul claims authority as an apostle of Jesus Christ based on his relationship with the risen Christ and *not* based on whether or not he exercises his right to marry or accept payment for his work on behalf of the church. And the work that he does on behalf of Christ as a vocation comes as a result of his call to follow Christ rather than as a means to support himself here on earth. His vocation is thus more accurately defined in terms of who he is as a disciple of Christ rather than as a set of job expectations and benefits.

What a powerful statement of discipleship! How can we give ourselves permission to train whales, or grow flowers, or rock babies for Christ? How do we give ourselves permission to grow into the disciples that Christ calls us to be? Paul says, "I do it all for the sake of the gospel." Can we do any less? (Mark D. Haines)

PRAYER AND HEALING

MARK 1:29-39

In the second healing story of the Gospel and the following verses, Mark describes an increasingly difficult ministry situation for Jesus. Everyone so far has been responding positively to Jesus, spreading his fame "throughout . . . Galilee" (1:28). Now the demand for his presence and attention becomes overwhelming.

I. Jesus the Healer

Let us not, in all our scholarship, fail to notice the obvious—Jesus heals. In 1:16–2:12, Mark treats readers to story after story about the kingdom of God coming near in Jesus' healing care and presence. The healing of Simon's mother-in-law is a very straightforward healing form: Jesus is made aware of the need (v. 30b), Jesus performs the healing (v. 31a), and the woman gives evidence of her healing (v. 31b). The response of the crowd is so intense as to press against credibility.

Tensions rise for the modern reader. At least in this section of the Gospel, Jesus heals with authority, power, and without failure. Yet, is this our experience of sickness and healing? If Mark is going to begin his story of the Good News with an assortment of healing stories, all of which go off without a hitch, then certainly Mark should permit readers to ask, "Why doesn't Jesus do this sort of healing when we bring our sick friends, relatives, or selves to Jesus?" We church folk tend to short-circuit serious conversation on this question by leaning on excuses which are theologically dumbfounding: "I guess I just don't have enough faith." "Healing must not be God's will for. . . ."

Is there a way to interpret these healing stories faithfully without resorting to pat answers that probably do more harm than good? Is there a way to promote authentic healing ministries in the sermon without becoming faith-healing "hucksters"? Can we both celebrate Jesus' healing presence and honor the integrity of faithful lives that remain in need?

II. Jesus the Prayer

Again, let us not overlook the obvious—Jesus prays. At night, the entire city of Capernaum responds to Jesus' healing authority by swamping Simon's house. Jesus rises early the next day and goes out by himself to pray. Why? This episode of prayer falls smack-dab in the center of a series of four healing stories. I think

Mark wants us to know that Jesus drew strength for healing from outside his own person—from God. To be a healing presence requires prayer and introspection. Interestingly, in 9:14-29 the disciples are unable to exorcise a spirit from a man's son. After Jesus casts out the spirit, the disciples ask, "Why could we not cast it out?" Jesus replies, "This kind can come out only through prayer." Apparently the disciples do not pray, or at the least, they do not associate prayer and healing.

We know that Jesus can handle the wilderness and any tempter or wild beast that might meet him there (1:13). It is the disciples who "hunt" him down (v. 36). The word translated "hunted" has quite hostile connotations. They are trying to force Jesus back into service. It seems that Jesus need not fear Satan; however, those closest to him will tempt him away from prayer. Jesus handles Satan's temptation in less than a verse. The disciples are even more adversarial, a point that Jesus underscores in 8:33.

What are the things that distract you from prayer? Typically for me it is no supernatural force, but my own sense of ministry. My own calendar and my unwillingness to carve out genuine time for renewal are far worse enemies than the evil one. Satan is no match for God's kingdom in Jesus. Sometimes, regrettably, Jesus' present-day disciples are. (Sam Parkes)

FEBRUARY 13, 2000

Sixth Sunday After Epiphany

Worship Theme: The cost of following Christ is always high, but the reward and riches of faith are unquestionable.

Readings: 2 Kings 5:1-14; 1 Corinthians 9:24-27; Mark 1:40-45

Call to Worship (Psalm 30:1-3, 11-12):

Leader: I will extol you, O LORD, for you have lifted me up, and did not let my foes rejoice over me.

People: **O LORD my God, I cried to you for help, and you healed me.**

Leader: O LORD, you brought up my soul from Sheol,

People: **restored me to life from among those gone down to the pit.**

Leader: You have turned my mourning into dancing; you have loosed my sackcloth and girded me with gladness, that my soul may praise you and not be silent.

People: **O LORD, my God, I will give thanks to you forever.**

Pastoral Prayer:
   So immense is your presence, Holy God, and so sure is your love. We praise your grace that redeems us and puts us on the road to your heavenly kingdom. Lord, you know that we stumble and fall. You know that we resist the price of following Christ. You know that too often we are proud and will not ask for your aid. Please lower our resistance, comfort our wounds, and help us

to discover the joy of humility. In the name of the humble One, Jesus Christ. Amen. (Thomas Gildermeister)

SERMON BRIEFS

LESSONS FROM A LEPER

2 KINGS 5:1-14

In Paul Cedar's *A Life of Prayer* (Dallas: Word Publishing, 1998, pp. 104-105), Rosalind Goforth relates a time of testing during her fourth year as a missionary to China. She, her husband, and their eighteen-month-old son were spending the hot season on the coast. Their son became ill with dysentery and was at the point of death.

Of that time she writes: "My soul rebelled. I actually seemed to hate God. I could see nothing but cruel injustice in it all; and the child seemed to be going fast. My husband and I knelt down beside the little one's bedside, and [God] pleaded earnestly with me to yield my will and my child to God. After a long and bitter struggle, God gained the victory, and I told my husband I would give my child to the Lord. Then my husband prayed, committing the precious soul into the Lord's keeping."

As Rosalind Goforth prayed, the rapid breathing ceased; and before the break of dawn, God's healing prevailed.

She writes: "To me it has always seemed that the Lord tested me to almost the last moment; then, when I yielded my dearest treasure to him and put my Lord first, [God] gave back the child."

The text deals with an army general who discovers the same lesson—yielding to God's will is a prerequisite to any type of healing. What lessons are to be learned from the healing of a leper general in need of God?

Lesson One: Disease Has No Favorites

It seems logical that disease would strike only the meanest, most cruel, ignorant scum of the earth and that God would protect everyone else. The truth is, it doesn't happen that way in a fallen world.

Everybody knows someone who has been vibrant with life but now suffers from some type of disease. Cancer, Alzheimer's, stroke, and heart problems represent a small fragment of common illnesses.

The general was a strong, rich, educated, intelligent, respected, and powerful man who no one dreamed would become ill. But disease is no respecter of persons, and Naaman, the general, contracts the most feared Old Testament disease—leprosy.

Lesson Two: Healing Methods Are Not All the Same, But God Is

A glance at Jesus' healing of people reveals that not everyone is healed in the same manner.

—Jesus orders the demons to leave, and they release their occupants (Mark 1:21 26; 5:1-18).
—Jesus touches Simon Peter's mother-in-law (Mark 1:29-31) and a man with skin disease (Mark 1:40-42).
—Jesus speaks words of healing to a paralyzed man (Mark 2:1-12) and a man with a crippled hand (Mark 3:1-6).
—Jesus feels healing leave him after his clothes are touched (Mark 5:25-34).

The text tells us that the prophet Elisha's method of healing differs from the normal way that Naaman and we think it ought to be done. Elisha sends a messenger in his place to talk with Naaman. Elisha instructs Naaman to go wash in the Jordan River seven times.

Naaman's reaction is one of disbelief. He is insulted. Elisha hasn't made the customary courtesy of meeting Naaman face to face. Then Naaman can't believe he has to wash in the muddy Jordan—not once, but seven times. Where's the magic in this? Where's the spectacularism associated with healing? Shouldn't Elisha be there and wave his hands and cry out loudly to his God?

God isn't interested in the spectacular TV-healing special, but only in your well-being. Naaman almost missed his opportunity for healing because he wanted to tell God and his prophet how to heal. Elisha made it clear that Naaman could not design his own healing method.

Lesson Three: Healing Comes

The bottom line is that Naaman was healed.

In *Windows of Hope* (Sisters, Ore.: Multnomah, 1992, p. 49), Richard Lee writes: "Should God see fit to heal you or your loved one, praise [God] for the added days . . . graciously given you. But if physical healing does not come—if you are left with weakness and pain where you desired strength, or an empty place where once the family circle was complete—know that out of that which you've experienced will come all the grace and strength you need to meet this trial as [God's] child."

There is a certainty that one day whole healing will come. Salvation is the true healing all of us need. (Derl Keefer)

RUNNING WITH A PURPOSE

1 CORINTHIANS 9:24-27

Simply stating one's intention to be a Christian is not the same thing as actively living the Christian life. Using athletes as an example, Paul emphasizes the difference between simply running a race, and running that race to win. "Do you not know that in a race the runners all compete, but only one receives the prize?" (v. 24). For Paul, it is the difference between calling oneself a Christian and striving with all of one's heart, mind, and soul for the physical manifestation of God's will on earth. In a race, there is a definite prize to be won, and a definite goal to be achieved. Being Christian, implies Paul, involves the same definitive purpose, and therefore the same diligent training and pursuit.

Paul's letters to the Corinthians are filled with responses to questions from the church in Corinth. They wanted Paul's opinions on whether or not to eat temple meat purchased in the market. They wanted to know whether or not women should have their heads covered in the worship service. They wanted to know how men and women should relate to one another in light of their understanding of the coming new age. Paul's concern is that the Corinthians have been trying to define their Christianity by what they do rather than by who they are.

Paul's contention is that defining the reason for the race is how one goes about defining the way one runs the race. Knowing the reason for the race will directly affect the effort that is put into winning the race. Knowing the reason for developing a relationship with God that will in turn direct the relationships people have with one another will directly affect the way people relate to one another in regard to food purchased in the market, and their marriage relationships, and how they appear in worship. We should not establish rules that illustrate a new morality without first establishing the reason for a new morality as a Christ-centered community of believers *from* which a new morality will come!

Runners run "to receive a perishable wreath, but we an imperishable one" (v. 25). What is this imperishable wreath? Why do we do what we do as the church? "I do not run aimlessly," says Paul, "nor do I box as though beating the air" (v. 26). Where are our foundations? Being the church is more than just knowing correct theological behavior. Being the church involves the God-centered reality that enables us to establish loving relationships with one another as we work towards the actualization of God's kingdom on earth. (Mark D. Haines)

WHAT IS THE KINGDOM ABOUT?

MARK 1:40-45

This is the third in a series of four healing stories from Mark 1:21–2:12. Jesus is on a preaching tour of Galilee (1:39), but Mark describes no preaching. In fact, this is the only story from the tour of cities related at all, and the event takes place away from crowds and disciples.

"Leprosy" was a term used to describe various skin diseases and was as much a legal and social problem as a medical one. Those with leprosy had strict codes to which to adhere (Leviticus 13–14). One primary burden placed upon those with leprosy was social isolation. Contact with healthy people was severely limited. Imagine being exiled from family, friends, and work. Imagine the endless days of waiting for something new to happen that might change the course of events. Imagine the sense of defeat and loss when such a change did not happen. So great was the fear of these diseases that even an apparent healing had to be validated by a priest before restoration to the community. That process took several days (Leviticus 14)—more waiting. When the healing presence of Jesus comes near the leper of Mark 1:40, there are two basic directions to pursue.

I. Thwarted Expectations

Mark, I believe, is trying to mess with readers' minds just a bit here. In the first two healing stories in this Gospel (1:21-28; 1:29-31), we see a Jesus who heals or exorcises in response to the initiative of others. Since there is little else in the way of teaching or instruction, the reader might be led to believe (as I believe Mark is attempting to do) that Jesus' mission is all about miraculous healing. After all, it is the healing that causes the crowds to search him out.

In this story, Mark turns the tables on the reader. In 1:40-42, everything goes according to formula—no problems. We even get the first glimpse of Jesus' emotional state: He is "moved with pity." If this were a screenplay, we'd read, "Healing, Scene 3. Setting: Lush hills in Galilee, sea in the background, lambs playing on the hillside, warm sunlight on Jesus." Jesus, full of pity, chooses of his own volition to heal the leper. "Close-up on the leper's tearful smile. Cue the swelling violins."

Suddenly verse 43 thwarts the reader's expectations. Jesus sternly warns the man and sends "him away at once," which is a mild translation. Jesus drives this guy away, commanding him not to tell anyone about Jesus' involvement in the healing. Look just off-camera and you will see Mark smiling and winking. This is not Hollywood after all! If the Kingdom were solely about healing, then surely Jesus would not try to suppress that fact. Jesus does not want to be understood only as a miracle healer, as attractive as that is to the crowds who clamor on Mark's landscapes. Soon enough, we will witness times when Jesus cannot perform such powerful deeds (6:5-6). What, then, *is* the Kingdom about?

How do you reconcile the fact that the One who heals is also the One who must suffer? How do you meld the images of a healing Christ with the suffering Jesus? People come from every quarter to be with the Christ who heals (1:45). Yet who will watch with Jesus on the eve of his suffering (14:37)? Does Mark's Jesus still mess with our minds and thwart our expectations?

II. Just Can't Wait to Tell Somebody About Jesus

This leper who has waited and waited and waited simply will not wait anymore. Having received what he asked of Jesus, having been sternly warned to shut his mouth and obey the law, he cannot help but proclaim freely what Jesus has done for him. Nothing, not Jesus' exhortation, not even the law's demands, seems more important to him. Jesus, who seems authoritative enough to silence demons and handle Satan's wilderness temptations, cannot control this healed leper. The news is simply too good.

I always wish that people in the pews would be a little more vocal about what God has done for them. I wish that I had more fortitude to encourage their witness and provide more opportunities for them to tell about God's work in their lives. In my own tradition, the emphasis on personal testimony is being lost though it is a profound part of our heritage.

What aspect of God's work in your life is so good that even Jesus' command cannot suppress your witness? What work of God in your life is so good that you just can't wait to tell somebody about Jesus? (Sam Parkes)

81

FEBRUARY 20, 2000

Seventh Sunday After Epiphany

Worship Theme: Through Christ we are being transformed from "the things of old" into a "new thing" altogether.

Readings: Isaiah 43:18-25; 2 Corinthians 1:18-22; Mark 2:1-12

Call to Worship (Psalm 41:1-3, 13):

Leader: Blessed are those who consider the poor! The LORD delivers them in the day of trouble;

People: **the LORD protects them and keeps them alive; they are called blessed in the land;**

Leader: you do not give them up to the will of their enemies.

People: **The LORD sustains them on their sickbed; in their illness you heal all their infirmities. Blessed be the LORD, the God of Israel, from everlasting to everlasting! Amen and Amen.**

Pastoral Prayer:

O Holy God, the source of all righteousness and atonement, we offer praise and thanksgiving for your creation—and for the possibility of re-creation in and through your Son, Jesus Christ. The world you have made is filled with the stuff of blessing and nurture. And when we delight in this goodness and share it, how pleasing and peaceful can our community be. But we seize and hoard. We turn our backs on the hurt of your children. Forgive us and release us once again from these mistaken choices, so that we can be the Body of Christ that you intended us to be. Amen. (Thomas Gildermeister)

SERMON BRIEFS

FAITHFUL MERCY

ISAIAH 43:18-25

The lessons of God's mercy and human sinfulness are woven throughout the Scripture in narrative after narrative. Continually even the casual reader will find that God does not discard unfaithful children. The call is for God's people to recognize the goodness of God, and the neglect of humanity toward God. The correct response is repentance and walking in obedience.

I. Self-Justification and Divine Reality (vv. 18-21)

It is in the best interests of Israel to forget the past and not argue for their accomplishments of faithfulness (cf. vv. 26-28). The Lord is willing to forget the past. Likewise for us, we would do well to stop dwelling on it and look to the present moment. God's chosen should have been focused on the present work being done in their lives. God was making a way of hope in the midst of a desert of hopelessness and providing a stream in the wasteland.

Nature cries out in praise as it receives the benefits of God blessing the people. Yet God's demonstration of grace, which should have garnered praise, was left unnoticed by Israel. It is far too easy to attempt justifying why we should be receiving a different treatment from God. In our minds that suffer from selective amnesia, our past accomplishments merit blessing. Yet our attention should be refocused on what God is doing now to bring about hope in our situation of difficulty.

II. The Charge Against the People (vv. 22-24)

Israel had not called upon God nor attempted to truly worship God in light of the mercy extended toward them. They were not burdened with great demands, and yet they did not honor God in any real respect. The Lord concludes that while they did not bring offerings and sacrifices, they did burden the Lord with their sins and they did weary the Lord with their offenses. God's perspective is an interesting one in comparison to ours. God does not receive worship but only receives our offensive disobedience. A principle at work here is that the disobedient heart does not raise sincere worship to the Lord. Worship is an act of obedience. The New Testament makes this clear in stating that we are to offer our bodies as living sacrifices, which is our reasonable worship. Obedience in our everyday life is an act of individual worship to be offered before God, and it is inseparably linked to our acts of corporate worship.

III. The Source of Restoration (v. 25)

It is clear from the previous verses that Israel did nothing to merit God's faithful grace. The Lord blotted out the transgressions of Israel for God's own sake. The act of forgiveness is a divine act independent of human justification. For Israel to find their way out of difficulty, they had to refrain from dwelling on their concepts of what they deserved or were owed as chosen people. The larger principle here is that to find restoration in the wilderness, one must focus on the present act of God's grace, and move in obedience and worship for the mercy received. It is in this process that one finds the way out of the desert toward a refreshing stream in the wasteland. All other paths just take us in circles. (Joseph Byrd)

THE GOD PLACE

2 CORINTHIANS 1:18-22

Paul had to change his plans and cancel his visit to the church at Corinth. Paul's opponents (perhaps those from the church in Jerusalem, or just local Corinthian adversaries) use this change of itinerary to malign Paul's character and devalue his ministry. The opposition spreads the word that Paul cannot make up his mind even about his travel plans, much less about the more important responsibilities of spiritual director for the Corinthian congregation (2 Cor. 1:17a). They accuse Paul of vacillating and making his ministry plans according to human standards (v. 17b). The opponents consider Paul's ministry ineffective because he cannot make definite travel plans. Paul's opponents are determined to undermine Paul's authority as an apostle as well as his work among the believers in Corinth.

Even if Paul had arranged his itinerary without any contingency plans, with every detail covered and every intended destination met at the appointed time, these persistent opponents would have found something to critique. Paul's work and life were offensive to them, and they were out to malign his reputation among the Corinthian church.

To attempt to undermine Paul's ministry by attacking his inability to follow a predetermined itinerary reflects more on the weakness of the opponents rather than serving as a statement of Paul's deficiency. The rhetoric of the opposition lacks potency. Who among us has not hesitated when making an important decision? While traveling down the unfamiliar highway of life, who has not first turned right, then turned left, only to have to return and travel straight with no turns at all? Who among us has not written a sentence, then read it, only to erase it and start all over? Who among us has never thrown out a batch of cookie dough because in haste we reached for the saltshaker rather than for the sugar canister? Who among us has not made an appointment, only to have to cancel it later?

However, who among us has turned harsh criticism from our opponents into a devotional thought? Paul's response to the opposition is far more potent than the criticism. Paul uses their criticism as a "homiletical moment." Paul has the gift to turn everything, even the harsh critique of his adversaries, into a spiritual lesson for the church. And he does it so well here. He acknowledges that we all are indecisive. You and I know that. Those great decisions of life—such as choice of life partner, vocational path, and purchase of a house—are usually not made without moments, even months of reflection. On a given day, you may be confident that you are doing the right thing. Yet on another day you might change your mind, find a new real estate agent, choose another career, and maybe not get married after all. Most of us know that kind of indecisiveness. The ambivalence is normal for major decisions. My mother often shared with me her philosophy: "When in doubt, don't do."

We wrestle with the decision until we get to that quiet place of resolve. You and I know the inner sacred space where we can rest

knowing that we have touched the will of God on that matter—
the place that appears after we have exhausted our resources—
and we begin to lean on the sacred wisdom of the One who created us. In that moment of peace, all is well. The decision has
depth and merit. We are in harmony with God and others. We
have tapped an inner strength that enables us to face whatever
outcome the decision might bring, because we know it is all in
order.

That is the God place where we can hear God's "yes" (v. 19).
Indecision fades and the definitive character of God shines
through our lives. In Paul's language, God establishes us, puts his
seal on us, gives us the Holy Spirit in our hearts (v. 21-22). We
are no longer tossed like the wind, but firmly planted in a life
with God that provides a foundation of rest and confidence.

Paul's opponents cannot win. Their critical rhetoric becomes
the center of Paul's homily. Paul says that we may say yes and no,
but God always says yes. And we can depend on God's "yes."

God has been affirmed, the opposition has been silenced, and
Paul's ministry to the Corinthians has regained focus. (Linda
McKinnish Bridges)

FAITH, FRIENDS, AND FORGIVENESS

MARK 2:1-12

That Jesus can no longer go into a town "openly" is an ominous
turn (Mark 1:45). Mark tells us that Jesus can no longer go into
the towns, but has to stay out in the country. So far, the author
has portrayed the wilderness as a place that is kind to Jesus. It is
there that angels minister to him (1:13) and that Jesus goes to
pray (1:35). The towns might be dangerous for him now. By 2:1,
however, he is back in Capernaum. Jesus is drawing people from
every quarter, and some of those quarters begin to oppose him.

The healing of the paralytic is the last of four healings before
Mark launches into a parallel section of four stories about controversy with religious authorities (2:15–3:6). The transition from
one set of stories to another, though, is bridged by Mark's insertion of conflict with scribes into this last healing (cf. 1:22). Mark
gathers many themes into these twelve verses, and all are worthy

of consideration by the preacher: the nature and origin of Jesus' authority (1:27; 11:28); the question of blasphemy (3:28; 14:64); the "Son of Man" title (8:31; 9:9; 9:31; 10:33; 13:26; and chapter 14); faith or belief (e.g., 1:15; 4:40; 5:34; 6:6; 9:24; 11:22; and 15:32).

I. Faith: Overcoming the Crowd

Let's look at the healing story without the elements of controversy. Imagine that the story was like this: Mark 2:1-5a, 11-12. What is unique about this portion of the story? The friends of the paralyzed man are forced to use drastic means to get their friend to Jesus. The crowds have gotten so big that they actually obstruct the way to Jesus. By extraordinary effort, the friends dig through the roof to place their friend near Jesus. In Jesus' vocabulary, there is a word for such effort—*faith*. In fact, Jesus only uses this word in reference to persons who with amazing effort get to Jesus by overcoming the crowd, such as the paralytic's friends, the woman with a hemorrhage (5:25), and Bartimaeus (10:46).

This story says something powerful about the value of Christian community and friendship. Jesus sees the faith of the friends and counts it to the credit of the paralyzed man, who never personally expresses confidence in Jesus. Recently I sustained several personal losses. One seemed to come right on top of another. Were it not for my friends "faith-ing" on my behalf, overcoming the obstacles that kept me from Christ, I do not know where I would be. Because of their faith, I have experienced healing.

Where have you seen your community expressing faith, the kind of faith that will dig through a roof, full of confidence in Jesus? Sometimes we simply cannot muster faith by ourselves. And even if we can, sometimes we still need the faith of others to help us reach the place where our own faith can be effective.

II. A Recognized Authority?

Like a hard pit in a ripe peach, the scribes are on the scene. People have recognized authority in Jesus before (1:21), the authority to teach and exorcise spirits. Now Jesus claims for himself the authority to forgive sins. The connection between sin and sickness is a long-standing debate, both among the scriptural witnesses and even people today. Even the word *salvation* has as its root the Latin word that is translated "to heal." Regardless of what we may or may not believe about the matter, Mark assumes a connection between the two in this passage. For Jesus to say "Your sins are forgiven" is little different in meaning from Jesus saying "Stand up and take your mat and [go to your home]." If we assume with Mark that the paralysis is the result of sin, then the effect is the same. Jesus is saying to the scribes, "Look, no matter which way I say it, the same result will occur. So, if you don't like one, then I'll use the other. Either way, you will still have to recognize my authority!"

Jesus shares the authority to forgive sins with the church (his Body). Every Sunday that we serve Communion in my parish, the Mass is preceded by a general confession, after which I pronounce the absolution, "In the name of Jesus Christ, you are forgiven." The congregation pronounces the same absolution to me. Somehow, I think my parishioners miss the radical act in which we are engaging. What does it mean to have not only the authority, but the responsibility, of forgiving one another's sins? Where do you witness this outside the context of worship? (Sam Parkes)

FEBRUARY 27, 2000

Eighth Sunday After Epiphany

Worship Theme: The love and light of God in Christ will overcome the darkness of any sin that we may commit.

Readings: Hosea 2:14-20; 2 Corinthians 3:1-6; Mark 2:13-22

Call to Worship (Psalm 103:1-8):

Leader: Bless the LORD, O my soul! and all that is within me, bless God's holy name!

People: **Bless the LORD, O my soul, and forget not all God's benefits,**

Leader: who forgives all your iniquity, who heals all your diseases,

People: **who redeems your life from the pit, who crowns you with steadfast love and mercy, who satifies you with good as long as you live so that your youth is renewed like the eagle's.**

Leader: The LORD, who works vindication and justice for all who are oppressed, has made known God's ways to Moses, God's acts to the people of Israel.

People: **The LORD is merciful and gracious, slow to anger and abounding in steadfast love.**

Pastoral Prayer:
O Savior of the world, of our lives, can it be true? Do you forgive and forget? Is the brokenness of the past erased, gone, removed? And all we must do is say yes to Christ's call to follow

him? O Lord, we believe. Help our unbelief. Too often we do not believe in the power of your love. Too often, in our utter arrogance, we believe that your love cannot defeat our sin. Forgive us. Give us the patience to wait on the miracle—the miracle that we will know in our minds and hearts the truth that our lives have been redeemed by the sacrifice of Christ. And as we wait, give us the grace to love your children as if we already fully embraced this truth of how much you love us. Amen. (Thomas Gildermeister)

SERMON BRIEFS

IN THAT DAY

HOSEA 2:14-20

Do you like the picture of God we find in Hosea? I do. The picture is not without problems, and I would not blame you if you found it disturbing.

In Hosea, God is portrayed in earthy tones as a husband who has been hurt by his wife's adultery. Immediately we encounter the usual problems when God is painted with the brush of a patriarchal culture. However, if we read this text as savvy interpreters, then we know that the word picture "God is like a husband" does not mean that husbands are God. Our friend Hosea should not take anything from the equal roles for women and men that we have come to know through our oneness in Christ. Once we overcome the initial hurdle of the husband picture, other difficulties appear. God is presented as hurt by the idolatry of the people of Israel, as jealous, as angry, and even passionate, like a lover bent on the seduction of the beloved. You may or may not find these bothersome, depending on how you usually think of God.

I. Seeing the Picture

Despite all its potential for offense, this picture of God is profoundly good news. In Hosea, God is not just any husband. God is the husband who is faithful. In our text in chapter 2, God professes an undying love for God's people and commitment to the covenant. The testimony of Hosea is that, although God's people may be unfaithful, God is always faithful. I would contend further that this may be the key theme of the entire Old Testament. The New Testament then carries on this theme by presenting Jesus as evidence of God's faithfulness and by declaring God faithful to the promises of the new covenant. And so, as we Christians gather to worship, the words of Hosea come to us as a fresh word from God.

I also appreciate the picture of God that we find in Hosea because it speaks to us with clarity and force. We never come to the Bible without remembering that it is a witness to us from another time and place. The faithful who wrote of the mighty acts of God had different habits and customs than we do. They organized family life differently than we do. This does not bother us but does affect how we listen to their stories. In this case, however, the message is not obscure. The concepts are familiar to us: marriage and promises—kept and broken. For example, many married people would like to return to the romance of their courtship. Through these familiar ideas and feelings we can begin to grasp the faithfulness of God to us.

II. Affirming the Picture

The real question, therefore, is not the value of this picture of God but its truth. Can we hear this witness and give our verdict, "Yes, God is faithful!"? Are we willing to trust God? That is our dilemma, and it is one we share with the Israelites of Hosea's day.

The prophet says some remarkable things on God's behalf—promises about peace with nature and neighbors, safety, love, righteousness, and justice. With all this talk of married bliss, we Christians cannot help but think of the marriage of the Lamb in the book of Revelation. We too desire peace and justice. We hope for fellowship with God, and resurrection to eternal life. The prophet Hosea is one of the first in a long line of witnesses who say that God has prepared a future for us. Are we open to that future?

Twice in our passage, and again in verse 21, God declares, "In that day . . ." (KJV). "That day" is the day of promise. It represents all the promises of God and all the hopes of God's people. God is not yet finished. There remains a work for "that day." Do you believe this? Can you say with conviction, "Yes, God is faithful!"? (David Mauldin)

LIVING LETTERS

2 CORINTHIANS 3:1-6

Anyone who has searched for a job knows the importance of letters of recommendation. A full resume for employment will include at least three names of persons who can write formal letters of recommendation. The letters provide additional information regarding the past work experience of the candidate, the strength of character, and the reasons why the candidate would make a successful employee. The letters of recommendation announce to the search committee that others think that this candidate is worthy of hire.

In first-century culture, notes of recommendation were equally important for business transactions and societal organization. Of particular importance in the social system of the ancient world was when a slave could buy his or her freedom and become a free citizen. To appropriately introduce oneself to society as a member who has full voting privileges, the former slave would announce this new status by erecting a stone in the center of the marketplace. The new citizen could be assured that members of society would see the stone of recommendation and would know of his new position in society. The tablet would be a monument of recommendation, noting the merits of the new citizen and providing introduction to the life of the city.

Perhaps the stone monument of recommendation, as well as the more familiar letter of recommendation with ink, is what Paul has in mind when he uses the metaphor of letters of recommendation being written on the hearts of members of the Corinthian church. Paul's relationship with the Corinthians is warm and personal. He has written at least two letters to them and visited at least twice. He has closely followed their progress in the advance of the Gospel. With this intimacy of relationship, it is clear that he does not need a letter of recommendation nor a stone monument in the marketplace to recommend him to them, or them to him. They know each other well. They do not need these avenues of formality.

The relationship between Paul and the members of the Corinthian church is written on their hearts. What a beautiful metaphor: Not stone, not paper, but the hearts of people become the living "letters of recommendation" for his apostolic credibility, for his seasoning in the ministry, for his personal validity. What a way to measure ministerial prowess. Gone is the temptation to carve pretty words about someone that you barely know. Gone is the temptation to say more than you really mean because you are trying to impress the reader with your own ability as well as the ability of the one seeking employment. Paul says that his ministry is measured by what happens in the hearts of people, not by the flowery words of a letter of recommendation or the quality of the grade of stone in the stone of recommendation.

What might that look like? How might these "living letters" appear in the city of Corinth? Perhaps someone would say, "Missionary Paul really helped me to understand the value of sexual morality" (see 1 Cor. 5:1-5). Another member might have said, "Paul gave me wise counsel regarding that pending lawsuit" (1 Cor. 6:1-11). "We had a disagreement here in the church regarding food sacrificed to idols, and Paul helped us settle it," another member might have said (1 Cor. 8:1-13). Many of the members may have commented on how Paul brought unity to the body when they were divided over several issues, including how to celebrate the Lord's Supper (1 Cor. 11:17-34). These are the letters of recommendation written on the hearts of people.

The mark of the minister is not how many letters fill his or her employment folio, nor how many digits describe the church's salary package. The clear mark of success is how many people's lives and hearts are changed through one's ministry. The success of ministry rests in the hearts of people. (Linda McKinnish Bridges)

A DIFFERENCE IN VIEWPOINT

MARK 2:13-22

Mark has told us that Jesus called disciples by the sea (1:16) and that Jesus claimed the authority to forgive sins (2:10). This time Jesus calls a disciple who is a sinner (2:13). This passage kicks off a series of controversy stories and may divide into two sections—verses 13-17 and verses 18-22, each containing one of these stories, which typically end with a pithy pronouncement by Jesus on the subject at hand. The first story relates a conflict over Jesus' mission. The second is over the disciples' response to that mission. One of Mark's favorite words in the previous section of the Gospel (1:16–2:12), *immediately*, is used sparingly in this section of stories. Mark is trying to slow readers down so that they may carefully consider what is happening in these exchanges between Jesus and religious leaders.

I. How Do You See Sin?

Verses 13-14 parallel 1:16-20. Jesus is by the sea. He sees a prospect at work in his trade. The Gospel even makes note of Levi's father (cf. 1:19). Jesus calls Levi in the same manner as Simon and Andrew; Levi responds with the same degree of interest. So what is the problem? For Jesus to call professional fishers as disciples is one thing, but to call a tax collector is quite another. Their contact with Gentiles and reputation for bilking people of their money makes them rate pretty low on the acceptability scale of that culture. Mark goes on to say, unabashedly, that these are the sorts of people who followed Jesus (v. 15).

Jesus shared table fellowship with social outcasts, an act of great toleration and intimacy that we tend to miss in our fast-food culture. Also, Jesus is not acting as a gracious host but as an invited guest in Levi's house! When the scribes of the Pharisees want to know why Jesus does this, they ask the disciples (a passive-aggressive action). Jesus, though, hearing their question, speaks directly to the accusers.

As in 2:12, Mark acknowledges, from the lips of Jesus, a connection between sin and sickness. While we stand in the world of modern medicine, skeptical and even scandalized by such connections, Mark calls us to understand something vitally important: The manner in which we view sin makes a big difference in how we relate to ourselves, others, and God. Let's look at a couple of popular points of view.

If we view sin solely as a debt incurred to God that we cannot pay back, then we need a redeemer (Jesus), someone with enough moral and ethical resources to pay our debts to our creditor (God). If we view sin as the legal violation of a covenant, then we need a mediator and advocate (Jesus) who can fulfill the covenant on our behalf before our Judge (God). Both of these perspectives assume that humanity is completely responsible for sin. They also assume that God is, in a sense, divided against Godself. Jesus is the Redeemer or Advocate who appeases the judgment of God, the Creditor or Judge. I am not saying that these are not valuable ways of looking at sin and redemption. They are just not the only ways. In fact, Mark uses a variety of images to help us understand how God is acting toward God's people (e.g., 10:45).

Here Mark invites us to look at sin as a sickness, an illness to be treated. While the sick person may or may not be responsible for his or her illness, the question of responsibility is rather irrelevant. The sick need healing regardless of how they got sick. In this view, there is no judge to appease, no debt against God to settle. Instead, we are freed to see the intention of God and Jesus as undivided, one intention, one divine physic in operation to heal a sin-sick humanity. Though some of you may not believe that all physical illness is the result of sin, how do you understand the work of God toward us sinners?

Mark sees Jesus as a physician who makes house calls to the sin-sick, to the outcasts. But is it the outcast or the Pharisee who is in greater need of Jesus' medicine? How you view sin makes all the difference in how you relate to sinners. How you view your own sin makes all the difference in how you view both yourself and God. (Sam Parkes)

DOORS AND WINDOWS

MARCH

Reflection Verse: "In everything do to others as you would have them do to you; for this is the law and the prophets" (Matt. 7:12).

The Golden Rule is so simple that it is complex. We are to love God first, and our neighbor as ourself—and this includes our intimates as well as the stranger!

The pressure on us is exquisite: We live in a glass house so that people see how we "do" with our spouses and children. Some of them even model themselves after us. For us clergy, sometimes loving our intimates is the hardest thing to do. Our commitments to God stand in the way of our being "regular" fathers or mothers, wives or husbands. It's not that the Golden Rule doesn't apply to laypeople; it does. But we are more visibly committed to its observance.

The Discipline:

March and Lent are good times to let our spouses, children, and parents know how much we love them. Even if all we can do is to sneak a letter to each one of them, then at least we and they will know that we didn't forget their importance to us.

Archibald MacLeish said of his wife: "The greatest and richest good / My own life to live in / This she has given me." Our intimates "give" us our lives to live in, and sometimes clergy steal the gift from them by not being properly grateful. Showing gratitude to those who support us is very important. Thank someone you love now. Make a list. Thank each one who gives you "your own life to live in."

Some of us are simply not a part of any family anymore. We may live alone and be alone; but still, there are people that we are closer to than others. In keeping with this month's observance of the Golden Rule, draw pictures of them and then thank them. Who would be the first person you would call if you discovered that you had cancer? Start your picture with him or her. For many of us, family relationships have been well tested and we may have to make amends before saying "thank you." Or, we might need to hold others responsible for their actions toward us. In either case, move toward gratitude through whatever pain you must. Remember: God is with us. There is nothing sentimental about the God of Lent!

The Meditation:

Some of us will know the joy of taking our loved ones with us into the next century. Others will not. Some of us will watch our children grow up in the next century. Others will not. How we accompany our intimates is one of the most important matters in any person's life. They make us; we make them. We become who each other is.

Those of us who are Christians understand that our lives were given by God, redeemed by Jesus, and are even now sustained by the Holy Spirit. We are closer to God than we are to our intimates—which only enriches our capacity to be close to them. What will we give our intimates in the coming time? Security. Adventures. Challenges. And one more thing—their own lives to live in.

We "give" freedom for those closest to us to be themselves. We "take" freedom to be ourselves. This constant connection and separation is a part of the doors and windows of relationships.

When any one self is not fully "there," there is no relationship, only the imitation of relationship exists. When both selves are fully there as themselves, there is full relationship.

Maybe this is why we call Jesus the true human. He was fully here among us. As we move through Lent, we know the beauty of Jesus' life story. We also know where it is going: Its destination is a complete gift—a giving up.

The Song:

The song is actually a poem by Lynda Hull titled, "Suite for Emily." In it, she expresses her decision to seek heaven on earth: "Over the seas, the powdery glow floating / the street with evening . . . saffron, rose, sienna / bricks, matte gold, to be the

good steam clanking pipes, that warm music glazing the panes /
each fugitive moment the heaven we choose to make."

The Prayer:

Thank you, God, for the color of sienna, for children whom we
love way too much, and for the heaven we choose to make of our
lives and relationships. If we don't have children, let us remember
that we were children and that someone loved us into the
fullness of life. Hear our thanksgiving for all whose destination
includes the fullness of our life, including Jesus Christ. Amen.
(Donna Schaper)

MARCH 5, 2000

Transfiguration Sunday

Worship Theme: The enormity of God in Christ is unimaginable; humankind cannot contain the love of God. Nothing can.

Readings: 2 Kings 2:1-12; 2 Corinthians 4:3-6; Mark 9:2-9

Call to Worship (Psalm 50:1-6):

Leader: The Mighty One, God the LORD, speaks and summons the earth from the rising of the sun to its setting.

People: **Out of Zion, the perfection of beauty, God shines forth.**

Leader: Our God comes, and does not keep silence, before whom is a devouring fire, round about whom is a mighty storm.

People: **God calls to the heavens above and to the earth, that the people may be judged:**

Leader: "Gather to me my faithful ones, who made a covenant with me by sacrifice!"

People: **The heavens declare God's righteousness, for God alone is judge!**

Pastoral Prayer:

Your glory, most sacred God, burns brighter than the sun and all the stars in your heavens. We cannot sing a song of praise to you that is too loud or too beautiful. And this shining light never was more magnificent than when it shone through Jesus. How can our brothers and sisters not notice him? How can we? In your mercy, let the scales of this world fall from your children's eyes so that we might all join the chorus of thanksgiving. Many here and many more beyond this place cannot see for the pain and hurt. Please heal them and give them peace. Allow us to take up the mantle of Christ Jesus so that we might be more fully his Body in this weary world. And so, in his precious name we pray. Amen. (Thomas Gildermeister)

SERMON BRIEFS

THE BUILDING OF A SPIRITUAL LEADER

2 KINGS 2:1-12

The Bible text describes the holy authoritative power of one spiritual leader, Elijah, transferred to another, Elisha. The spectacular transference of leadership is not in question. The focus shifts from Elijah to Elisha. Such a thing actually happens on a continual basis, from local congregations with church boards, department heads, and pastors to national spiritual leaders. Someday Billy Graham will be off the national scene; who will God raise to take his place?

What we need in the world and local scenes are spiritual leaders. George Barna wrote, "A Christian leader is someone who is called by God to lead; leads with and through Christlike character; and demonstrates the functional competencies that permit effective leadership to take place" (*Leaders on Leadership* [Ventura, Calif.: Regal 1997], p. 25).

Elijah demonstrated certain qualities as a leader that were later bestowed upon Elisha. If we are leaders, certain qualities will be demonstrated. This list is limited.

I. Building a Leader Through Attitude (v. 2)

One of my favorite quotes is from L. Thomas Holdcroft: "Life is a grindstone. But whether it grinds us down or polishes us up depends on us" (Albert Wells, Jr., *Inspiring Quotations* [Nashville: Thomas Nelson, 1988], p.12).

Many know the story of Viktor Frankl, the courageous Jewish doctor who became a Nazi prisoner during World War II. He endured suffering, humiliation, and indignation by the Gestapo. The regime stole away his family, home, freedom, and possessions. He realized that he was homeless and a prisoner of a sadistic organization whose goal was to make his life miserable. After a period of time, it dawned on him that there was one thing his captors could not rob him of—his attitude. Despite their abuses, he could choose forgiveness over bitterness, love over hatred, and determination over self-pity.

Leaders understand the power of attitude.

II. Building a Leader Through Teamwork (v. 4)

Elijah and Elisha walked together; they formed a team. Leadership on all levels occurs best in the context of a team of people working, suggesting, thinking, and supporting the called leaders. No one person has all the gifts or abilities needed to run a church, home, office, or corporation. The strong leader pulls together a leadership team to make life or the organization a success.

In the words of Barna: "The church would infiltrate American society to its very core if we had leaders in charge, people who experiment, take risks, and create new possibilities through casting God's vision. Leaders are the missing link to the health of the church" (*Leaders on Leadership*, p. 29).

III. Building a Leader Through Concern (v. 9)

People and their relationships are at the heart of the leader. Leaders are to make a difference in people's lives. God cannot use hardhearted people to make that difference. What God wants are leaders who have a deep concern for the people they lead. Even if the decisions made are tough, the leader does it out of love and concern. This can be achieved by

— **being an encourager.** The word *encourage* can be translated as "support" or "sustain."
— **being a complimentor.** Sincere compliments for qualities we observe developing in people's lives.

— **being a letter writer.** Pen notes that uplift and inspire.

— **being a phone caller.** Use the phone to communicate something positive to one of the "followers."

— **being a visitor.** Face-to-face contact helps develop trust and confidence in your leadership.

IV. Building a Leader Through Availability (v. 10-12)

Personal presence develops real leadership qualities. Elisha observed Elijah, which would have been impossible if Elijah wasn't around. There were tasks that Elijah gave to Elisha to begin building his own leadership qualities, but as they were together, Elisha saw for himself what needed to be done. Hands-on experience is an important aspect of leadership training.

One of the best things we can do is latch on to a leader to follow and catch the vision, understanding, and concerns they have for their people. One day the baton will be passed; who will be there to receive it? (Derl Keefer)

POWERFUL RAYS OF LIGHT

2 CORINTHIANS 4:3-6

Recently I visited Iona, an island in the Inner Hebrides off the coast of Scotland where missionary Columba developed a Christian community in 563. Iona is a special place for many reasons—the abbey, the rich worship experiences, the primitive beauty of the island, the holy places where saints have been praying for centuries.

The island is a thin place where heaven and earth meet. Of special interest is the light that shines on this small piece of land lying in the Atlantic Ocean. The light is special as it shines on the water lapping on the shore, giving multiple shades and hues to the rock formations, varying the colors of the ocean depths, changing the colors of the grass in the sheep pasture, and even the shades of color on one's own face. I wish I were a painter and could capture light on canvas like Monet or Cezanne would have been able to do there on Iona. Or, I wish I had the ability to describe in a poem or narrative the majestic power of the light.

Even if I could describe the light on Iona—identifying the angle of the sun, noting the exact colors of the sea and sand—I would have to constantly rewrite the analysis because the light, as it moves up and down the horizon, is always changing the appearance of the island.

For travelers who use landmarks to find their way around, this place presents a challenge. For example, the angle of the light drastically changes the appearance of the rock formation to the extent that you are no longer sure it is the same rock that you passed a few hours ago on your way across the island. Light is powerful.

Artists and pilgrims gravitate toward places that have unique light, such as Aix-en-Provence, France, and Iona. We are not surprised that when Jesus wanted to describe his own life and work, he used the image of physical light to talk about matters spiritual: "I am the light of the world" (John 8:12). Paul uses the same metaphor to describe the "gospel of the glory of Christ, who is the image of God" (2 Cor. 4:4).

Paul writes that some people are so blinded that they cannot see the light. The question of this text is, How can that be? Light is such a powerful force. How could anyone not see light unless one's eyes were totally impaired? A mere veiling would not shut out the powerful rays of light (v. 3). The nuance is slight, but an important one to make.

God's revelation cannot be ignored. Nature cries out the name of God. The life, death, and resurrection of Jesus Christ shouts God's name. The ancient prophet Isaiah wakes us up from our slumber, "Arise, shine; for your light has come" (60:1). We know light, or so we think. We know God, or so we think. The power of light and of God is so mighty that no one can miss it. But we can miss the depth of the experience of God. We can miss seeing the intensity, the variations, the majesty of the light. We can know that the room is dark or lit, that the sun is shining or not, that the sun does not shine at night. We can know the bare basics about light.

To notice the beautiful hues of light; the wonders of the variation of the angles; the majesty of light's reflection on the waters' edge, on rock formations, on the faces of those we love, is to know light intimately. To see how God works in the life story of Jesus Christ, the life story of the early church and Paul's missionary activity, the life story of those people around you, and, finally, your own life story, is to know God intimately. We can know light and we can know God from superficial, rational descriptions. To know the God of light intimately in all manifestations of life is the goal of the believer. (Linda McKinnish Bridges)

LESSONS LEARNED IN THE HIGH COUNTRY

MARK 9:2-9

The term "mountaintop experience" has become a cliche, but it certainly fits the events of this text.

I. They Saw Something

We can never fully explain what they saw. One minute Jesus was dressed in the rough homespun robes of a peasant carpenter, and the next minute he was dressed in dazzling white. We are not surprised that it was white. White suggests purity (see Ps. 51:7; Rev. 3:4; 7:13), and Jesus is pure (1 Pet. 2:22; Heb. 4:15; 2 Cor. 5:21). We are not surprised that it was light. Light suggests deity (John 1:6-9), and Jesus is divine (John 14:9, 10; Col. 2:9; Rom. 9:5). The sight must have been impressive beyond description. It was also instructive: Moses represented the law, Elijah represented the prophets, and Jesus was the fulfillment of both.

II. They Said Something (v. 5)

Possibly the apostle Peter spoke of things he and the others had been discussing. The idea of staying here seemed most appealing. The idea of honoring each of the three figures seemed most appropriate. Who would not want to prolong so rich an experience as this?

We are not surprised that it was the apostle Peter who spoke these words. He was often outspoken, and he often spoke hurriedly. These traits that we see in Peter so often in the Gospels we do not see in him in the book of Acts. He must have learned something along the way.

III. They Heard Something (v. 7)

We can only wonder what the voice of God sounded like. We can imagine it as deep and resonant, and certainly unforgettable. We are certain, however, that we know the intonation of God's voice. We are certain that the emphasis was on the last word: "Listen to *him!*"

Most important is what God said. Did the Twelve remember that they had heard the voice of God before? Did they remember that God spoke at the baptism of Jesus, saying something very similar to what God said on this occasion. There is much we need to know as Christians, but the most important thing we need to know is who Jesus is.

IV. They Learned Something (vv. 8-9)

Here was an important lesson about Jesus. They learned that Jesus was greater than all who had gone before. They learned the preeminence of Jesus (see Col. 1:18).

Here was an important lesson about life after death. They learned that there is life beyond the grave. It must have been reassuring to see Moses and Elijah—long dead—alive and conscious and talking with Jesus. They had survived death.

Here was an important lesson about patience and timing. Jesus wanted everyone to know eventually who he is. But he wanted the world to be prepared to receive the message; he did not want it to be given prematurely. They were only ordered to keep silence until the Resurrection. After the Resurrection, they were to tell everyone. We can never see what they saw nor hear what they heard, but we can learn what they learned. When the apostle Peter wrote about this event, he said that we have a more sure word of prophecy (2 Pet. 1:19).

Thankfully, we have Scripture to teach us what they learned by experience (Robert Shannon)

MARCH 12, 2000

First Sunday in Lent

Worship Theme: The season of Lent is our time to wander in the wilderness, examining the darkness of our lives, reclaiming God's calling on our lives, and preparing to reengage God's work in and for the world.

Readings: Genesis 9:8-17; 1 Peter 3:18-22; Mark 1:9-15

Call to Worship (Psalm 25:1, 4-5, 8-10):

> *Leader:* To you, O LORD, I lift up my soul. Make me to know your ways, O LORD;
>
> *People:* **teach me your paths.**
>
> *Leader:* Lead me in your truth, and teach me,
>
> *People:* **for you are the God of my salvation; for you I wait all the day long.**
>
> *Leader:* Good and upright is the LORD; therefore the LORD instructs sinners in the way, and leads the humble in what is right, and teaches them their way.
>
> *People:* **All the paths of the LORD are steadfast love and faithfulness, for those who keep the LORD's covenant and testimonies.**

Pastoral Prayer:

Great God of mercy, we praise you for meeting us in the wilderness, in the dark night of our souls, and calling us by name. O Lord, your love song brings us courage as we discover and claim our sin during this season of Lent. Your love song beckons us, woos us. Please let us see the light of Christ Jesus so that our wanderings might soon end. There is pain in body and mind, as well as in spirit, here in your house. And how great is the pain beyond your church. Heal us. Use us to heal others. Help us to cling to one another, for we are needy; we long to meet the needs of our needy sisters and brothers. We are willing. We believe. Help our unwillingness. Help our unbelief. Amen. (Thomas Gildermeister)

SERMON BRIEFS

A NEW BEGINNING

GENESIS 9:8-17

The story of Noah and the ark is one of the most well known, and well loved, of all biblical stories. Why is that? Perhaps it's because it shows us that God is a God who makes and keeps promises. Promise is, after all, another word for covenant. God made his covenant with Noah, Noah's descendants, and every living creature that was with Noah. The rainbow was a sign of the covenant "that never shall all flesh be cut off by the waters of a flood" (v. 11). The rainbow was a symbolic bridge between human shortcomings and God's divine plan.

In the truest sense, the rainbow, as a sign of the covenant, was also a sign of new beginning. Noah and his family represented the highest devotion of loyalty to a loving and caring God. Noah was "a righteous man." He was "blameless in his generation." In addition, he "walked with God." God's favor was upon Noah because Noah's heart was right with God. Noah's life was in harmony with God. Noah represented the best of what one could become by ordering one's life in relationship to Almighty God. And in return, God took Noah's life of devotion and loyalty, and sent him forward to begin again.

Noah's faithfulness is followed by an expression of God's gracious faithfulness, not just to Noah, but to all humankind. Note that in the biblical text the covenant that God makes with Noah and his descendants is a covenant of grace. Human sinfulness had accounted

107

for the flood in the first place; after the flood, it would be God's faithfulness that guaranteed that never again would the world and its people be devastated as it had been in the days of Noah.

God offers us a new beginning in Jesus Christ. Just as God established a covenant with Noah and all living creatures of the earth, so God has established a new covenant through the blood of his Son. Just as God graciously provided a way of salvation for Noah and his family during the flood, and just as God graciously provided the rainbow as a sign of the covenant with Noah, so has God graciously provided a new covenant in Jesus. Anytime we accept what God has done for us in Jesus Christ, and commit our highest and best in devotion and loyalty to God, we are empowered to begin again through the blood of our Lord Jesus Christ. Christ is our bridge between human shortcomings and God's divine will for our lives. Noah's sign of remembrance was a rainbow flung across the sky. For us, the sign is now a cross—and an empty tomb. Looking to Jesus, remembering the way of life he modeled, the sacrifice he made, and the conquest of death he achieved, we are given a new beginning every bit as special as Noah's. God calls us to live lives worthy of that new beginning. (Harold L. Martin)

BAPTISM AND CHRISTIAN LIFE

1 PETER 3:18-22

Two key liturgical injunctions appropriate to the reflective season of Lent are "Repent, and believe the gospel," and "Remember your baptism, and be grateful." These two go together—the rethinking of life and all reality in light of Christ, and pondering the meaning of our baptism into Christ. This scripture text is well suited for such spiritual disciplines as these. Martin Luther placed 1 Peter alongside the Gospel of John and Paul's letter to the Romans as the three foremost witnesses to the gospel in the New Testament. It may further have originally been a baptismal homily.

I. The Gift of Salvation

Although not the consensus of scholarship on the original purpose or form of 1 Peter, still, a persuasive minority advances the view that in 1 Peter 1:3–4:11 we have a homily to newly baptized believers from the first Christian century. The homily interprets life in Christ in terms of exile and alienation from the world. It was later expanded into epistolary form in order to give encouragement to Christians undergoing actual persecution resulting from this alienation.

Of particular importance is suffering. The verb *paskein* occurs more in 1 Peter than in the rest of the New Testament. Exile and alienation from the world through participation in the gift of salvation bring the possibility that Christians too will suffer. Yet this must be understood in light of Christ's suffering, which is accorded salvific significance by virtue of the Resurrection. The suffering of Christ and of Christians, while still real and painful, thus takes place under the pledge of victory.

These realities are set forth under the language of a nascent confessional tradition in 3:18, 22. These are utilized to interpret baptism in 3:19-21. The elements thus given suggest possible approaches to preaching.

II. Confessions and Baptism

1. The cost of our reconciliation (3:18a-c): These phrases do not address random, senseless suffering. They are confession that the mystery of our reconciliation to God includes Jesus' suffering and death. This is the cost of the salvation given to us as a gift (1:3-5).

2. Christ's victory (3:18d, 22): The last part of verse 18 does not reflect a dualism of being. It does not say, in essence, "They killed his body but not his spirit." It is, once again, a confession that Jesus truly suffered death as a human being among human beings. Yet this death has been vindicated by God, who raised him up into a spiritual, eschatological mode of existence.

3. Our baptism (3:20-21): These difficult verses offer two implications of baptism. First, there is an element of separation from the world as a result of baptism. The image of the ark (which became a symbol of the church in early iconography) conveys a sense of protection, safety, and hope in a dying world. It is not of the world. Still, it sails in the midst of it.

Second, the sacrament of baptism is instrumental (though not causal) in our salvation because through it the power of Christ's resurrection is made effective in our lives. This gives Christians assurance in the state of exile. The pledge spoken of in verse 21 promises preservation in baptismal life. A Baptist baptismal prayer from the eighteenth century holds both aspects together: "Henceforth be thou his, and he thine; for it is his will to put on Christ by baptism . . . to take thy yoke and burden on his shoulder; and to learn obedience of the meek and lowly Jesus! Let his life be alike figure to his baptism . . ." (Morgan Edwards, *The Customs of Primitive Churches* [Philadelphia: n.p., 1774], pp. 81-82). (Philip E. Thompson)

GOD'S INTENTION FOR THE WORLD

MARK 1:9-15

Only in Year B does the lectionary give us the opportunity to see the link between the baptism of Jesus and the temptations read in the Scriptures. Like Moses the lawgiver, who fasted while receiving the law, Jesus withdraws for forty days (Ex. 34:28). Unlike Moses, who received the covenant from God, Jesus receives temptation from God's adversary. Like Elijah, in conflict with authority and running for his life, Jesus endures the wilderness and is waited on by angels (1 Kings 19).

Clearly, Mark wants the reader to understand Jesus as one who stands in the prophetic tradition. Standing in that tradition means communion with and validation by God's Spirit. It means expressing God's intention for the world. Also, it means preparing for conflict and for being a lone voice over against powerful enemies. Mark, even from the inauguration of Jesus' prophetic ministry, is figuring both the intention of Jesus' ministry plus the conflict that ministry will arouse. Only after baptism, validation by God's voice, withdrawal, and temptation is Jesus ready to proclaim God's good news. Only after formation for ministry can information about God's kingdom be proclaimed with decisiveness and with a call to others.

A caution: There is no description from Mark about Jesus' emotional or physical state before, during, or after the wilderness experience. We simply do not know how Jesus felt about this trial. I think we miss Mark's point when we preachers attribute such characteristics to Jesus. Emotive elements are not as important to Mark as the symbolic ones; Mark wants us to see Jesus as a fulfillment of the prophetic line, as one prepared to proclaim a message given to him by God.

I. Between Jordan and Galilee

One thing that Matthew and Luke are quick to "clean up" from Mark's telling of the Jesus story is the role of the Spirit. They see Jesus as "led" by the Spirit into the wilderness, not "driven," as Mark tells it. All three agree, though, that a trial initiated by God's Spirit follows God's claim on Jesus. Somehow the Christian communities that I have served do not seem to get this point. Lord knows, I don't want to get it either! Somewhere between being captured by God's vision and intention for our world and going out in a ministry consistent with that vision, God wants us to do the hard work of withdrawal and self-denial. God wants us to wait on the message. Between receiving the identity of Son-Beloved and going out to proclaim a specific word, Jesus waits, alone, tempted, accompanied by beasts and angels. We do not know precisely what happened, but we are invited to experience this for ourselves.

In an age when pastors are endlessly calling churches to "catch God's vision" for their ministries, is there a prophet who will call the church to deep formation as a mature body, tempted and honed? Perhaps God will inaugurate the most effective ministry as we let God drive us into that wilderness between the Jordan and Galilee, between call and action. What would this look like in your community? Are you about to embark on a new ministry without enough wilderness time? Or, are you letting the Dove do the driving?

II. Who's Doing the Preaching?

Mark points out a transition between John and Jesus, between the old age and the new. John is arrested, and Jesus arrives in Galilee. John preached for repentance and forgiveness, a recommitment to the old covenant. Jesus' message includes repentance, but the sort of repentance that moves us in an entirely new direction—toward the-Kingdom-come-near.

As I write, a national conversation is going on about the nature of moral authority and leadership. Sometimes I want to preach John's message: "Stick to the law!" Yet in Jesus, a new kind of covenant has come near, one that includes not only repentance and forgiveness for sins but also good news accessible through belief. The time for this Kingdom is fulfilled in Jesus. The moment is decisive. What are the practical differences between the two ages? Is this Lenten season a time of decision, of the Kingdom's fulfillment for this parish? Who is calling this community to repentance? John or Jesus? (Sam Parkes)

MARCH 19, 2000

Second Sunday in Lent

Worship Theme: The cost of following Jesus Christ is high.

Readings: Genesis 17:1-7, 15-16; Romans 4:13-25; Mark 8:31-38

Call to Worship (Psalm 22:25-31):

Leader: From you comes my praise in the great congregation;

People: **my vows I will pay before those who worship the LORD.**

Leader: The poor shall eat and be satisfied;

People: **those who seek the LORD shall praise the LORD! May your hearts live for ever!**

Leader: All the ends of the earth shall remember and turn to the LORD;

People: **and all the families of the nations shall worship before the LORD.**

Leader: For dominion belongs to the LORD who rules over the nations.

People: **All who sleep in the earth shall bow down to the LORD.**

Leader: All who go down to the dust shall bow before the LORD, and I shall live for God.

People: **Posterity shall serve the LORD;**

Leader: each generation shall tell of the LORD, and pro-
             claim his deliverance to a people yet unborn.

People: **Surely the LORD has done it.**

Pastoral Prayer:

O Lord, our promise-making and promise-keeping God; O
Lord, our God of covenant and faithfulness, we turn and flee
from your loveliness, but you pursue. We praise you for the ever-
present offer of freedom and peace through your new and final
covenant, Jesus, the Christ. Why cannot we accept your perfect
gift? Why do we clutch this diaphanous, shadow life and reject a
true and redeemed life? At least for this instant, God, we lay
down our fruitless efforts to create our own life. At least for this
moment we take up a cross and follow Jesus. We are ready for
this tawdry illusion to die. We are ready to be genuine, to be as
you intended since the beginning of time. In your mercy, hear
our prayers. Amen. (Thomas Gildermeister)

SERMON BRIEFS

ON FAITH AND A PROMISE

GENESIS 17:1-7, 15-16

God said to Abram, "I am God Almighty; walk before me, and
be blameless. And I will make my covenant between me and you,
and will make you exceedingly numerous." What did God mean
by calling Abram to "walk before me and be blameless?" I believe
God was calling Abram, as he calls to us today, to be upright, to
be forward-looking, and to be full of faith.

I. God Calls Us to Be Upright

God's desire is that we live life to the fullest. Take what each
day brings and use it to your best advantage, seeing every good
thing as a gift from God. Do not hold back for some tomorrow,
nor dwell too much on some past yesterday. Engage life for what
it offers you right now. Live to the fullest in God's will for you.

II. God Calls Us to Be Forward-looking

To be forward-looking is to look with anticipation to what God has in store for you. Life is not a random meandering from one uncertainty to another. Rather, as Christians we know that we are part of God's divine plan and that "all things work together for good for those who love God, who are called according to his purpose" (Rom. 8:28).

God calls us to live life expecting God to do great things in us and through us for the benefit of others. "For surely I know the plans I have for you, says the Lord, plans for your welfare and not for harm, to give you a future with hope" (Jer. 29:11). We will never realize all that we can become and all that God can do through us without looking forward in faith and believing God's promises.

III. God Calls Us to Live in Faith

To live in faith is to trust God to honor his promises. It does not mean we will never have doubts. However, it does mean we will never let our doubts get the best of us. It does not mean we will never become fearful. Nevertheless, we will replace fear with trust in God to do what God has promised.

Abram was obedient and believed God. He acted on God's promise in faith and belief, for himself and for his wife, Sarai. It was an act of faith on Abram's part, and blessings bestowed upon him on God's part. God blessed Abram because of his faith and trust in God's promises. Abram's name was changed, and he was given the place and privilege of being the first of a great nation. Abram was not only blessed, but he was the source of blessing to his wife and a multitude of others. However, Abraham would have never realized and experienced all that he had become without acting on his faith and believing God's promises to him.

God calls us today to "walk before him, and be blameless." This is only possible through our Lord Jesus Christ.

Trust that Jesus gave his life that we might have abundant life. Walk before God in uprightness. Move forward in faith and trust, and be blessed to be a blessing. (Harold L. Martin)

LIVES OF GREAT MEN ALL REMIND US

ROMANS 4:13-25

We remember the words of Longfellow's beloved poem:

Lives of great men all remind us
We can make our lives sublime,
And, departing, leave behind us
Footprints on the sands of time.
("A Psalm of Life")

No one ever left more indelible footprints than Abraham. He is honored by three of the world's great religions: Judaism, Islam, and Christianity. Today's text tells us why.

I. He Is an Example of Faith

We see it in his leaving home for an unknown land. We see it in his unselfish sharing with his nephew Lot. We see it in his stubborn belief that God would give him a son. We see it in his willingness to sacrifice that son, if God required it. We see it in his belief in the resurrection (Heb. 11:17-19). We see it in his belief in the eternal city of God (Heb. 11:10).

While none of us has a life experience exactly like his, most of us will, at some point in life, find a connection to him. We may travel to an unknown land. We all move into an unknown future. We may find that faith is easily eroded unless we cling stubbornly to it. We may have to make great sacrifices. We may have to face great sorrows. And we all have to look beyond this world and beyond this life to things eternal. It is appropriate that Abraham should be called "the father of the faithful."

II. He Is an Example of Hope

When we discuss faith, hope, and love, it is hope that usually gets the least attention. But in the Bible, hope garners much subject. Abraham hoped against hope. This tells us two things: We could not see any earthly way that his hope could be realized; only God could bring it to pass. On the other hand, his hope was no fragile thing. It was not a case of being quite sure it wouldn't happen, yet desiring it all the same. It was not just wishful thinking. Biblical hope—Abraham's hope—was a strong and virile thing.

Those who cherish hope are, in the words of an old song, "standing on the promises." Many people put little stock in promises, but you can count on the promises of God. And in the long run, there really is no other place to stand except on the promises.

III. He Is an Example of Grace

It was the grace of God that brought Abraham to the new land. It was the grace of God that sustained him there. It was the grace of God that made him victorious in battle. It was the grace of God that used him despite his sin (Gen. 20:1-16).

It was grace that brought him a son. It was grace that stayed his hand when he was ready to sacrifice that son. While grace is more prominent in the New Testament than in the Old (and better understood), Paul makes it plain that grace was there in the dramatic events of Abraham's life. And surely every believer, looking back, can see God's grace in his or her life over and over again.

The focus of these verses shifts, and the spotlight falls not on Abraham, but on Christ. Paul followed his own principle, that Christ should have the preeminence (Col. 1:18). The focus shifts to Christ—and us. For us Christ lived a sinless life. For us he died a saving death. For us he rose in power and glory. For us he ascended to God. For us he returns to claim his own. (Robert Shannon)

NEVER MAN SPAKE LIKE THIS

MARK 8:31-38

People were amazed at the teaching of Jesus (Matt. 7:28-29; Luke 4:22). They said that no one else taught as he did (John 7:46). These verses from Mark's Gospel are an example of some of the ways Jesus taught.

117

I. Sometimes He Spoke Plainly (vv. 31-32)

On some occasions Jesus spoke in parables. His meaning was veiled from casual or insincere listeners. His disciples, on the other hand, would think about those parables and find their inner meaning.

On some occasions he spoke of his death in symbolic language. "I have a baptism to undergo," he said in Luke 12:50. "Just as Moses lifted up the snake in the desert, so the Son of Man must be lifted up," he said in John 3:14.

But this time he spoke plainly. He did not want the cross to be a surprise to his followers. He tried to prepare them for it. Even so, they were shattered by it. While we sometimes enjoy plumbing the depths of difficult passages, we should spend most of our time asking the question, "What does the Bible plainly say?" There are enough plain passages to keep us occupied.

II. Sometimes He Spoke Bluntly (v. 33)

We are surprised at the way Jesus turned on the apostle Peter and called him Satan. It must have shocked the disciples as much as it shocks us. It was intended to shock. It was shock therapy. It may also be that the severity of the response is partly due to the strength of the temptation. For Jesus was tempted to avoid the cross. The Garden of Gethsemane proves that.

III. Sometimes He Spoke Cryptically (vv. 34-35)

Did they understand what Jesus meant by "taking up the cross"? Certainly we fail to understand it. We say of all sorts of things such as,"That's a cross I'll just have to bear." But Jesus meant to be taken literally. Some of his followers would have to die for him. It is in the light of that that the riddle of verse 35 suddenly makes sense: If you save your life, you lose it.

Imagine a person who never takes any chances. He denies himself tasty foods lest he gain weight. He denies himself exercise lest he strain his heart. He denies himself fresh air; it might be polluted. He doesn't go out, for he might be run over by a car or hit by a bicycle or struck by lightning. And he loses his life by trying to save it. Jesus is not advocating recklessness. He would not advise us to take unnecessary chances. But danger is a part of life for all of us—and it was very much a part of life for the first believers.

IV. Always He Spoke Practically (vv. 36-38)

Every businessman must consider profit and loss. Some merchants will sell an item at a loss to get customers into the store, for they know that they can then sell them other things at a profit.

Would it be worth it to gain the whole world and lose your soul? If it would not be a good deal to gain the whole world, it is certainly not a good deal if we gain some small piece of the world and lose our souls. Yet people give up eternal life for one more acre of land, or one more dollar in the bank account, or one more hour of fame, or one more moment of pleasure. It's a poor bargain. They make a very bad trade.

There is one fair trade in this text. If we are ashamed of Jesus Christ, he will be ashamed of us. That's fair. But if we confess him, he will confess us. That's wonderful! (Robert Shannon)

MARCH 26, 2000

Third Sunday in Lent

Worship Theme: The Crucifixion is God's "foolishness" and God's "weakness." And it is the salvation of humankind, wiser and stronger than millennia of sin.

Readings: Exodus 20:1-17; 1 Corinthians 1:18-25; John 2:13-22

Call to Worship (Psalm 19:7-10):

> *Leader:* The law of the LORD is perfect, reviving the soul;
>
> ***People:*** **the testimony of the LORD is sure, making wise the simple;**
>
> *Leader:* the precepts of the LORD are right, rejoicing the heart;
>
> ***People:*** **the commandment of the LORD is pure, enlightening the eyes;**
>
> *Leader:* the fear of the LORD is clean, enduring for ever;
>
> ***People:*** **the ordinances of the LORD are true, and righteous altogether.**
>
> *Leader:* More to be desired are they than gold, even much fine gold;
>
> ***People:*** **sweeter also than honey and drippings of the honeycomb.**

Pastoral Prayer:
 Holy God, our perfect lawgiver, you are just in your judgments, and we praise you. Yet we delight in the assurance that

your mercy exceeds your judgment. No words of thanksgiving can be enough. Forgive us, precious Redeemer, we are enamored with the wisdom of the world, with the security of economics, with the strength and power of the wonders that science performs. Yet the wonder and majesty of the cross of your beloved Son makes our works seem pale and shriveled. Lord, bind us, heal us, continue your sacred call to us. In the name of Christ, the crucified and risen Lord. Amen. (Thomas Gildermeister)

SERMON BRIEFS

LOVE IS THE GREATEST

EXODUS 20:1-17

The law was given as a way to help God's chosen people live before God truly as God's own people. It was a means by which one could take note of how to live in order to please a righteous and jealous God. While there are many ways to respond to life, and many things in which to make the object of one's pursuits, there is only one right way.

Several years ago when I was in the military, there were manuals with procedures on how to accomplish just about everything a person can imagine. They were designed to show us not the quickest way nor the cheapest way, but instead the surest way to do things, which would produce the desired result. Within these procedures were "Warnings," "Cautions," and "Notes." A "Note" was given with the understanding that if the procedures following it were not followed, the end result may be that one may not accomplish the desired task. On the other hand, a "Caution" was given to indicate that if the procedures were not followed, the end result may be damage to the equipment and possible injury in addition to not accomplishing the task. Of extreme importance were the "Warnings." They came with the understanding that if one did not follow the procedures after a "Warning," the end result, in addition to damage and not accomplishing the task, may result in loss of life—the life of the one performing the task and of others. We all paid particular attention to the "Cautions," and certainly to the "Warnings."

God gave the law to help his people live in the right way before a righteous God. God said, "You shall have no other gods before me. You shall not make for yourselves an idol. . . . You shall not bow down to them or worship them; for I the Lord your God am a jealous God . . ." (vv. 3-5). These words come as cautions and warnings. However, who can keep all the laws? Jesus said we have already sinned and broken the law if we think wrongly in our hearts. In addition, when we break one law we are guilty of them all.

What are we to do? The answer is in knowing that Jesus came to save us from our sins and the law. Jesus said, " 'You shall love the Lord your God with all your heart, and with all your soul, and with all your mind.' This is the greatest and first commandment. And a second is like it: 'You shall love your neighbor as yourself.' On these two commandments hang all the law and the prophets" (Matt. 22:37-40). These words of Jesus from the manual of life come not as "Warnings" but as good news of how to prevent loss of spiritual life. If we follow this procedure that Jesus has issued, we will accomplish the task of all the law through the help of the Holy Spirit that God gives to all who accept his Son. The law came through Moses, but grace and truth came through Jesus Christ. Thanks be to God. (Harold L. Martin)

CROSS WORDS AND CROSS ROADS

1 CORINTHIANS 1:18-25

A preacher announced one Sunday morning that his evening sermon was entitled "The Foolishness of God." It was, obviously, based on today's text. The following Monday morning, he was soundly criticized by one of his members who had not heard the sermon and apparently had never read the text.

It is, of course, a riddle. If there were such a thing as foolishness with God, that foolishness would be wiser than the wisdom of men.

I. Paul Did Not Preach Christ Crucified Because It Appealed to the Jews

Sometimes it seems that politicians determine their views by the polls. Whatever position seems popular is the one that they declare. If a poll had been taken in the Jewish community, the crucified Christ would not have been ranked as a popular position. If the apostle Paul had determined his preaching by what was popular, he would never have preached about the cross.

Even today, the temptation to preach what is popular remains. People want preachers to condemn the sins they themselves love to hate (omitting, of course, the sins they commit). They want the preacher to lift up the virtues they possess (eliminating, of course, the virtues they lack). Every true preacher of the gospel must continually resist this temptation.

What deeds could Jesus have done mightier than the deeds of his life and ministry? What greater miracle, what greater sign, could have been given than his crucifixion and his resurrection? But to many in the Jewish community it was not enough. Perhaps no miracle would have been enough for those who did not want to believe.

II. Paul Did Not Preach Christ Crucified Because It Was Appealing to the Greeks

At the time, Greece was the center of philosophy. Great wealth gave the Greeks vast amounts of leisure time, and they loved to spend it thinking thoughts no mortal ever dared to think before. It seemed incredible to them that one could build a religion on the death of its founder. It seemed even more incredible that a religion could be built on the shameful execution of its founder. Most incredible, though, was a religion that could be built on the death of one they said was divine. Gods don't die. That seemed so obvious that the preaching of the cross seemed like foolishness.

But we see a deeper wisdom in the death of Christ. We reckon that few great causes ever came to fulfillment without somebody making a sacrifice. That's true of the rise of nations. It is true of the discoveries of modern medicine. It's true of every great advance in human thought or human achievement. Always there was an accompanying sacrifice.

What is, of course, unique about the Christian religion is that the sacrifice is made by deity, not by man; by the offended, not by the offender; by the innocent, not by the guilty.

III. Paul Preached Christ Crucified
Because It Was the Power of God

God often astounds us by doing the unusual. He walls the sea with sand. He warms the earth with snow. He clears the air with storms. The wisdom of God is not apparent at first glance, but if we look deeply we can see that wisdom. Followers of Christ are never called upon to make a sacrifice greater than the sacrifice that Christ himself made. Over the years we can see that there is something appealing about the cross. There is something comforting about the cross. There is something encouraging about the cross. There is something inspiring about the cross. It is no wonder we sing "In the cross of Christ I glory." (Robert Shannon)

JESUS THE RADICAL

JOHN 2:13-22

In the Gospel of John, the cleansing of the temple is the second public act of Jesus' ministry. For John, Jesus' ministry begins with a radical act of rebellion against the greed and injustice of the religious establishment. John shows us Jesus' anger and righteousness right out of the gate.

As a result, we cannot ignore the passion, the "zeal" (v. 17), and the anger of Jesus that this passage offers. Many congregations are reluctant to hear the stories of Jesus' anger. They don't like to think about Jesus as a radical who stirred up trouble. Images of Jesus as a shepherd, as a friend, as a nice person, prove more comforting and satisfying for many believers. But John makes it clear from the very beginning that Jesus was all about stirring up trouble and challenging the status quo. Niceness was just not a priority for him. Here we witness Jesus' zeal and anger. And we are reminded in this story of how important it is for us as Jesus' followers to combat greed, injustice, and "marketplace mentality" in the church. Examples of marketplace mentality are not too difficult to come by, since all around us we see moneymaking schemes in the name of Jesus Christ.

In the story, Jesus was enraged at the money changers, not only because they turned God's house into a marketplace but also because they took advantage of and discriminated against the poor. Likewise, we in the church also ought to watch out for ways that our practices might shut out or even discriminate against the poor. Do we assume in our programming, our fellowship, and in our worship that persons must have resources to participate? Can everyone pay for Wednesday night dinner? Can everyone afford to buy something at the bazaar? Can everyone afford to have a suit or a dress on Sunday morning?

Following this passage through to the end, we discover that Jesus is offering his followers something far beyond buildings and institutions. When Jesus said to the Jews, "Destroy this temple and in three days I will raise it up" (v. 19), John makes it clear he was talking about the temple of his body (v. 21). Jesus replaces buildings and institutions with his own body. For us, then, who are his followers and who make up the Body of Christ in the world, this passage calls us to examine our church and our institutions. It calls us to clean out the mentality of the marketplace and to remember that our calling is not to an institution but to a community of faith that is open to all. (Carol Cavin)

DOORS AND WINDOWS

APRIL

Reflection Verse: "But you have kept the good wine until now" (John 2:10).

The Discipline:

Become new. Don't become altogether new; simply become new in one or two ways. If you are carrying too much weight around, lighten up. If you are carrying too little weight around, pick up something heavy and carry it a while. If you are bored stiff, do something exciting. If you are excited, do something boring. If you are too free, make a commitment. If you are too committed, do something freeing. (My teenage daughter eats a chocolate-coated cereal every now and then, so as not to be too much of a goody two-shoes. You don't know how glad I am for this serious a rebellion.) If you are too serious, do something silly. If you are too silly, do something serious. The Resurrection is for you. It is as real as any reality: Ordinary people have been pushing stones off tombs for centuries. Go find one and give it a shove.

The Meditation:

Many consider April the cruelest month. But it is also the month of Easter and resurrection and new life. God saves the good wine until Easter—and then we truly drink.

We live in a time when "somebody done turned the wine into water," as the Reverend James Forbes, of Riverside Church in New York City, says about the Christian Right. Instead of enchantment and fairy tales promising that straw can become gold, the reverse is happening.

How can we keep the gold gold and the wine wine? By hoping well. By hoping personally. By hoping articulately. For what dare we hope? That nobody substitutes an outer battle for an inner one among us. That the water turns to wine. That the straw becomes gold. That enchantment returns. That we become poets of our own lives. That our congregations mature into the fullness of Christ. That we dare not fear death so much as fear not living. That we not get scared.

We may dare to hope, in the spirit of the many mansions of John 14:2, that we don't get cramped in too small a space. We may hope to keep the doors of our work so open that they can breathe and sense the breeze of our promises. We can dare to hope for as rich an interior as exterior life. We may dare to hope for place consciousness. For time consciousness. We may hope to be fully aware of the wonder of this day. We may dare to hope for animation. For art in our work. For God as our Muse. For wiggle in our walk. For our water to turn into God's wine.

The Song:

Hum a hymn at least once today and really consider the meaning of the words. "Praise God from Whom All Blessings Flow" (the doxology) is often a good hum.

The Easter Prayer:

Sanctify and renew my labor, O God. Make it good. Let it bring me growth and you praise. As I prepare my Easter message, let me move beyond performance into joy. Let me worry more about my knowledge of your victory over death and less about my words.

Not all I do will succeed. In some things I will fail. Come, Holy Spirit, and lead me through my incompleteness to something that honors you and what you would have from me.

Use me, O God, for a fountain. Let my water spring forth. Let my joy emerge from the very details of living. Let there be gladness in my associates; let me be a part of the fun today. Give me good jokes to tell, deep laughs to belly forth; and when things become hard, deepen my gladness in you. Let the power and truth of the Resurrection be visible in me.

Elizabeth Clephane, a Scottish hymnodist, in "Beneath the Cross of Jesus," wrote about "the burning of the noontide heat, and the burden of the day." I will know the burning today. I will know the burden. Let each be easy. Let each be expected lest my innocence cloud your vision, lest my sloth disturb your presence.

You want rebirth from me. You want something from me today, O God. Let me know what it is. Do something with me, O God, that connects me to the song of the age. Let me be a part of your grand globe. Let me watch the news as one who belongs here and cares here and acts here. Don't let me feel small, but enlarged by the size and scope of human community. Connect me. Let my Easter be so rich that other people have Easter because of me.

My broken dreams are in my pocket, my dashed hopes still dismay me. Release me to live with my sorrows—as opposed to above my sorrows. Acquaint me with your sorrows, and let me not be afraid. Remind me of the certainty of your victory over every kind of poverty. In the name of my baptism and your resurrection and the good wine. Amen. (Donna Schaper)

APRIL 2, 2000

Fourth Sunday in Lent

Worship Theme: The darkness of this world and our lives cannot overcome the light and grace of God in Christ Jesus.

Readings: Numbers 21:4-9; Ephesians 2:1-10; John 3:14-21

Call to Worship (Psalm 107:1-9):

Leader: O give thanks to the LORD, who is good, whose steadfast love endures for ever!

People: **Let the redeemed of the LORD say so, whom the LORD has redeemed from trouble and gathered in from the lands, from the east and from the west, from the north and from the south.**

Leader: Some wandered in the desert wastes, finding no way to a city in which to dwell;

People: **hungry and thirsty, their soul fainted within them.**

Leader: Then in their trouble, they cried to the LORD, who delivered them from their distress,

People: **and led them by a straight way, till they reached a city in which to dwell.**

Leader: Let them thank the LORD for his steadfast love, for his wonderful works to humankind.

People: **For the LORD satisfies those who are thirsty, and fills the hungry with good things.**

129

Pastoral Prayer:

O God, our help in ages past, our hope for years to come, can it be so? Can you love and care for this fallen world—the whole fallen world—so much that you sent your own precious Son to redeem it, redeem us? We praise you; your goodness is infinite, and in you nothing can be too good to be true. Dear Lord, please help us to remember that your promise is not to remove troubles but to meet us in the midst of troubles. Forgive us when hurt and difficulties take root in our souls, and we doubt your love. Forgive us when we forget that your Holy Promise is to save us in the world and not from it. Give patience to all of your troubled children. Help us to wait on the peace and comfort of your Son and our Savior, sweet Jesus. Amen. (Thomas Gildermeister)

SERMON BRIEFS

ANOTHER DIFFICULT ENCOUNTER

NUMBERS 21:4-9

The journeying Israelites' graphic encounter with poisonous snakes is one more difficulty in the Israelites' long trek and can be considered from three different perspectives. One approach would be to focus on despair and the snakes as the poisonous consequence of becoming stuck in despair and fixated on complaint and bitterness.

Review the preceding events: The Israelites have attempted to pass through Edomite territory, promising to use little water and do no harm to the people, but they are refused. Aaron, the trusted priest, has died; and Eleazar, a new mediator, has been appointed, which is another source of insecurity. Still, God has enabled them to defeat the Canaanites, so there is much to be hopeful for. However, instead of gratitude, they complain—again.

Complaining leads to bitterness and is the opposite of gratitude, which focuses on the giftedness of life. Complaining assumes one knows what is better than *this* reality; gratitude implies trust in *another* ("This for which I am thankful is good; the One who provides is good"). Much like snakes that slither quietly, almost unnoticed at first, complaint and bitterness can erode our faith in God before we even realize it; and then we are dying spiritually, poisoned by our own discontent.

The solution given to Moses by God is for the dying ones to confront their poison, raise it up on a bronze pole where they can look it full in the face. In this one whom God has appointed to lead, the people are given a chance at honesty, comparable to confession. Moses is the one who reminds them repeatedly of God's faithfulness; in this is their hope. Remembering God's faithfulness and hope heal the poison of despair.

A second approach is that this experience of looking back later becomes a source of idolatry (1 Kings 14:15). Remembering gives hope, but if the *memory* of being rescued is the focus of worship rather than worshiping the God who did the rescuing (and still does save), an idol has been made that must be destroyed.

Where are the sacred poles in our lives? A sacred pole can point beyond to the One who has blessed us and continues to bless. The church is a sacred pole. Ritual can be a sacred pole. Soul friendships can be sacred poles. Experiences that enhance our relationship with God and give us enough security to enable us to be honest with God and with ourselves so that God can continue to transform us are sacred poles. They are means for healing (as in the snake poison story).

But when the memory, the nostalgic longing for the past, becomes our source of faith rather than a living, growing relationship with God, the sacred pole becomes an obstacle. Later, during Josiah's reform, the sacred pole had to be destroyed because it had become an obstacle for God's people. So *our* idols, our sacred poles that have become ultimate in our lives, must be confronted and destroyed.

A third approach could be to examine the role of the leader who holds up the sacred pole. It is not a winsome object to place in the middle of folk who are coming for answers. The one who would be used by God to bring healing will not have an easy or attractive task.

Like Moses, the leader who would confront the poisonous snakes in life, must be in a living, consistent relationship with God. This person must be willing to go where sent, even when the map is incomplete and the journey is through the wilderness. The answers for healing come not from one's own bag of tricks, but at the instruction of God. "Moses prayed [to God] for the people." Moses is not praying for himself, nor is he coming up with self-vindicating chastisement of the people for all the grief he has endured on their behalf.

Moses is willing to be obedient and *act* on God's orders, even though it may seem strange and, in fact, the last thing one would want to do in such circumstances. It is obedience on the part of Moses and the people that results in their healing. It is obedience that will heal our lives and our church and our world of the poison which kills us. (Kay Gray)

TAKE YOUR NEW POSITION TO SERVE GOD

EPHESIANS 2:1-10

A minister attending a conference took a bus to the beach on a free afternoon. Soon a peculiar-looking lady boarded. She sat next to him, cooing, "Cross my hand with a dollar, and I'll tell you your past, present, and future." He eyed her for a moment and then thought, "Well, she asked for it."

"That won't be necessary," he cooed back. "I have a little book in my pocket that tells me my past, present, and future."

"You have it in a book?" she replied, not really believing.

"Yes, and it is absolutely infallible. Let me read it to you." Then he read Ephesians 2:1-3. "That's my past."

"Oh, yes. That is plenty. I do not care to hear more." However, he took her arm and said, "But I want you to hear my present," and read verses 4-6. "No more," she cried. "But hear my future," he insisted, reading verses 7-10.

Finally she broke from his grasp and ran down the aisle shouting, "I picked the wrong man!"

In Ephesians 2:1-10, Paul tells us, along with the believers at Ephesus, our past, present, and future with God.

I. We Were Dead to the Things of God (vv. 1-3)

In the past we were spiritually dead because of sin. God says that without Christ we were *dead*. God doesn't say *sick*, in need of surgery or a shot. He doesn't say *asleep*, in need of a shake or a shout. He says *dead,* in need of life. *Dead* means powerless. *Dead* means rotting. In God's sight, we were powerless to serve God and rotting in sin. As a result, we could expect nothing from God but wrath.

There is paradox here: We were dead, without God, yet active against God. We served the world, the devil, and our fleshly desires. Because we didn't live to please God, we set ourselves up for God's wrath.

II. God Made Us Alive with Christ Jesus by Grace Through Faith (vv. 2:4-9)

"But God." What wonderful words! In our present, God invades our death march and makes us live. We couldn't work for it, don't deserve it, haven't earned it. God gifted salvation to those who believe, because Jesus earned it for us on the cross. And now we share his resurrection life.

When David was hunted by King Saul, all those who were in distress or in debt or discontented gathered around him like dead men walking (see 1 Sam. 22:2). But when the chase was over and David was crowned king, those men ate at the king's table, sharing his glory. Even the king's former enemies confessed, "All my father's house were doomed to death . . . but you set your servant among those who eat at your table" (2 Sam. 19:28).

We too were dead, enemies deserving wrath. But by God's grace through faith in the Lord Jesus Christ, we feast at God's table.

III. We Were Re-created to Serve God (v. 10)

We who were dead are now alive, not *by* good works but *for* good works. In this exceptional verse, Paul pictures our future in a series of metaphors. We have become God's workmanship, God's masterpiece in this world of sin and death. We have been re-created, made alive and new in Christ Jesus. God has prepared a road map of good works for us to accomplish.

When a child models good manners, the parent finds favor. When a student attains the prized scholarship, the teacher receives recognition. When an athlete wins the championship, the coach enjoys esteem. When we take up our new position in Christ to serve God, God gets glory. (Timothy Warren)

AN ASSENT OF THE HEART

JOHN 3:14-21

A passage such as this one in the third chapter of John proves challenging. In fact, we might be tempted to set it aside and look to another of the lectionary passages for the week. Another temptation might be to focus solely on John 3:16, the beloved verse that rings true for adult and child alike.

However, such a challenging passage invites us to resist these temptations and struggle with the passage as a whole. In exploring this passage, it is crucial to remember that these words of Jesus are part of his conversation with Nicodemus. When Nicodemus comes to him and is unable to understand Jesus' teaching about being born anew in the Spirit, Jesus tells him that he is failing to receive Jesus' testimony. Nicodemus is not getting it. He's missing out on the Kingdom.

As if to drive this point home, Jesus continues to differentiate between those who believe and those who do not. Verses 15, 16, and 18-21 reveal how those who believe are set apart from those who do not believe. He clearly states that Nicodemus has a choice—he can choose to believe or not. The end of this conversation with Nicodemus leaves the reader uncertain as to the choice that the Pharisee makes. Nevertheless, Jesus paints for him a clear picture of the choice Nicodemus has in front of him.

As Jesus talks with Nicodemus, he wants him to know exactly where God stands on the matter. God wants Nicodemus to choose belief. God wants him and all the world to be redeemed. Verse 16 says that "God so loved the world." Verse 17 claims that God sent Jesus to save the world, not to condemn it. God wants the whole world to be redeemed. God did not pick and choose whom to love and redeem. God did not decide just to love the righteous or the good or the certain. God loves those who are sinful and confused and uncertain, like Nicodemus, and God wants them to believe in Jesus Christ.

This is a wonderful passage to reassure all of us that God longs for us to believe and be faithful. God wants the whole world to be redeemed. God does not want to condemn the world. God longs to be in relationship with us; God loves us. What, then, is our response to such a God?

The response that Jesus urges in this passage is *belief*. By *belief* he does not mean simply an intellectual assent. He does not mean the willingness to speak the magic words "I believe in Jesus Christ." He does not mean having sound doctrines and correct theology. The word *belief* means much more than that. It means an assent of the heart. It means trusting that God loves us and is at work mending and healing the world. It means living a life that reflects God's love for the whole world.

While Jesus is urging Nicodemus and us to live a life of belief (an eternal life that begins here and now), he points out that our belief does not give us cause to judge other people. He makes it clear in verse 17 that God is not interested in condemning the world. God is only interested in redeeming it. Thus, we are not called to beat other people over the head with our doctrines but to invite them into loving fellowship and relationship with Jesus Christ. We are called to want nothing less than the redemption of the whole world. (Carol Cavin)

APRIL 9, 2000

Fifth Sunday in Lent

Worship Theme: In Christ, God writes a new covenant on the hearts of humanity, a covenant that is offered to anyone who will follow Jesus to the cross.

Readings: Jeremiah 31:31-34; Hebrews 5:5-10; John 12:20-33

Call to Worship (Psalm 51:1, 6-9, 14-15):

Leader: Have mercy on me, O God according to your steadfast love;

People: **according to your abundant mercy blot out my transgressions.**

Leader: Behold, you desire truth in the inward being; therefore teach me wisdom in my secret heart.

People: **Purge me with hyssop, and I shall be clean; wash me, and I shall be whiter than snow;**

Leader: Make me hear with joy and gladness; let the bones which you have broken rejoice.

People: **Hide your face from my sins, and blot out all my iniquities.**

Leader: Deliver me from death, O God, God of my salvation,

People: **O LORD, open my lips, and my mouth shall show forth your praise.**

Pastoral Prayer:
 We thank you and praise you, holy and gracious God, for opening the doors of our stormy hearts to the love that enlivens your

136

new covenant. We stand in awe that all are called, all are welcome to your table of joy. Regardless of gender, race, nationality, age, or the sins of the past, you call all of us to be one in your Son, Jesus Christ. Please, O Lord, burn into every soul the truth that the power of your love always surpasses the messes we make of our lives. Teach us to hate the dark paths that we have followed so that we might journey in the light of Christ. Amen. (Thomas Gildermeister)

SERMON BRIEFS

A FAITH THAT LOOKS FORWARD

JEREMIAH 31:31-34

Faith looks forward. While the people of God are told to remember what God has done for them in the past, no real progress can be made by staring into the rearview mirror. Jeremiah tells his contemporaries a "time is coming" (NIV). He helps them look forward to a time in the future when their condition would improve. Jeremiah promises a new covenant. The new covenant would face the people forward and help them live life as it came toward them. Consider how this happens.

I. Faith That Looks Forward Is Based on the Love of God

Jeremiah's description is arresting. God would set aside the old covenant. In its place God would give a new covenant. Its foundation would not be on written laws and regulations. The Lord's spirit would be put directly into the hearts of people. It would be based on God's nearness—on God's love.

Truly, love is a healer of all manner of human hurts. Even medical research is discovering this truth. Dean Ornish is the author of the book *Love & Survival: The Scientific Basis for the Healing Power of Intimacy* (New York: HarperCollins, 1998). Dr. Ornish writes: "Love and intimacy are at the root of what makes us sick and what makes us well, what causes sadness and what brings happiness, what makes us suffer and what leads to healing.

If a new drug had the same impact, virtually every doctor in the country would be recommending it for their patients. It would be malpractice not to prescribe it" (*Love & Survival*, p. 3.). This wise physician realizes that love, or the lack of it, affects us in positive or negative ways, but it is never neutral. For people who have read the Bible, that news comes as no surprise. Why? Because, as 1 John 4:16 (NIV) puts it, "God is love. Whoever lives in love lives in God, and God in him."

God chooses to be close to people who accept God. God's love points us in the right direction.

II. Faith That Looks Forward Comes Naturally from Within

The covenant described by Jeremiah was natural and internal. People were not forced to learn of God. Instead, they knew God naturally. This does not mean that disciplined study of religious matters is useless. It simply means that God wants to be known by people everywhere. The knowledge of God has been given to everyone, as we can see from Romans 1:20. This comes about as we give ourselves to God through Christ. Knowing God this way establishes us and strengthens us. In times of trouble we will already have a relationship with God that we can count on.

Aesop told this old story: A wild boar was busily whetting his tusks against a tree in the forest when a fox came by. "Why are you wasting your time in this manner?" asked the fox. "Neither a hunter nor a hound is in sight, and no danger is at hand." "True enough," replied the boar, "but when the danger does arise, I shall have something else to do than to sharpen my weapons."

III. Faith That Looks Forward Results in Forgiveness

Jeremiah 31:34 is a most comforting passage: "For I will forgive their wickedness and will remember their sins no more." Gaining God's forgiveness is not a matter of following minute rules or loathsome regulations. It is knowing and trusting God. That trust can help us walk through incredible times.

Forgiveness is ever necessary. It is much in the news in contemporary times. For example, after the White House sex scandal, President Clinton wrote to his home church in Little Rock and asked for forgiveness from his fellow church members. In the letter, Clinton "expressed repentance for his actions, sadness for the consequence of his sin on his family, friends and church family, and asked forgiveness" (*Baptist Press*, October 22, 1998). Christ calls us to a faith that looks forward. Which way are you facing? (Don M. Aycock)

ONE GREATER THAN MELCHIZEDEK

HEBREWS 5:5-10

The catchword in the discussion binding the end of Hebrews 4 with the truths of Hebrews 5 is *empathy*. Jesus is able to identify with our temptations and sufferings because he too has undergone suffering and temptation, and has learned obedience through his sufferings on our behalf. In chapter 5, the nature of Jesus' high priesthood is further unfolded.

I. The Qualifications for Old Testament Priesthood

In verses 1 through 4, the writer points out two qualifications of the ordinary high priest. First, he must be from among men, so that he can feel the infirmities of those on whose behalf he ministers. As a man, however, he too is sinful and must offer sacrifices not only for others but also for himself. Second, he must be called of God, as was Aaron.

II. Jesus, the Successor of Melchizedek

While the writer stresses Jesus' ability to sympathize with and strengthen his followers, the writer also stresses the divinity of Jesus and his unique priesthood. Jesus comes to the priesthood not through human lineage but as a priest after the order of Melchizedek (Gen. 14:17-24). An ancient commentary on these verses in Genesis points out that Melchizedek's priesthood was not for the fulfilling of legal sacrifices but for the offering of bread and wine, symbols of Christ. There came a time when animal sacrifice ceased, but the sacrifice of the bread and wine, the sacrifice of Christ, never ends in terms of its power to redeem men.

We notice also that Melchizedek combined kingly and priestly functions, even as does Jesus, and Melchizedek appeared only once, giving no clue to his background or his progeny. Jewish writings speculate that Melchizedek may have been Shem, the son of Noah. He could perhaps have survived to this time, but this is only guesswork. The significant point about Melchizedek is that he is seen as a symbol of a priesthood that has no human beginnings or endings; he comes out of nowhere and then vanishes (Heb. 7:1-3). He foreshadows the eternal priesthood of Jesus (Heb. 7:24-25). Jesus comes out of eternity to forge an eternal priesthood on behalf of sinners.

III. Jesus, the Source of Eternal Salvation

The Jewish sacrificial system offered, even in the minds of its best thinkers, a hope for temporary salvation, a release from sins until another sacrifice was made. Jesus is not only the final and eternal, once-and-for-all sacrifice to erase the guilt of our sins (Heb. 9:24-28), but he is also the slayer of death (Heb. 2:9-15).

We should not overlook the aspect of obedience in this passage of scripture. The writer is addressing a group of believers who are in danger of falling away from their commitment. As we come to chapter 5, we have before us the spectacle of the unfaithful Israelites in the wilderness who could not enter into the promised land because of unbelief and disobedience. Jesus is held up as a model of obedience to God, his obedience being perfected through suffering.

IV. The Gift of Our Priesthood

One glorious outcome of this reinterpretation of the nature and role of the priest, and its fulfillment in Christ, is the concept of the priesthood of every believer. The role that was the privilege and responsibility of one man in the Old Testament, the high priest, has now become the privilege and responsibility of all Christians, all the time, through our great high priest, Jesus, who has gone beyond the veil and bids us approach him for one another. He who is the perfect sacrifice and the perfect priest to offer the perfect sacrifice once and for all has called us, his people, to fulfill that part of the earthly priestly role that is uniquely suited to our sinful pilgrimage. The privilege of the Old Testament priest was to approach God without needing any human mediator. Each Christian now has that boldness through the blood of Christ, in spite of our sinfulness (Heb. 10:19-25). We have no need for another person to usher us into the presence of God, or to grant forgiveness to us, or to tell us what we must believe. Each of us, as a priest of God, is competent to relate to God for ourselves and to approach God's throne on behalf of others.

The priestly responsibility is to do the ministry of a priest. We are responsible for offering our lives as sacrifices to God (1 Pet. 2:5; Rom. 12:1; Phil. 2:17). We are likewise charged with interceding for others. We need to recover this concept of "a priest at your elbow" and find the healing power of sharing and confessing our hurts to our brothers and sisters. The acceptance of this great truth means that we come to church not primarily to be ministered to but to be equipped to minister to others. It also means that, as priests, we each have our parish, whether it be in the office, home, or classroom. (Earl C. Davis)

A LIFESTYLE MODEL

JOHN 12:20-33

A single seed is planted in a cup of soil. A bit of water is poured onto the soil, and some plant food is added. The cup is tenderly placed on the window sill of the schoolroom so that the sun will shine on it. Before long, a plant begins to show. Then the plant is removed from the cup and placed in an old barrel or the family garden. In a few weeks that single seed produces a vine from which tomatoes are picked to grace the family table. The second-grader who began and completed this simple biological experiment has experienced the truth of Jesus' words in a natural sense.

Jesus, who was ever cognizant of both the simplicity and profundity of children, often drew analogies from the natural world that served to communicate spiritual and eternal truth. Here he says that "unless a grain of wheat falls into the earth and dies, it remains [alone]; but if it dies, it bears much fruit." Jesus remains true to his understanding that his coming death will be for the purpose of blessing multitudes of people. And when the hour of his death comes, there will be "glory" in it. The Greek word from which *glory* is derived is the same word from which our word *doxology* comes. During the worship in most of our churches we sing, "Praise God from whom all blessings flow." The glory is in the blessings.

But Jesus is thinking not just of his own death. He has in mind his followers, who also would be willing to lose their lives. Those who lose their lives find it, and those who hate their lives in this world will keep it for eternal life. What is about to happen to him at Calvary is the lifestyle model for his followers. Dying to self, dying to life, is the only path to fulfillment. It's paradoxical, but it's true.

Susanna Wesley found her life by giving it up to those in her care. Her life continues wherever there is a Wesleyan or United Methodist witness in the world. My mother had nine children. After I became an adult I asked her, "How were you able to give each of us all your love." Her reply was, "I loved the one who at the time needed me the most." I would like to think that this one who gave her life and love for her family lives on through her now maturing children.

Jesus' commitment is to the kind of life that finds meaning in the willingness to die. Jesus certainly has some anxiety about the coming Passion. But he knows that the suffering is the seed that will produce a harvest of blessings, and it's only by yielding his life that he will really gain it. (Jim Clardy).

APRIL 16, 2000

Passion/Palm Sunday

Worship Theme: The crowd's joyous adulation of King Jesus will give way to their mocking and derision. A genuine disciple holds fast to Christ in bad times as well as the good.

Readings: Isaiah 50:4-9*a*; Philippians 2:5-11; Mark 14:1–15:47

Call to Worship (Psalm 118:25-29):

Leader: Save us, we beseech you, O LORD!

People: **O LORD, we beseech you, give us success!**

Leader: Blessed is the one who comes in the name of the LORD!

People: **We bless you from the house of the LORD.**

Leader: The LORD is God, who has given us light.

People: **Lead the festal procession with branches, up to the horns of the altar!**

Leader: You are my God, and I will give thanks to you; you are my God, I will extol you.

People: **O give thanks to the LORD, who is good; for God's steadfast love endures for ever!**

Pastoral Prayer:
O most sacred Lord, you have poured the fullness of your life and love into your Son and our precious Savior, Christ Jesus. How can we thank you? Let us not join with the crowds to lay down palm branches and cloaks if we do not intend to follow Jesus to his

day of horror. May we all remain on this path of Christ, sometimes smooth and sometimes more abrasive and difficult than we could imagine. And we pray this for more than ourselves. Use us to tend the wounds and broken spirits of our brothers and sisters who lack the stamina to carry on with the journey home to God through their days of horror and sorrow. Help us to serve as the peace and comfort and healing of Jesus Christ. By your grace and in his name. Amen. (Thomas Gildermeister)

SERMON BRIEFS

WHAT IT TAKES TO BE A DISCIPLE

ISAIAH 50:4-9A

On this Palm Sunday we remember the ride Jesus took into Jerusalem on the last week of his life. But we remember more than that. We remember a prophet who lived before Jesus and who laid out his life as a testimony to God. Isaiah wrote about a servant of the Lord who was willing to pay any price in the cost of discipleship.

Discipleship still calls us to have certain qualities of the Spirit. Here are some qualities that show us to be disciples.

I. A Nature That Is Teachable

Being open to the truth is a quality needed for all disciples. How can we learn if we are closed-minded? Like Isaiah's servant, we can remain receptive to whatever God has for us. The servant has an "instructed tongue."

When we are younger we may be like that. But what happens as the years roll by? We can be instructed by an event in the life of Thomas Edison. His laboratory was virtually destroyed by fire in December of 1914. Although the damage exceeded $2 million, the buildings were only insured for $238,000 because they were made of concrete and thought to be fireproof. Much of Edison's life work went up in spectacular flames that December night. At the height of the fire, Edison's twenty-four-year-old son, Charles, frantically searched for his father among the smoke and debris. He finally found him; Edison was calmly watching the scene, his face glowing in the reflection, his white hair blowing in the wind. "My heart ached for him," said Charles. "He was sixty-seven—no longer a young man—and everything was going up in flames. When he saw me, he shouted, 'Charles, where's your mother?' When I told him I didn't know, he said, 'Find her. Bring her here. She will never see anything like this as long as she lives.' "

The next morning, Edison looked at the ruins and said, "There is great value in disaster. All our mistakes are burned up. Thank God we can start anew." Three weeks after the fire, Edison managed to deliver his first photograph ("By the Sower's Seeds," from *A 3rd Serving of Chicken Soup for the Soul* by Jack Canfield and Mark Victor Hansen [Deerfield Beach, Florida: Health Communications Inc., 1996], p. 235).

II. A Conscience That Is God-formed

The servant in Isaiah has his ears opened by the Sovereign Lord. He has not been rebellious nor has he drawn back from the task. Even physical violence did not deter him. The description in verse 6 of the abuse is appalling. But the servant did not run. Disciples have their consciences formed by the Lord.

Our consciences keep us moving in the right spiritual direction. Regular communion with the Lord and worship with God's people keep us sensitized to God's spirit. Some people have dropped out of regular worship attendance, however. Someone has come up with a perfect Sunday for them. Consider these options in a "No Excuse Sunday":

To make it possible for everyone to attend church next Sunday, we are going to have a special "No Excuse Sunday."
Cots will be placed in the foyer for those who say, "Sunday is my only day to sleep in."
There will be a special section with lounge chairs for those who feel that our pews are too hard.
Eye drops will be available for those with tired eyes from watching TV late Saturday night.
We will have steel helmets for those who say, "The roof would cave in if I ever came to church."

Blankets will be furnished for those who think the church is too cold, and fans for those who say it is too hot.

Scorecards will be available for those who wish to list the hypocrites present.

Relatives and friends will be in attendance for those who can't go to church and cook dinner, too.

We will distribute "Stamp Out Stewardship" buttons for those that feel the church is always asking for money.

One section will be devoted to trees and grass for those who like to seek God in nature.

Doctors and nurses will be in attendance for those who plan to be sick on Sunday.

The sanctuary will be decorated with both Christmas poinsettias and Easter lilies for those who never have seen the church without them.

We will provide hearing aids for those who can't hear the preacher and cotton for those who can!

Hope to see you there!

III. An Assurance That God Will Ultimately Triumph

Discipleship is not up to us alone, thankfully. Following the Lord is not a do-it-yourself project. It is living with the awareness that God will bring all things together and under control in the end. Waiting is difficult, but the wait will be worth the effort.

Carl Sandburg wrote a multivolume set of books on the life of Abraham Lincoln. One volume has a chapter entitled "Palm Sunday '65." It was about the date of April 9, 1865, when Robert E. Lee surrendered to Ulysses S. Grant at Appomattox Court House in Virginia. On that Palm Sunday the war ended and peace began to reign. A few skirmishes flared up here and there until everyone finally got the word that the war really was over.

That is not a bad Palm Sunday. God was ready to present peace plans to men. There would be no compromise. Although a skirmish broke out on Friday, it was because the men did not realize that the battle was over.

Palm Sunday is the day when Christ proclaimed his victory over the hostile forces opposed to him. He faced these forces armed only with power of self-giving love, but that was enough. God is still seeking to let everyone know the battle is over and

146

that Christ won. Jesus' life itself was the treaty. Discipleship is the honor of signing the peace treaty with God.

These qualities help us understand what it takes to be a disciple—a nature that is teachable, a conscience that is God-formed, and an assurance that God will triumph. (Don M. Aycock)

A GIFT FROM A GRACIOUS GOD

PHILIPPIANS 2:5-11

Take off your shoes. Cover your head. Prostrate yourself on the floor. You are in the presence of God, and humility is the only response imaginable. Though you do not deserve it, you are about to experience the loftiest expression of God's exaltation of his Son, and the greatest demand that God will ever make on your life. The name for this experience is grace.

I. Why Did Paul Write These Words?

It is clear from the preceding four verses that there were problems in the church at Philippi. Though the specifics remain nameless, the nature of the problem is clear enough—self-righteous disciples were creating division in the church. In our day, we might consult a work on conflict management in the church and arrive at an eminently practical, and pragmatic, response to this congregational dysfunction.

Paul, however, took an approach which some writers have likened to hunting a hare with a howitzer. He disavowed pragmatic solutions to theological problems and responded by using the greatest Christological hymn of the New Testament to call the self-serving sinners to become sacrificial servants.

II. What Was Paul Trying to Say?

Verse 5 is the key to understanding this passage in context. As a corrective to conflict, he says, conform your attitude about life to that of Christ. Verse 5 is difficult both to understand and to apply to our own lives, and so verses 6 through 11 are a commentary on how to have the mind of Christ. This commentary is a hymn to the lordship of Christ and a command to take up our own cross and to honor Christ by duplicating his self-sacrificing service. The problem with pettiness is that it diverts our attention from what is essential. Paul's response to pettiness was to call the church to remember the cost of its freedom.

III. How Can We Understand This Text?

There are many volumes which deal with the critical problems raised by this text: Was it original to Paul, or did he quote it? Was the background of this hymn Jewish or Gentile? Does it contain two or three strophes on the work of Christ? What kind of Christology is Paul espousing here? If Paul is quoting, what did he add to the hymn himself?

The study of these issues is crucial to the growth of each minister as an exegete and student of the Scriptures, but to dissect this scripture passage adequately would require a year of sermons and likely still miss Paul's point: How should we react to Christ? This scripture, like the great work of art that it is, must be experienced as a whole in order to do it justice. Also, we must remember when looking at Scripture that frequently the simplest way of understanding a complex text is to start at its end and to work backward.

The greatest confession is that "Jesus Christ is Lord" (v. 11).

The greatest name is the name given to Jesus of Nazareth—Christ (v. 10).

The greatest location is the highest in heaven—where Jesus reigns (v. 9).

The greatest attitude is humility—a paradox of salvation (v. 8).

The greatest example of humility is Jesus Christ (vv. 6-7). In the words of the early church: "He became as we are so that we might become as he is."

The greatest demand on our lives is that we have the mind and live the life of our sacrificial Savior, Jesus Christ (v. 5).

The greatest grace is that God has made it possible for us to receive the mind of Christ as a gift through the Holy Spirit.

In the movie *Saving Private Ryan*, the last words of Captain Miller to the private he sought to save from the ravages of war are "earn it." By the grace of God and the sacrifice of Christ, we do not have to earn either our salvation or the abundant life salvation brings. We enjoy them in the way of the new covenant, as a gift from a gracious God. (Mickey Kirkindoll)

IS THERE MEANING IN THE DEATH STORY?

MARK 14:1–15:47

Who wants to be on a losing team? The TV sportscasters contrast the glory of winning with the "agony of defeat." On that black Friday forever marked in the annals of history, defeat seemed to be written indelibly even on the clouds of heaven. The events of those last days spoke thunderously of doom and failure. For the disciples who accompanied Jesus, those painful events were seared into their memories. Indeed, in the Gospel of Mark the story of Jesus spans sixteen chapters, but a very long two chapters encompass just a few hours. Why is so much ink used on such a brief and painful time? Is Mark a weird misanthrope who likes to detail sad events? And what is the point of those events anyway?

I. A Wasteful Anointing (14:3-9)

After a brief introduction, the reader is confronted with a tear-jerking story of a woman who poured precious ointment on Jesus. It was worth the equivalent of a year's wages, enough for a dowry. It could have been a bride-price. Is that not wasteful? Why didn't the woman use the valuable ointment and get married? Does such an action make any sense?

II. The Betrayer's Role (14:1-2, 10-11, 43-46)

The enemies of Jesus wondered how they could get rid of him. Their goal was realized when one of Jesus' own disciples who knew the value of money became a stool-pigeon and agreed to betray him. What's more, he did it with a kiss. What gets into a man to do that? Was something wrong with him?

III. The Tragic Peter Story (14:26-29, 32-38, 66-72)

Then Peter, the leader of the disciples, if there was one, boasted that he was more faithful than all the rest and that he would never compromise his commitment to Jesus. But he could not even follow instructions about prayer, and he ended up denying Jesus, even with a cursing oath. What kind of crummy disciples did Jesus choose to follow him? Didn't he know any better how to make his choices?

IV. The Horrible Way to Die (15:16-32)

Then Jesus' captors mocked him, beat him up, spat at him, stretched him on a cross and nailed him to it, stuck it into the ground, and let him hang there in the hot sun and gasp for breath. And when he hung there suffering, they teased him mercilessly. Is that not "cruel and unusual punishment" by any definition? What makes people torture others that way? Is there something wrong with them?

V. The Eerie Cry (15:33-34)

The pain and anguish of Jesus reached such a pitch that it was unbearable, as the sense of utter loneliness encompassed the one who was a friend of sinners and people who were abandoned. The cries of the suffering and forsaken ones of the world were all caught up in the eerie cry of Jesus from the cross. Why was the pain so intense? Was he really abandoned by God?

VI. The Meaning of the Death Story (15:37-39)

The death story leaves us with many questions, as we seek to make sense out of the acts of love and the ways of evil and failure. What is eminently clear is that (1) evil here became unmasked in all its horror and showed that humans are capable of the worst atrocities; and (2) well-meaning followers of Jesus are very weak and that Jesus knew all about evil and human nature before he died.

While the pain was extreme, it is clear that God did not actually abandon Jesus. Mark indicated this fact with two points. The first was the tearing of the veil of the Temple (15:38). The people of God had rejected their Savior, and the God who suffered with Jesus judged the people's rejection. The second was that an outsider, a Gentile centurion, recognized that it was not a mere mortal but the Son of God who died on the cross; thus death actually opened the way of salvation to the whole world.

The story does in fact make sense, but its sense is not the way of the world. (Gerald L. Borchert)

APRIL 21, 2000

Good Friday

Worship Theme: Without the Crucifixion there can be no Resurrection. "Good" Friday is despair and death before it is faith and hope.

Readings: Isaiah 52:13–53:12; Hebrews 10:16-25; John 18:1–19:42

Call to Worship (Psalm 22:1-5):

> *Leader:* My God, my God, why have you forsaken me?
>
> ***People:*** **Why are you so far from helping me, from the words of my groaning?**
>
> *Leader:* O my God, I cry by day, but you do not answer;
>
> ***People:*** **and by night, but find no rest.**
>
> *Leader:* Yet you, the praise of Israel, are enthroned in holiness.
>
> ***People:*** **In you our forebears trusted; they trusted and you delivered them.**
>
> *Leader:* To you they cried, and were saved;
>
> ***People:*** **in you they trusted, and were not disappointed.**

Pastoral Prayer:

We remember that day so many years ago, dear God, and we sit in its darkness and heaviness. Even now that we know how the story ends, Lord, the sadness is suffocating. For us, Jesus? Did you love us that much? Do you still? Most Holy Christ, of course your love endures our worst sin, our worst choices. Indeed, this love is the object of all our faith and hope. And it is the source of any life and love that was, is, or ever will be. We sit in silence now, waiting on Resurrection. Amen, sweet Lord, Amen. (Thomas Gildermeister)

SERMON BRIEFS

THE MEANING OF JESUS' DEATH

ISAIAH 52:13–53:12

Jesus died on a cross as a convicted criminal. Questions of guilt or innocence became largely meaningless once punishment was carried out. With him died his mission. And it was his mission that had brought him to the cross, not a suicidal tendency or ignorance of the forces aligned against him. His mission, as I believe he saw it, was to proclaim the coming kingdom of God; and wherever he went the Kingdom came with him. With him it came, and with him it died. After Easter the picture changes. By raising him from the dead, God vindicated Jesus and his mission. Hope was reborn, but how could one make sense of Jesus' death?

I. The Witness to Our Lord from Isaiah

Whenever I read Scripture in worship, I always preface the reading with the words "Hear the witness to our Lord from . . ." and then the name of the book. Following the reading I say, "You too are witnesses. Thanks be to God." I do so to highlight how the Bible functions in our lives and especially our worship. We live by faith in a God we have learned to trust and love. We gather to celebrate God's mighty acts, past, present, and future. The Bible, of course, is an indispensable and authoritative witness to these things. My formula, however, draws frequent criticism from those who say the Hebrew Scriptures have a witness of their own, quite apart from any reference to this man we Christians call the Messiah. My response is that there are many ways to read the Bible and many levels on which to interpret it. Certainly the books we call the Old Testament have an integrity that stands on its own. However, when we read them in Christian worship, we are appropriating them as a witness to our Lord.

Jesus' first followers turned to their Scriptures to make some sense of their experiences with him. Because Jesus proclaimed the God of Abraham, Isaac, and Jacob, the Jewish Scriptures could not be abandoned. Henceforth, the Scriptures would be interpreted by Christians as a witness to the One whom they knew to be their Lord and God. Could those early Christians have read this passage without thinking of Jesus? Clearly they did not. New Testament writers quote this servant song seven times and make many more allusions and references to it. Look for it in such diverse writings as Romans, John, Matthew, Luke and Acts, and 1 Peter. As Jesus' followers wrestled for an understanding of his death—the very thing we do on this day—this passage resonated with what Jesus had done and said.

II. A Death for You

Thus, we modern Christians make our pilgrimage back to this text so precious to our faithful ancestors. And here we find the answer they found. Jesus' death is a death for us—a death for you. "He was wounded for our transgressions, crushed for our iniquities; upon him was the punishment that made us whole, and by his bruises we are healed" (53:5).

He became a sacrifice; an example; a victor who overcame all the consequences of sin; the last scapegoat; a sign of God's love; and more. How his death works for our benefit is a question for another time. That his death was for you is the answer we seek today. It is enough for you to contemplate the cross on this Good Friday and recognize the love of God for you.

The cross, you see, is something other than it first appears to be. Not an accident of history, it is part of God's great plan. And because Jesus died for you, you must somehow fit into that plan. Can you even begin to understand such great love? Try. Believe the Good News, and try. (David Mauldin)

FOR US AND FOR OUR SALVATION

HEBREWS 10:16-25

On Good Friday the church remembers Jesus' death. The lections provide an occasion for proclaiming the meaning of this death. Precisely here lies a problem, however. "Objective" theories of atonement, focusing on Jesus making satisfaction to God or serving as a substitute for us, are problematic for many Christians. Conscience makes an explanation of Jesus' death that rests upon divine necessity intolerable. A merciful God that requires suffering and death is a contradiction. These theories are said to ascribe to God what was done to Jesus by the history of human injustice.

Other Christians are equally adamant that "subjective" theories of atonement reduce Christ to no more than a good example. Such interpretations rob the event commemorated this day of any integral role in the mystery of salvation beyond testimony to God's love. This lection offers another way to approach the issue of the atonement.

I. The Lection and the Book

Our assigned portion of this early sermonic interpretation of the meaning of Jesus relates his life and death to God's promise to establish a new covenant and to forgive sin. In him is the fulfillment of the promise given in Jeremiah 31:31-34. According to the Hebrews preacher, God has indeed acted on our behalf and for our salvation in Jesus' death on the cross.

Yet, rather than interpreting this event as the payment of a penalty, Hebrews declares that it has made new life a living possibility for us. This view is exposited in verses 19-25 in what we might call a "rhetorical flourish." In the Greek, these verses are a single sentence underscoring the implications and consequences of Jesus' death for Christian life.

II. The Message and Themes

The first theme is obedience. Hebrew prophets had translated the concept of sacrifice into the arena of ethics long before the days of Jesus' flesh. They did not completely remove sacrifice from the cultic realm. Rather, they extended it into everyday life, to be lived in obedience to God (cf. Amos 5:22-24 and Mic. 6:6-8). Given Hebrews' reliance upon messianic interpretation of the Jewish Scriptures, this ethical understanding of sacrifice is proper for speaking of Jesus' death (cf. 10:5ff.). The power operative in his death is that of his unfailing obedience. His blood is not the sacrifice itself as much as it is testimony to the perfect degree of Jesus' sacrifice.

At the same time, Jesus' obedience unto death was not merely an example, no matter how perfect. His obedience served to open the way for our life of obedience to God. Eduard Schweizer illustrates this from his boyhood in the Alps. In deep mountain snows, his father would walk before him. Young Eduard would follow along, placing his feet in his father's footprints that were larger and deeper than young Eduard could make himself (Gerhard Krodel, ed., *The General Letters: Hebrews, James, 1-2 Peter, Jude, 1-3 John* [Proclamation Commentaries] [Philadelphia: Fortress Press, 1975], p. 18.). Further, our undeniably imperfect obedience is, by the gracious will of God, taken up into Jesus' perfect obedience. He is, as the preacher of Hebrews says, "the pioneer and perfecter of our faith" (12:2).

A second theme from this lection is that of Christian life that responds to Jesus' sacrifice on our behalf. In particular, the three hortatory subjunctives of verses 22-25 call hearers to new life marked by what are called "the Christian virtues." This new life is defined by:

1. The assurance of faith: Christ's work has been accomplished in us, even if the fullness of it is as yet unseen. We are thus bold (the meaning of the word translated "confidence") to live before God and for God.

2. The confession of hope: Hope is faith oriented toward the future, a confident expectation of the final fulfillment of God's promises.

3. The life in community characterized by love and good deeds: Christ's sacrifice of obedience has made communion with God and our fellow human beings possible, communion marked by the self-giving love seen in Jesus' sacrifice. (Philip E. Thompson)

THAT YOU MAY BELIEVE

JOHN 18:1–19:42

Several years ago *The Door*, a humor magazine published by American evangelicals, produced an issue that seemed to be about Diana, Princess of Wales. The cover had no fewer than four photographs of the princess, and advertised the following articles: "Simon Mayo on the Media Treatment of Princess Di and Fergie"; "Susan Howatch on the Novel Based on the Life of Princess Di"; "Graham Cray on the Inside View of the Spiritual Life of Lady Di"; "Steve Lawhead on the American View of Princess Di"; and "Beavis & Butthead Asked to Palace by Princess Di."

The not-so-subtle commentary being made by *The Door*'s editors was that anything to do with the Princess of Wales helped sell magazines, therefore suggesting that a "Diana connection" (however far-fetched) with their regular articles would increase circulation.

The lesson suggested by the magazine cover was not about the world's most-photographed woman; rather, it was about motives. The editors implied that in any kind of public discourse we would do well to consider why a story is being told, and how it is being presented.

In the narrative covering Jesus' passion and death, it is easy to discern the writer's *why* and *how*. John 19:35 (RSV) reads, "He who saw it has borne witness—his testimony is true, and he knows that he tells the truth—that you also may believe." Later in the Gospel (20:31 RSV), the writer reiterates, "These [things] are written that you may believe that Jesus is the Christ, the Son of God, and that believing you may have life in his name."

The gospel was recorded with a single purpose in mind—to bring people to faith and new life in Jesus Christ. As for how, the writer presents his material in such a way that points to Jesus as the fulfillment of Old Testament prophecies. The miracles are signs of who Jesus is. The Master's teachings are revelations of the divine nature and purpose. And the portion of Scripture traditionally read on Good Friday, the "Passion narrative," is presented in a way that focuses our attention on what Jesus suffered for our sake. This doesn't "sell" well in popular culture, and not just in a marketplace where Easter candy and clothes bring in profits that a crown of thorns cannot. We live in a time when Christian radio stations play music celebrating the Resurrection weeks before Easter, mistakenly call Holy Week "Easter Week," and switch back to their usual musical potpourri the day after Easter. Why? Because people prefer listening to upbeat, happy songs and messages. In addition, ours is a self-absorbed generation, prone to psychologize any and every text in service to our narcissism.

Good Friday isn't good, however, unless we set aside "what sells" and attend to the *why* and *how* of the story. The suffering of our Lord cannot be likened to the suffering or oppression of any other person or group in history, because only Jesus' grief and pain are the means for the world's redemption. For our sake was he seized and bound, spat on, and struck by his tormentors. For our sins, the Redeemer wore a crown of thorns and a purple cloak. For love of a people yet unborn, Jesus carried a cross and was nailed through his hands and feet. The anguish of being denied and abandoned by his closest friends, and his terrible thirst and death by asphyxiation and blood loss—all these were for our salvation. These things were written that we may believe and that, believing, we may have life in his name.

What story are we, as a church or as individuals, telling on Good Friday? How are we telling it, and why? This is a day to find our places in the story, to take our places at the foot of the cross, to fix our attention solely on what Jesus Christ has done, and then to repeat the story for others that they too may believe. (Carol M. Noren)

APRIL 23, 2000

Easter Sunday

Worship Theme: May we have eyes and ears to see and hear the living Christ in our midst.

Readings: Acts 10:34-43; 1 Corinthians 15:1-11; John 20:1-18

Call to Worship (Psalm 118:21-24, 28-29):

Leader: I thank you that you have answered me and have become my salvation.

People: **The stone which the builders rejected has become the cornerstone.**

Leader: This is the LORD's doing; it is marvelous in our eyes.

People: **This is the day which the LORD has made; let us rejoice and be glad in it.**

Leader: You are my God, and I will give thanks to you; you are my God, I will extol you.

People: **O give thanks to the LORD, who is good; for God's steadfast love endures for ever!**

Pastoral Prayer:

O God, Almighty, and Everlasting, we are dumbfounded by your love, a love so powerful that even death cannot stand up to its strength. Christ is risen! Christ is risen, indeed! Hallelujah! You truly have finished the story, our story, and all the stories of your children. Dear Lord, we praise your name. The tomb really is empty. Nothing can separate us from your love and your life now. But, precious Redeemer, for many gathered here today, and many more beyond this sacred place, your love seems distant, your promise seems impossible. Just as beloved Mary Magdalene lingered at the tomb of her grief, hurt, and sorrow, so too we ask for your grace so that our broken brothers and sisters may wait and be patient. Because you are risen! And their eyes will finally be opened. And they will know a peace and grace that is beyond their wildest dreams. Amen. (Thomas Gildermeister)

SERMON BRIEFS

THE CHALLENGE TO CHANGE

ACTS 10:34-43

Today's text is about a man whose view of the world changed radically. His neatly ordered ways of thinking were challenged and shattered. He had to learn to cope with the fact that God is much bigger than he had ever imagined.

God cared for Gentiles just like Jews. What a revelation! What a change! This challenge is also faced by everyone who tries to follow Jesus.

I. Acknowledging Change

An understanding of the context of this passage is necessary. In Acts 10:1-33, two men are called by God in separate visions to accomplish the same thing. The men are Cornelius and Simon Peter. Cornelius, a devout soldier, was called to go to Peter and bring him back to the other Gentiles. The Lord wanted to teach the Gentiles through Simon Peter, a Jew.

Peter's vision was of a banquet spread out before him, but the items on the menu were disgusting to him. The key verse is 15 (NIV): "The voice spoke to him a second time, 'Do not call anything impure that God has made clean.'" The Lord was about to show him that Peter's idea of "clean" and "unclean" extended to people, too.

Cornelius went to Joppa where Peter was staying, and asked Peter to return with him. Both men knew that God was doing something significant in their lives, but at first they were unsure what it was. When the two arrived back in Caesarea, Peter went into the house of the Gentile. In verse 29, he asked, "May I ask why you sent for me?" What strange evangelism! Some people say that Peter opened the door to the Gentiles; it would be closer to the truth to say that the Gentiles opened a door to a larger world for Peter.

In verses 34-36, Peter tells the Gentile listeners that he made an enormous discovery. He had come to realize that God shows no favoritism but treats everyone alike. His comments demonstrate that Peter is surprised at the discovery and that he also understands the magnitude of the discovery. If God does not treat people with favoritism, then what about the Jews? What about the Gentiles? What about the nationalism Peter and countless others had believed in all their lives?

Simon Peter realized that the gospel that Jesus had taught and died for was for all people. Think of that—all people. It was a revolutionary idea. Peter begins his address in verse 34 with the words, "I now realize. . . . ." This literally means, "I am catching on." But why had he not known before then? If he and other Jews had been familiar with their Bible, what we call the Old Testament, they would have realized God's attitude much sooner.

II. The Gospel of Change

The great realization of God's universal love was the most compelling motivation in Peter's life. When he speaks to the Gentiles in the home of Cornelius, he touches briefly on his association with Jesus. Peter also lays out the facts of Jesus' death and subsequent resurrection.

The facts are these: Peter and the other disciples were witnesses to Jesus' life; the Jews killed Jesus by hanging him on a tree; God raised Jesus on the third day, and many people saw Jesus; some people ate and drank with Jesus after he was raised; Jesus commanded the disciples to preach about him, that he will be their ultimate judge; the prophets testified about him; and everyone who believes in him will receive forgiveness of their sins through his name.

Peter's "sermon" was not a rhetorical masterpiece, but it was a recitation of the facts of the life, teachings, death, and resurrection of Jesus, and of Peter's own involvement in that life. The message was not just for the Jews. The message of the cross is that all people everywhere are equally guilty before God, and therefore equally deserving of God's love.

It demonstrated how, in the midst of change, God was faithful to God's promise. God's people are called to be faithful in the changes we face, too. Change is difficult for most of us to face and conquer. But it is necessary, as Peter found out. Let us follow him. (Don Aycock)

HOW TO DEAL WITH DEATH

1 CORINTHIANS 15:1-11

If ever there was a worthy "how to" sermon topic, surely this is the one. Death is the universal experience, equaled only by birth. All of us, if Jesus tarries, will experience death. We may deny the reality, seek to cover it up, but it is there.

A minister was seeking to console a parishioner who had lost her husband, and in the conversation the minister reminded the lady that her husband was in heaven. She responded, "Oh, I suppose he's enjoying eternal bliss, but I wish you wouldn't speak of such unpleasant things."

We need to hear Paul's words on how to deal with death. In these opening verses of this "resurrection chapter" of 1 Corinthians, we find three great principles of Christian comfort.

I. Don't Be Carried Away with Spiritual Fads About the Afterlife

The church in Corinth, like the church today, was full of fads. They had their "wisdom" group, their divisions, their immorality, their confusing ideas of worship. Paul seeks to deal with their weird ideas of death and the afterlife. While we do not know their exact situation, apparently there was a group who did not believe in a bodily resurrection. Maybe they thought that when a man died, he died like a dog ("I had a dog named Rover; when he died, he died all over"). Perhaps they felt that Christians had already been "resurrected" in their conversion and were already ruling with Christ. (This kind of thinking, heresy, has always been dangerous because it carried within it a portion of truth, but fatally mixed with error.) Maybe they bought into the Greek idea of the immortality of the soul, but the destruction of the body at death. A sort of "John Brown's soul goes marching on," but his body's through! Possibly some of the Corinthian Christians felt that only those who remained until the return of Christ would live on, and all the rest who died had perished.

Now, if you think the Corinthians were all mixed up in their thinking about the afterlife, just take a poll of Christians today. There is the gospel of speculation. A rash of books in the last decade or so tout "near death" experiences and a return to this life with knowledge of the hereafter. Prominent catchwords include "warm, full of light, peaceful, a desire to remain." That clearly will not be the universal experience!

There is the gospel of reincarnation. "Here today, back tomorrow." We need to remember that Christian truth depends on the revelation in the Bible, not on what movie stars or sports figures may think or wish. New Age thinking has given a sense of legitimacy to spiritualism, to reincarnation and the idea that we get another shot at this world.

Recently a member of my congregation lost her father through death. I listened as she said that her father was not a Christian, but then a few minutes later she spoke of her confidence about the conversation her father was having with Christ, and that his life of good deeds would give him a passing grade. This woman, who had grown up in the church, clearly knew Christian doctrine. With great care I talked with her about what it truly means to be a Christian, and the basis for eternal life.

II. Be Sure to Lay Our Foundation of Faith in Jesus

In the midst of all the speculation surrounding the Corinthians—and us—Paul is urging Christians to get a grip on true faith. "This faith which I preached," he says, "and this same faith in which you stand—surely you were serious—will lead you on to salvation" (vv. 1-2 paraphrased). In verses 3-5 we find the heart of the Christian faith. Perhaps it is an early confession of faith; in any case, we cannot sum up our Christian faith better than this: Christ died for our sins; he died according to the Scriptures, proving he is the Messiah. He was buried, enduring all that death means. He was raised on the third day, against all the experience of mankind. He was seen by his followers. In verse 6 we read that many who actually saw Jesus after his resurrection were still around when Paul wrote, and could be questioned about that wonderful time. Paul continues on to name people and groups to whom Christ appeared after the Resurrection, naming himself last. The preacher doesn't matter; the message of the Gospel does! The question Paul raises for the Corinthians—and for us— in the midst of competing doctrines, is this: Can you affirm in your own life this good news, this gospel?

III. Keep the Resurrection of Jesus in Focus When We Deal with Death

If, says Paul, Christ has not been raised from the dead, if the resurrection of dead men is impossible, then Christ is still in a tomb somewhere. And, if so, that has shattering consequences for the Christian faith. Our preaching is empty, and the faith of all of us, pastor and layperson, is misplaced. We preachers are then false witnesses, and all of us are still in our sins. More than that, our Christian relatives who have died have simply perished forever.

If, on the other hand, Christ has been raised—and this is the unashamed proclamation of the Bible and Christian preaching— then good news has broken into this world. And that has tremendous consequences. The resurrection of Jesus means that our Friend and Lord has come through all the terrors of death which we face. We will never go in death anywhere he has not been and conquered. It means Jesus has pulled the sting of death. As the King James translation beautifully expresses it: "O death, where is thy sting? O grave, where is thy victory?" (1 Cor. 15:55). Thanks be to God he has given us the victory!

The resurrection of Jesus is the power, the proof, the catalyst for our own resurrection. His resurrection gives a meaning, a purpose, a direction to our life.

> Because I know he holds the future,
> And life is worth the living just because he lives.
> ("Because He Lives")

"Therefore, my beloved brethren, be ye steadfast, unmoveable, always abounding in the work of the Lord, forasmuch as ye know that your labour is not in vain . . ." (1 Cor. 15:58 KJV). (Earl Davis)

A MOVING ANNOUNCEMENT

JOHN 20:1-18

One of the most enduring images of the Easter story, as recorded in John's Gospel, is that of Mary Magdalene's encounter with the risen Christ in the garden. Perhaps it engages us because there is dialogue here rather than the narrative prevalent in the first part of the chapter. We are not told what Peter and John felt as they saw the empty tomb; we're only told what they did. But in verses 11-18, we find ourselves identifying with Mary's tears, her misunderstanding, and finally her amazed joy. Some of us come to church on Easter Sunday hoping that we will be moved in a similar way, delivered from the bondage of sorrow and lostness and to the assurance that He is risen indeed. One of the most-loved gospel songs of a previous generation, "In the Garden," makes use of the imagery found in the story of Mary's meeting with Jesus:

> I come to the garden alone,
> While the dew is still on the roses,
> And the voice I hear,
> Falling on my ear,
> The Son of God discloses.

Is it so surprising that on Easter morning we turn our churches into something resembling that garden? Lilies and spring flowers fill every available space. Soft candlelight is reminiscent of the half-light of early dawn that Resurrection morning. In some churches, the smell of incense permeates the air, just as the aroma of the spices brought to the tomb did. We hear the proclamation, "Christ is risen, just as he said!" and wish to feel the same awe and wonder Mary did when the truth became real to her.

According to John's account, Mary Magdalene was alone when Jesus appeared to her. In Luke's Gospel, only two disciples were walking on the road to Emmaus when the resurrected Christ joined them and transformed their faith. And when Jesus later appeared to the disciples in an Upper Room, the doors were locked for fear of the Jews. Whether in a garden or along the road or in someone's house, these moments of revelation were essentially private. Our risen Savior *did* appear to other followers during the forty days between Easter and Ascension but not to mixed crowds of believers and unbelievers. We may not focus on this aspect of the post-Resurrection narratives, but it can shape our religious aspirations more than we realize. You see, while more people come to church on Easter than on any other Sunday of the year, many of us come hoping for an experience that satisfies and inspires but makes little claim on us. We sing "The joy we share as we tarry there, none other has ever known," making a religious encounter a commodity to be pursued and treasured rather than something that equips us for mission and service.

Make no mistake: Mary Magdalene did not "stay in the garden with him" to savor his presence in solitude. As the Gospels present it, Easter was an action-packed day, with people coming and going constantly in response to the death and resurrection of Jesus. Mary *came* to the tomb, and when she found it empty, she *ran* to tell Peter and John. Then they *ran,* and *stooped, looked* around, and *went home.* Christ told Mary, "*Go* to my brethren and say to them, I am *ascending,*" and Mary *went* and *told.*

The thousands who came to faith in Christ in the first few years after the Resurrection did so not because they met Jesus of Nazareth in the flesh. They encountered the risen Lord in the testimony and praise and actions of those who bore the name Christian. As we thrill to the glorious music of Easter morning, as the Spirit touches our hearts through the Word proclaimed, as we drink in the beauty of the sanctuary, let us remember that God is moving us, and not just to a deeper knowledge of Jesus Christ for ourselves. The Lord's commission is to move us into the world to share the glad news with everyone: Christ is risen indeed! (Carol M. Noren)

APRIL 30, 2000

Second Sunday of Easter

Worship Theme: The Resurrected One enters into our lives of despair and doubt, offering us peace and the power of the Holy Spirit.

Readings: Acts 4:32-35; 1 John 1:2–2:2; John 20:19-31

Call to Worship (Psalm 133:1-3):

Leader: Behold, how good and pleasant it is when we live together in unity!

People: **It is like the precious oil upon the head, running down upon the beard, upon the beard of Aaron, running down on the collar of his robes!**

Leader: It is like the dew of Hermon which falls on the mountains of Zion!

People: **For there the Lord has commanded the blessing, life for evermore.**

Pastoral Prayer:

The pageantry and clamor of our Easter celebration subsides, dear God, and life goes on. We believe, Lord, that you are risen. We believe, and we praise your holy name. But this past week, the dull ache with which so many live has returned. Belief and faith wane. Doubt creeps under the door as life's everyday problems distract and overwhelm. And yet, Lord, here you are, risen and crashing into our ordinary lives with your extraordinary offer of life eternal, of peace, of the home for which we all long. Lord Jesus, forgive us when our doubts and crises numb our awareness of your Holy Spirit. Free us from the prison of our own making.

We pray in the name of Jesus Christ, above which there is no other. Amen. (Thomas Gildermeister)

SERMON BRIEFS

ONE HEART AND SOUL

ACTS 4:32-35

What does it mean to be of one heart and soul as a community? This may not have been as big an issue for a Jewish people, who could look at thousands of years of historical precedence as a people who needed to keep a communal presence strong, but it is certainly a valid question for a modern society. To be Jewish meant being part of a community focused on covenant with God. The judicial part of the community was God-centered. The social aspects of the community were God-centered. The political aspects of the community were God-centered. Being Jewish meant being God-centered *as a community.*

The early Christians were grounded in this communal understanding of a relationship with God. And as they drifted farther and farther from the mainstream Jewish consciousness, for they were already being viewed as outsiders in the Roman society, they naturally drew upon their Jewish backgrounds for strength, and this showed most visibly in the ways in which they drew strength and comfort from each other as a community.

So what does it mean for Christians today to be of one heart and soul as a community? Luke, in Acts 2:44, says that the Christians "had all things in common." In this passage he says again that "they had everything in common" (v. 32 RSV). This means that the concerns of daily living regarding education and work and shelter and food were shared. Each person truly thought of the community as an extended family. Everyone was aware of every blessing and every sickness that took place within the community. In Acts 2:46-47 (RSV), Luke says that "day by day, attending the temple together and breaking bread in their homes, they partook of food with glad and generous hearts, praising God and having favor with all the people." Regular communication and connection was thus an important part of maintaining "everything in common." Our once-a-week hour in the sanctuary detracts greatly from a true understanding of all that is going on in our church communities today. We've lost that "day by day" connection. We still share many of the same worries about life that those who have gone before shared, it's just that the same concerns for daily living that we have today in our individual and family lives were simply expanded in the life of the early church to cover a community and not just the individuals within the community.

This does *not* mean that everybody thought the same thing and said and did all the same things; it simply means that everybody had the same focus on being a Christ-centered community concerned with the welfare of all who gathered together. In Acts 4:37, Barnabas sold a field and gave the proceeds to the community because of his awareness and concern for the community. He did not sell all of his fields and give up his own understandings of how he could best serve the community, but he did share in the common mind-set of the community, doing whatever he could do to contribute. A modern parallel might be the understanding of opposing political parties *not* sharing the same understanding of how to solve political problems, but nonetheless sharing a common mind-set about the political necessities of how to meet the needs of the modern nation.

We won't always agree on how to do God's will in a changing world, but we can agree on the primacy of seeking that will and doing all that we can do to implement Christ's vision for our communities as we strive for truly attaining one Christian heart and one Christian soul. (Mark D. Haines)

THE REALITY OF GRACE

1 JOHN 1:1–2:2

John writes to the early Christians much as a firsthand witness testifies at a trial. No hearsay evidence in this pericope. Instead, John confesses, "This is my experience as a person—and a Christian." Verses 1 and 3: "We declare to you what . . . we have heard . . . and seen . . ., so that you also may have fellowship with us;

and truly our fellowship is with the Father and with his Son Jesus Christ."

As a person, an observer of life, a full participant in its glories and pitfalls, John declares, "What I declare to you is the universality of sin." Verse 8: "If we say that we have no sin, we deceive ourselves, and the truth is not in us." It is easy, of course, to assume that others "sin" and I merely commit "errors of judgment." Jesus called that seeing a speck in my neighbor's eye and ignoring the log in my own.

A friend confessed chastising an acquaintance for being politically narrow-minded. The acquaintance asked, "How often have you voted for someone in my party?" My friend confessed that he had never voted for anyone in that party. Still he argued, "But you vote because of party loyalty, and I vote from commitment to social principle, and those are entirely different things." Really? It is too easy to judge others for that which we do ourselves.

John points out in this lesson that we are all in the same boat together. Paul says it this way: "*All* have sinned and fall short of the glory of God" (Rom. 3:23 italics mine)

However, there is a note of good news that overpowers the bad. John goes on to say that what he declares is also the reality of grace. "If we confess our sins, he who is faithful and just will forgive us our sins and cleanse us from all unrighteousness" (v. 9). Why is that the case? The answer: Because Jesus loves us.

J. Winston Pearce tells of a family that had a daily breakfast table ritual. Each family member, on a rotating basis, would read scripture verses and offer the morning prayer. Obviously, children too young to read were not expected to take a turn. One morning, however, Angela, age four, asked if she could do the devotional. Her brothers laughed. "She can't read. She can't do the devotional!" But their mom intervened and said, "Let her try." Little Angela opened the Bible to Genesis, appeared to peer hard at the page, then said, "Jesus loves me." She flipped a few pages over to Daniel and repeated the exercise, ending with the same words: "Jesus loves me." Twice more from Mark and Hebrews, she did the same. Her brothers could not contain themselves. They burst into laughter, one of them saying, "See! She can't read. She doesn't know what the Bible says." Their mom quieted them with a look only moms possess, and answered, "You are mistaken. You need to learn what your sister knows—

that written bold on every page of God's Word is the message that Jesus loves us."

"We declare to you what we . . . have heard . . . and seen . . .," wrote John. In other words, "Let me share with you what I have experienced as a person and as a Christian. As a person, there is the troubling news that sin is universal. But as a Christian, there is the good news that "he who is faithful and just will forgive us our sins and cleanse us from all unrighteousness." We may be sinners, but we are loved. (Michael B. Brown)

MORE THAN WAS ASKED FOR

JOHN 20:19-31

"Have you believed because you have seen me? Blessed are those who have not seen and yet believe." This statement addressed to Thomas, whose first name is not Doubting, has been used as the basis for countless moralizing sermons. The preacher exhorts us to have more faith than Thomas did when he required hands-on proof, as though it is a bad thing to wonder about the Resurrection and downright wicked to harbor the question, "Is it true?" Thomas becomes a caricature, singled out from the other disciples as a symbol of recalcitrant unbelief.

Yet Thomas was not different from the others. *Every* witness to the Resurrection mentioned in John 20 was slow to believe that Christ was risen. It is true that Thomas wanted evidence, but so did the other followers of Jesus, both before and after the Passion. At the Last Supper, Philip said, "Lord, show us the Father, and we shall be satisfied." When the women who encountered the risen Christ at the tomb told the disciples the news, the Bible says their words "seemed to [the disciples] an idle tale." The truth is that singling out Thomas is majoring in the minors and making a false distinction between him and other disciples. We all have moments of faltering faith and flawed understanding. Rather than looking at Thomas as a skeptical loner, the narrative's central character whose change of heart must be weighed and analyzed, our attention should be focused on the risen Christ. What is the Gospel writer proclaiming about Jesus' divine nature, and what does it have to do with us?

Modern communication theory suggests a means of discerning what is important in this passage—observe what is mentioned or focused on most often. In today's text, Jesus' name, and pronouns referring to him are more numerous than Thomas'. The writer's primary concern is bearing witness to the risen Lord rather than tattling on Thomas. The first words out of Jesus' mouth are "Peace be with you" (v. 19). Quite a statement to people who had denied him and left him to die. Jesus said it a second time, and a third time eight days later when he presented himself to Thomas and the assembled group. This peace is not simply a greeting such as some Christians exchange during worship or spiritual thrill-seeking. The peace Christ offers is the dawning awareness that God's promise has been kept. The Lord who died for us loves us while we are yet sinners, and he will never leave us or forsake us.

Peace is the first gift Christ offers to his disciples. He also gives them power. In verse 22, it says he breathed on them and said, "Receive the Holy Spirit." The Spirit breathed into them power to do God's work—to proclaim the Gospel in word and deed, to exercise discipline among believers, and to preserve and "contend for the faith delivered once for all" in the face of challenge and compromise (Jude 3).

In this scene we also find an implicit promise of everlasting life. When the disciples saw the risen Lord, they would have remembered his words: "I am the resurrection and the life. Those who believe in me, even though they die, will live, and everyone who lives and believe in me will never die" (John 11:25, 26). Christ stood before them, the first fruits of those who have fallen asleep (1 Cor. 15:20).

Peace, power, and the promise of eternal life—they're all in this story. Thomas didn't think to ask for any of them. What he wanted—physical proof—couldn't begin to measure up to what Jesus offered. But grace overcame the poverty of his request. In asking, Thomas opened himself to all that the risen Christ gives to those who call upon him, including the power to believe and confess him as Lord and God. (Carol M. Noren)

DOORS AND WINDOWS

MAY

Reflection Verse: "And all your fortresses shall be destroyed" (Hos. 10:14).

The Discipline:

Meditate on a spider's web. If you can't find one, find a picture of one. Take a long look at it. A spider's web is what passes as a house or a fortress for a spider. Imagine that.

Let me tell you the story of one web. The light was slant and fall-like. I could see the web in its full complication in the garden only because it was 7 a.m. Earlier, no. Later, no. Only right then, as light from the east found it and exposed it, was it visible.

I found the web breathtaking and beautiful. I enjoyed it for quite the long morning time, ten minutes easy of not weeding or clipping. Then I decided to clean and weed and fix around the area where the spider had spun its glory. I wasn't going to get too close; I knew not to get too close. I knew about its delicacy.

You know what happened: I destroyed it, unintentionally. I robbed morning of its web, transition of its time, light of its own remorse. I knocked down the spider's house, doors, windows and all. The spider web is gone. But the lesson in delicacy lingers. We must be careful. We must be very, very careful.

The Meditation:

What Hosea really means about destroyed fortresses is all said in the word *your.* Your fortresses. What he means is that all the casings we put around ourselves will be spoiled—if they do not issue from God. In God's house, we live and move, not in our own fortress or armor or box or house or camouflage or web. We live in God's fortress for us, which is creation, not something we make for ourselves. As we prepare to lead the people of God in worship during this month, we need to pay attention to our houses. We may need a spring-cleaning or an "interior decorator." It may be time to redecorate.

Old-fashioned people redecorated their homes on a regular basis. They also spring-cleaned them. This regularity kept their houses in a proper place: they didn't become grandiose and idolatrous so much as humble and clean. The habits of spring-cleaning and regular redecoration have gone out of style, but spiritually they remain quite useful.

Moving into a new century is more like moving into a new house than even spring-cleaning or redecorating. We change locations. We pick up and move. We open doors. We close doors. We move "on."

Moving involves us with the serious question of what kind of housekeeper we really are. We can keep a house too clean. We can let a house go. We can tidy at the time when we should be letting be, and we can let be when we should be tidying. We can fail to appreciate the beauty of a messy coffee table with leftover joy from the night before. Or, we can enter Christmas with the bittersweet still hanging, and arrive at Easter with the mistletoe still up.

I learned some of this sense of delicacy and housekeeping when my eldest son left for school. I *insisted* on cleaning out his room—right after he had already done so. I kept some of the wrong things. I threw out some of the things that should have been kept.

Isaac, at age fourteen, had just left for boarding school. Within days his voice dropped, and he redid his room. He threw out boy and moved in teen. Video games, stuffed animals, guns, rockets, and large-print books were replaced by CDs, sci-fi novels, a computer, and an alarm clock.

I kept some old wooden trains that looked way too "baby" to him; I threw out an old stuffed monkey. Isaac's pet bear, "Cuddles," long lost under the bed, in full woozy, came out in this major interior redecoration. Cuddles is having a hard time with Isaac's maturing, as you might imagine, or at least he gave me a way to tell Isaac that I was.

Some of us are having a hard time making the move into the next century. We may need to locate our lost bear and have a long talk with it. Then maybe we can move on. God will provide us with enough foundation and enough fortress to get through the transition. We will have to make the decisions about what to keep and what to let go. God will be the interior decorator—and we will move the furniture and paint the walls.

The Song:
A mighty fortress is our God, our strong and sure protection;
Our God, who loves us, has resolved to free us from subjection.

(*The New Century Hymnal* [Cleveland: Pilgrim Press, 1995], 440)

The Prayer:
   Substitute your fortress for ours, O God. (Donna Schaper)

MAY 7, 2000

Third Sunday of Easter

Worship Theme: Christ Jesus presents his wounded body to us so that we might believe, know God's love, and be free to love as God loves.

Readings: Acts 3:12-19; 1 John 3:1-7; Luke 24:36b-48

Call to Worship (Psalm 4:4-8):

Leader:	Be angry, but do not sin;
People:	**commune with your own hearts in your beds, and be silent.**
Leader:	Offer right sacrifices,
People:	**and put your trust in the LORD.**
Leader:	There are many who say, "O that we might see some good!
People:	**Lift up the light of your countenance upon us, O LORD!"**
Leader:	You have put more joy in my heart than they have when their grain and wine abound.
People:	**In peace I will both lie down and sleep; for you alone, O LORD, make me lie down in safety.**

Pastoral Prayer:

You come and amaze us with your grace, dear Lord. Your gift of life is free, and we praise your unending name. Indeed, your mercy and grace sometimes shock us, even terrify us. But you never withdraw. You are with us in all seasons. Forgive us when we try to withdraw, when we try to flee. You come to us so often, Surprising God, with wounds in your body—the wounds of your children, our own wounds, for we are the Body of Christ. Have mercy on us, Lord, so that we may not be repulsed by broken bodies and souls. Dear God, help us to believe. Help us to know your perfect love. Help us to realize our freedom in your Son, Christ Jesus. Amen. (Thomas Gildermeister)

SERMON BRIEFS

WHY DO WE QUESTION?

ACTS 3:12-19

Our society spends a lot of time and effort enabling and encouraging each individual to be the very best that he or she can be. The Army even uses the slogan "Be all that you can be!" In our schools and businesses, good work is rewarded, and we begin to rely more and more on our own abilities and talents. And in our churches it is the dynamic youth program or the powerful preaching that receives credit for bringing in the people and being responsible for growth in the Christian community. We sometimes forget to give credit to the source of energy and integrity that undergirds the healthy Christian focus that drives our ministries. This passage calls us away from self.

Peter quite correctly asks, "Why do you wonder at this, or why do you stare at us, as though by our own power or piety we had made him walk?" We are bluntly and clearly reminded by this passage that it is not the administrative board that makes a difference in the lives of the hurting community. It is not the council on ministries that brings healing to those in need. The "power [and] piety" of the music director or the children's minister is not enough to make the lame walk or the blind see. We take credit for the ministries that seem to be going well, and we question God when things do not flow as smoothly. Peter could have just as easily asked, "Why have you lost an awareness of the power of God?" This is a passage that recalls us to God's purpose on earth.

177

Peter takes the opportunity of a successful ministry not to ask for a raise or implement another ministry that is meaningful to him but to point out to observers just who Jesus is and why good things are possible through faith in him. We sometimes get caught in the glow of meaningful ministry, patting ourselves on the backs for the good work being done. We sometimes also forget in whose name this good work is being done. When the people of God drift away from an understanding of God's presence in the ministries of the church, Peter quickly uses this success story to bring them back into a stronger relationship with the God who wants to be active in the world.

That's why this is a passage of repentance. "Repent therefore, and turn again," says Peter (v. 19 RSV). If we are not walking with God, we are walking away from God. If we are not connected to the focus and direction and energy of the Holy Spirit in the work of God, we are disconnected from the message of Jesus Christ concerning the calling of his church. If we have forgotten the role that God plays in our lives as the living representatives of Jesus' ministry here on earth, we too are in need of repentance and a turning back towards the God who guides and directs and energizes all that we do as a faithful community of believers. (Mark D. Haines)

OUR JUDGE AND OUR SAVIOR

1 JOHN 3:1-7

These words seem so out of character for John. Thus far he has written of the exceeding love that God feels for us, a love revealed in the selfless sacrifice of Jesus. Even here he begins that way:

> "See what love the Father has given us, that we should be called children of God; and that is what we are. The reason the world does not know us is that it did not know him. Beloved, we are God's children now; what we will be has not yet been revealed. What we do know is this: when he is revealed, we will be like him, for we will see him as he is." (vv. 1-2)

How wonderfully reassuring to know that God chooses us as children.

Karl Stegall tells of two brothers in the same class at school. The teacher, asking their birth dates, was told that one brother was born in March of 1994 and the other in May of the same year.

"How is that possible?" she asked.

One little boy answered, "One of us is adopted."

"Which one?" queried the teacher.

The child replied, "When Mommy tucks us in at night, she always says one of us is adopted, but she can't remember which."

What a beautiful parable of how God loves us. We are chosen. We belong to God. There are no distinctions among us. This is the God we have come to know and trust, the one John has proclaimed thus far in his Epistle.

Suddenly, though, John changes tracts and we find ourselves hit with the equivalent of a theological bombshell. It is unexpected, and we feel blind-sided by it: "Everyone who commits sin is guilty of lawlessness; sin is lawlessness. . . . [I]n him there is no sin. No one who abides in him sins; no one who sins has either seen him or known him" (vv. 4-5)

Now, that is bad news for some of you. Personally, I "make unwise choices," am "the victim of my environment," or at worst have "momentary lapses in good judgment." But you? You sin! No question about it. Sin. Capital S.

The temptation is all too real for any of us to adopt that posture. No one likes to confess his or her own sinfulness. But the truth is, we are all guilty. And this passage implies that God has no part in those who sin. "No one who abides in him sins; no one who sins has either seen him or known him" (v. 6). Does that mean you and I live without hope? A friend told me of the response of his wife following a serious indiscretion on his part. "Don't contact me ever again," she demanded. "To me, you no longer exist." Is that the sort of barrier sin builds between us and God?

Fortunately, there is an additional word in the lesson. "You know that he was revealed to take away sins. . . ." He who is our Judge is also our Savior. The sin that builds a barrier between a person and God is destroyed by one atoning act on the cross. There the gap is bridged. Jesus is sent to us ("revealed," as John puts it) to reestablish the bond our sins have broken. Thus, this passage leaves us with a Trinitarian formula of God-person relationships: (1) God chooses us as children; (2) we sell our birthright through sin; and (3) Jesus buys us back that we may become God's children again.

Thus was John's fundamental theme unchanged. Love still triumphs. (Michael B. Brown)

PEACE BE WITH YOU

LUKE 24:36b-48

There can be no doubt at all that the New Testament clearly teaches that Jesus rose bodily from the grave. The witnesses are clear. This important Resurrection text reveals Jesus' commission to his disciples to go to all nations.

I. The Message of Christ's Resurrection

The context indicates various reports of Jesus' resurrection appearances. The momentum of his appearance is stacking up. Even as the disciples are sharing reports, Jesus stands among them and utters the triumphal words "Peace be with you." The traditional greeting of that day now carries new significance because of the Resurrection. The Resurrection means the end of anxiety, the promise of God's blessing, and the continuation of God's plan. Yet the disciples are frightened. They are not yet accustomed to the idea of resurrection. Some in the group thought they were seeing a ghost.

II. The Meaning of Christ's Resurrection

Jesus' words of personal testimony were important for them and for us: "Why are you frightened, and why do doubts arise in your hearts? Look at my hands and my feet; see that it is I myself. Touch me and see; for a ghost does not have flesh and bones as you see that I have" (vv. 38-39).

Great care is taken first by Jesus and then by the Gospel writer to establish that the body in which Jesus appeared was a real body, no phantasm or mere manifestation of the Spirit. The text says "he showed them his hands and his feet." It was the body of the cross and the tomb, still bearing the marks of suffering. Yet he belonged to a different order of existence. He appeared, disappeared, and reappeared. The disciples struggle to make sense of it all. They are at once paralyzed by the awareness that Jesus has been raised from the dead.

On the one hand, they still did not believe. On the other, they were filled with joy and amazement. To help them in this unusual moment, Jesus asks for something to eat. Broiled fish is available. Jesus takes it and eats it. How can this happen?

The opportunity opens up for Jesus to enable them again to hear the significance of the cross and Resurrection. "This is what I told you while I was still with you," he says (vv. 44 paraphrased). He opens their minds by pointing them to the testimony of the Holy Scriptures.

The Old Testament portrays the Messiah as one who would suffer (see Psalm 22 and Isaiah 53) and rise from the dead on the third day (Ps. 16:9-11; Isa. 53:10-11). The crucified and resurrected Messiah is hardly an adjustment in God's plan. This was the design all along, for everything written about the Messiah in the Law, the Prophets, and the Psalms must be fulfilled.

III. The Mission of Christ's Followers

Now the important commission comes to all who would be Christ's followers: Proclaim repentance and forgiveness of sins to the nations.

Upon hearing the good news, people everywhere are to repent (the necessary response). Those who repent will be forgiven (the appropriate effect). Repentance involves a changing of heart, a changing of mind, a changing of perspective. No, Jesus is no longer dead. He is risen. The message is to be taken to all nations. Those who repent and receive forgiveness know true peace.

Jesus' greeting, "Peace be with you," is the promise he provides to faithful followers. The Old Testament anticipated, and the New Testament confirms that God's peace is mediated through the Messiah. True peace with God comes only by the death and resurrection of Jesus Christ. The true peace of God comes only by Christ's presence with us, among us, in us, and through us. We have the privilege to witness this marvelous truth, as Peter witnessed to Cornelius, telling the good news of "peace by Jesus Christ—[who] is LORD of all" (Acts 10:36). (David S. Dockery)

MAY 14, 2000

Fourth Sunday of Easter

Worship Theme: Listen to the voice of the Good Shepherd.

Readings: Acts 4:5-12; 1 John 3:16-24; John 10:11-18

Call to Worship (Psalm 23:1-6):

Leader: The LORD is my shepherd; I shall not want.

People: **The LORD makes me lie down in green pastures,**

Leader: leads me beside still waters, restores my life,

People: **leads me in right paths for the sake of the LORD's name.**

Leader: Even though I walk through the darkest valley, I fear no evil;

People: **for you are with me; your rod and your staff, they comfort me.**

Leader: You prepare a table before me in the presence of my enemies;

People: **you anoint my head with oil, my cup overflows.**

Leader: Surely goodness and mercy shall follow me all the days of my life;

People: **and I shall dwell in the house of the LORD as long as I live.**

Pastoral Prayer:

The valley is filled with wolves, sweet Jesus, but you are our Good Shepherd. We thank you for the lilting song of your voice that calls us home to safety, making your truth and your way unimaginably more luring than the wolves' false cries to sin and death. But, Lord, the temptations upon us are great. As breathtaking as your voice may be, the call of cheap grace and the empty security of this world draw us away from your protection. Holy Christ, help us to realize that you call us to safety not to languish and boast of some special blessings, but to venture out into the valley, offering good news in our words and our actions to people no less lost in the forest than we. And please give us the wisdom to know that words are not enough. You call us to ministries of love and justice wherever hate, poverty, and oppression thrive. Use us, Savior Christ, to heal the wounded spirits and bodies of your broken children. In the name of the One who has healed us and will always call us home. Amen. (Thomas Gildermeister)

SERMON BRIEFS

NO OTHER NAME

ACTS 4:5-12

I. Miracles Done

In chapter 3 of Luke's accounts of the acts of the apostles, Peter heals a lame man in the name of Jesus Christ. Here in chapter 4 he is being questioned by the Jewish religious authorities about that act. The problem is *not* that Peter healed a man. The problem is that Peter healed a man in the name of Jesus Christ. The question is *not* about whether or not miracles happen. They do. We have our own miracle stories of both the explainable and the unexplainable. Flowers, our own healing stories, and the birth of new life can be seen as miraculous or can sometimes be taken for granted when we drift from our awareness of God's presence in all that has been and is being created.

The authorities do not question Peter about whether or not a healing took place, they question him about the source of that healing. Miracles *do* still happen, and our recognition of them is often simply an indication of how close we still are to an ongoing relationship with God. Peter thus uses this miracle not as an end unto itself but as a means of pointing towards a greater truth. The first steps, therefore, taken by Peter and John to attract attention from society were *not* taken in order to draw attention to themselves, but rather to the One in whose name these actions were being taken.

II. Questions Asked

Luke points out that the friction between Peter and John, and the religious authorities focuses on the source of power for this healing action and not the action itself. The authorities ask, "By what power or by what name did you do this?" (v. 7). They do not ask how the healing took place; they ask about the need to give credit to Christ for the healing. In effect, they are asking Peter and John about the reality of Jesus as Christ. God is all around us, but like the religious rulers of Peter's day, we allow distance to come between God's presence and the ebb and flow of life. We have a tendency to remove God from the process of life around us. The authorities did not recognize God in the person of Jesus, and we ourselves don't often recognize God in the many miracles of modern life.

In Paul's letter to the Romans, he writes, "What can be known about God is plain to [people], because God has shown it to them. Ever since the creation of the world his invisible nature, namely, his eternal power and deity, has been clearly perceived in the things that have been made" (Rom. 1:19, 20 RSV). And yet, we continue to allow ourselves the possibility of finding other ways to explain life and the wonders of it. We continue to overlook the very real presence of Christ as a means of entering into relationship with God our creator.

III. Answers Given

Peter is thus steadfast in his efforts to point his accusers back to the reality of Christ. He speaks of how the leaders have drifted from God's presence and how Jesus was sent to bring them back.

Refusing to accept the reality of Jesus as Christ was in effect refusing to accept the very cornerstone of their salvation. Where have we missed God's presence in the world around us? How are we being called back to an affirmation of Jesus as Christ? Peter says we are in need of being saved, and that it is in the very name of Jesus Christ "by which we must be saved." Let us renew our own efforts to open our eyes to the loving presence of God in our lives. And let us remain firm in claiming the salvation offered by Peter in the name of Jesus Christ. (Mark D. Haines)

PUTTING FAITH INTO PRACTICE

1 JOHN 3:16-24

John offers his readers a strong model for living out one's faith. In fact, the model he offers is not merely strong, but exceedingly difficult. Using Jesus as his example, he says, "We know love by this, that he laid down his life for us—and we ought to lay down our lives for one another" (v. 16).

The immediate argument from most of us, of course, is, "Hey! I'm not Jesus."

And that is true. But if we are "CHRISTians," then we are by definition persons who are like him. And that involves selfless service and serious sacrifice. It involves a willingness to work at putting faith into practice.

Gary Player is one of the greatest golfers ever to carry a club. Years ago, he was part of the tour's "big three"—Nicklaus, Palmer, and Player. One particularly long and grueling day at the close of a round, a tired and frustrated Player heard a fan shout out, "I'd give anything if I could hit a golf ball like you!"

Player, a devoutly religious and usually polite man, fell to his fatigue and answered in an uncharacteristic manner, "No, you wouldn't. You'd give anything to hit a golf ball like I do if it were easy. Do you know what you've got to do to hit a golf ball like that? You've got to get up at five o'clock in the morning, go out on the course, and hit one thousand golf balls. Your hand starts bleeding; and you walk up to the clubhouse, wash the blood off your hand, slap a bandage on it, and go out and hit another thousand. That's what it takes to hit a golf ball like I do."

John advises the early Christians that putting faith into practice is not easy and often requires sacrifices we would prefer not make. It may require forgiving those who have trespassed against us. It may require allotting time to spend with our kids or our spouse when we have other personal or business plans. It may require listening when we would prefer to talk. It may require attention to church, to personal devotional disciplines, to faith development. It may require charity and generosity. "How does God's love abide in anyone who has the world's goods and sees a brother or sister in need and yet refuses help?" John asks. To possess faith is a key to salvation. But unless one takes it a step further and puts faith into practice, belief is shallow and powerless.

When Frank Sinatra died, famous performer Steve Lawrence remarked that he had made a successful career of imitating Sinatra. Discipleship is to make a spiritual career of imitating Jesus, bearing crosses, serving a needy world, celebrating God's goodness, and passing that goodness along through word and deed. "We know love by this, that he laid down his life for us—and we ought to lay down our lives for one another." (Michael B. Brown)

THE REICH, THE REIGN

JOHN 10:11-18

I. He Gave His Life for No One

One of the most chilling pictures of World War II, to my mind at least, is that one of Adolph Hitler walking amidst the rubble of bombed-out Berlin, stumbling over the remains of his dreams, there to review the ragged band of boys who will soon give their lives to defend what's left of the city. The Russians are coming from the east. Other allies are coming from the west. The end of the Third Reich is very near, and the end of Hitler is even nearer. He had promised these boys that the Reich would last a thousand years. Most of them will not live long enough to grasp that he only missed it by about nine hundred and ninety.

And look at the führer, awarding Iron Crosses and patting the cheeks of the children who will give their lives for him and his twisted imaginings. Look as he smiles at them, pleased, I guess, with their devotion and sacrifice, their willingness to die for him. He, of course, is unwilling to give himself or even his surrender that these children might live. Better that they all die together than for him to die alone.

Maybe this picture stays with me so vividly because I was about twelve years old when first I saw it. But now, and long after reading about Bonhoeffer, Barth, and the rest, it speaks vividly as to why these brave Christians could never address Hitler as führer, which, of course, is the German word for "lord." For while millions of Jews, millions of Germans, and millions of children died on account of this one man, he gave his life for no one.

II. The Good Shepherd Lays Down His Life for the Sheep

In our lesson, the real Lord distances himself from all those who do not care about the sheep but who leave the sheep in the breach as a buffer against the wolves. The Good Shepherd affirms that he is willing to lay his life down for the sheep, because the sheep are his and he cares for them. He loves them. Whether or not Hitler knew those boys who were ready to die for him is anyone's guess. My sense, though, is that Hitler knew no one and loved nothing other than his hatred. But the Good Shepherd knows his sheep, and they know him. They recognize his voice, the Scripture tells us; and even if the voice is a call to die, it is a call to die with the Shepherd who has already died for us.

III. The Difference Between Reich and Reign

The Reich was a dream of world domination. The Reign—the kingdom of God—is a plan for universal reconciliation. The Reich destroyed others in its vain attempt to gain power. Jesus gave up his power, and died, to defeat the opposing powers. The Reich murdered or enslaved many to service "the master race." The real Master brings all of his children together so that they might be one flock. The Reich was willing to sacrifice even its children in a lost cause. The Reign refuses that any be lost, and most especially its children.

187

IV. Wise Christians Know the Difference

Fifty years ago, a crazy man asked for the ultimate allegiance. Wise Christians said no. Today, many crazy things ask for pieces of our allegiance, and if we are not careful, we will find ourselves enslaved. Wise Christians can still tell the difference between führers and the Lord, between reichs and the Reign. (Thomas R. Steagald)

MAY 21, 2000

Fifth Sunday of Easter

Worship Theme: God calls us to produce a love that nurtures and sustains, but this fruit is only possible when we remain connected to God through Jesus Christ.

Readings: Acts 8:26-40; 1 John 4:7-21; John 15:1-8

Call to Worship (Psalm 22:25-31):

Leader: From you comes my praise in the great congregation;

People: **my vows I will pay before those who worship the LORD.**

Leader: The poor shall eat and be satisfied;

People: **those who seek the LORD shall praise the LORD! May your hearts live for ever!**

Leader: All the ends of the earth shall remember and turn to the LORD;

People: **and all the families of the nations shall worship before the LORD.**

Leader: For dominion belongs to the LORD who rules over the nations.

People: **All who sleep in the earth shall bow down to the LORD.**

Leader: All who go down to the dust shall bow before the LORD, and I shall live for God.

People: **Posterity shall serve the LORD;**

Leader: each generation shall tell of the LORD, and pro-
                 claim his deliverance to a people yet unborn.

People: **Surely the LORD has done it.**

Pastoral Prayer:

You have called us to participate in your Kingdom-building project, and we praise you, Almighty God. And you offer to us each day through that lovely Vine, your Son, Jesus Christ, the one true link to you, the one true source of all the love that ever has or will exist in this world of woe. But your commandment, that holy and singular law of love, is difficult even in the church. And as we attempt to love the outcast and outside, our failure looms more horrible. O Lord, forgive us. Don't allow us to be satisfied until we have loved with every ounce of our being and our doing. Help us, sweet Holy Spirit, to recognize the gifts that you have given to each one of us that allow our efforts to bear the abundant fruit of the vine of Christ. By your grace and in his name we pray. Amen. (Thomas Gildermeister)

SERMON BRIEFS

THE SURPRISING GOSPEL

ACTS 8:26-40

Some events grab our attention with urgency and power. Today's text is one such event. We learn about a man who is on the outskirts of society. He hears the story about another man who was pushed to the outskirts of society. People turned their backs on him and even killed him. But that man rose from the dead and gives eternal life to anyone who trusts him for it.

Today's text introduces us to a man who is a eunuch. His encounter with Philip teaches him that he is acceptable to God as much as everyone else is. The story he hears is, first, the gospel of reversal.

I. The Gospel of Reversal

Eunuchs were forbidden to enter the Temple to worship. They were told that God would not accept them because of their physical limitations. But Philip helps this man realize that circumstances such as his are overcome in the gospel. The gospel reversed many of the standards set up by men. A so-called outcast was included in God's family.

The modern call to Christians is to rise above our fears, prejudices, and misgivings, and to reach out to other people, especially new Christians. What a good thing it is to be called "brother" or "sister."

You never know what you will be doing when you help someone spiritually. On April 21, 1855, a man named Edward Kimball led one of his Sunday school boys to faith in Christ. That boy had been a "nobody" to many people. His name was Dwight L. Moody, and he became the world's leading evangelist in his era. His preaching led multiple thousands of people to faith in Christ.

Are there people around you who need to be "touched"? Do you know new Christians in your church who need a bit of extra help? Are there people who might be seen as the "wrong" kind of people? What can you do to reach out to them?

II. The Gospel of Inclusiveness

The Ethiopian eunuch wanted to know if he could be baptized after hearing the good news about Jesus. Philip obliged him as soon as possible. He was baptized into the death of Jesus, and therefore included in God's work.

Throughout my ministry, I have noticed that often a person's former weakness is turned into an asset by God. I have a friend who was once a "character" and an alcoholic. One night, while he was drunk, he was in a wreck. His fiancée led him to Christ that night in the emergency room. This man is now a powerful preacher of the gospel. The same forces and power he formerly used to "raise hell," as he used to put it, are now used by God to raise heaven.

When we reach out to new Christians and help them get started on their pilgrimage, we fulfill the command of Christ to love one another. Public baptism is a way of following Christ's commands and of being initiated into fellowship in a church. The eunuch needed both. So does every Christian.

III. The Gospel of Future Hope

One of the important things about the eunuch's faith was that it gave him hope for the future. He would never have children to carry on his name or to support him in his old age. But he had hope for the future because of his faith in Christ. Everyone needs hope.

While a company of people were having dinner together, one man in the party, who had spent many summers in Maine, fascinated his companions by telling of his experiences with a little town named Flagstaff. It was to be flooded, as part of a large lake for which a dam was being built. In the months before it ceased to exist, all improvements and repairs in the whole town were stopped. What was the use of painting a house if it were to be covered with water in six months? Why repair anything when the whole village was to be wiped out? So, week by week the whole town became more and more bedraggled, more gone to seed, more woebegone. Then he added by way of explanation, "Where there is no faith in the future, there is no power in the present" (Halford Luccock, *Unfinished Business* [New York: Harper and Brothers, 1956, p. 54]).

Yes, the gospel is full of surprises. God loves us. Isn't that the biggest surprise of all? (Don Aycock)

REMEMBERING WHOSE WE ARE

1 JOHN 4:7-21

Each night at bedtime I still say prayers with my children, kiss them, and tuck them in—even the teenager, who probably wishes Dad would "grow up" a bit. Still, he indulges me in this bit of parental nostalgia. And each night as I profess my love to the kids, each of them responds, "I love you, too, Dad." As often as you hear them, the words remain musical.

I believe that my children do love me. But I recall a time when they probably did not. They needed Mom and Dad. They relied on us. They were utterly and totally dependent. They could not prepare nor deliver their own food, change their own diapers, move about unless carried, and the list goes on. As newborns, our children were dependent. However, had they been removed from our care to the equally sufficient care of someone else, they would have survived nicely enough. For them initially, love was not the issue. That came later. It was learned. And the learning was in response to a greater love that was already there—ours for them. From my first sight of our children, from the very first touch, the first sound of a cry, the first cradling, I was head over heels in love with them. I loved them simply because they were mine. They didn't earn it. They didn't necessarily deserve it. They demanded a lot. They were costly. They woke their mother and me up in the night. They prided themselves in putting baby food on my clean shirts just prior to my leaving for the church office. But above and beyond any of that, they were my children. And nothing they could do would ever stop me from loving them. Eventually, growing up in that environment, they began to love their parents. And now, when they profess such before drifting off to sleep, I take them at their word.

John says God's parental relationship with us is similar to ours with our children. "We love [God] because [God] first loved us" (v. 19). Nothing we can ever do will stop God from loving us.

But there is something more. As my children grow and mature, I have certain expectations of them. I expect them to be honest in their relationships, to be fair, to be kind, to go to church, to do their best, to try hard, to celebrate life, and so forth. And God's children are likewise greeted with expectations from our Parent: "Those who say, 'I love God,' and hate their brothers or sisters, are liars; for those who do not love a brother or sister whom they have seen, cannot love God whom they have not seen. The commandment we have from him is this: those who love God must love their brothers and sisters also" (vv. 20-21).

A friend of mine keeps his father's picture on his desk. "I look at it during business transactions," he confessed. "I remember whose I am, and it keeps me honest."

In remembering whose we are, we too are kept honest—honest in our confidence of being loved, and honest in our efforts to pass that love along to others, even as our Parent calls us to do. (Michael B. Brown)

IS IT TIME TO TRIM YOUR TREES?

JOHN 15:1-8

There were four maple trees in front of one of the parsonages in which my wife and I lived. The branches had grown on to the roof of the house. They were not symmetrical, and not really that beautiful. One day while my wife and I were talking, one of us suggested that the trees be trimmed. It took me two days to cut them back. Members of the church, afterwards, stopped by and told us that the trees had been trimmed too closely and that they would not survive what we had done to them.

The next spring, however, those trees came to life. As they grew, they put on limbs where there had been stubs. Before long, they had grown into magnificent ornaments to decorate the parsonage lawn. What did the members say? You guessed it. They remarked, "Those are the most beautifully shaped trees we have ever seen."

Hopefully this will serve to introduce this text in a way so as to demonstrate the principle that pruning produces. In this case the pruned trees became four distinctively magnificent specimens of God's creation. Jesus, horticulturist par excellence, observes that a branch on the vine that doesn't produce fruit is taken away. In fact, the purpose of the pruning is to make a branch produce more fruit.

In this parable, the branches represent the disciples. The disciples have the potential not only to produce fruit but also to be unfruitful. Should disciples who have never brought other persons to Christ be considered unfruitful? The older preachers that I admired when I was a child would say, "The fruit of a Christian is another Christian." They were teaching me that to be fruitful I must share the love of Jesus with others. They never considered evangelism an option unless, of course, one was satisfied with the inevitable consequence of being pruned off the vine. There is an affirmation of one's fruitfulness in the kingdom of God in knowing that one has been responsible for bearing spiritual sons and daughters.

These days there is much fruit waiting to be harvested right in front of our churches. A few weeks ago I received a call late one afternoon. The lady told me that her grandfather had died. He had left written instruction that his funeral was to be conducted by a United Methodist minister. I agreed to do the funeral and told her I would visit them the next day to plan the funeral. I was later to learn that she was also the daughter-in-law of one of my former district superintendents. I also learned that her deceased grandfather lived directly across the street from our church. What was stunning to me personally was my being reminded that, for whatever reason, I had failed to cultivate the fruit trees at my own front door. My experiences during those two days with that family was what Jesus said had already happened to his disciples. They had been pruned by his Word. So had I. And with that pruning I was prepared to be more fruitful. Sometimes God has a way of reminding us that we are branches on the vine.

Think about the times you have been "trimmed." Perhaps it occurred when the dead branches of selfishness were pruned so that you could see the poor at your front door. Maybe it was the branch of poor concentration that deafened you to the voice of the little child as she kept trying to tell you in very simple language what God was doing in her life. Maybe you were listening in the wrong language. Perhaps it was a theological language, or the language of the market, or the latest technological lingo you were accustomed to hearing. So you were programmed to tune out the simple voice of God, and God pruned those branches so that you could hear the special little creation of God. You were able again to hear the voice of God through your child.

Don't always look for what it is God is going to do. Think about what God has already done. That kind of memory is what gave the Israelites their self-awareness and God-awareness. The Passover deliverance, the sustenance in the wilderness, deliverance from captivity—all these became a function of memory which kept them aware that the God who had acted in the past could be counted on in the future.

Is it time to trim your trees? Get all the dead wood out of the way and give the fresh sprouts of the Spirit room to grow. Don't be afraid of a good trimming. The One who brought forth a sprout from the stump of Jesse is waiting to bring forth from the new growth, which will produce the fruit of the Spirit. (Jim Clardy)

MAY 28, 2000

Sixth Sunday of Easter

Worship Theme: To be a friend of Christ requires more than belief. It requires obedience to the rule of love.

Readings: Acts 10:44-48; 1 John 5:1-6; John 15:9-17

Call to Worship (Psalm 98:4-6):

> *Leader:* Make a joyful noise to the LORD, all the earth;
>
> ***People:*** **break forth into joyous song and sing praises!**
>
> *Leader:* Sing praises to the LORD with the lyre, with the lyre and the sound of melody!
>
> ***People:*** **With trumpets and the sound of the horn make a joyful noise before the Ruler, the LORD!**

Pastoral Prayer:

You have called us to be your friend, dear Jesus? It is almost too wonderful to bear! We lift up voices to praise you and thank you. When we suffer from disease and bad fortune, begging for your comfort, your friendship seems to cool and drift away. But this is not so. Your love remains warm, provides the strength to survive, and even thrive, when we were not certain whether we could have endured another moment of this world. In you, Holy Christ, our life can continue forever, and our joy can be neverending. In you, Great God, our vision might be raised above the crisis and torment to see even beyond the horizon to a timeless time of perfect peace. Hallelujah! Amen. (Thomas Gildermeister)

SERMON BRIEFS

"WHOSOEVER" MEANS ME

ACTS 10:44-48

I had a conversation with a woman in her eighties. As we talked about her long and eventful life, I asked her about some of the difficulties she had experienced. She smiled and said, "Just keeping up with the changes I've seen. Most people don't like changes. We want everything to stay smooth. But along comes all these changes, and you have to start thinking again. But that's not too bad when you think of it."

"You have to start thinking again." That is the phrase that stands out from our conversation. My friend was right. Many people, if not most people, like things to stay the same because they are used to them. Changes bring new challenges, and we have to start thinking. This is especially true with religious faith. Simon Peter learned to think again about his faith. Here is what Peter learned that will help us.

I. The Gospel Is for All People

Simon Peter realized that the gospel that Jesus had taught and died for was for all people. Think of that—all people! But why had he not known that before? If he and other Jews had been familiar with their Bible (what we call the Old Testament), they would have realized God's attitude sooner.

What Peter learned is that God welcomes all who come to God. God sees the rich variety of humanity as precious, and, like a gardener, loves the roses, the chrysanthemums, the pansies, dahlias, lilies, and even the dandelions. God greatly loves the kaleidoscope of humanity. Who can overrule God and exclude people whom God includes?

II. Salvation Is Available to Everyone

Verse 44 indicates that while Simon Peter was still speaking to the Gentiles, the Holy Spirit "fell upon all who heard" the message. One commentator notes that God the Father interrupted

Peter on the Mount of Transfiguration (Matt. 17:4-5). God the Son interrupted Peter regarding the temple tax (Matt. 17:24-27). Now God the Spirit interrupted him before he could even finish the sermon. Any preacher would gladly accept such an interruption.

But what did it mean? Among other things it meant that when the early Christians shared their faith with people different from themselves, some of those people would be saved. This is still true. As mentioned above, there are no "right" or "wrong" people where the gospel is concerned. Anyone who says yes to Christ is the right person.

I once read a statement that said people are like piston engines—we move along through a series of internal explosions. These internal explosions are the sometimes shocking events and discoveries that happen to us. The Jews certainly were in for a shock, as God sent the Holy Spirit upon the Gentiles.

III. Salvation Is Worth Celebrating

Jesus once told a parable about jealousy. Some workers were hired to work all day, while others, hired later in the day, worked only a short time. When the pay was handed out, they all got the same amount. After hearing some workers grumble, the employer asked, "Are you envious because I am generous?" (Matt. 20:15 NIV). Some people really are jealous of johnny-come-lately people. A very sticky situation could have developed when the Jewish Christians saw that the Gentiles were given the Spirit. They could have been jealous and felt that they were being slighted in some way. How would they respond?

Peter asked the important question in verse 47 (NIV): "Can anyone keep these people from being baptized with water?" No one objected, so the group of Gentiles were baptized in the name of Jesus Christ. That action brought the Gentiles into the fold of the church.

Peter learned his lesson. The gospel is for everyone. Salvation is available to all. And salvation is worth celebrating. Let us learn it, too. (Don Aycock)

EMPOWERED BY THE SPIRIT

1 JOHN 5:1-6

The book of 1 John concerns itself with the connection between believing God, in Jesus, and our actions as a result. In other words, it addresses how our faith intersects with our deeds. The particular text for consideration, 1 John 5:1-6, considers the triumphant life of God's people as empowered by the Spirit. The Spirit empowers us for this life; however, it is power for the new time, a time yet to come. This Kingdom power manifests itself in loving God's people now as if the Kingdom has already come.

Let's consider these questions: What does it mean to live "into new life?" What does it mean to behave victoriously when the team is losing? How does one act when the evil ought to lose but does not?

These questions require a faith discussion. The activity of faith building and faith sharing, equipping disciples with an authentic trust is a necessary prerequisite in this arena. What are the possible avenues we can use to address this issue?

First of all, we must ask what 1 John says about faith? Moreover, we must explore faith from this character-building perspective. What are the qualities of a life that is built through faith? What are the examples, the models, that disciples need to construct a Christian reality? How are Christian principles embodied by believers? Answers to these questions allow us to really begin to engage with the text.

Harry Emerson Fosdick's *The Meaning of Faith* (Nashville: Abingdon Press, 1982) offers a fine point of departure for faith discussion. Another splendid model for this kind of living is Maya Angelou's biographical *I Know Why the Caged Bird Sings.* Each of these books offers faith examples that will stretch our perceptions and help us discover relevant character models.

Next, we must ask what 1 John means related to Kingdom living? What are the implications for individuals who seek this life? What can be predicted? What are parallels to this in the present age? Along this line, we can ask ourselves: What have Christians endured through the ages as they tried to live for God in the midst of a secular world?

Walter Brueggemann's *The Prophetic Imagination* (Minneapolis: Fortress Press, 1978) makes some interesting observations about serving God when power seems vested elsewhere. Also, Carlyle Fielding Stewart's *Street Corner Theology* (Nashville: Winston-Derek Publishers, 1995), a treatment of culturally relevant inner-city theologies, can help broaden our quest for a biblical, postmodern era, culturally relevant projection regarding Kingdom living.

Finally, we must ask this question: What difference does this make for us? As these issues become clear, we must relate them specifically to ourselves. How can we as Christians gear this message of Kingdom faith to the commonalities we all share—the struggles, stresses, and strains that we each encounter on a daily basis? In answer, we must take note of how we are living. Then we must ask ourselves: How will a vital faith impact my present circumstances? (Vance P. Ross)

DANCE WITHIN THE HEART

JOHN 15:9-17

My wife has always wanted me to dance with her. I've always refused. I am not a dancer. I never did learn. However, recently we were in Pittsburgh, Pennsylvania, where I conducted the service of worship during which my nephew and his fiancée were married. After the wedding, at the dinner, the DJ put on the music. The music and the occasion turned me into a child again. I really felt happy. I guess I got a bit carried away. Of course I take seriously our covenant to abstain from alcohol, so this transformation was not due to substance inducement. I did, however, recall the first miracle Jesus performed at the wedding in Cana of Galilee. As a matter of fact, I had just quoted that story as part of our United Methodist ritual for marriage. Anyway, the music stirred something in me. I found myself on the dance floor and facing my nephew's mother (my wife's sister). She said, "You want to dance?" And before I knew it I had responded in the affirmative. Afterwards, I asked my wife if she would like to dance. Thankfully I was able to fulfill my longstanding obligation to her. Finally, I took the hand of my mother-in-law, who had not danced in years. We followed the music like two kids would.

For some reason, in thinking about this passage, my mind went back to that happy occasion. But I also thought of a statement by Barclay Newman and Eugene Nida in *A Handbook on the Gospel of John* (New York: American Bible Society, 1980). There they present an interesting possibility for understanding verse 11*b*: "So that your joy may be complete." They suggest that the word *joy* here may be expressed idiomatically as "dance within the heart."

The "dance within the heart": What a powerful concept! And it is experienced in the most unexpected places and ways.

Some years ago I was driving with some friends through Southern Mississippi. We stopped at a small restaurant that, though clean, was not like anything I have been used to visiting. As we walked in, a man began playing the piano. He played beautifully. When I turned the second time to get a look at this musician, I discovered that he was blind.

I asked the waitress to see if he would play "The Tennessee Waltz." She whispered in his ear. Shortly she returned with this comment: "He doesn't know that one." Then I gave her a twenty-dollar bill and asked her to hand it to him. Without hesitation he played my request so that a wave of chill bumps swept over me. "I once was blind, but now I see," wrote Newton. Some people can see more with their hands and hearts than others of us can with 20-20 vision. That's one of the many amazing things about grace.

The dance within the heart. Wasn't it there in the heart of the prodigal's father when he first saw his penitent son in the bend of the road (Luke 15)? Mary rejoiced that God had looked with favor upon the lowliness of the Almighty's servant (Luke 1). The dance within the heart? The Philippians were Paul's "joy and crown" (Philippians 2). The woman in one of Jesus' parables rejoiced over the discovery of her lost coin (Luke 15). Again, the dance within the heart? Wasn't it there in Mary Magdalene when finally she realized that she was in the presence of the resurrected Christ (John 20)?

Friend, take your authority to preach this Word. Preach it with joy and power. Turn your heart loose, and let it dance.

> Dance, then, wherever you may be;
> I am the Lord of the Dance, said he.
> ("Lord of the Dance")

(Jim Clardy)

DOORS AND WINDOWS

JUNE

Reflection Verse: "I have said these things to you so that my joy may be in you, and that your joy may be complete" (John 15:11).

The Discipline:

Consider how we conduct services. Do we bid God, or does God bid us? Who issues the invitation to worship? June is a good month to evaluate what is happening in worship for us, for God, and for our people. Where is the joy?

Worship services are rehearsals of the good time God has promised as destiny for the world. They are times to remember the ancient texts and to think about them in a contemporary context. They are a time to sing. They are a time to forget about ourselves. A time to be quiet together. A time for filtered light. A time for lit candles. A time for preludes and postludes, marked beginnings and endings. Worship is a time to let go of the past, to receive a blessing, to be told that it is possible to go on. It is a time to learn more about the core of the universe, a time to prepare for the week, and a time to end the week. It is a time to be in sanctuary, a safe space, to look out the windows and know we are safe inside.

Worship is time out of time. It is time that ends one week and begins another. Worship keeps time by keeping the beat. It gets us out of one kind of time into another kind of time on behalf of the very time we left. Without worship, the weeks get weird. In worship, we learn to press our stop key and our start key.

Clergy may need to worship *both* in church *and* elsewhere. I have learned to be less "churchy" about worship. I have learned that God is not caged in the church and that worship is not, either. Most certainly, God is not the end point of my liturgical efforts! We can find God in almost any regular practice. We can even find God in irregular practice. God is not present only at our bidding: God is also present in our lives unbidden.

This month, evaluate your practice of preparing and leading worship. Change something if it's appropriate. Make sure God is in charge and not you.

The Meditation:

For a strange set of reasons, I once attended Sunday worship in four United Church of Christ churches in four states in two months. The services were more alike than different, but each was full of quirky joy.

Notably, the pattern of prayer in each service was the same—pastoral prayer interspersed by populist, personal intercessory prayer by the people. So why did I, who loves both personal prayer and populism, become increasing uncomfortable during this national form of piety?

A dear friend gave me the first reason. He is dealing with cancer in a private part of his body, and has stopped going to church because he is afraid that that part of his body will be mentioned during prayer. Personal prayer can cross the border into prayer that is too personal.

A second reason came to me as I left the fourth of these otherwise magnificent worship services. None of the prayers mentioned anything public; all the intercessions were individual, individualistic even. Why did the people of Indonesia receive no intercessions? Or the poor in town? Or the people we don't know? Does an in-law's cancer warrant more attention than a stranger's needs?

A final reason was the attention-getters. In each service, there was one or more persons who simply talked too long. He or she was not calling attention to the power of God to intercede, but to the power of personal pain. Pious exhibitionism is no better than any other kind.

What might have made me feel differently? Perhaps intercessions that included the stranger, where tendencies toward exhibitionism had been tamed, and that respected the privacy of people for whom prayers were being sent. Minimally, we might ask permission from someone we're about to "out" in prayer before we pray for them. Piety is important for prayer. So are good manners.

The Song and the Prayer:
This great bidding hymn is a great one to memorize.

> Come, my Way, my Truth, my Life: such a way as gives us
>   breath, such a truth as ends all strife, such a life as kil-
>   leth death.
> Come, my Light, my Feast, my Strength: such a light as
>   shows a feast, such a feast as mends in length, such a
>   strength as makes his guest.
> Come, my Joy, my Love, my Heart: such a joy as none can
>   move, such a love as none can part, such a heart as joys
>   in love.

("Come, My Way, My Truth, My Life")

(Donna Schaper)

JUNE 4, 2000

Seventh Sunday of Easter

Worship Theme: Christ Jesus is the Word of God. Whoever has this Word has life.

Readings: Acts 1:15-17, 21-26; 1 John 5:9-13; John 17:6-19

Call to Worship (Psalm 1:1-3):

> *Leader:* Blessed are those who do not walk in the counsel of the wicked;
>
> ***People:*** **or stand in the way of sinners, or sit in the seat of scoffers;**
>
> *Leader:* but their delight is in the law of the LORD,
>
> ***People:*** **and on God's law they meditate day and night.**
>
> *Leader:* They are like trees planted by streams of water that yield their fruit in season, and their leaves do not wither.
>
> ***People:*** **In all that they do, they prosper.**

Pastoral Prayer:
O Master of the universe, you speak your perfect word in Jesus, and eternity becomes possible even for the likes of the broken-down, stumbling souls who gather here today. Even for me the infinite journey is offered. Even for me! (Can we all say that—"even for me"?) But many will not say these priceless words, for they are too overloaded with the shame and guilt of the past. O Savior, let these suffering brothers and sisters hear this Word, accept this Word, live into this Word. Burn into their very being the good news that Christ is the Word of forgiveness

and acceptance. He is the Word of unconditional love. Let them recognize that the love of Christ Jesus for them clears the thorniest debris of a life filled with mistaken choices. Free each one of us, Almighty God, from the outrageous claim that our sin is greater than even your Word, your love, your Son, Jesus Christ. Amen. (Thomas Gildermeister)

SERMON BRIEFS

MOVING FORWARD

ACTS 1:15-17, 21-26

I. Our Task Has Been Determined

Jesus told his disciples what was expected of them, and told them that they would be given the strength and power to do God's will. "You will receive power when the Holy Spirit has come upon you; and you will be my witnesses in Jerusalem, and in all Judea and Samaria, and to the ends of the earth" (Acts 1:8). Their task (and ours) was to witness as fully and completely about God our creator and the relationship with God that is possible because of the presence and reality of Jesus Christ. They were to continue the mission to which they had been devoted for the last three years, not on the strength of the personality of Jesus, but on the power of the presence of Christ in the Holy Spirit. This was hard to understand and there was some confusion, but the task was stated clearly by Christ in his reappearance to the apostles.

We have been called to the same task and have been given the same assurances of the gift of the power of the presence of the Holy Spirit. Everything we say and do as representatives of Christ here on earth is still very much related to our primary task.

II. We Sometimes Have Setbacks

There are as many possibilities for setbacks in our task as there are people. In this story of the early disciples, their leader has been crucified, having been betrayed by one of their friends. They are no longer a movement of any strength or direction. This is as low a moment as they have ever experienced. We also have leadership changes. Sometimes this is good, and sometimes this is bad. But it always feels as though we lose a step or two trying to recover our momentum. We have scandals. Tornadoes and hurricanes and other natural disasters damage our church facilities. Questions about ministry possibilities can split our congregations. Our own human weaknesses lead us into difficulties time after time.

Whether or not we bring on these setbacks ourselves or they are simply a part of our life experience, the fact remains that setbacks are a regular part of our life. And in this context, the setback is seen specifically in light of our Christ-directed task to witness "to the ends of the earth." As individuals and as church communities, this particular passage speaks to those low moments in our lives, whatever they might be.

III. We Are Called to Move Forward

Even at their low moments, this passage suggests, the apostles know to move forward with Christ. First, the apostles take stock of their need to focus on their task and not their difficult circumstances. Their task, as they see it, is best accomplished from a structure that includes twelve apostles, not eleven. This means replacing Judas with a new representative who will "become a witness . . . to [Jesus'] resurrection" (Acts 1:22).

We also are called to replace staff members, reevaluate budget requirements, and evaluate our mission statements. This passage reminds us of the context under which such evaluations are to take place. How will our new staff members and new budgets and new administrative boards speak to a "witness to Jesus' resurrection"?

Second, the apostles knew not to continue in their task without the help of the Holy Spirit promised by Jesus. Casting lots for a replacement for Judas was *not* placing their confidence in fate or change but *was* very definitely placing confidence in the Holy Spirit. How can we do less? (Mark D. Haines)

207

THE GIVER OF ETERNAL LIFE

1 JOHN 5:9-13

The first epistle of John presents challenges to the contemporary Christians. We may be stirred by its pastoral tones and encouraging qualities that are clearly discernible in a reading of the text. However, as contemporary listeners, its intended meaning may prove confusing because we do not share in their particular struggles, theological questions, and assumptions as a community of believers. What was at stake in this Johannine community that makes the letter so timely, and how may its message inform and guide us?

It is generally held that the conflict within the Johannine church arose over the nature of incarnation and its relationship to Jesus' salvific mission. Eventually, a group that emphasized the significant moment of Jesus' baptism (in which God's spirit anointed him) while minimizing the salvific importance of his death, brought about an open division and departure from the church (see 2:19). The passage in chapter 5 seeks to address those left behind by encouraging a reexamination and commitment to a faith that "conquers the world" (5:4). The author's authority is rooted in his own experience as one who inherited the testimony concerning Jesus' life and death through the beloved disciple (as seen in John's Gospel [19:30] and in the epistle's Prologue [1:1]) and now as a part of the Johannine community.

Earlier passages in chapter 5 address the significance of both Jesus' baptism (water) and death (blood) as testimonies for hearing and believing from those who witnessed the events. By rooting the theological points, the writer seeks to convey in the actual witness of some who saw and heard Jesus, and is now able to establish an even greater witness in God's own testimony.

Three major themes from this text may be explored.

I. Understanding the Testimony of God

According to the text, the actual testimony of God is greater than any human testimony to the Son of God. That is, God's own testimony is found in the giving of eternal life to believers, an eternal life that is found in God's own Son (5:11). Unlike earlier testimonies, namely the witness of the Spirit to Jesus' own baptism and his death on the cross (see 5:6-8), God's testimony becomes even more powerful when one believes "in the Son of God." The belief itself is the agent for making the testimony of God known and understood within oneself. That testimony is eternal life, an eternal life that comes from believing Jesus, who in a similar way received it from God as God's Son. The indwelling of the Spirit in the believer speaks to God's own testimony to his Son. Eternal life signifies that indwelling testimony. Jesus is, in a most profound sense, our eternal life.

II. The Significance of Testimony for the Life of the Community

The fact that witness or testimony is central to these passages concerning belief about and in Jesus ties the living community to the events of Jesus' own life. The witness of the Spirit of God is made known in the witness of the community of believers. The Spirit reveals to believers the very testimony of God that in turn offers assurance and a faith that overcomes the world. To know is to have witnessed Jesus in the life of faith. The testimony of the church stands in a long tradition of witnesses.

III. Assurance of the Knowledge of Eternal Life

As in the Gospel of John, the author states the chief reason for writing the epistle in verse 13: "That you may know that you have eternal life." Offering assurance of their belief in the midst of conflict, disagreement, and schism is more than a pastoral concern of the writer. It is a theological affirmation that on the one hand pastorally addresses doubts some believers may have in light of their present circumstances, and on the other hand ties the community to Jesus himself as giver and embodiment of eternal life. Jesus gives assurance. Jesus gives himself. (Scott Hudgins)

WHAT IS TRUTH?

JOHN 17:6-19

Truth appears in verses 8, 17, and 19. This concept of *truth* occurs in other places throughout the Gospel of John. For example, the disciples see the incarnate Word "full of grace and truth" (1:14). Grace and truth came by Jesus Christ (1:17). The one who does the truth comes to the light (3:21). Worship of God must be in truth and in spirit (4:24). John the Baptist bears witness to the truth (5:33). The disciples will know the truth that will make them free (8:32). This word is also found in 8:40; 8:44; 8:45; 8:46; 14:6; 14:17; 15:26; 16:13; 17:8; 17:17; 17:19; 18:37; and 18:38. Obviously, truth is a very important concept for the author of this Gospel.

There are three affirmations about truth in the lection. The first is *the disciples' knowledge that Jesus is from God.* This knowledge will be an empowerment they will desperately need to fulfill their roles as disciples after Jesus is gone. It would be for them the greatest motivator of all. In a world where Caesar was proclaimed as God, this knowledge would often bring them into conflict that threatened their very lives. They would be willing to die for the truth. The very religion in which many of them were reared would often bring the accusation that they had been deceived by a lie.

The second affirmation is that *truth is equated to the word Jesus has spoken to them.* Today we can hardly trust that what we read or hear is truth. But what Jesus spoke to his disciples was truth. There are the leaks from grand juries to the news media. But do we dare trust those leaks to be true? Jesus spoke the truth, the whole truth, and nothing but the truth. Sometimes truth was not accepted as truth. This did not, of course, change the value of Jesus' words. He even said, "I am . . . the truth" (14:6).

One of the most difficult experiences of my ministry was the death of a baby who suffered from terminal heart disease. The baby was the child of a couple in the church I was serving at the time. I never had prayed as fervently for anything as I did for the healing of that child. I never, ever believed anything anymore than I did that the child would get well. But he died. To this day, I still have times when I say to God, "I just don't understand." Friends told me, "You got too emotionally involved." My only response has been, "Yes! I did."

I am still waiting for their truth to set me free. I believe that a word of truth will be revealed to me by Jesus in some way through someone or some other experience at sometime. My prayer is that it will come soon.

Third, Jesus prays that *the disciples may be **sanctified** in* truth. What does that mean?

Years ago, while in seminary, I was required to write a project on the meaning of **hagios**, the word in the New Testament usually translated *holy*. This term is used in the Septuagint to translate the Hebrew word *qodesh*. Early on in my research I discovered that conjugates of the word *sanctify*, as found in many of our English translations, are from the same Greek root word known in adjective form as *hagios*. At that time it was a very enlightening experience for me to learn that God was *holy* because there was no other god like Jehovah. The temple was *holy* because there was no other building like it.

In the text at hand, Jesus' followers are not like other persons, because the disciples have been **sanctified** in *truth*. There are no other persons like them except those who have themselves been sanctified in the truth. Though these who are sanctified maintain the same human characteristics as other humans, they have become different from other humans. They do not change in size or shape or color, but they are different because something else has changed. It is an inward change, known to us as a change of heart. The truth in this sense can set one free. (Jim Clardy)

JUNE 11, 2000

Day of Pentecost

Worship Theme: Through the love of Christ working through the Holy Spirit, we can be united with God regardless of our sin, and united with our neighbors regardless of the differences and affronts that once threatened us and kept us alienated.

Readings: Acts 2:1-21; Romans 8:22-27; John 15:26-27; 16:4*b*-15

Call to Worship (Psalm 104:1-4, 35*b*):

> *Leader:*   Bless the LORD, O my soul!
>
> ***People:*   O LORD my God, you are very great!**
>
> *Leader:*   You are clothed with honor and majesty, and cover yourself with light as with a garment;
>
> ***People:*   you have stretched out the heavens like a tent, and have laid the beams of your chambers on the waters;**
>
> *Leader:*   you make the clouds your chariot, and ride on the wings of the wind;
>
> ***People:*   you make the winds your messengers, fire and flame your ministers.**
>
> *Leader:*   Bless the LORD, O my soul!
>
> ***People:*   Praise the LORD!**

Pastoral Prayer:
O God, we praise you, for the chasm has been bridged. O Lord, we thank you, for the distance of our own making that once sepa-

rated your children from one another has been closed. But we act as though the magnificent diversity of race, language, gender, journey, and circumstance is a threat to our peace and joy, and not the blessing that you have intended. O Jesus, forgive us for the walls we build, walls torn down by your death and resurrection. Forgive us for forgetting that we all are one in and by your Son, Jesus Christ. We have placed the shackles of fear and hate squarely back on our wrists. Precious Redeemer, help us to realize that our freedom is already won in your name. And in that freedom, give us courage to breathe into our souls the power of your love, the power of your Holy Spirit. Amen. (Thomas Gildermeister)

SERMON BRIEFS

HOW WILL WE BE HEARD?

ACTS 2:1-21

I. "Whoever Calls on the Name of the Lord Shall Be Saved"

There are two primary foundations in this passage upon which the rest of the book of Acts is built. There is the message that must be proclaimed concerning who Christ is and what he means for the world, and there is the important understanding of what the Holy Spirit is and the Spirit's responsibility for both the content of that message and the strength to share it.

No one can read Luke's accounts of the early church without an understanding of the importance of the presence of the Holy Spirit in all that was to happen in those formative years. No speech or action or event took place without first being ordained or directed or encouraged by the Holy Spirit. And although Luke wants his readers to have a better understanding of the beginning years of the church, this is not just a passage about what did happen, as much as it is a confession about what does happen. Each historical story told by Luke serves as an example of how to act in the future. Our first lesson therefore involves the necessity of each and every word or action being Spirit-directed.

Our second lesson, according to Luke, involves the content of those Spirit-led words and actions. Peter says in his first speech that "whoever calls on the name of the LORD shall be saved" (Acts 2:21 RSV). We are in need of being saved. Jesus saves. We saw in chapter 1 that the apostles were told to witness to the world. In chapter 2 we are told where the strength will come from for that witnessing, and we are told more specifically the content of that witnessing.

II. "How Is It That We Hear, Each of Us, in Our Own Native Language?"

One of the true inspirations of this particular passage comes from the description of how the apostles spoke to the people of the marketplace in the people's own languages. One cannot stress enough the primacy of relying on the Holy Spirit for purpose and direction, but the passage also beautifully leaves open the question of how to best communicate the message of Jesus to people of different languages and backgrounds. It becomes an illustration for the difference between speaking to different people in different ways and simply babbling. When is liturgical dance a means of presenting the message in a different language to a different people, and when is it simply a means for showcasing talent? When is a contemporary service a means of having people hear "each of us, in our own native language," and when is it simply a performance? This passage gives us permission to continually seek out different ways of communicating to different people the message of God's wish for relationship with us as shown in the life of Jesus Christ but keeps clear the foundations upon which our search is to be built.

III. "What Does This Mean?"

This means that Pentecost Sunday is *not* just a celebration of what was. This is *not* just a story of the church's beginning; this is also a call to our task as the church to share with as many people as possible, in as many ways as possible, the message of Jesus Christ. There is no one way to share that message; but, in fact, in our diverse and complex society we are called to find a number of different ways of communicating with one another. If we remain true to the presence of the Holy Spirit in our midst, and if we remain true to the mission to which Jesus has called us, we too will be heard by different people in different languages and will be responsible for bringing people into relationship with God. We will be heard by the accountants and the nurses. Each with his or her own language and way of viewing life. We will be heard by the housewives and the policemen. "And it shall be that whoever calls on the name of the LORD shall be saved" (v. 21 RSV). (Mark D. Haines)

TWO VALUABLE PARTNERSHIPS

ROMANS 8:22-27

I. We Have a Partnership in Pain

We do not know why there is pain in the world. Without doubt God could have created a world without pain. But God did not. There are some benefits to pain. If there were no pain, we would never see the doctor. If there were no pain, we would never take our medicine. If there were no pain, we would never have the operation that saves our lives. If there were no pain, we might not appreciate pleasure. We can see some benefits from pain. Still, we would much prefer to live without it. But none of us will manage that. Our pain may be physical, it may be mental, it may be emotional. But it is pain nonetheless, and we would prefer not to have it.

According to this text, pain is universal. All created beings suffer pain—fish, fowl, animal. Indeed, the environment itself suffers something like pain. The idea is that the perfect world of God's creation was greatly damaged by sin, and that damage is universal.

While this may be difficult to understand, we do know that all of our fellow human beings suffer pain. There is some comfort in that. We know that we are not in pain because of something we have personally done that is wrong. We know that we are not in pain because of something that we have personally left undone. Pain for us may be the collective result of sin in general, but it is not necessarily the personal result of something we have done as individuals. We know this because God also suffers pain. Often we fail to grasp the broken heart of God. Only when we see Jesus suffering mental pain, physical pain, and emotional pain do we grasp the idea that God experiences pain.

II. We Have Partnership in Prayer

It helps us a little to know that we are not alone in experiencing pain. And it helps us a lot to know that we are not alone when we pray. Certainly there is enormous value in private prayer. In fact, Jesus recommended it in Matthew 6:6. Conversely, there is great value in collective prayer. Jesus recommended it as well (Matt. 18:19). But the verses in Romans emphasize that we all have a prayer partner in the Holy Spirit, and this touches us deeply.

We are touched even more by the knowledge that Jesus is also our prayer partner. We cannot visualize the Holy Spirit. We can visualize Jesus. So near the end of this chapter we are given a picture of Jesus at the right hand of God. What is he doing there? He is praying for us (Rom. 8:34). The picture is emphasized again in Hebrews 7:25. Surely Simon Peter was touched when Jesus said he would pray for him (Luke 22:32). Surely the Twelve were touched when Jesus said he would pray for them (John 14:16; 17:9). Like them, we are touched to know that Jesus prayed for us on the night before the cross (John 17:20). And now we can add to that these verse from Romans and Hebrews and know that he is praying for us still.

III. We Learn Patience from These Partnerships

Patience is not easily learned. But knowing that we are not alone in suffering helps us to endure patiently. Knowing that we have a divine prayer partner gives us patience when we must wait for our prayer request to be granted. This patience is nourished in the rich soil of hope. Never forget that hope stands alongside faith and love as an equal (1 Cor. 13:13). As long as we have hope for something better (and we always do), we can be patient with the present, even when it is unpleasant, even when it is painful. (Robert Shannon)

GETTING ACQUAINTED

JOHN 15:26-27; 16:4*b*-15

The disciples are sorrowful. Why? Because Jesus is going away. The truth of his impending death has finally dawned upon them. We might be tempted to say that the experience of death is exceptional, but in the larger scheme of things death is just another component of life.

Sorrow has many causes. The disciples' sorrow is a sense of loss for someone near and dear to them. This is not just anybody, however. This is the One who has protected them and cared for them, though they are not blood relatives with him. The realization of his death is shocking.

I remember the killing of two policemen at the U.S. Capitol. Officers John Gibson and Jacob Chestnut were shot to death as they sought to protect the Congress at work in the halls of our Capitol. There was a sorrow not often displayed by our public officials. The bodies of the two slain officers were memorialized in the Capitol Rotunda, a honor reserved for presidents, while the American flag flew at half-mast over the Capitol. Respect makes the sorrow more piercing. This experience was not something Congress or the American public was prepared for. Many were in shock.

Here Jesus is endeavoring to prepare the disciples for the shock of his death. He prepares them by seeking to turn their sorrow into confidence and power. The resource for this conversion from sorrow to joy is the assurance that when Jesus leaves, the Spirit will come. The Spirit will guide and empower them.

This Spirit works in many ways. For example, the Spirit is active through many who have the gift of communication through the printed word. Raymond Brown, author of *The Community of the Beloved Disciple* (Mahwah, N.J.: Paulist Press, 1979), was a brilliant Johannine scholar. At the time of Brown's death, I was a member of a computer list through which one could correspond with persons around the world who were interested in the use of Koine Greek not just in the Gospel of John, but also in the entire New Testament and the Septuagint. One person on the list, commenting on Brown's death, wrote: "I had the feeling I was reading the work not only of a brilliant scholar, but of a generous heart well steeped in the spirit of what John was trying to convey. I would love to have met the man."

"I would love to have met the man": That's my sentiment as I think of Jesus. But through the Holy Spirit, what would otherwise be impossible has been made possible. I can get acquainted with Jesus through the Spirit as revealed through the writings of good people.

John Wesley would advise that the Spirit is revealed through spiritual disciplines such as Bible reading, prayer, the Sacraments, and accountability through the sharing of the state of one's soul. (Jim Clardy)

JUNE 18, 2000

Trinity Sunday

Worship Theme: The Holy Trinity is not so much who God is but how God loves the creation.

Readings: Isaiah 6:1-8; Romans 8:12-17; John 3:1-17

Call to Worship (Psalm 29:1-4):

Leader: Ascribe to the LORD, O heavenly beings, ascribe to the LORD glory and strength.

People: **Ascribe to the LORD the glory of his name; worship the LORD in holy splendor.**

Leader: The voice of the LORD is upon the waters; the God of glory thunders, the LORD, upon many waters.

People: **The voice of the LORD is powerful, the voice of the LORD is full of majesty.**

Pastoral Prayer:
We are awestruck, most sacred Lord, by the many facets of your love for us. You are our Creator, our Redeemer, and our Sustainer; Father, Son, and Holy Spirit. You love as a parent, as a friend, as an advocate. You love us by standing back, allowing us to experience the consequences—good or bad—of your gift of our freedom to choose. You love us by standing on our behalf, dying on a cross. You love us by standing with us, binding all your children together in a common peace and a shared language of love. So often, mysterious and triune God, we feel unlovable. So often we refuse all the many ways through which your love is offered. Let the scales fall from our eyes. Help us to see first how beautiful and precious we are in your sight. And then help us to

219

see how beautiful and precious all your children are to you, and consequently to us. In the name of Jesus, the Christ, the One who makes any receipt of God's grace possible. Amen. (Thomas Gildermeister)

SERMON BRIEFS

COMMISSIONED

ISAIAH 6:1-8

Isaiah's commission is recorded here before he delivers the judgment oracles. Perhaps the occasion is one of sadness for him, as his friend and godly king Uzziah has died a miserable death as a leper. Our times of calling can also come during tragedy.

I. Vision of Glory (vv. 1-4)

In this time of testing for Isaiah, he envisions the temple of God. At the center of the temple is the throne of God. The "train," representing God's glory, fills the temple where the Lord is high and exalted. We must keep perspective in the time of our testing or tragedy. There is unseen by us a realm in the presence of God Almighty in which there is no concern or wrenching of hands because of circumstances. In our difficulty, we would do well to consider this vision of the flying angelic beings who humbly sing the praises of God. They focus upon the holiness of God in their song, noting that the earth (our circumstances included) is filled with God's glory. The proclamation shakes the temple and should shake our thoughts. God's glory, imperceptible to us perhaps, surrounds all of our circumstances and us. Our prayer should be, "Lord, open our eyes."

II. Sanctified Perspective (vv. 4-5)

To behold such a vision of glory is to have our perspective changed. When we see God and His glory, we see the pale comparison of our realm of reality. His reality is a much more ultimate reality. Yet, part of the vision process is purposely reflective, to view where we live in relation to God. Isaiah laments, "Woe to me, I am ruined" (v. 5 NIV). This is not poor self-esteem but a perspective of viewing oneself as dependent and in need of something beyond personal resources.

He recognizes the "unholiness" of his context (unclean lips) and his personal association with such unholiness. What makes him aware of such problems? He knows he has envisioned the King, the Lord Almighty. If we really desire to be holy, as our God is holy, to be used for sacred and profound purposes, we begin that process by focusing on the Holy God who is enthroned. This entails moving from the trivialities of our existence, and to the priorities of God's kingdom.

III. Sacred Purposes and Sacred Tasks (vv. 6-8)

The heavenly beings, recognizing the task to which Isaiah will be called, prepares him by curing his ailment of unclean lips. Taking a hot coal from the fire of the altar of sacrifice, one of the seraphs presses it to the prophet's lips and declares atonement and sanctification. The altar represents sacrifice and something totally outside of the realm of the prophet's accomplishments. It is, in short, a "God thing." The only way to be adequately prepared for a sacred purpose is to be sanctified through a touch or encounter with the holy presence of God.

Although we may want to focus on Isaiah's positive response to the call, we may miss the point. A positive response is the only natural response to the call when one has been adequately prepared. The key to the response is that Isaiah is enabled to "hear" the call. Verse 1 begins with the saddened prophet "seeing"; here we view the prophet "hearing." So it is with us after a proper perspective of God and ourselves, and the preparation that comes only by being touched by God, are we ever prepared to hear what God is calling us to be or to do. What a true sense of purpose in life awaits for the one who is willing to encounter God by focusing on God enough to allow God to touch and call her or him. (Joseph Byrd)

THREE SIDES TO OUR SALVATION

ROMANS 8:12-17

Today's scripture text shows us a three-sided faith.

I. We Have a Debt to Pay

Our debt is not to the flesh. We owe the flesh nothing. Our debt is not to the world. We owe the world nothing. Our debt is to the Spirit, to God, to the suffering Christ, to the church, and to the gospel of God. We owe a debt to all who have gone before us. They wrote down hymns, they preserved our gospel, they built our buildings. We have a debt to the past and a debt to the future.

It is a pleasure to make payments on this debt. Ordinarily, we do not like paying debts and we do not like making payments, but it is a pleasure to make payments on this debt. We will, however, never get it paid. Until the day we die we will be in spiritual debt.

II. We Have an Adoption to Celebrate

Many families adopt children. Often these families not only celebrate the child's birthday, but they also celebrate the child's adoption day. A part of the celebration may involve looking at photographs of the building where they got the baby, and pictures of the first time they held that treasured child.

Christians also have been adopted. Sometimes the Bible speaks of our conversion as "being born again," and sometimes it speaks of our conversion as "adoption." This does not mean that there are two different ways to be converted. It only means that conversion is so grand a thing that one picture is never enough to illustrate it. It is also called "our redemption" and "our resurrection." No one word will do to describe what God's grace has done for us.

In worship we celebrate our adoption. In Christian fellowship we celebrate our adoption. In evangelism we celebrate our adoption. For we are not selfish children who do not want others to join the family. We want to share the joys of our salvation with as many as possible.

III. We Have an Inheritance to Claim

People are often surprised when they inherit money or land that they did not expect to receive. We are told so much about our inheritance, and yet we know only a little of its magnitude. We share this inheritance with others, and we share this inheritance with Christ. He is our older brother, and the family's wealth is his as well as ours. The apostle Peter described it as "an inheritance incorruptible, and undefiled, and that fadeth not away" (1 Pet. 1:4 KJV). Psalm 37:11 and Matthew 5:5 say the meek shall inherit the whole earth. Revelation 21:7 says we shall inherit all things. The apostle Paul said that "all things are yours" (1 Cor. 3:21 KJV).

But between the present moment and the glory of receiving our inheritance, we may have to suffer. Since we were buried with Christ in baptism, and since we will be heirs with Christ in heaven, it should not surprise us if we also have to suffer with Christ. When Paul wrote to the Romans, persecution was a real and present danger. For most Christians today, persecution is a far distant thing. But we may suffer in other ways. Christians are not exempt from physical pain, mental anguish, or emotional pain.

We must remember that sharing with Christ is a many-sided thing. It makes our pain bearable when we know we suffer with him. It makes our joy all the greater when we rejoice with him. It makes our future all the more inviting, because we will be glorified with him. (Robert Shannon)

TRANSFORMING A PHARISEE

JOHN 3:1-17

Although this passage from John includes the well-loved and often memorized John 3:16, the bulk of these verses focus on the late-night encounter between Jesus and Nicodemus. This story, told only in John's Gospel, allows us into the mind and heart of a Pharisee. Nowhere else in the Gospels do we see a Pharisee struggling, doubting, and longing to understand. Thus, the invitation to delve into the character of Nicodemus is quite enticing.

No doubt most congregations have heard at least one sermon, if not hundreds, on the character of Nicodemus. Very often he is portrayed as courageous and promising. Most times we want to say, "Good for him for breaking rank with the Pharisees! Good for him for seeking out Jesus and trying to understand."

However, it is important not to shower too many accolades too soon onto Nicodemus, as if this one encounter changes him immediately into a faithful disciple. True, he does defend Jesus in chapter 7 by asking for a fair trial. And he does join Joseph of Arimathea in burying Jesus in chapter 19. Both of these events are clues that Nicodemus is *in the process* of being transformed into a disciple.

But in this passage in chapter 3, Nicodemus does not become an unequivocal disciple of Jesus. He does not come to Jesus ready to give up everything—including his status as a Pharisee—to follow him. No, Nicodemus comes to Jesus in the middle of the night, afraid that someone might see him. He is curious. He is tentative. He is confused.

His first words to Jesus are, "Rabbi, we know that you are a teacher who has come from God." Does he seek Jesus out just to tell him that? Does he want to reassure Jesus that the religious powers recognized his ministry? Does he even know why he came?

Even if Nicodemus does not know why he is there or what he is really seeking, Jesus knows what he needs. He begins to talk about being "born from above" (v. 3) and being "born of the Spirit" (v. 6). In his practical, Pharisaic, institutionalized mind, Nicodemus cannot understand what Jesus is saying. Jesus is surprised that one who is supposed to be a spiritual leader among the Jews cannot grasp the truth of spiritual rebirth. In verse 11, Jesus sees that Nicodemus has not yet set himself apart from other Pharisees when he says, "You do not receive our testimony."

All in all, this seems like a failed encounter between Nicodemus and Jesus. Nicodemus does not say another word after verse 9. He remains confused and unenlightened. Jesus chastises him for his lack of understanding. There are no words of parting. There is no closure between them. And that is exactly the point. The story does not end here. John gives us clues (7:50 and 19:39) that Nicodemus continues to chew on Jesus' words and is slowly being transformed into a disciple. Nicodemus' story gives us hope and encouragement about our own transformation. We would like to think that discipleship is a one-time decision that in a moment leaves us transformed forever. Wouldn't that be nice and neat? However, most of us are more like Nicodemus. It takes time as we struggle for understanding and faith.

Nicodemus had many obstacles to becoming a disciple. He was wealthy; Jesus had a lot to say about riches and the kingdom of heaven. Nicodemus was powerful and ranked high among the Jewish authorities; Jesus had a lot to say about the powerful. Nicodemus was a man of common sense; and Jesus asked his disciples to be foolish. We struggle with many of the same obstacles. Yet the Word of God continues to work on us, helping us to grow more sure and more bold in our faith. (Carol Cavin)

JUNE 25, 2000

Second Sunday After Pentecost

Worship Theme: Authentic faith is confidence in the presence of the Lord. God is with us. We are not alone. Thanks be to God!

Readings: 1 Samuel 17:(1a, 4-11, 19-23) 32-49; 2 Corinthians 6:1-13; Mark 4:35-41

Call to Worship (Psalm 9:11-14):

> *Leader:* Sing praises to the LORD, who dwells in Zion!
>
> ***People:*** **Tell among the peoples God's deeds!**
>
> *Leader:* The LORD who avenges blood is mindful of them,
>
> ***People:*** **and does not forget the cry of the afflicted.**
>
> *Leader:* Be gracious to me, O LORD! See what I suffer from those who hate me;
>
> ***People:*** **You are the One who lifts me up from the gates of death, that I may recount all your praises, and, in the gates of the daughter of Zion, rejoice in your deliverance.**

Pastoral Prayer:

O Lord who calms the waves and storms of our lives, we give thanks to you. We frolic on the mountain in the warmth of the light, and we know you are with us. But when we stumble into the valleys, dark and frightening, sometimes you seem distant, and we feel forsaken. When we struggle in crisis, failure, and loss, we often feel so very alone. Merciful Savior, forgive us for our faithlessness. Remind us of your promise. Give us the courage to sit in the darkness, to listen intently when we cannot see, to

226

watch with focused attention. Help us to wait—not on your presence, for you are always with us—on our pain and fear to subside enough so that we can recognize your blessed assurance once again. O God, in your mercy, hear our prayer. Amen. (Thomas Gildermeister)

SERMON BRIEFS

RITE OF PASSAGE

1 SAMUEL 17:(1a, 4-11, 19-23) 32-49

The story of David and Goliath is as familiar to us as "Goldilocks and the Three Bears." It is a heroic tale of a boy coming to age, of the weak overcoming the strong, of good versus evil. The story of David and Goliath resonates with the child within each of us, the child that wants to get out and dance and play and sing.

But more than a child's story, it also tells of how an older value needed to be overthrown. A simple shepherd-boy had the solution to a problem that could not be solved by King Saul. Israel had been held captive by the Philistines and was now at war with the enemy, which had a champion of gargantuan proportions. Saul's army had none. But little David overcame all odds. He relied on past experience, how he had dealt with lions and other wild beasts that had threatened his livestock. Goliath was dispatched similarly.

By the end of the story, David has grown in stature. He has become conscious of what is possible—the conquering of the champion. He initiates a new relationship to the tribe, Saul respects him as a man, and David is accepted by the Israelite army, whose morale he has boosted by defeating Goliath, the only thing standing in the way of their certain demise. And, he has grown in his relationship to God, who was directing the whole affair, including Israel's captivity at the hands of the Philistines, an on-again, off-again situation since the days of Samson the judge.

But beyond becoming the man of the hour, David was being made a steward of the mysteries of God in the midst of his tribal community. He underwent a rite of passage from shepherd-boy to manhood. It was a kind of death-to-new-life experience, not unlike the sacrament of baptism. Someone has said that a warning label with large letters should be affixed to the word *baptism*—"Warning: Baptism Is Dangerous!"—because we suffer the death of our old sinful selves in order to receive new life in Christ. If baptism is so dangerous, what about ordination? For here again we are denying our old selves in favor of putting on new clothes, or as Paul put it, clothing ourselves with Christ.

In this there is something inherently dangerous, from the world's perspective. Can you hear it? Sarcasm. Snickering in the dark. Pointing its finger at those funny-looking new clothes we've all put on, because they're not normative, and perhaps they're out of date, if not completely out of step with the rest of the world and its latest trends and fads. David found himself in a curious situation. He was called to be an example for the flock. No longer a herder of sheep, David shepherded people. (Eric Killinger)

THE OTHER SIDE OF THE STORY

2 CORINTHIANS 6:1-13

Paul's language here is commendable: "Our heart is wide open to you. There is no restriction in our affections" (vv. 11-12). Behind this assertion is a mountain of experiences that we as the reader of Paul's Epistles will never know but only surmise. From Paul's language we can assume strained relations between the missionary and the people. Evidence from this letter and others show that Paul had many enemies who continually tried to discount his ministry and his life. In some places, the opponents were successful.

From what Paul writes in refutation to the opposition, one can assume that those church members influenced by the adversaries considered Paul to be lacking in integrity (v. 3). He may have been accused of placing obstacles in the way of salvation rather than clearly presenting the truth. Paul postponed his visit to Corinth. The opponents used the change of travel plans as an opportunity to criticize Paul as an indecisive leader who speaks from both sides of his mouth (2 Cor. 3:1-6). Constantly Paul is having to refute their accusations of inadequacy, defend his apostolic status, and reiterate his missionary goals.

In this passage, Paul reminds the congregation that his ministry has not been easy. He has not taken the easy road but rather has experienced great hardship with many afflictions (vv. 4-10). If the opponents are saying that Paul is in ministry for the plush lifestyle, then they are mistaken. And if church members want to believe the troublemakers and agree with them, then Paul wants equal opportunity to set the record straight. He has endured beatings, imprisonment, riots, sleepless nights, and hunger for the gospel's sake. "Listen to my side of the story," Paul is saying here.

Finally, Paul saves the best argument for last. Perhaps it is not enough to defend himself against the accusations with simply another litany of responses to his credit. For his final appeal is from his heart to their hearts, not from his list of tribulations or his job resume. Ultimately, Paul wants to appeal to them because his "heart is wide open" to them.

What does it mean to have your heart wide open, even to people who are hostile to you, to those who are working to devalue you and undermine your work? This appeal is the basis for life.

Perhaps Paul's motives were not perfect; that would be no surprise, for he was human. Perhaps the members of the congregation were not perfect, either; that would be no surprise, because many of us know the sting of church folk. But what if, in the final analysis, the success of the gospel message in the Corinthian church did not depend on the level of Paul's ministerial portfolio, nor on the persuasive arguments of the opposition, but on how much both Paul and the congregation were willing to "open their hearts" to one another. The appropriate conduits of the gospel message are not perfect vessels, just ones willing to be used and used and used. (Linda McKinnish Bridges)

CONFLICTED AND CHAOTIC

MARK 4:35-41

"On that day," Mark tells us, Jesus and the disciples got into a boat. This is the same day in which Jesus had both taught and interpreted to the disciples several parables about the Kingdom. Jesus had been sowing the Kingdom, and it had been received in a variety of ways (4:1-20): The growth of the Kingdom is out of the sower's control (4:26-29); the Kingdom will grow in surprising ways (4:30-32). In short, the disciples can have faith and trust in the natural, growing process of the Kingdom's birth and growth.

In this miracle story, the reader discovers the natural enemy of that faith—fear.

I. "Why Are You Afraid?"

Thus far in this Gospel, the sea is a place over which Jesus has much authority; he calls disciples there (1:16-20); he teaches there (4:1). Still, the sea is the sea. It can be a chaotic place that inspires fear of being swamped, fear of death. For that reason, we can understand the sea as symbolic of Mark's world. Mark's Gospel is a story over which Jesus seems to exercise much authority. Still, Mark fills it with turbulent conflict and abrupt transitions. When the weather looks quite good for the Kingdom (1:1–2:12), the prevailing winds change the character of the water (2:13–3:6). Ominous clouds form on the horizon and threaten Jesus' life and the lives of those near him (3:6).

In this passage, the metaphor is finely focused on a small boat in a big sea, tossed by a windstorm. Look at the characters. The disciples are fearful for their very lives; and some of them, we know, are quite experienced with the sea (1:16). Jesus rests in the stern, full of sleeping confidence, upon a cushion. This Jesus trusts in his own parables; he has faith that the Kingdom will take root, will find an anchor in the midst of the chaos.

Often the presence of the Kingdom also means the presence of opposition and conflict. In the local church, most people avoid conflict like they would avoid the tossing seas. In our individual interiors, too, we often experience life as chaotic, threatening, and frightening. We tend to view conflict as "unholy," an infringement of secular "chaos" into sacred "calm." Mark, however, is telling us that this is simply how life is, conflicted and chaotic. The Kingdom's presence does not mean the end of conflict in our communal or individual lives. It does mean, though, that we have another lens through which to look at life.

Though Jesus expresses divine power in calming the sea, the

point seems to be that he calms the disciples. He is clearly not afraid of the storm, and he doesn't calm the storm to soothe his own fears. He exercises his authority so that the disciples will know that they do not have to be afraid in the midst of storms, either. They too can be confident because Jesus is in authority. He does not promise to calm every Kingdom-quenching storm. Indeed, we know that the seas of conflict in this Gospel will eventually overwhelm even Jesus. Yet we also know that not even the storms of death are beyond the scope of Jesus' authority. Like the farmer who does not know how grows the seed (4:26-29), so also we cannot know when will come the crashing waves. In either case, we can give up our fears of being out of control, even of perishing. We can have faith that the Kingdom will last and grow. God will not have it any other way.

II. "Who Then Is This?"

This miracle caused the disciples to take another look at who Jesus was. It is as if those who were the closest to Jesus' mission were seeing him for the first time: "Who then is this, that even the wind and the sea obey him?" The same type of thing happens as Jesus walks on the water (6:51). The disciples seem to transfer their fear of the storm to Jesus! Such divine power is frightening when you do not expect the rabbi with whom you have been traveling to manifest it. At the end of the Gospel, the manifestation of divine power in raising Jesus from the dead was not a cause for celebration by the disciples, but for trembling and fear (16:8). Their understanding of who Jesus was and what Jesus was about had to shift. Again, it is as if they were seeing him for the first time.

Have you ever witnessed the manifestation of divine power in your midst and then been scared of it? How has your understanding of Jesus had to change? What events or thoughts have filled you with awe, changed your perspective about the Kingdom, or scared your faith to life? (Sam Parkes)

DOORS AND WINDOWS

JULY

Meditation Verse: "For if justification comes through the law, then Christ died for nothing" (Gal. 2:21).

The Discipline:

Create a religious form with various questions. Then fill it out. Be honest about who you really are when answering the question. Remember this is an imaginative exercise, not a grade school assignment.

Kathleen Norris, the writer of *Dakota*, has gone from being one who filled out the religious section on college applications with the word *nothing* to one who overflows those lines with "Roman Catholicism and two versions of Protestantism." One of her grandmothers was Methodist; the other was Presbyterian. Both religions, as well as others, are incorporated into Norris' mature faith. Note that I said mature, not perfect, faith. One of the short essays in her book *Amazing Grace: A Vocabulary of Faith* (New York: Putnam Publishing Group, 1998) is on perfection. In the essay, she translates Paul as meaning maturity by perfection, and manages to use the overly perfect Martha Stewart to prove her point.

Make two columns as you fill out your newly created form. Label one "perfect faith." On a scale of 1 to 10, measure how perfect your faith is. Above the second column write the word *maturity*. Now measure how mature your faith is. Then return to describing yourself religiously. Let what you learn in this simple exercise filter into your preaching this month. Are you trying to mature or perfect your people? There is a difference. Moreover, there is a big difference between belief and doubt and sacred ambiguity. How sacred is your ambiguity about God?

One of the marks of mature faith, according to Norris the ecumenist, is the practice of "Lectio Divina," learning to read and speak the Bible "by heart." If you found the exercise too difficult, simply tell the form that "I am a reader of the Bible by heart."

The Meditation:

The Dalai Lama helps people recognize the value of where they have come from. One of his quotes tells people not to become Buddhist but to go home and become what they were meant to become.

When Christians go home, we go home to the cross, to the Trinitarian God, the one Catholics and Methodists and Presbyterians all know. Norris claims to have understood most everything about Christianity except Christ. "I often felt a void at the center of things: Christianity with the center missing." Mature Christians know the cross, experientially and by "biblical heart."

Norris also employs the image of quark to explain her understanding of the Trinity. Only quarks could show us the dance of communal interrelationship at the heart of God. Similarly, Norris' preaching criteria is that people remember the scripture that she used, not what she said about it, after she is done. Having read her book, I'd love to hear her preach. Her humility is winning: "I often think that if I am a Christian, I'll be the last to know" (*Amazing Grace*, p. 232).

She also appreciates the so-called unchurched. She recounts a story of a preacher who tries to get a deal from a delicatessen owner. He orders his meal in the name of the "unchurched." When his food arrives, in the center of the plate is bologna in the shape of a cross (p. 289).

The preacher was put in his place. He had misunderstood the cross in the name of Christianity. As Jesus could easily have told him, the "little people," many of whom are quite deeply unchurched, often are the strongest reminders of the cross we can find. They know what it is to be called names—like "unchurched." They know what it is to be ignored and left out from the center of things. But Jesus puts them right there at the center of his love. Can we, as pastors, want to do anything more? Or less? If people can see through our maturity to the cross, to Jesus, and beyond, then we are fine. If they cannot, we are not, and then Jesus died for nothing, as far as we are concerned. But if, in our lives and our reading of the Scriptures and the cross, we show deli owners the meaning of the cross, then Jesus died for something.

The Song:

> So I'll cherish the old rugged cross, till my trophies at last I
> lay down;
> I will cling to the old rugged cross, and exchange it some-
> day for a crown.
>
> ("The Old Rugged Cross")

The Prayer:

Mature us, O God, into people capable of your Scripture and your cross. Mature us into mattering to the so-called little people, the ones who stand outside your church but not outside the body of Christ. And when we tell the world who we are, let us articulate you, not just us. Amen. (Donna Schaper)

JULY 2, 2000

Third Sunday After Pentecost

Worship Theme: Our faith in Christ can make us well and give us peace. But the miracles we seek are not always the miracles we find.

Readings: 2 Samuel 1:1, 17-27; 2 Corinthians 8:7-15; Mark 5:21-43

Call to Worship (Psalm 130:1-8):

Leader:	Out of the depths I cry to you, O LORD! LORD, hear my voice!
People:	**Let your ears be attentive to the voice of my supplications!**
Leader:	If you, O LORD, should mark iniquities, LORD, who could stand?
People:	**But there is forgiveness with you, that you may be worshiped.**
Leader:	I wait for the LORD, my soul waits, in the LORD's word I hope;
People:	**my soul waits for the LORD more than those who watch for the morning, more than those who watch for the morning.**
Leader:	O Israel, hope in the LORD! For with the LORD there is steadfast love, with the LORD is plenteous redemption.
People:	**And the LORD will redeem Israel from all iniquities.**

Pastoral Prayer:

O great God of salvation and sustenance, we come today to offer nothing more and nothing less than our lives as a living sacrifice in praise of and thanksgiving to you. Every one of us brings a broken life to the altar of your power and love; some have broken bodies, others have broken minds, still others have broken spirits. But Lord, these are the only lives we can bring to you. Forgive us when we overlook the miracles that you provide because they are not the miracles for which we came begging. We know, dear God, that you are all-powerful and all-knowing and that you cannot be manipulated or cajoled by whims and wishes, no matter how desperate those wishes might be. But we also know that you are compassionate and merciful. And so we come begging. Your Son and our Lord, Jesus Christ, taught us to ask you to meet our needs. He taught us to ask and not to worry, to ask and be aware of the gifts in our midst that you intend for us to claim. O God, thank you for your greatest gift, the gift of life and love in and through Jesus. By his name we pray. Amen. (Thomas Gildermeister)

SERMON BRIEFS

LIFE LESSONS FROM A FUTURE KING

2 SAMUEL 1:1, 17-27

How do powerful and famous people cope with the trials of life? It is the stuff that keeps magazines publishing, big-name biographies booming, and "insider" books on the bestseller list.

Today's text, from 2 Samuel, is an intriguing account of a precarious time in the history of David and his people. He has been successful in defeating the Amalekites, but the deaths of his king (Saul) and his best friend (Jonathan) make the victory seem hollow. David, blessed with remarkable gifts and abilities, has an appeal that brings him both admiration and respect. At this particular time, however, he has not yet been crowned king. Through this unusual passage, composed mostly of David's lament, we catch a glimpse of his humanity, his loyalty to God and God's anointed, and his gift for poetry and hymnody. We also can discover three important lessons for living.

I. No One Is Immune from Loss

Neither wealth nor fame nor power can stop death, or the often tragic unfolding of life's story. Our life's journey is an adventure in which both wondrous and wicked, terrific and terrible things may occur. David was respected as a soldier, admired for his good looks, and revered for his leadership ability. It was his time in history's spotlight. He stood on the eve of uniting the Southern and Northern Kingdoms. Even so, he could not stop the deaths of Saul or Jonathan.

Our own time is not without examples of death's relentless pursuit. Power and prestige cannot always sway death. Diana, Princess of Wales, captured the hearts of the world with her beauty, charm, grace, and candor. She was a fabulously wealthy woman of great influence. Her smile faded from our memory as death claimed her body from this life. We cannot cheat death for long. Though we need not live as victims, we also cannot completely defend against life's trials and losses. David's lament is powerful because David's loss is genuine.

II. True Humanity Is Revealed in Authenticity

David has appeal because David is "one of us." He is the shepherd boy who becomes the shepherd king and the predecessor of the ultimate shepherd, Jesus Christ. David's power comes from being blessed by Yahweh, who has evidently singled him out to be the future king of Judah (chapter 2) and Israel (chapter 5). David will be the first to unite the two kingdoms and to establish Jerusalem as the political and religious center of Israel.

Israel was in a life-or-death struggle with the Philistines, and the death of Saul came as a personal and political blow to David and his kinspeople. That alone would be significant, but the loss of Jonathan doubled the blow. Jonathan was more than a brother to David, for they were the closest of friends. Theirs was an intimacy that transcended the physical intimacy of lovers ("your love to me was wonderful, passing the love of women" (v. 26c). Such an intimacy was born out of shared hopes and dreams, self-sacrifice, and the bonds that form when souls struggle together for righteousness (see 1 Samuel 20). David's lament characterizes him as a great man because of his willingness to disclose his feelings. David's authenticity is revealed through this passionate narrative of loss, grief, and remembrance.

III. Music and Scripture Are Powerful Medicines for the Soul

According to 1 Samuel 16:23, David played the lyre, and his name is included in the superscriptions of sixty of the one hundred and fifty psalms. As a gifted poet and musician, David uses his abilities to express his grief and to call others to remembrance of Israel's loss. Saul, though at times an adversary of David, is still revered by him as "the LORD's anointed." It is for this reason that David strikes down the messenger from Saul's camp who lies about killing Saul (2 Sam. 1:14-16). This narrative builds to the lament which concludes chapter 1. A moving expression of grief, David uses it to express and assuage his own grief and as a national anthem of mourning and remembrance.

Bill Winter was not known for what he did during his forty-year career in real estate, but for what he did upon his retirement. He built his retirement home on the grounds of a church camp and nurtured young saplings so that one day the grounds might be covered with beautiful shade trees. A mere six months after, having completed his home at the camp, he died of a heart attack. In the brief span between his retirement and his death, he had planted more than two hundred trees at the camp for future generations to enjoy.

Chris Rhoads, a Christian songwriter, wrote a ballad called "Old Man Winter" to tell the story of Bill Winter's legacy. For the family, that song became a family hymn and a reminder of faithful service. David's lament becomes a living testimony of a tiny nation's loss, an articulate expression of one man's personal grief, and a reminder to us all of the power of music and Scripture to touch our soul and liberate our pain. (Gary G. Kindley)

GRACE-FULL GIVING

2 CORINTHIANS 8:7-15

Every adult in our congregation is immune to appeals for more giving. They have heard it all—the guilt-raising statements of duty, the gut-wrenching stories of human need, and the God-angry promises of divine retribution for shirked responsibilities. Mark Twain, when faced with such an appeal for cash, wrote that he became so disgusted that he not only did not give what he had planned, but that he also took a dollar out of the collection plate. In this scripture passage, Paul suggests a new pattern of "grace-full giving."

I. Be Motivated by Your Love for Christ

Paul walks a tightrope of motivation in the first verses of this passage. He uses the example of the Macedonian Christians to encourage the Corinthians to give: "They gave themselves first to the Lord . . ." (v. 5). Then he compliments the Corinthians on the spiritual development, but adds a further task necessary to complete their maturity—they are to excel in the grace of giving. Like the rich young ruler, they were exemplary in their faith, yet they withheld their possessions from the exercise of their faith. This is also a twenty-first century story, isn't it?

The answer to this problem, Paul says, is simple: Follow the example of Christ in your giving. Paul cuts to the heart of this issue by using the fundamental Christian doctrine of incarnation as the fundamental example of Christian stewardship. Since this Sunday precedes Independence Day, it is easy to utilize stories of sacrifice and commitment to illustrate the nature of Christian giving, but this would sell our motivation short. Nothing less than the love of Jesus Christ for us will do.

II. Don't Let Your Good Intentions Grow Stale

The Corinthians reacted with "spontaneous enthusiasm" (Calvin) when they first heard of the offering for the church in Jerusalem. They gave immediately to the offering, but never completed their offering to the best of their abilities or to Paul's satisfaction. Perhaps their fiscal circumstances changed for the worse, and now the Corinthians lacked the will to complete their part in the offering. Instead of criticizing them, Paul offered them a principle for giving: Give what you can, not what you cannot.

III. Let Your Heart Regulate Your Hands

In support of his argument, Paul quotes Exodus 16:18. Rather than the equality of the supply, however, he emphasizes the equal opportunity of all Christians to respond to the needs of fellow believers. If each church will only give what it can when it can, then all churches will be adequately supplied for ministry. This Scripture applies directly to the situation that faces the congregations of every major city where inner-city churches struggle to minister with inadequate resources while suburban churches struggle to find appropriate ways in which to expend their resources. Paul's advice to the Corinthian church rings with sanctified common sense: "[Let your] heart regulate [your] hands" (The Message).

IV. Excel in the Grace of Giving

It is not enough in God's eyes that we excel in faith, speech, knowledge, enthusiasm, and in love for others apart from grace-motivated giving. This is a stern challenge to twenty-first century Christians. What good will we have done if we evangelize the entire world, yet we give our God-provided financial resources out of soul-less duty? In this scripture passage, Paul calls us to re-create our motivation for giving, and in so doing, to re-create our own lives in the image of Christ's life. Martin Luther wrote that three conversions were necessary for us—the conversion of the heart, the mind, and the purse. Let us work out with fear and trembling the conversion of our whole selves to God. (Mickey Kirkindoll)

FROM DEATH TO LIFE

MARK 5:21-43

One of Mark's stylistic devices is the insertion of one story into the middle of another. By giving us some clues, Mark encourages the reader to interpret the two together, to look at one story through the lens of another story. Today we will focus on how we can do just that. How does the healing of the women with the hemorrhage relate to the raising of Jairus' daughter, and vice versa? These stories are the last two in a series of four miracle stories (Mark 4:35–5:43) that describe the conflict between faith and fear.

Jesus and the "Daughter"

The stories begin as Jairus, a religious leader, falls at Jesus' feet. This posture is generally one of faith in Mark's Gospel (1:40; 5:6; 7:25; for examples of Mark's irony, see 10:17 and 15:19). He begs Jesus to come heal his very sick daughter. Jesus responds to such faith. On their way to Jairus' house, the crowd presses in on Jesus. They interrupt his present mission. I can't help but think of poor Jairus on the fringes of the crowd, standing on one foot, biting his lip.

Mark describes a new, nameless character—a woman suffering from hemorrhages for twelve years. She is destitute, hopeless, and her disease incurable. She also would have been an outcast, shunned by the community as unclean (Leviticus 12). This incredible person, overcoming her poverty, her exclusion, her disease, and this pressing crowd, takes the initiative to reach out to Jesus in faith, that if she could touch Jesus' clothes, God would heal her. She is right. Jesus' power goes forth to heal her, restoring her to her community. Jesus asks who it was that touched him, and the faithless disciples chide him for asking such a dumb question. Still, here this woman comes in that same faithful posture of Jairus (v. 33), scared to death of Jesus but nonetheless telling her story. She had more faith than fear. Jesus calls her "daughter" and sends her on her way, saved, peaceful, and reconciled (v. 34). One "daughter" is given life. What about the other?

Even while this last sentence comes from Jesus' mouth, some people come from Jairus' house to tell him of his daughter's death. Jesus calls Jairus to have the same balance of faith and fear that the woman with the hemorrhage had (v. 36). Of his followers, Jesus allows only Peter, James, and John to accompany him, just as they will go with him to the Mount of Transfiguration (9:2), the Mount of Olives (13:3), and Gethsemane (14:33). By stating the guest list, Mark is clueing the reader that this is a critical moment in Jesus' ministry. The suspense is thick as Jesus calls the young woman to rise, and she does. At this point, Mark thinks it important that the reader know she is twelve years old, the same number that appeared in association with the woman in the other story. Two daughters go from death to life, one figuratively and one literally. What is the requirement for either resurrection, according to Jesus? "Daughter, your faith has made you well . . . Do not fear, only believe" (vv. 34, 36). The key to overcoming death is faith in Jesus' power and authority. Here is the radical thing: Faith in Jesus may overcome all sorts of "death" because Jesus himself overcame all sorts of death. Unjustly railroaded to execution as a criminal and a sinner, betrayed and abandoned by his own community of disciples, Jesus looks an awful lot like the woman with the hemorrhage. He is like this outcast "daughter" whose faith in God caused her to stretch out over the pressing crowd (compare 15:13-15), even over skeptical disciples (compare 14:37, 50), to receive healing for her physical, social, and economic "deaths." He is also like Jairus' daughter in that, having physically died, his crucified body was raised (16:6). At the cross, Jesus bound his own suffering self to our sufferings (our virtual deaths) and to our physical death.

In these daughters, we see our hope. No matter what kind of death we are enduring, Jesus has life for us; he has salvation, healing, reconciliation, even resurrection for us. In our suffering, we can know that God is with us. In our death, we can know that God will vindicate us. More than that, we can become as Jesus. Through faith in his resurrection, we are set free, even in our own sufferings, to bind ourselves to the suffering of others. Our worst obstacles are skepticism and fear, which appear about as death-dealing in Mark's Gospel as do clubs, swords, and spears.

How is the church binding itself to the suffering and death of the "daughters" in the community, those who are poor, outcast, and sick? Considering our culture's neurotic fear of illness and death, can we speak a good word to those who are ill or dying without promising them cures for their ills? Is there a difference between curing and healing? God promises them healing because, through the cross, God is with them. How can we help them find that hope? How have you found that hope? How have you experienced life as a "daughter"? (Sam Parkes)

JULY 9, 2000

Fourth Sunday After Pentecost

Worship Theme: We must respond to God's grace in Christ Jesus if we are to experience its power.

Readings: 2 Samuel 5:1-5, 9-10; 2 Corinthians 12:2-10; Mark 6:1-13

Call to Worship (Psalm 48:10-14):

Leader:	As your name, O God, so your praise reaches to the ends of the earth.
People:	**Your right hand is filled with victory; let Mount Zion be glad!**
Leader:	Let the daughters of Judah rejoice because of your judgments!
People:	**Walk about Zion, go round about it, number its towers,**
Leader:	consider well its ramparts, go through its citadels, that you may tell the next generation,
People:	**"This is God, our God for ever and ever. God will be our guide for ever."**

Pastoral Prayer:

Precious Lord of the cross, your power was made perfect in weakness. Your power is not strong as this fallen world measures power, for it is the power of love—sacrificial, unconditional, eternal love. O dear Jesus, we praise you. We stand before you, wideeyed in wonder of this vulnerable love, too vulnerable it seems for so many of us to try. O God, O Christ, forgive us for our cowardice. Forgive us for trying to cover up this fear of loving as you love with our judgments of our broken brothers and sisters as not worthy of healing. Forgive us for our hypocritical pronouncements that these folks are getting what they deserve. O merciful Lord, forgive us. We shudder to think of receiving your judgment on our lives. And we relish the freedom in Christ from judgment. By your grace, use us as conduits of your love and forgiveness. And help us to remember that you have called us not to judge our neighbors, but to love them. In the name of the One who loves us. Amen. (Thomas Gildermeister)

SERMON BRIEFS

DO YOUR VALUES NEED A CLEARANCE SALE?

2 SAMUEL 5:1-5, 9-10

When I was child, whenever there was a big bargain-basement clearance sale at our downtown department store, shoppers frothing in anticipation would form lines that stretched around the block. The amazing thing was that people would stand in line to buy on sale what no one else wanted. They did so because they believed that they were getting a bargain. Occasionally, everyone needs to take inventory and clean out the unwanted stuff in our life, including unwanted values.

This text tells of the tribes of the Northern Kingdom of Israel gathering before David at Hebron. They are now very interested in the shepherd boy becoming the shepherd of Israel. It is David's value of faith in God, loyalty to God's anointed (King Saul), and obedience to God's will that has brought him and the united Israel to this point. David's values challenge us to examine our values and consider what is truly important for our lives.

I. David Placed His Faith in God

It was David's desire to place his trust in God that had brought him success. Even as a youth, he stood before the Philistine giant, Goliath, proclaiming, "I come in the name of the LORD."

There is a plaque by an unknown author that hangs on the wall of my friend's office. It reads: "When you stand at the edge of all the light you have, and you step off into the darkness, you can be sure that there will be a ledge on which you can stand, or you will be taught to fly!" That is the truth of faith.

II. David Was Loyal to Those Whom God Called

Saul was no easy man to serve. He was prone to bouts of depression and rage. He was jealous of David's personable nature, great success, and unswerving faith. He raged at his own son, Jonathan, for his loyalty to and friendship with David. David had every reason to be disloyal to Saul. Yet he recognized that he was God's anointed. This was a theocratic culture, and the king was king by God's desire, not human will.

A woman was criticizing her pastor for his less-than-inspiring sermons. Another lifelong church member spoke up and said, "I have never failed to be nurtured by any pastor whom we have ever had. Some I have had to pray for more than others, but all have blessed me because God called them to be my pastor."

Loyalty blesses the loyal as well as the revered.

III. David Sought God's Will

Second Samuel 5:12 says, "David then perceived that the Lord had established him king over Israel, and that he had exalted his kingdom for the sake of his people Israel."

David desired to be obedient to God. He desired to follow God's commandments and to do what was best for Israel. This is a younger, less cynical David who is not yet drunken with power. He has built up Jerusalem as the city of David and established Zion (the name of the mount on which Jerusalem rests) as the new political and religious capital of the united Israel.

When my best friend died during our senior year in high school, I did not understand why God had allowed a senseless accident to claim a life of only eighteen years. My pastor gave me Leslie Weatherhead's *The Will of God* (Nashville: Abingdon, 1987), and I read it cover to cover. I still did not know exactly why Chad died, but I knew what the biblical writer affirmed about King David: "For the LORD, the God of hosts, was with him" (v. 10b). (Gary G. Kindley)

PARADISE, PROMISE, AND A PARADOX

2 CORINTHIANS 12:2-10

The best-selling Christian book of 1997 was Philip Yancey's *What's So Amazing About Grace?* (Grand Rapids, Mich.: Zondervan). In his book, Yancey recounts the story of a British conference on world religions in which the subject of debate was what, if any, belief was unique to the Christian faith. C. S. Lewis happened to walk into the room where the conference was being held and, being told of the subject, replied: "That's easy. It's grace." Grace, both as a doctrine and as an experience, is the crowning glory of the Christian church and the Christian faith. In this sometimes baffling passage of Scripture, the apostle Paul describes three ways in which he experienced the grace of God.

I. Paul Experienced Paradise with the Empowering Grace of God

Why did Paul speak of himself in the third person in verses 2 through 6, when verse 7 clearly states that Paul himself was the subject? Perhaps he sought to separate himself from the braggadocio of the false teachers. Perhaps he felt that it was more becoming to refer to himself in the third person. Perhaps, as some have suggested, he was following an unwritten rabbinic convention by his use of the third person. Clearly Paul's role in this experience was passive—"[I] was caught up." Similarly, the nature of his body seemed unimportant (vv. 2-3), and he heard things in heaven that were inexpressible, both because they were beyond the power of words to express and because he was forbidden to tell them to others.

Why did Paul wait fourteen years to tell of such an experience? He certainly did not wish to brag of his own experiences. Why then did God seek to keep him from being conceited by giving Paul a "thorn in the flesh"? Perhaps this Paradise experience was Paul's Pentecost, the catalyzing and empowering experience that

would motivate Paul's evangelistic mission for the rest of his life.
What was it like to experience Paradise? Paul gives us only a glimpse of what it must have been like. In 2 Corinthians 5:8, he wrote that he would prefer to be away from his body so that he could be "at home with the Lord." Perhaps he meant to tell us that Paradise is like "going home," where all is natural and right and at harmony. Paul's experience of grace empowered his service to God.

II. Paul Received a Promise of the Sufficient Grace of God

No one will ever know what Paul's "thorn in the flesh" was, and no one who has ever sought to serve the Lord can doubt the reality of his experience, for it is played out anew in the life of each of his servants. He prayed three times (numerologically, often enough to invoke the power of God for change, if that was God's will), but the source of his pain was not removed from his life. In fact, the "messenger of Satan" was allowed to use his bare knuckles in pounding Paul (v. 7).

Paul's claim to apostolic authority came from his experience of seeing the risen Lord on the road to Damascus. In this instance, Paul received the grace of a spoken promise from the Lord: "My grace is sufficient for you, for my power is made perfect in weakness." Paul did not receive a release from his suffering; rather, he received a promise to help him persevere and conquer his suffering. His promise from Jesus convinced him to trust the sufficiency of God's grace.

III. Paul Resolved a Paradox Through the Transforming Grace of God

Paul embraced these growing pains of the soul and accepted both the discipline and the delight in them. He became a "wounded healer," boasting that his weaknesses were nothing more than an opportunity to reveal the strength of God. Someone once said that the sacrifice of Paul's life was for the purpose of his delight in the presence of his Lord and in the maturing faith of his disciples.

The transforming grace of God empowered Paul to transform a paradox of self-sacrifice and spiritual power into the secret of ministry that transforms lives. When we, in confessional transparency, allow our weaknesses to become God's strengths, we will experience a new spiritual power in our lives and in our churches. (Mickey Kirkindoll)

FORFEITING FAITH

MARK 6:1-13

Mark 6:6 (NCV) says, "He was amazed at how many people had no faith." Mark reports two intertwining incidents in the beginning verses of the sixth chapter of his Gospel, and both deal with the results if faith is forfeited.

The first part pertains to people one would least expect to forfeit their faith—Jesus' hometown friends. It would seem that a friend would readily accept a hometown celebrity, but it was not the case in Nazareth. The New Century Bible translates Mark 6:3 this way: "So the people were upset with Jesus." Upset? "At what?" one may ask. The answer: Christ's dynamic teaching, powerful authority, and miracles of healing (v. 2). How foolish! Yet, today many mimic the Nazarenes of Jesus' day.

The second phase occurs as Jesus commissions his twelve disciples to place in their hands the divine authority to battle demonic powers of evil—and win! He gives them power to heal the sick as well as the powerful preaching of holy truth. Salvation was at hand to those with a changed heart and lifestyle.

Jesus tells his followers if the people forfeit faith, the disciples were to "leave that place. Shake its dust off your feet" as a symbol of God's holy displeasure of their lack of faith (Mark 6:11 NCV). What a frightening thought—to displease God. That is the essence of sin. Forfeiting faith results in the loss of several things. Acceptance brings much to life, while rejection costs much.

I. Rejection Costs: Power

Power for many equals a competitive, muscle-packed person or program poised to take on any challenger. That describes one type of power, but another power deals with a self-emptying lifestyle sacrificed to God. God is the source of genuine power.

In *Holiness and Power* ([Cincinnati: Revivalist Publishers, 1897], pp. 283-84), A. M. Hills quotes William Booth of the Salvation Army: "[Sacrifice] is the presentation or giving away of all we have to God; a ceasing any longer to own anything which we have hitherto called our own, but all going over into God's hands for him to order and arrange. . . . [It] can only be done in the might of the Holy Ghost . . . then the fire descends and burns up all the dross and defilement of sin, and fills the soul with burning zeal and love and power."

The power God offers include:

1. The power to live holy. Mother Teresa said, "Our progress in holiness depends on God and ourselves—on God's graces and on our will to be holy. We must have a real determination to reach holiness" (Reuben Job & Norman Shawchuck, *A Guide to Prayer for Ministers and Other Servants* ([Nashville: Upper Room, 1983], p. 216).

2. The power to acknowledge our limited resources and dependence upon God.

3. The power to minister to others in need.

II. Rejection Costs: Healing

The townspeople of Nazareth could have had a great healing, a supernatural touch from God, but they rejected God's hands of healing.

The new millennium ushers in a renewed opportunity for a new hope, a new trust, a new experience, a new healing, which rests in the hands of God. God reaches out for all of us to be touched by God for healing of our minds, emotions, splintered families, social decay, loneliness, hatred, and more. "Jesus touched the untouchables of the world. Will you do the same?" (Max Lucado, *Just Like Jesus* [Dallas: Word Publishing, 1998], p. 37).

III. Rejection Costs: Changed Hearts

The bottom line of rejecting Jesus is the rejection of his salvation. Sin dominates hearts, demands its own way—completely selfish, inconsiderate, hell-bent.

Salvation changes self-centeredness to God-centeredness.

Repentance is not a sentimental sorrow, but a revolution centered in God that turns us from the sinful road to the righteous road.

Don't forfeit your faith for a false feeling of self-sufficiency. Has Jesus come to your hometown today? If so, let him touch you now. (Derl Keefer)

JULY 16, 2000

Fifth Sunday After Pentecost

Worship Theme: Our love of God must come first, preceding social convention, and even family ties.

Readings: 2 Samuel 6:1-5, 12*b*-19; Ephesians 1:3-14; Mark 6:14-29

Call to Worship (Psalm 24:7-10):

Leader: Lift up your heads, O gates! and be lifted up, O ancient doors! that the Ruler of glory may come in.

People: **Who is the Ruler of glory?**

Leader: The LORD, strong and mighty, the LORD, mighty in battle!

People: **Lift up your heads, O gates! and be lifted up, O ancient doors! that the Ruler of glory may come in.**

Leader: Who is this Ruler of glory?

People: **The LORD of hosts, the LORD is the Ruler of glory!**

Pastoral Prayer:
  Almighty Friend, all-loving Lord, we praise you for giving us examples of joy and conviction that we find in David and John the Baptist. Help us to follow such faithful saints. And we thank you for giving us bad examples, examples like Herod, whose terror of your power could never sustain him against temptation. Help us to reject a life of terror for a life of adoration and praise. Help us to rely on you because you, and only you, are trustwor-

thy in all seasons and in every circumstance. But, Lord, many of us rely on family. We do lean on friends, and they disappoint us. Our loved ones die or sometimes leave. Our wounds are deep. Our pain takes our breath away. God, we ask you to heal those who are broken in body, soul, and spirit; to forgive those who rely on your gifts and not only on you; and to lighten the load of those whose burden seems unbearable. We pray in the name of the One whose burden is light indeed. Amen. (Thomas Gildermeister)

SERMON BRIEFS

PARTYING IN THE PEWS

2 SAMUEL 6:1-5, 12b-19

A sister of the faith once confessed that she was raised with the belief that a dancing foot and a praying knee could not grow on the same leg. What a sad belief that faith in God must rob one of joy and abundant living. Life is meant to be a celebration. It is sin and evil that rob life of its full joy.

Today's text describes the wondrous celebratory nature of divine worship as David dances before the ark of the covenant, and Israel celebrates being a nation under God.

I. David Honored the Sacred

The ark of the covenant was both the mercy seat of God and a symbol of God's presence among the people. In reclaiming the ark for Israel, David was reminding the people of God's presence in their lives. By bringing the ark to Jerusalem, David established Jerusalem as the worship center for the newly united kingdom.

Today we also use symbols to acknowledge God's presence and work in our lives. Through baptism and the Lord's Supper, we experience God's grace. Through the water of baptism or the bread and cup of Communion, we acknowledge God's sacred presence and claim Christ's marvelous grace. Honoring the sacred through acts of worship and praise is a means of drawing closer to Christ and enriching our soul.

II. David Humbled Himself Before God

Much ado has been made about David dancing naked before the ark. Though not nude, it is true that he was clothed in a ceremonial apron that covered only the front of the body. Ironically, this apparently was done in an act of humility and worship. David was praising the God who created all flesh, who had redeemed Israel from her enemies, and who had empowered David and his people to regain the ark. Here we see Jesse's son as the royal worship leader, the kingly shepherd who leads his people in the praise of the Lord. Certainly not everyone saw David's actions as the humble worship of God.

It is difficult to interpret the feelings of Michal (v. 16). Perhaps she was bitter over having not conceived. Perhaps she was contemptuous of David for paying less attention to her than the other women in his court. Whatever her concern, it is offset by David's enthusiastic celebration of God in leading the whole people of Israel in ecstatic praise.

III. David Celebrated Joy

"David danced before the LORD with all his might" (v. 14a). Observing the holy rituals, David made preparations and offerings before the ark of God. He recognized how God had blessed him, and he passed on God's blessing to his people. In an act of joyous benevolence, he provided food to every person in the kingdom, men and women. The text is specific in stating that it was not only a portion of bread, but meat and fruit as well. This was a most generous celebration on the part of a most generous king.

The church is a place where the kingdom of God is manifest and God's presence is realized. In Christ's church, everyone shares what he or she has (Acts 2:44-45), puts his or her whole heart into glorifying God, and after the benediction all return home to live their life in faithful, joyous obedience. Perhaps if the church is to look more like God's kingdom, we should follow King David's example and throw a party for God each Sabbath. (Gary G. Kindley)

PRAISE GOD FROM WHOM ALL BLESSINGS FLOW

EPHESIANS 1:3-14

During each episode of *The Millionaire* someone received $1 million. Viewers marveled over the responses of the people who received these incredible gifts. Have you ever dreamed about being given $1 million?

Suppose we all were handed a valid check for $1 million. Attached to each check is a note that says, "When you exhaust this, I have more—just for you." Both check and note are signed, "Bill."

How would you respond to Bill? Would you refuse to shake his hand? If he asked you to mow his lawn, would you tell him to get lost? Would you go around town telling people he was a fraud? Or, would you look forward to seeing him? Would you help him in any way you could? Wouldn't you spread the word that he was a great guy?

As the apostle Paul begins his letter to the Ephesians, he reminds them that God deserves praise. The word *bless* (used three times in verse 3) means "to say or do good." God deserves blessing because God has blessed us with every spiritual blessing. In Trinitarian fashion, Paul enumerates God's blessings, which evoke our praise.

I. Praise God the Father Who Chose You (vv. 3-6)

God chose you; that's election.

We struggle with God's sovereignty and our responsibility. What Paul says reminds me of the near-frozen traveler who saw a sign over the entrance to a cabin: "Whosoever will may come." He went inside and was saved from the storm. Only later did he see another sign over the same door, but from the inside: "Chosen before the creation of the world."

God the Father chose you to be his child; that's adoption.

Suppose I went to an orphanage to adopt some hopeless children. I walk into a room full of children. Every one may grow up homeless and unloved unless I decide to adopt them. I say, "I'll take that one and that one."

254

Do I walk out condemned because I didn't choose them all? No, I'm praised for choosing those I chose. God's choice is to blessing, never to reprobation.

II. Praise God the Son Who Redeemed You (vv. 7-12)

Jesus the Son redeemed you to show you his grace.

When Richard married, he anticipated a long life of love and joy but soon discovered his wife's unfaithfulness. Rather than abandon her in his shame and anger, he sought to restore their marriage. She would have none of it, running off to prostitute herself.

Years passed. While visiting a distant city, he was told that his long-lost wife was being held in the mental ward of a public hospital, diseased and despondent. He went to her, paid her bills, and brought her home to nurse her to health and to rekindle her love.

She had been redeemed, "bought back." She had been his wife; now she was also his devoted love.

III. Praise God the Spirit Who Sealed You (vv. 13-14)

God the Holy Spirit sealed you to secure your eternity.

Ephesus supported a thriving lumber business. Logs were floated down the rivers of Europe and Asia into the Aegean Sea. Raftsmen guided them down into Ephesus' harbor.

When the logs arrived, notice was sent to the various lumber companies. These firms sent out their representatives to evaluate the timber, choosing those logs they would eventually turn into lumber. After the down payments were made, representatives carved an identifying wedge upon every log each firm had agreed to take. Each company had its own brand or seal that secured its logs until the day the logs were taken out of the water.

The Holy Spirit is God's seal on true believers. We belong to God, waiting only for the day we are claimed for eternity.

> Praise God, from whom all blessings flow;
> Praise Him, all creatures here below;
> Praise Him above, ye heavenly host;
> Praise Father, Son, and Holy Ghost.

(Timothy Warren)

255

SIN'S ENTANGLEMENT

MARK 6:14-29

The textual scene from this scripture takes place in one of the most lonely and grim fortresses in the world—the Castle of Machaerus. The fortress stands as a symbol of all life's evil. The dungeon stank with the rot of human flesh and the stench of human dung. Rats played hide-and-seek in the muck, as merciless guards ravaged the wretched souls languishing in exile. John the Baptist spent his last days chained to the walls of this desolate dungeon. All who pass by this ungodly place—then and now—ought to hang their heads in disgust and despair that such a place could exist.

Many today are in dungeons because of sin's entanglement in their lives. The characters in the text exemplify a phase of sin's web of deceit, hatred, temptation, and victimization.

I. Herod Antipas: Sin's Villain

Herod Antipas was a master of arrogance, superiority, immorality and pride. He was the first ruler of Galilee. His half-brother Herod Philip lived in Rome as a rich private citizen. While still married to a Nabataean princess, Herod visited his half-brother Philip. In Philip's own home, Herod seduced Philip's wife, Herodias, and took her back to Galilee. Herod's wife escaped and went back to her Arabian family, leaving Herod free to marry Herodias. By marrying Herodias, Herod broke the Jewish law (Lev. 18:16, 20-21) and fathered indecency and immorality. His deliberate seduction of Herodias was but one of his many acts of public improprieties. Luke wrote of Herod in his Gospel: "John rebuked Herod the tetrarch because of Herodias, his brother's wife, and all the other evil things he had done" (Luke 3:19 NIV).

Sin is evil. Comedians poke fun at it. People downplay its devastating effects. Satan encourages it. But the bottom line is that sin is evil. Sin hurts God and people—forever! Antipas did evil things. Don't follow his lead.

II. Herodias: Sin's Vengeance

We say that Herod seduced Herodias away from Philip. The truth is, she willingly left Philip for Herod's bedroom. No force was used. She did not go by spear point. She simply left Philip for Herod.

John the Baptist bluntly told her and Herod how wrong this situation was in God's sight. There was no repentance or sorrow, but a defiance of John and God.

Herod feared John but paradoxically respected him. Thus, he would call John up from the dungeon to preach occasionally. Herodias' vengeful spirit desired to kill John.

William Barclay wrote: "The trouble with Herodias was that she wished to eliminate the one man who had the courage to confront her with her sin. She wished to do as she liked, with no one to remind her of the moral law. She murdered John that she might sin in peace. She forgot that she need no longer meet John, but that she still had to meet God" (William Barclay, *The Daily Study Bible* [Philadelphia: The Westminster Press, 1954], p. 155).

A chilling commentary: "She still had to meet God." Anyone who cuts off communication with God still must meet God in the end.

III. Salome: Sin's Vamp

The word *vamp* means "temptress, seductress, flirt." That describes Salome perfectly. She must have been exotically beautiful, yet ugly of character. Through Salome's veins ran the blood of royalty, yet she demeans herself and her stature as princess by dancing the licentious dance of the professional prostitute. The horrific fact is that her mother, Herodias, not only allows it, but encourages her to dance in front of Herod and his guests. Herod was Salome's stepfather and uncle, all in one. She tempts him beyond his control. Drunk with wine, lust, and in a stupor, Herod is so charmed that he offers Salome anything she wants. Her price for the dance—the head of John the Baptist! Herod fears the palace guests' laughter if he does not comply. Then he fears either John or his God. John is executed. Temptation comes full circle, and sin destroys.

J. Williams Chapman said, "Temptation is the tempter looking through the keyhole into the room where you are living; sin is your drawing back the bolt and making it possible for him to enter" (Albert Wells, Jr., compiler, *Inspiring Quotations* [Nashville: Thomas Nelson, 1988], p. 198).

IV. John the Baptist: Sin's Victim

John lay rotting in a stinking dungeon because he challenged Herod and Herodias' illicit affair and subsequent marriage. He demanded repentance. I wonder if John, as he laid there, thought: "Where are my friends?"

"Where are my disciples?"

"Where is Jesus?"

"Where is God?"

Alone! John was all alone, but God was there. Though chains bound John, God entered his prison cell and ministered to him. God assured him that he was not alone.

When you feel like a victim, rise up! God has not abandoned you. (Derl Keefer)

JULY 23, 2000

Sixth Sunday After Pentecost

Worship Theme: Fear is a sickness that keeps God's children from loving one another. If we seek the living Christ, he will heal this deadly disease.

Readings: 2 Samuel 7:1-14*a*; Ephesians 2:11-22; Mark 6:30-34, 53-56

Call to Worship (Psalm 89:1-4, 28-29, 36-37):

> *Leader:* I will sing of your steadfast love, O LORD, for ever; with my mouth I will proclaim your faithfulness to all generations.
>
> *People:* **Your steadfast love is established for ever, your faithfulness is firm as the heavens.**
>
> *Leader:* You have said, "I have made a covenant with my chosen one,
>
> *People:* **I will establish your descendants for ever, and build your throne for all generations.**
>
> *Leader:* My steadfast love I will keep for him for ever, and my covenant will stand firm
>
> *People:* **I will establish his line for ever and his throne as the days of the heavens.**
>
> *Leader:* His line shall endure for ever, his throne as long as the sun before me.
>
> *People:* **Like the moon it shall be established for ever; it shall stand firm while the skies endure."**

Pastoral Prayer:

Our dear God in heaven, that holiest of "placeless" places where life is forever and love is without blemish, we stand in open-mouthed awe of your love for us and for all of creation. That you would make us all so splendid. That you would send your own Son to redeem us. That your Holy Spirit is with us and in us, guiding us, and healing us. How great is your love for us; we are humbled by your compassion. It is so enormous, while our caring is so puny. We allow our fear of the differences between us to build walls of hatred and suspicion. We run from neighbors who are ill, maybe even dying, because we are afraid. Teach us to love. Teach us to live in the shadow of Christ Jesus. Teach us to be "wall breakers" and not "wall builders." In the name of the One who destroyed every wall. Amen. (Thomas Gildermeister)

SERMON BRIEFS

WHICH END OF THE BINOCULARS ARE YOU HOLDING?

2 SAMUEL 7:1-14a

How significant it is that David proposes building a temple for the ark of the covenant. David is not responding to God's admonition nor to pressure from others, but he is led by his holy vision. It is this same vision that leads faithful persons to serve, give, and pray as an act of discipleship. Yet, there is something missing in David's vision—grandeur. God has bigger plans, a larger scheme, a grander scale. So it goes when we look at life through the wrong end of the binoculars, and miss God's wondrous, holy vision.

I. David Places God As His First Priority

When David observes, "I am living in a house of cedar, but the ark of God stays in a tent" (v. 2b), his statement declares his priority and humility. David's words reflect his thoughts, values, and priorities. In everything that we do, we make choices as to what we value and what we feel is important.

A woman at her church's capital fund banquet declared that she had nothing more to spare for the church's need. She then went outside and drove away in her $38,000 sport utility vehicle. She had already made her choice and declared her priority. Such is the subtlety of our values, but it is still a matter of choice.

II. God Redefines David's Vision

The difference between personal ideas and a holy vision is the selfless and God-inspired nature of the holy. Through the prophet Nathan, whom God uses to guide and admonish David in good times and bad (see chapter 12), the Lord redefines David's vision. David is to be a house for God in that he will bring forth a line of faithful from his seed. It will be his offspring, Solomon, who builds the house for the ark of God. Sometimes the most important part of being visionary is being flexible enough to change our vision when God leads us in new directions.

I still remember my woeful complaints about inadequate nursery facilities at my first student pastorate. "How can we expect to attract young families to church, with no safe, clean place for their children to play and rest?" was my plea. I was not inaccurate; my vision was simply too small. I wanted to remodel a nursery. The next pastor built a separate child care facility to reach out to an entire neighborhood. What a change has been wrought in that little church, which now ministers to dozens of families and their precious children.

III. God's Vision Surprises Our Small Thinking

David wanted to build a house (temple), but God wanted him to build a house (dynasty). Abraham and Sarah wanted to parent a child, but God wanted them to be parents of millions. Judas wanted Jesus to be a redeemer of Israel, but God wanted Jesus to be the redeemer of the world. The trouble with human vision is that it is usually too small. God's vision bursts into our world with holy rainbows and resurrection signs.

He wanted to be a doctor and save lives, but God called him to be a pastor and save souls. She wanted to be an accountant for large corporations, but God called her to account as a missionary to a foreign land. He wanted to soar with the birds as a pilot, and God piloted him to be an aviation missionary in the African Congo. (Gary G. Kindley)

COME TOGETHER NOW

EPHESIANS 2:11-22

What kind of church building glorifies God? Some say, "It ought to be conservative, because we have a conservative God and a conservative faith." Others favor a more modern design, since "God is up-to-date, relevant, speaking to today's people about today's needs." Still others would choose a structure ten to twenty years old: "Not too old-fashioned, but not too modern—right in the middle." Everybody has an opinion.

Hopefully most would agree that the church building ought to be a testimony to the world of our faith, who we are in Christ and what we are about. Exactly what that building would look like, I don't know.

The church, however, is not made of wood and stone. *The church is that community of believers who are committed to the Lord Jesus Christ.* Now, if the church building ought to reflect who we are in Christ and what we are about, how much more should the people of Christ (the church) reflect the same? That is what the apostle Paul tells us in Ephesians 2:11-22.

I. You Were Once Far Off (vv. 11-12)

God wants you to remember who you used to be. You used to be an alien, far from God. You were once without privilege (v. 11*b*), the Messiah (v. 12), citizenship (v. 12), promises (v. 12), hope (v. 12), and God (v. 12).

Perhaps you have experienced being an outsider. You don't have the look, the language, or the lifestyle to fit in. Some people experience race, age, gender, economic, political, religious, or some other kind of exclusion daily. But to be alienated from God because of sin, nothing could be worse.

II. But You Have Been Brought Near (vv. 13-18)

As Paul often says, "But now" things have changed. Now you belong. You are near, intimate with, God. How did this transformation take place? No change in race, age, gender, economic status, politics, or religious affiliation could make the difference. Only Christ Jesus himself can make such a difference. You were brought near through the blood of Christ, (v. 13). True peace with God is possible because of Jesus' cross work.

But there's more. True unity among believers is possible because of Jesus' cross work, (v. 14-18). The apostle has in mind the barrier of exclusion that existed for centuries between Jews and Gentiles. In the temple, a barrier separated Gentile worshipers from Jewish worshipers. Jewish people had "special access" into God's presence.

But Jesus died to abolish all such physical divisions. Now the only spiritual barrier that divides people from one another and from God is sin. When God looks down upon people, God sees *one*. And God desires that the world see *one* as well.

III. You Are One in Christ with All True Believers (vv. 16-22)

— One new body (v. 16).
— One new nation (v. 19*a*).
— One new family (v. 19*b*).
— One new church (vv. 20-22).

When people look at this church—not the building but the people—do they see racial, cultural, economic, or political subgroups? Or, do they see the *Body of Christ*?

Do they see nationalities siding against each other, or *one nation* of heavenly citizenship?

Do they see families lined up across from one another, or *one loving family* of God?

Do they see old denominational champions hanging tightly to mere traditions, or *one true church* reflecting its new nature in Christ and his love through us to the world?

Romeo and Juliet were star-crossed lovers. Their families were at war. Though caught in the middle of that bitter battle, which had turned the entire town into turmoil, they lived out their sacrificial love. Their sacrifice led to the ultimate reconciliation and new unity between the Capulets and Montagues.

Jesus' sacrificial love on the cross made your union with God and unity with one another possible. Do you, in this church, show it? (Timothy Warren)

THE TOUCH OF THE MASTER'S HEART

MARK 6:30-34, 53-56

Max Lucado relates the story of "one of my sadder memories" that included a fourth-grade friend named Jerry. He was one of a half dozen boys who were "an ever-present, inseparable fixture on the playground." One day Lucado called Jerry to see if Jerry could come out to play, but instead of talking to Jerry, he spoke to his dad. The voice of Jerry's father was loud, cursing and slurring the words saying that Jerry could not come over that day—or any other day! Lucado writes: "I told my friends what had happened. One of them explained that Jerry's father was an alcoholic. I don't know if I knew what the word meant, but I learned quickly. Jerry, the second baseman; Jerry the kid with the red bike; Jerry, my friend on the corner, was now 'Jerry, the son of a drunk.' Kids can be hard, and for some reason we were hard on Jerry" (Lucado, *Just Like Jesus* [Dallas: Word Publishing, 1998], p. 321). Outcasts, the hurting, the ill, the hungry, the elderly, the young, the lost, the weary—Jesus had compassion on them all. Today, we Christians are called by Christ to have compassion on the "Jerrys" of life. He asks us to choose to touch those who need help.

Our text tells us that the master's heart touched a wide variety of hurting people.

I. Jesus' Heart Touched the Weary of Life (vv. 30-32)

Mark, the Gospel writer, places the beheading of John the Baptist prior to the text, but that is an interlude in writing. Flip back a page to discover that Jesus gathered his disciples and commissioned them to preach, heal, and drive out demons. Exhausting work! The truth is that a person who does that kind of work is drained physically, mentally, and spiritually. The disciples were no exception. They returned to the Master Preacher, Healer, and Authority to report all their experiences. The apostles could barely recount their experiences because of the continuous interruption of people coming to talk to Jesus. It was a madhouse of confusion. Christ saw and felt the frustration and weariness of his men, and had compassion. In wisdom he said, "Come on, let's go to a quiet place—just you and I." They got into their boat and sailed away four miles to the other side. A windless day or a contrary wind would make travel a bit lengthy, so they would be on the lake long enough to relate their experiences. It was a good thing, because as soon as they stepped out of the boat, they were met by thousands of people anxious to hear from Jesus.

William Barclay says of this text that we find what might be called the "rhythm of the Christian life." Barclay writes, "For the Christian life is a continuous going into the presence of God from the presence of men, and coming out into the presence of men from the presence of God" (Barclay, *The Daily Study Bible* [Philadelphia: The Westminster Press, 1954], p. 156).

Two thoughts entwine in this passage. First, there is action in the Christian life. One of the verses of the hymn "Work for the Night is Coming" says, "Give ev'ry flying minute something to keep in store: Work, for the night is coming, when man works no more." We sing it with conviction because the time is coming for Christ's return. Second, this is no time to dillydally in the Christian work, but there must be respites. Times of spiritual, physical, and mental relaxation enable us to continue the pace God sets for us.

I went out to the garage and found that my rechargeable flashlight was unplugged from its source of energy. It was dead. No light. When I recharged it, the light came back on. Prayer, devotion, and sometimes rest are just what God orders.

Jesus understood and had compassion on his weary men.

II. Jesus' Heart Touched the Lost of Life (vv. 33-34)

As the people throng the place where Jesus and his disciples landed, Jesus looks into the lostness of their hearts.

1. The people stood at the crossroad of life bewildered. Jesus came to help them on their journey. He points to what we now call the Christian life and to heaven. Only through his divine touch can we be changed.

2. The people needed strength for the journey. Jesus is the Bread of Life. Only Jesus fills our hunger and thirst for righteousness.

3. The people needed a defender of faith. Only in the presence of Jesus can people walk in holiness and love with faith filled to overcome the world. He is our Defense, our Rock!

III. Jesus' Heart Touched the People's Illness (vv. 53-56)

After the miracle of the feeding of the five thousand, Jesus sends his disciples ahead by boat. He crosses by foot. He walks on the water, another in a succession of miracles. When they finally arrive at Gennesaret, the whole countryside comes to see this miracle-making machine. From everywhere the people came to be healed by Jesus. In this setting, he fulfills their desires.

David McKenna, in *The Communicator's Commentary* (Dallas: Word Publishing, 1989), makes three good observations about Jesus' ministry of healing.

1. Their healing was not selective. No one was left out.

2. Some demonstration of faith and determination is required of people who are sick.

3. When a person is made well, it carries the connotation of "freedom from the disease that has enslaved a person. The other is the wholeness that comes to the person who touches Christ."

Ministry occurs through compassion. Have we missed the ministry of compassion in the church today? This scripture suggests we follow Jesus' example of compassion. (Derl Keefer)

JULY 30, 2000

Seventh Sunday After Pentecost

Worship Theme: Only the One who walked upon the sea can satisfy our deepest longing.

Readings: 2 Samuel 11:1-15; Ephesians 3:14-21; John 6:1-21

Call to Worship (Psalm 14:1-3, 6-7):

Leader: Fools say in their hearts, "There is no God."

People: **They are corrupt, they do abominable deeds, there is none that does good.**

Leader: The LORD looks down from heaven on all people, to see if there are any that are wise, who seek after God.

People: **They have all gone astray, they are all alike perverse; there is none that does good, no, not one.**

Leader: You would confound the plans of the poor, but the LORD is their refuge.

People: **O that deliverance for Israel would come from Zion! When the LORD restores their fortunes, Jacob shall rejoice and Israel shall be glad!**

Pastoral Prayer:
   Ruler of time, Master of the farthest reaches of space, we offer thanksgiving to you for granting the peace and grace of Christ Jesus. We know deeply in our souls that when we look beyond our Lord for security and comfort, we only find misery. But still,

we do. Rescue us from the prison of our own making. Deliver us from this living hell that we call our existence. Help us to follow Jesus. Guide the leaders of our church, our community and state, our nation, and our world so that all of us might realize that weapons, popularity, money, career-building, and the incessant drive to please our bodies can never bring anything that even approaches the unsearchable riches of our beloved Jesus Christ. Thank you, Holy God, for the gift of your creation. Yet, let us worship only the giftgiver and not your spectacular gifts. Amen. (Thomas Gildermeister)

SERMON BRIEFS

STEPS TO MURDER

2 SAMUEL 11:1-15

Kenneth Chafin tells in *The Communicator's Commentary* (Dallas: Word Publishing, 1989) that Hollywood had a special liking for the story of David and Bathsheba. It had all the makings of a blockbuster movie, with characters of interest including a passionate warrior-king, a beautiful but passive woman, a naive trusting husband, an obedient but amoral army general, and a prophet of God without fear. The plot would appeal to the baser side of life—lust, adultery, deceit, murder, blackmail, intrigue, confrontation, and tragedy.

This sad story reminds us that no one is exempt from temptation. Left to run wild, temptation leads to devastating circumstances and sin. Truthfully, it can be a step to murder.

Step One: Lust

The story of David and Bathsheba begins on a warm evening in early summer. The glance of David down from the palace balcony to the rooftop of Uriah's house settles into a lustful stare at a woman's back. Uriah's wife, Bathsheba, unaware of David's eyes, takes a ritualistic bath marking the end of her menstrual period. The author makes a point of indicating that "the woman was very beautiful" (v. 2), setting the stage for the reader. Temptation seldom begins with ugliness. The normal bait is something beautiful, and the eye becomes lustful for more.

Step Two: Adultery

David should have stopped with the glance, could have stopped with the stares, but rather he sent for Bathsheba. David ignored all the warning signals surrounding him:

— his conscience;
— "daughter of Eliam," probably a prominent loyal Jewish family;
— "the wife of Uriah the Hittite," a woman committed to one of his loyal subjects;
— the sacred law that points to the sin of adultery and describes its consequences.

Adultery is the act of taking another person's spouse for sexual relations. It is the act of stealing another's affections, emotions, care, and stealing from that person the body of the one to whom that person is committed. That is exactly what David did, he stole Bathsheba's body from Uriah. He could have said to himself, "She's off limits; she's committed to Uriah." But David didn't.

Step Three: Deceit

When David learned of Bathsheba's pregnancy, he should have faced his sin, but he didn't. He tried to worm his way through the affair with deceit. He conceived a masterful plan to bring Uriah back home. David expected Uriah to go home and have sex with Bathsheba. David hadn't counted on a wrench being thrown into the plan. Uriah's commitment to God and country overrode his own personal desires.

Step Four: Murder

Thwarted in his sinister scheme, David sent Uriah with his own death plan to Joab. The bottom line: Uriah dies because of David's sin.

J. Wilber Chapman said, "Temptation is the tempter looking through the keyhole into the room where you are living; sin is your drawing back the bolt and making it possible for him to enter." David had "drawn back the bolt."

The gruesome story of how an Eskimo kills a wolf offers insight into the consuming self-destructive nature of temptation that leads to sin.

The Eskimo coats his knife blade with several layers of animal blood and allows it to freeze in the cold. The hunter fixes his knife in the ground, with the blade sticking up exposed. A wolf gets a whiff of the blood bait, follows the scent to the source, and begins licking it feverishly to the point that the blade is bare. But by now his craving has become so great that he doesn't recognize that he is licking his own blood. Dawn comes, and he lays dead in the snow. The temptation of lust has overpowered him. (Derl Keefer)

PRAY FOR GLORY'S SAKE

EPHESIANS 3:14-21

Some people are window-shoppers. They go to the mall not to buy but to look, to try on, to put back—wishing they could buy but going on to the next display. They fear they may deplete their precious resources. As a result, some people never appropriate what they need to accomplish life's tasks.

Some believers merely window-shop and never buy into the Christian life. They cautiously examine the product. They may even do some "trying on," but they quickly realize they do not have the necessary resources to appropriate what they need to accomplish the demands of the Christian life. Unfortunately, they never live out of the riches of Christ in them.

God has another plan. God desires that we go into this world not only enlightened, but also enabled by every spiritual resource from God's unlimited resources in Jesus Christ.

In Ephesians 1:1-14, the apostle Paul informed the church that God had blessed them with every spiritual blessing. The Ephesians, however, had not known of their rich spiritual status. So, Paul prayed that they might experience spiritual enlightenment

(Eph. 1:15-23). All of God's resources were available because Jesus had died to make God's blessings accessible (Eph. 2:1–3:13). It's one thing to have unlimited potential and to know that every resource is available. It's quite another to act upon that knowledge. That is why Paul interceded again for the Ephesians in chapter 3. This time he prayed for spiritual enablement. Once they had comprehended their blessings, they needed to apprehend them.

Paul prayed to the God of creation and redemption. Every family in heaven acknowledges God as the Father of their eternal salvation. Every family on earth acknowledges (or will acknowledge, see Phil. 2:10-11) God as the Father of their human existence. Only through the unlimited physical and spiritual riches of God's glory do we accomplish every breath and every victory.

I. Pray to Be Strengthened Through the Spirit (vv. 14-16)

Living the Christian life demands strength through the Spirit. God has given his spiritual children the Spirit as an inner resource. The various enablements of the Spirit have no limit. Imagine what you could accomplish if you apprehended the fruit of the Spirit—love, joy, peace, patience, kindness, generosity, faithfulness, gentleness, and self-control (Gal. 5:22-23), to mention only a portion of God's rich provision.

II. Pray to Be Indwelled by Christ (v. 17b)

Living the Christian life requires Christ living in us. Paul means more than simply "Christ in [us], the hope of glory" (Col. 1:27). That reality is true of all true Christians. Rather, Paul prays that Christ will be "at home" in us because of our faithful obedience.

To accomplish all that God desires us to accomplish, Jesus Christ must be welcomed and congenially hosted. His enablement does not come to those who resist him.

III. Pray to Be Established in Love (vv. 17b-19)

Living the Christian life necessitates love as our foundation. When we comprehend and apprehend God's love that forgives, unifies and fills, we become eager to accomplish all God desires. There's no limiting the loving enablement of God on behalf of those who turn to God for spiritual resources.

IV. Pray to Give God Glory (vv. 20-21)

The result of our living out the Christian life will be that God gets glory. Paul prayed that we would apprehend what we comprehend so that God might receive the glory God deserves. When we experience the joy of being all we were intended to be, our lives will be rich and God will be blessed.

The Germans have a word for it—*verstehen*. It means not simply "to understand" but "to be grasped by." Prayer seeks not only "a comprehension of" our spiritual resources but also "a being apprehended by" them. God desires that we know and live out the riches of God's blessings. (Timothy Warren)

CAPTURING GOD'S MIRACULOUS VISION

JOHN 6:1-21

The story of the feeding of the multitude appears in all four Gospels, but John recounts the event with some unique details.

One thing that is clear in John's account is that Jesus is using this miracle as a teaching tool for the disciples. As John is apt to do in his Gospel, he gives an editorial comment in verse 6 that makes it clear what Jesus is thinking. He is testing Philip and the other disciples. There are at least five thousand people with them that day, and Jesus asks, "Where are we to buy bread for these people to eat?" He's already made the decision that they *are* going to feed them; there's no debate there. He just wants to see if the disciples can envision the possibilities for ministering to the crowd.

The first one to speak up is Philip, who has no solution to the problem. He cannot envision anything but helplessness. "There's no way we'd ever have enough money!" he says (paraphrase). The second to respond is Andrew, who actually makes a halfhearted suggestion. He points to a boy who has five loaves and two fish, but almost as soon as the words exit his mouth, he feels embarrassed and doubts himself. He says, "But what are they among so many people?" After Jesus hears these two disciples and their doubts, he takes over and begins giving instructions.

This story has a great deal to say to us as disciples. Are we like Philip, so overwhelmed by the needs and the tasks ahead of us that we feel helpless? Or, are we like Andrew, recognizing a few gifts here and there but failing to see how God can use them? There are many examples of ways in which the church sees only its limits, and so fails to capture the miraculous vision of what God can do.

The person we need to emulate in this story is the nameless little boy who presents his lunch to Andrew. He knows that he only had five loaves and two fish. He knows his meager little lunch is not enough for thousands. Yet he offers it up. He shares what he has. His sharing reveals not only complete trust in Jesus, but also quite a bit of imagination.

Maybe that's why Jesus held up children as an example of faith. Children are willing to believe in miracles. They don't have adult experience and rationality to tell them that some things are impossible. If Jesus wanted to feed thousands of people, this little boy believed he could do it, and he wanted to help.

In the same way, we ought never to put limits on what God can do. So often in the church we want to put limits on God's power, God's compassion, God's forgiveness. We have a hard time believing that God feeds us so miraculously, loves us so extravagantly, and forgives us so completely. We have a hard time envisioning the miraculous work that God can do, and so we fail to offer up our best resources. We don't want to hope for great things, because we pragmatic adults don't want to be disappointed. Yet childlike trust and wide-eyed idealism is the life that Jesus calls us to. If we are willing to loosen our tight grip—if we can let go of our lunch—then God can and will do marvelous things. (Carol Cavin)

DOOR AND WINDOWS

AUGUST

Reflection Verse: "I have removed the boundaries of peoples, and have plundered their treasures; like a bull I have brought down those who sat on thrones. My hand has found, like a nest, the wealth of the peoples; and as one gathers eggs that have been forsaken, so I have gathered all the earth; and there was none that moved a wing, or opened its mouth, or chirped" (Isa. 10:13-14).

The Discipline:

What are your boundaries? Although we hear the word *boundary* used everywhere, I don't think we quite know what it means.

There is a clear pro-boundary movement among white, middle-class people. Right next to these kinds of thoughts are those that are basically pro-immigration. We want immigrants; we want multiculturalism. We approve of "mixt" couples. We welcome the stranger who crosses the boundary to come to the United States.

In *Shifting the Borders*, an interview with Trinh Minh-ha, we are brought to realize how "thoroughly hybrid . . . things are. Other is between us, not out there. Cultures are far from being unitary. We no longer have clear borders. One constantly threads the fine line between positioning and depositioning. One travels transculturally while engaging in the local habitus which links inhabitants."

Chung Yung Kuhn joins her in a basic appreciation of the postmodern "mixt-up-edness." She teases her detractors with these words: "You don't like my syncretism, but you do like the syncretism of orthodox Christianity . . . ?"

One theologian likes boundaries; the other enjoys mixing things up. What can personal boundaries mean, theologically, under these circumstances? Does "boundary theology" have anything to do with Christianity, which mixes God and human in a way that makes it different from all other world religions? What does God really have in mind for the next century? Are we ready? Are we ready to be mixed up?

What are your boundaries? Do you need fence repair? Or, do you need to open some doors?

The Meditation:

God both loves and hates boundaries. God wants people to know themselves and be careful about trespassing on each other. And God also loves the strangers, the ones who cross borders into other lands. This love of the stranger begins early in the Hebrew Scriptures:

> "Strangers shall stand and feed your flocks, foreigners shall till your land and dress your vines; but you shall be called priests of the LORD, you shall be named ministers of our God; you shall enjoy the wealth of the nations, and in their riches you shall glory." (Isa. 61:5-6)

Strangers bring wealth; they do not take it away.

There is going to be a lot of spiritual travel in the next century. A lot of borders are going to be crossed. We might even call our passage a "time travel." How can we cross the right borders and not cross the wrong borders? How can we keep from trespassing while we keep moving?

One way, surely, is through self-definition. When we are aware of the power dynamics in a situation, we are very close to understanding the matter of good adventuring and bad adventuring. Men have at times crossed too many boundaries that women were trying to keep. Why? They didn't understand the self-definition of women. They thought they had permission to violate what was more "his" than "hers."

Simultaneously, many have refused the stranger who might have made them rich in their homes. Many have kept pure thoughts on the matter of interracial or interreligious marriages when they would have been better mixt.

How will we know what to do? By staying close to God, who does show us the way if we simply listen up.

The Song:

You who dwell in the shelter of the LORD,
  who abide in his shadow for life, say to the LORD,

275

"My Refuge, my Rock, in whom I trust." . . .
And God will bear you up
On eagle's wings, bear you on the breath of dawn,
   make you to shine like the sun,
   and hold you in the palm of his hand.
                             (adapted from Psalm 91)

The Prayer:

Spirit of the Edge, let us look both ways—out from where we are and in to where we are, and across the table at the one some think of as other. Let us see ourselves in others, and let others see themselves in us. Let us be so careful of our boundaries that sometimes we cross them and sometimes we keep them. Amen. (Donna Schaper)

AUGUST 6, 2000

Eighth Sunday After Pentecost

Worship Theme: We are nurtured by the gifts of God in Christ. God expects us to use these gifts not only for our own benefit,but also for the benefit of the world.

Readings: 2 Samuel 11:26–12:13*a*; Ephesians 4:1-16; John 6:24-35

Call to Worship (Psalm 51:1, 6-7, 15-17):

Leader: Have mercy on me, O God according to your steadfast love;

***People*: according to your abundant mercy blot out my transgressions.**

Leader: Behold, you desire truth in the inward being; therefore teach me wisdom in my secret heart.

***People*: Purge me with hyssop, and I shall be clean; wash me, and I shall be whiter than snow; O LORD, open my lips, and my mouth shall show forth your praise.**

Leader: For you have no delight in sacrifice; were I to give a burnt offering, you would not be pleased.

***People*: The sacrifice acceptable to God is a broken spirit; a broken and contrite heart, O God, you will not despise.**

Pastoral Prayer:
   Holy and all-loving God, we praise you. In Christ Jesus you have given to us the bread and water of life, living nourishment for our

bodies, souls, and spirits. And can it be? We read in your Holy Scriptures that you have given to us gifts that can help to build your kingdom. Do you really choose to need us? We are staggered with the responsibility. We do not feel up to the task. Many of us, Lord, are so burdened by a deep and long-held sense of worthlessness that your call in our lives seems ludicrous—like a bad joke, and we are the punch line. Heal us and our broken sisters and brothers. Let all know in a deep place in our souls how much you love us, how many gifts you have given to us, and how to use those gifts to increase your love and your justice in this weary world. In Jesus' name we pray. Amen. (Thomas Gildermeister)

SERMON BRIEFS

GOD'S SECRET WEAPON

2 SAMUEL 11:26–12:13a

The naval battles of Trafalgar in 1805 eventually led to the demise of Napoleon by the British. Trafalgar was won because Admiral Horatio Nelson possessed a secret weapon—signal flags.

The technique of communicating over long distances by coded flags had only recently been invented by her majesty's Royal Navy. It revolutionized naval warfare for decades.

The new system allowed the British ships to blanket the vast expanses of ocean, on its search-and-destroy missions, while remaining in close circuit contact with the fleet commander. It also allowed tactical flexibility once the battle raged. While rigid inflexible battle plans bound other navies, the British maneuvered from one place to another with its ships, all because of this secret weapon of signal flags.

God has a secret weapon in the war against satanic ships—conviction. God used it on King David.

I. Conviction: The Displeasure of God (v. 27)

Today's passage, in the words of Kenneth Chafin, "pictures one of the most dramatic moments in the Old Testament, a God who cares, challenging the action of one of his children. A year had passed and even the gossips at the palace had quit talking about what David had done, while a few cynics were still complaining, 'I told you nothing would happen.' David's sin, however, did not go unnoticed nor unchallenged by God" (*The Communicator's Commentary* [Dallas: Word Publishing, 1989], p. 305). David's indiscretion absolutely repulsed and displeased the Lord. Conviction informs us of God's displeasure about something in our lives.

II. Conviction: The Voice of Spiritual Conscience (vv. 1-4)

A year passed before God's prophet Nathan moved to confront David and his "secret" sin. We have the opportunity to look back on the incident, but Nathan did not. It could have been quite a long time before he learned of the possibility of the affair. As he listened to the gossip, he had to sort out the difference between true and false. He observed David's actions and reactions. He talked with God, planned his approach, and weighed the timing of his approach. Nathan desired to be right before he became the voice of David's spiritual conscience.

III. Conviction: The Birth of Inner Turmoil (vv. 5-6)

Nathan's parable penetrated the facade of smugness that David used to cover himself. This masterful sermon wove the tapestry of David's deceit from the fabric of sinful behavior. Nathan dared to preach the truth through a parable. What David heard caused outrage at the sheep stealer in Nathan's story. He asked himself, "Who could be so arrogant, self-centered, self-righteous, greedy, and mean-spirited?" David's soul burned within him in a turmoil of thought.

IV. Conviction: The Pointing of God's Finger (vv. 7-10)

David's angry response was, "The man who did this deserves to die!" No sooner had David's words poured from his lips, Nathan pointedly said, "*You* are the man." Nathan pronounced God's judgment on David's actions. Interestingly, Nathan lists God's blessings on David:

— anointing
— deliverance from Saul's wrath
— David's wives
— God's protection in unfriendly circumstances
— provision for his needs

Yet David mocked God's goodness by rebelliously disobeying God's commandment against adultery, which led to deception and ultimately murder. No sin is hidden from the eyes of God.

V. Conviction: The Author of Repentance (vv. 11-13a)

David finally had enough spiritual sense to come to his knees in repentance. "I have sinned against the LORD" (v. 13a). No sin can be forgiven until a conscious acknowledgment of wrongdoing is admitted. Conviction brought David back to God, and forgiveness followed.

God's secret weapon is being signaled to your heart by the Holy Spirit at this moment. What sin do you need to repent to the Lord? (Derl Keefer)

BODY BUILDING

EPHESIANS 4:1-16

Can one get enough exercise in prison? Indeed, Paul, writing from prison, proves that there are areas in which one can always get enough exercise and that he is a "trainer" par excellence in those disciplines. The body that Paul is so concerned with building up is, of course, the church, which is greatly enhanced as its members practice those primary virtues of humility, gentleness, and patience, which Paul highlights here. As these are exercised, they are strengthened. These particular qualities also especially encourage growth in unity of the body (one of Paul's main concerns) because they "do not quench the Spirit" (1 Thess. 5:19).

I. Biceps and Gray Matter, Too

Within the unity of this "one body and one Spirit," there are special gifts given to each person or part. You may have heard the riddle about the child who was in a terrible car accident with his father. The father was dead on arrival at the hospital. But when they took the young boy into the operating room for emergency surgery, the doctor said, "I can't operate on him. He's my son." How can that be?

Well, the history of this riddle charts one area of our awareness in exercising various gifts and skills. When I heard it for the first time some years ago, no one could figure out the answer to the riddle. Today it is much more likely that, even if the person hasn't heard it before, someone will come up with the solution, which is, of course, that the doctor is the child's mother. This can remind us of how very recent in Western culture the victory of women's freedom to use their gifts as doctors really is.

Paul, a captive, writes of freedom from the captivity of small imaginations, especially since Jesus has been here, there, and everywhere and so can "fill all things."

II. Growth of God-given Gifts Rules

Paul, the peace-loving conservative, still challenges the church to let each one be all that he or she can be. For the very same reason, Frank Sinatra was well known as someone absolutely against prejudice, because he wanted all races to be allowed to perform in the clubs. For instance, a black entertainer's skin color could not be used as a means of preventing that person from using his or her musical talents because that person's gifts were a gift to everyone. Sinatra fought hard for that in a time when it was generally a very unpopular position.

But it is certainly the same enlightened stance urged by Paul for the same most reasonable reason: Everyone's gifts are valuable and needed by the whole, so they should all be carefully cultivated, aligned by awareness of the truth, and generously equipped with the necessary resources to fulfill the promise of each person or part.

III. The Mind-body Connection

Right knowledge is as essential to coordination in this body as virtue, because those who are confused by tricks and lies are no longer reliable parts of the community. So sometimes a word of clarification must be spoken. The church would usually rather "be nice" than speak the truth when it's painful. But Paul's qualifier, that it be spoken "in love," makes this absolutely necessary "word of truth" possible, bearable, and even helpful to build up the body "in love."

In deference to the importance of the free and encouraged exercise of all of God's gifts in all of God's people, the church did, and will continue to, equip all the saints for its ministry in Christ, with an ever-broadening imagination and vision about how big a circle that "all" can be drawn around. (Kathleen Peterson)

WORKING FOR THE GIFT

JOHN 6:24-35

Come spring and summer in our loop of the Bible Belt, Wednesday nights, choir programs, missions activities, prayer meetings, and Bible studies are diminished by all the various practices, games, and dance rehearsals that we call "enrichment activities." Sadly, I fear that many of the coaches, players, and families involved do not feel themselves to be in any way impoverished by these pursuits.

That story applies to many other people and during many other seasons. How hard we chase after and work for things that won't endure. How easily we abandon the seeking that can manifest eternal life. How often we "enrich" ourselves into spiritual impoverishment. This deep irony is at the heart of the human predicament.

Ironies abound in the Gospel lesson, ironies that began last week as Jesus fed the five thousand, and which will continue throughout this section from John 6. In our text, many of those Jesus fed came looking for another of his caterings. Among the many ironies mentioned in the lesson, these are key:

— There are many "seeking" Jesus, but they do not want to "follow" him.

— The people call him Rabbi, but they are not willing to learn.

— The people clamor after bread, but they do not want to be filled.

And while the people spend considerable energy locating

Jesus, Jesus considers it wasted energy: "Do not labor for the bread which perishes, but for that which is imperishable." This is a lesson the people will not easily hear.

It's an odd imperative, really, to work for a gift. Normally we work for wages; gifts come effortlessly. But here in our lection we see one more irony, one commanded by Jesus and echoed by the desert fathers and mothers in their quest for spiritual progress. They maintained that unity with God, or eternal life, is the goal of all spiritual striving (requiring all our energies and efforts), but it is utterly unreachable by any work or program. Requiring all our work, the results are yet a gift.

Put another way, consider that the second clause of the Shema ("You shall love the LORD your God with all your heart, and with all your soul, and with all your might") is both a command and a promise. We are required to love the LORD with everything we have, and we have not the ability to do so lest God enables us.

The crowds that sought after Jesus were filled to the point of starvation. They chased after him, but were unwilling to follow. They wanted what he would give, but were unwilling to give in return.

Many in the crowds following Jesus even today could be described in much the same way, and we ourselves likewise. But we may prove ourselves disciples instead by hearing the command to work for the bread that lasts, by believing in the One whom God has sent, and by working for the gift of eternal life. (Thomas R. Steagald)

AUGUST 13, 2000

Ninth Sunday After Pentecost

Worship Theme: A life in Jesus Christ is a life for all time and beyond all time; eternity can begin now.

Readings: 2 Samuel 18:5-9, 15, 31-33; Ephesians 4:24–5:2; John 6:35, 41-51

Call to Worship (Psalm 130:1-8):

> *Leader:* Out of the depths I cry to you, O LORD, hear my voice!
>
> ***People:*** **Let your ears be attentive to the voice of my supplications!**
>
> *Leader:* If you, O LORD, should mark iniquities, LORD, who could stand?
>
> ***People:*** **But there is forgiveness with you, that you may be worshiped.**
>
> *Leader:* I wait for the LORD, my soul waits, in the LORD's word I hope;
>
> ***People:*** **my soul waits for the LORD more than those who watch for the morning, more than those who watch for the morning.**
>
> *Leader:* O Israel, hope in the LORD! For with the LORD there is steadfast love, with the LORD is plenteous redemption.
>
> ***People:*** **And the LORD will redeem Israel from all iniquities.**

Pastoral Prayer:

Eternal God, everlasting Christ, we are so very humbled to hear the good news that coming to you and believing in you means we begin life anew. That the slate is wiped clean. That eternal life and perfect love can start now. That as risky and frightening as a life with you may seem, we are never alone. You are with us. God, with our mouths we claim that we want to help bring your kingdom to earth. That we want to help reduce to rubble the walls of oppression and intolerance. That we want to love as your Son, Jesus Christ, loves. But our actions suggest another intention. Our daily lives are all the evidence any jury would need to convict us of apathy, and even complicity, in the dire problems of our time. Forgive us. Help us to walk with Jesus. Help us to have integrity and a life that is pleasing in your sight. Amen. (Thomas Gildermeister)

SERMON BRIEFS

THE LOVE OF DECEPTION

2 SAMUEL 18:5-9, 15, 31-33

My father is an avid fisherman. In retirement, he does it almost exclusively. His grandson, my son, also enjoys the sport of fishing. When I go with them I hold a pole in my hand, but I get bored quickly. Dad must have a hundred lures, one for each species of fish, and he knows exactly which one to use. Occasionally we will get a school of fish that we can't haul out fast enough. They seem to just jump onto the line, as the lure seems to possess magical powers. The fish have a weakness for that color or wiggle of the lure, and the temptation is too great for them not to bite.

King David's son Absalom bit at several lures, but the one he liked best was deception.

— Absalom deceived his brother Amnon and had him killed (2 Sam. 14:23-33).
— Absalom deceived the people of Israel by telling them lies about the king (2 Sam. 15:5-6).

— Absalom deceived his father for his own rebellion (2 Sam. 15:7-12).

The lure of his deceptive heart ultimately kills him.

I. His Deception Ushered in Through Lies (vv. 5-9)

There are many avenues for people to stumble and fall, and Satan drives each one of them. Satan exploits each weakness we exhibit. The devil aimed at Absalom's deficient power—lies.

1. He lied to Amnon. The story of Amnon's rape of their sister, Tamar, enraged Absalom so much that Absalom seduced Amnon to believe for two years that the not-so-secret sin was forgotten. Absalom tricked and lied his way into Amnon's good graces and, while Amnon was drunk, had his brother killed.

2. He lied to his father in order to steal Dad's throne. Casual reading of the Scripture reveals David's love for his son Absalom, but Absalom's total rebellion demonstrated his disrespect toward his father. Sad. Oliver Wendell Holmes stated, "Sin has many tools, but a lie is the handle which fits them all."

A mother was shocked to discover that her son had told a fib. Taking the boy aside for a heart-to-heart chat, she graphically explained the evil of lying. She said, "A tall green man with one red eye and two sharp horns grabs little boys who tell lies and flies them to Mars. On Mars, the little boys are forced to dig in a dark deep canyon for fifty years. "Now," she concluded, "you won't tell a lie again, will you, Junior?" He replied, "No, Mommy, because you tell better ones."

Lying destroys our credibility.

II. Deception Is the Wrong Choice (v. 15)

If we choose to be deceptive with people, we have chosen to hurt them. God wants the best for people, and desires for God's people to want the very best for others. The biblical standard for the Christian is agape love, a love that stems from our will, not our emotions.

In a sermon on May 19, 1998, Tom Hermiz said, "Agape love means that my will says I must treat my neighbor with respect." Philia love is the warm fuzzy emotional attachment to self and others. Agape love has a richer meaning, for it is bonded to the "will" of the person. I *choose* to treat my neighbor, spouse, friend, enemy, and God right. That is why I can love my neighbor, because I *choose* the right; but I don't have to like his or her personality, because that goes by feeling while focusing on self.

Deception robs me of my choice of right relationship.

III. Deception Destroys in the End (vv. 31-33)

Second Samuel 15:14 says that David told his men they must leave, "or we shall not escape from Absalom." This son would kill his father if he had the opportunity. Deception has destruction as its goal:

— destroys marriages   — destroys peace
— destroys children   — destroys hope
— destroys churches   — destroys salvation

Don't be lured by deception lest you too shall be destroyed. (Derl Keefer)

LIVING IN LOVE

EPHESIANS 4:25–5:2

My prayer for this congregation is that Paul's description of the church in Ephesians will always come true more and more here. This letter seems to have been circulated to all the churches, and it is a celebration and description of how life in the church should be different from the life the "pagan" Gentiles led, and much of the world still leads.

The big idea is that there can be a community that is so different from the world that it is strikingly distinctive, and not because of any particular outward appearance of any kind. The distinguishing thing about it would be how the people lived together in love. Notice how this is not every man, woman, and child on their own in an isolated relationship with God. It's about how they live in love with each other, God helping them. "But that's so general," you say. "Love means different things to different people. How do you 'do' that?" Paul's instructions here are precise and his answers provocative.

287

I. First, Stop Lying

This tells us a lot about the people in the early Greek church. They must have been well known for their lying, which, in fact, was quite acceptable in that culture if it was expedient. Darius told Herodotus, "When telling a lie will be profitable, let it be told." Paul told the new Gentile Christians, "Let all of us speak the truth to our neighbors."

Paul gives reasons, too. Why not lie to each other? Because "we are members of one another." We really are connected. What hurts you, hurts me, and vice versa. And lies really hurt, because they keep us in a bondage of confusion. To give someone false information is like giving him or her an incorrect road map; that person tries to find his or her way then with information that can only get them more lost because it's not true.

We had a frozen custard stand in our family when I was growing up. I remember my father coming home one night very angry. It seems a customer had asked the guys working there how to get somewhere and the guys made up long, complicated, phony directions and sent the customer off on a wild goose chase. They were talking and laughing about it; they didn't hear my father come in the back. He fired them all, on the spot.

It's even more serious to send someone off on a wild goose chase in their mind because you've given them false information. And of course that can have very real consequences in the physical world. Remember Jesus' words: "You will know the truth, and the truth will make you free" (John 8:32 NRSV)?

We really are on a search for the truth, the whole truth and nothing but the truth, together. Anyone who clouds the issue clouds the revelation of the truth for everyone. There is an awareness in the world that is opening on the truth, and we want to work for and with that, not against it.

This is really more than the Old Testament commandment "Thou shalt not lie." It goes beyond that to "Let us speak the truth."

II. Anger Is No Excuse for Sin

Paul is probably quoting Psalm 4:4, and this also sounds a bit like James 1:19-20. If anger isn't a justifiable cause for sin, a lot of anger would immediately be found useless. Best we take the psalmist's advice and ponder in silence on our beds what we can do with righteous indignation that can promote righteousness.

III. Stop Stealing

Work honestly with your own hands so you have something to give. The change of heart that goes with honesty is generosity, adding to the garment rather than "ripping it off."

IV. Give Grace in Your Words

What marvelous power we have to build up one another with simple good words, as is so beautifully shown in Job 4:4, and as Moffatt translates: "Your words have kept men on their feet." (See also Proverbs 25:11 and 15:23.)

V. Be Kind to One Another

Tender hearts and forgiveness make it possible for love to be "practiced" over and over again, until we get it all right. (Kathleen Peterson)

EDUCATION FOR THE SOUL

JOHN 6:35, 41-51

Simone Weil once suggested that real spiritual transformation could begin only when pilgrims let go of their "imaginary position as the center" of things (*A Guide to Prayer for Ministers and Other Servants* [Nashville: Upper Room, 1983], p. 73). Since "self" will ever be humans' abiding idolatry—"false divinity," she calls it—the denial of self is part and parcel of true discipleship. Our selfishness is so insidious, however, as to prevent easy detection. Its malignancy is so invisible as to prevent easy eradication (cf. Psalm 19:12). And how often we imagine, never thinking ourselves vain, that our wishes are God's commands and that our expectations constitute hope.

Last week we saw a sad irony—full-bellied followers staring at their toothpicks, idly asking Jesus for some sign that would prove to them that he truly was God's gift to the world, someone, in other words, who met their expectations of what a Messiah ought to be. The crowds had been willing to concede that Jesus was a prophet on the order of Moses: His provision of bread and walking on the water connoted the manna eaten by their forebears and deliverance at the Red Sea. So full of the moment were the crowds that they were going to proclaim him king, and in their minds the best kind—a provider who makes no demands. Of course he will be king, but not as they imagine. Sure enough, in our lesson the sermon has begun and Jesus is proving grander than Moses in both his giving and in his requiring. "I am the bread of life," he says, the first of his seven "I am" sayings, and in so saying he promises to satisfy more than their hungry stomachs. But they must believe to be filled. And to believe, of course, they must see past their expectations. They must renounce their selfish and vain imaginings. "We know this guy, don't we?" Such was the crowd's response. "Why, he's only Mary and Joseph's son. How can he be the Bread of Life?"

"We know this guy, don't we?" Such is often our response. "He's a peasant/sage/guru/cynic. How can we responsibly say there is more to him than that?"

"We know this guy, don't we? We know how God works. We'll believe as we've always believed. We want from God what we want from God." We seldom wonder if what we want from God bears any relationship to what God wants from us. That, of course, is the bad news. The good news, though, is that there is mystery at work in and through Christ that is greater than all our objections, and ultimately more powerful than all our idolatries.

In verse 45 of our text, Jesus says that all who come to him do so because they have been taught by God; they have heard and learned from God. Disciples are those, in other words, who have been "educated." The word means "drawn out."

True disciples, those being truly transformed, are being drawn out of their selfishness, idolatry, and idle expectations; they are drawn out of the "world" and toward Christ. They are able to renounce their place at the center, and find their centering in him. (Thomas R. Steagald)

AUGUST 20, 2000

Tenth Sunday After Pentecost

Worship Theme: The sacrifice of Jesus Christ is the proof of God's love for and in the world.

Readings: 1 Kings 2:10-12; 3:3-14; Ephesians 5:15-20; John 6

Call to Worship (Psalm 111:1-3, 10):

Leader: Praise the LORD.

People: **I will give thanks to the LORD with my whole heart, in the company of the upright, in the congregation.**

Leader: Great are the works of the LORD, studied by all who have pleasure in them.

People: **Full of honor and majesty are the works of the LORD whose righteousness endures for ever. The fear of the LORD is the beginning of wisdom; all those who practice it have a good understanding. The praise of the LORD endures for ever.**

Pastoral Prayer:
   Our God in heaven, we lift up a song of gratitude, of thanksgiving and praise that burns in our hearts. You have loved us so much, offering to us a life of challenge and a life of joy through the body and blood of our Lord Christ Jesus. But have we refused your love? So many of us claim to know you, but we live a life of possessiveness, greed, corruption, and resentment. We acquire more and more stuff, declaring our allegiance to it and not to you. We can never get enough, as we look upon our destitute brothers and sisters who lack the basic necessities of food,

clothing, homes, family, health, and freedom. O Lord, forgive us. Give us the faith to eat only of the body of Christ, so that we might be more like him. O God, in your mercy, hear our prayer. Amen. (Thomas Gildermeister)

SERMON BRIEFS

SOLOMON'S PRAYER: MODEL OF SINCERITY

1 KINGS 2:10-12, 3:3-14

David Polish wrote, "Prayer is not an investigation, it is experience. Prayer is not a shopping list in the supermarket of the universe. We should not pray 'Help me win,' but rather 'Help me live'" (C. Neil Strait, *The Speaker's Book of Inspiration* [Atlanta: Drake House, 1972], p. 135).

On a continual basis Solomon offered sacrifices to his God at the tabernacle in Gibeon. It was here that Solomon met God in an encounter that would forever change his life. Russell Dilday wrote, "Here the God of heaven bends down to grant the supplication of a man and graciously puts the key to all his treasures in the young king's hand. Within the bounds of reason, Solomon could have obtained anything he wished" (Lloyd Ogilvie, *The Communicator's Commentary: 1, 2 Kings* [Dallas: Word Publishing, 1987], p. 68).

Solomon's request and God's response provide a classic study of the subject of prayer.

I. Prayer As a Lifestyle

In their book *Fully Alive* (Kansas City, Mo.: Beacon Hill, 1997), Jerry and Larry Hull remind us that people are to live a life of wholeness. This includes "integration," meaning that life is built around a single purpose or unified focus. Another ingredient of wholeness is "harmony," living with inner tranquility and in proper relationship to the Creator and the creation. When integration and harmony combine, they produce a balance in life. The Hull brothers define that as "steadiness and stability in all areas of life."

Praying becomes a lifestyle that allows us to become spiritually connected with God for a lifetime through open communication—prayer.

II. Prayer with a Persistent Heart

In *A Life of Prayer* (Dallas: Word Publishing, 1998, pp. 151-52), Paul Cedar quotes Wesley Duewel's hard-hitting words:

> The great need of our world, our nation, and our churches is people who know how to prevail in prayer. Moments of pious wishes blandly expressed to God once or twice a day will bring little change on earth or among the people. Kind thoughts expressed to him in five or six sentences, after reading a paragraph or two mildly religious sentiments once a day from some devotional writing, will not bring the kingdom of God to earth or shake the gates of hell and repel the attacks of evil on our culture and our civilization. Results, not beautiful words, are the test of prevailing prayer.

Our task in prayer is not to twist God's arm into doing what we want, but to singly let God know of our needs. The gospel truth is that we do not insist, we persist.

III. Prayer with a Listening Heart

Several years ago I thought I was having hearing problems. People would have to repeat themselves because I could not hear them. Finally, I made an appointment with a hearing aid company for hearing testing. The morning appointment had me a bit nervous because I worried about the outcome. The test went smoothly. After a few minutes, the man administering the test told me I had "perfect" hearing. I'll never forget what he said: "Mr. Keefer, your problem is that you aren't listening. You have selective hearing. You've tuned people out."

After that day, I began to focus more on what people were saying to me. Unfortunately, many of us do the same with God. We tune God out. My challenge is for you to listen more intently to God. It's amazing what God has to say, if we just listen.

Dear friends, it's time to pray. (Derl Keefer)

SINGING HEARTS

EPHESIANS 5:15-20

All these spiritual disciplines that Paul shares here in Ephesians are to help us handle our lives with care. They are gifts, as words to the wise. They are treasures we can carry with us everywhere and still travel light.

I. Internal Equipment

My daughter Cara, who is in her twenties now, has two big dogs. One is almost as big as she is and weighs more. When Cara comes to visit us, she usually brings the dogs. She can just let them, without a leash, run out the back door, and when she calls them they come right back.

My younger son, Aaron, asked her, "How come your dogs don't run away?"

"Because I've trained them," Cara said.

I said I had wondered if it would be good to have a dog whistle. But Cara said that she has trained them to respond to her voice and her hands because "those are things I always have with me."

Cara continued, "For something so important, you can't depend on something you might not have with you. You don't train them with treats or whistles. If there's a car coming, and the dog doesn't respond because you don't have treats or whistles with you, the dog could get killed."

I thought, "What a wonderful way to look at our lives and respond to each other, too, in terms of what we always have with us—*who* we are and *how* we are." We may have a nice house and car and clothes today; but tomorrow, who knows? It's the character traits inside us that we always have with us, such as kindness, thoughtfulness, honesty, and so forth. If we have cultivated these, we can *depend* on their availability, and no one can snatch them away. God, Jesus, and the Holy Spirit are the other resources promised as always being accessible to us, in one form or another.

II. Strength in Repetition

Paul knows the law of life, that the more something happens, the more likely it is to happen again. You don't stop smoking by smoking another cigarette, even if you *call* it your last cigarette. You stop smoking by not smoking another cigarette. Things gain momentum by way of repetition. Instead of becoming a drunkard with addictive beverages, let the Spirit lift you.

III. Singing Strength

Songs travel light, too. Paul gives the oft-unnoticed counsel that music and singing are very important and healthy for the good life in Christ. How many times lately have you heard it prescribed to go about "singing and making melody to the LORD in your hearts"?

This is right up John and Charles Wesley's alley. They took popular melodies of their day, many of them tunes from tavern songs, set glorious words of wisdom and faith to them, and gave them out as rich, sumptuous spiritual food in the form of about nine thousand hymns and poems.

John Wesley's directions for singing, in the 1761 hymnal for which his brother Charles wrote so many hymns, tell us how seriously they took these "heaven-sent" songs:

Learn these tunes before you learn any others; afterwards learn as many as you please.

Sing them exactly as they are printed here, without altering or mending them at all; and if you have learned to sing them otherwise, unlearn it as soon as you can.

Sing all. See that you join with the congregation as frequently as you can. Let not a slight degree of weakness or weariness hinder you. If it is a cross to you, take it up, and you will find it a blessing.

Sing lustily and with a good courage. Beware of singing as if you were half dead, or half asleep; but lift up your voice with strength. Be no more afraid of your voice now, nor more ashamed of its being heard, than when you sung the songs of Satan.

Sing modestly. Do not bawl, so as to be heard above or distinct from the rest of the congregation, that you may not destroy the harmony; but strive to unite your voices together, so as to make one clear melodious sound.

Sing in time. . . . Do not run before nor stay behind it . . . and take care not to sing too slow.

Above all sing spiritually. Have an eye to God in every word you sing. Aim at pleasing him more than yourself, or any other creature. In order to do this, attend strictly to the sense of what you sing, and see that your heart is not carried away with the sound, but offered to God continually. . . .

The Wesleys' vision of music, carried in the heart and mind as the happy bearer of their theology (its content *and* spirit), was precisely what Paul was commending here as one of the great and so easily portable resources of our lives. (Kathleen Peterson)

SYMBOLS AND SACRAMENTS

JOHN 6:51-58

Lee, a wonderfully crotchety old Presbyterian, used to scold me—and all Methodists—saying, "You Methodists don't take doctrine seriously." He was slopping the paint with too big a brush, to be sure, but you can understand his pique. Though Wesley was a formidable thinker, his heirs have tended toward the experiential rather than the formulaic; we are inclined to consider too-precise expressions of faith as prescriptive rather than descriptive, and thus more divisive than inclusive. Since we are sure that no doctrine can "photograph reality" (H. A. Williams, cited in *A Guide to Prayer for Ministers and Other Servants* [Nashville: Upper Room, 1983], p. 120), we content ourselves with other expressions of faith. As I assured Lee, there is a doctrinal basis for such a stance, but he only growled.

Still, I can't help thinking that our practical dismission of doctrine in favor of "hertzenreligion" is a false deconstruction. After all, as Henri Nouwen so aptly put it, "doctrines are not alien formulations which we must adhere to, but the documentation of the most profound human experiences which, transcending time and place, are handed over from generation to generation as a light in our darkness" (*A Guide to Prayer*, p. 262).

In our lesson, we have doctrine pure and simple, though not so simple as to be easy, and not so pure as to be without controversy. It is, of course, the eucharistic theology of the early church, or at least of John's church, for next week we will see that even some of Jesus' disciples (other churches?) are unable to abide this particular doctrine. Whatever historical nuances may lie behind the text, this sermon is doctrinal as Nouwen would describe doctrine.

It is not an alien formulation designed merely for the adhering, but a description of the most profound experiences of disciples with their Lord—those who know that without Christ feeding us and giving us the nourishment of his own life, we have no life in us.

This description is the basis of our understanding of Sacrament.

Coming to Methodism after growing up Baptist, I had to come to peace with the Methodist understanding of the Sacraments. (Later, I came to see such doctrine as not Methodist but "catholic.") Comparing and contrasting with, and not wanting altogether to jettison, my received tradition, the formula I derived is essentially this: An ordinance (the normal designation in Baptist life for baptism and Lord's Supper) is what we do as a pledge to God. It is our way of saying that we will remain true to God come what may. Since the ordinances are voluntary, participation in them must be preceded by an understanding of and accession to the faith. Consequently, as my grandmother used to say, one "has to be old enough to know what he's (or she's) doing."

Nor would Methodists disagree entirely. When one is baptized, all the baptized renew their vows to God in light of God's grace. Still, in harmony with many other traditions, we Methodists affirm that the first movement of baptism and Holy Communion belongs always to God. The Sacraments are God's "ordinary" way of pledging to us that presence and power and strength will stay with us come what may. Consequently, the only one who has to be old enough to know what's going on is God.

In this lesson, set at the time of Passover and recalling God's deliverance of Israel from Egypt, Jesus preaches a doctrinal sermon on the deliverance provided for his followers. It's not the most palatable of sermons, but those who abide in Christ will come to understand that what Jesus says is true, both theologically and experientially. Those who abide in him will do so because they feast upon him. Life will be theirs. (Thomas R. Steagald)

AUGUST 27, 2000

Eleventh Sunday After Pentecost

Worship Theme: The good news of God in Christ is spirit and life, yet offensive and repulsive to many.

Readings: 1 Kings 8:(1, 6, 10-11) 22-30, 41-43; Ephesians 6:10-20; John 6:56-69

Call to Worship (Psalm 84:1-4):

Leader: How lovely is your dwelling place, O LORD of hosts!

PEOPLE: **My soul longs, indeed it faints for the courts of the LORD; my heart and flesh sing for joy to the living God.**

Leader: O LORD of hosts, my Ruler and my God, at your altars even the sparrow finds a home, and the swallow a nest for herself, where she may lay her young.

People: **Blessed are those who dwell in your house, ever singing your praise!**

Pastoral Prayer:
Dear God, in your Son and our Lord Jesus Christ you have loved us beyond measure and offended us to the bone. The life to which you call us is sweet and full of joy, when we take the risk to live such a life. But to consider this life of costly discipleship seems horrid to many of us. O holy Lord, open our eyes. Please show our brothers and sisters who want to flee from your love that life with you is sweet. It is filled with peace. And for those who have set their course on the path of Christ, assure them that they are protected by the armor of truth, righteousness, peace, faith, salvation, and the Spirit. Amen. (Thomas Gildermeister)

SERMON BRIEFS

GOD IN THE SANCTUARY

1 KINGS 8:(1, 6, 10-11) 22-30, 41-43

During the Kennedy days, Robert Kennedy visited villages in the jungles of the Amazon. There he conversed with several of the Brazilian Indians. He met one who had recently been converted to Christianity. Through a translator, Kennedy asked, "What do you most like to do?" Kennedy expected an answer like, "Hunting with bows and arrows, or canoeing."

The villager gave an interesting answer: "Being occupied by God." Kennedy said to the translator, "Ask him again. Something may be lost in translation." The truth was the man knew exactly what he was saying. He gave an authentic definition of true worship (Roy Zuck, *The Speaker's Quote Book* [Grand Rapids: Kregel Publications, 1997], pp. 425-26).

In the text, the occasion is the completing of the Temple in Jerusalem and bringing of the ark of the covenant (Agreement) into the Holy of Holies (the most holy place in the Temple) by the priests. The ark is set under the wings of the golden creatures as a special place of honor. The people of Israel and their king make a presupposition about this occasion in their nation, a guarantee of God's presence, no matter what they do. Walter Brueggemann wrote that this section is a long, complicated one that developed over a long period of controversies in Israel.

Solomon's prayer of dedication of the sanctuary of God offers three concepts of God in the sanctuary.

I. The Sanctuary: A Place of Meeting (vv. 1-6)

The sanctuary structure reveals a place set apart for meeting with God.

A place for the family to meet with God: Robert Couchman wrote that "a true family consists of two or more people who care unconditionally for one another and share in the collective health and security of the unit as well as in supporting and helping each member to secure his or her full potential and achieve personal fulfillment" (Albert M. Wells, Jr., compiler, *Inspiring Quotations* [Nashville: Thomas Nelson Publishers, 1988], p. 69).

The sanctuary is a place where the family love unit bonds with God.

A *place of holiness:* The sanctuary is a holy place where the awe of God inspires, convicts, and redeems the person because it is one of the places where individuals meet God.

II. The Sanctuary: A Place of Promise (vv. 22-30)

Solomon reminds the people through his prayer that God's promise offers unfailing love for all. There are four basic premises of promise:

— God's justice and holiness, which will not allow God to deceive;
— God's grace and goodness, which will not allow God to forget;
— God's truth and honesty, which will not allow God to change;
— God's power and might, which will not allow God to fail.

Solomon's hope lies in the God of forever.

III. The Sanctuary: A Place of Prayer and Praise

"The unmistakable mark of a living faith is a readiness to praise," says Howard H. Jones. What better place to praise than in the sanctuary of God.

Praise in worship: J. H. Morrison stated that worship is an inward reverence as the spirit bows down in the presence of a holy God, an awesome dependence on God, in a solemn consciousness of the divine in revelation.

Praise in miracles: Observing the power and inherent ability of the supernaturalness of God.

Praise in respect: In our age of familiarity, we tend to view God as the "man upstairs" or "the big guy in the sky." Such familiarity breeds contempt.

A wholesome need for respect must not cloud our view of God's closeness and availability to us.

A little boy whose dad had been promoted to brigadier general asked, "Do you think he will mind if I still call him 'Daddy'?"

In our respect, God still loves for us to call him "Abba" ("Daddy").

As the psalmist wrote, "LORD all-powerful, how lovely is your Temple! I want more than anything to be in the courtyards of the LORD's Temple. My whole being wants to be with the living God" (Psalm 84:1-2 NCV). (Derl Keefer)

NOT A ROSE GARDEN?

EPHESIANS 6:10-20

So, you say you were sure the invitation said "tea and biscuits in the rose garden" and not "mortal combat in the desert"?

It's always interesting to me when people seem surprised that something bad happened to them. Everyone except the very youngest child knows that bad things happen. Still, many seem to think that this badness is not to be taken seriously until it directly affects them. Then when it does affect them, they want to know why them. Well, that's a perfectly understandable question that deserves careful examination. But it is simply the age-old question of evil, and often not answerable.

I. There's a War Going on Out There

Here in Ephesians, Paul is turning his attention from his good words about how loving and gracious life *within* the church can be, to the warfare it will be subjected to from *without*. There is evil, he says simply. It's out there. It will attack you. Be ready. Arm yourself. Don't imagine you will have special immunity from it.

This reminds me of my daughter Cara saying that she told a friend, "You know, there are a lot of poisonous snakes in Southern Illinois."

Her friend answered simply, "Yes, that's why you have a shotgun." It turned out that the fellow was *from* Southern Illinois. He said he remembered his mother standing on the front porch in the mornings with the shotgun shooting rattlesnakes so the family could go outside.

When Cara visited that area one autumn, she heard on the radio one day that certain roads were closed for "the annual snake crossing" because the snakes were about to migrate. "At certain times," she said, "you just don't go outside in certain places if you're not armed."

You would want to know about that if it were happening in your neighborhood, wouldn't you? And about how to protect yourself.

Well, we may not feel like we're under direct attack a lot of the time. We may not be aware of the poison lurking around us. But this is a spiritual battle Paul is talking about, not one "of flesh and blood." So it is more subtle, but even more serious, because our spirit is at stake.

I recently heard Herbert Schiller, professor emeritus of communications at the University of California, San Diego, talk about the "mysterious and sophisticated manipulation" of our minds today. He said there are very powerful forces of evil that "we don't see so much, so they're harder to deal with." He said that "what's going on is literally a silent massacre of peoples' hopes, peoples' lives, and peoples' futures."

Now, this man is not a preacher, but he sounds a lot like Paul. And he too is saying, "You better arm yourself." He starts just where Paul does, with the armor of truth. "I would not have you uninformed," says Paul, with Jesus. We have to be careful to study the Word, to think and pray, and study and think, and then pray some more.

II. Just to Stand with the Saints

When Paul talks about "the sword of the Spirit, which is the word of God," he means the living word. Not just Holy Scripture. Right in the next line Paul says "Pray *in the Spirit* at all times in every prayer and supplication" (v. 18). This is the same thing Jesus was talking about in Luke 12:12.

There are many things we need to arm ourselves with, to "be able to withstand on that evil day, and having done everything, to stand firm" (v. 13). Which also tells us that we win not by slaying the enemy. This is not a battle in which we attack. We win just by standing firm and holding our own ground.

III. Poison-proof Gear

A lot of people know life is no rose garden, so they can't be taken unaware. But hardship can wear down the spirit, and many lives have been just used up or totally distorted by too heavy doses of adversity. Protect your life, Paul says, the very life of your Spirit, with these invisible armors—first truth, then righteousness—and take the high ground. Put on readiness to proclaim the gospel of peace.

Faith, Paul says, is like a big, deep shield, with which we can quench the flaming arrows of the evil one. Fiery darts were one of the most dangerous weapons in ancient warfare. And we know how faintheartedness and the loss of faith's vision can strike us down like a fiery arrow in the heart. Faith protects the vision of God's goodness from doubts, fears, and distractions that can really kill it.

Salvation is the ultimate lifesaver and keeper. But don't just pray for yourselves, Paul concludes. Pray for all the saints—everyone in the church—and for him too, he says, as he continues to teach that even prison chains need not prevent boldness in unlocking the "mystery of the gospel." (Kathleen Peterson)

DEFECTIONS AND CONFESSIONS

JOHN 6:56-69

When I was in seminary, full of brash and pop, there were many others just as brash who would pop off now and then as to how the church they served was doing. Only, we couldn't always agree on the criteria for comparable evaluations. The bookstore was full of "church growth" manuals which proposed that attendance and membership increases were the very definition of successful ministry. Full pews meant faithfulness, and those student-preachers whose churches were growing held fast to the manuals' doctrine.

There were other, grimmer students, however (and mostly guys in the Old Testament department, now that I think of it), who countered that in Samaria, for example, church attendance was booming, but God sent prophets to thunder at these church-loving people for adhering to a "form" of religion without its disciplines. Flush with remnant theology, these preachers as much as implied that the only good pew was a near-empty pew; the few made them proud. Faithful, prophetic ministry could entertain no more.

I was never happy with those alternatives, and have since come to imagine that "full pews vs. empty pews" is a false disjunct. At least that seems to be the lesson of John 6; in the course of seventy-one verses, we see both big crowds and no crowds, lots of disciples and few disciples, miracles that draw standing-room-only crowds, and teachings that empty the house. Oh, and we see one more thing—a wonderful confession of faith.

This text is one of the most critical and poignant passages in all of the New Testament, and not just for Jesus, either. C. H. Dodd once remarked that this text remembers a moment of powerful crisis in the ministry of Jesus; and I think it must echo through crises in John's own time. I try to imagine how John must have felt as he wrote this material, aware that the defections he recounts are not just those of ambivalent or malevolent outsiders, but of some who considered themselves disciples. Apparently there was a division in the early church as to the nature of Jesus' self-giving. Was this a eucharistic debate, along the lines of our own disagreements regarding sacraments and ordinances?

Was it a controversy fueled by the gnostics, offended by the very notion that eternal life is somehow tied to Jesus' flesh? Whatever the particular rub, it is clear that some clusters of believers abandoned the faith, as John records it. Like Demas forsaking Paul, these had walked out of the Teacher's class. The author of 1 John summed it up this way: "They went out from us, but they did not belong to us; for if they had belonged to us, they would have remained with us. But by going out they made it plain that none of them belongs to us" (2:19). One can almost sense the pain behind the pen.

Likewise, if our lesson provides a narrative expression of this kind of phenomenon—that disciples, even, may abandon the One if they cannot abide in the teaching of John's Jesus—then surely the pain in Jesus' question to the disciples is a pain John shares.

"Will you go, too?" Jesus asks the Twelve, soon to be eleven. From twenty thousand to twelve to eleven—no church growth here. But we also know that the eleven will become one hundred and twenty, which will become thousands, then millions, and then billions. Perhaps it is safe to say that faithfulness sometimes gathers them up, sometimes scatters them out.

"To whom can we go?" Peter responds. Indeed. Having heard the words of life, even these difficult teachings, Peter speaks for all who remain. Even if we don't always understand the *what*, we have come to believe the *who*. "We have come to believe and know that you are the Holy One of God."

People defect the faith for all sorts of reasons. However, they confess for only one, because they too have come to believe and know that Christ is the One who has the words of eternal life. (Thomas R. Steagald)

DOORS AND WINDOWS

SEPTEMBER

Reflection Verse: "Very truly, I tell you, no one can see the kingdom of God without being born from above" (John 3:3).

The Discipline:

Walk along a beach, a lakeside, or on a mountaintop and find an object such as a shell or a stone. Pretend it can hear you speak. Tell the shell or stone about the person you want to be this fall. Keep the object with you as a reminder of your intentions and your promises to yourself for those times when your schedule turns crazy, demands increase, and fear sets in about how much everybody wants from you.

Make sure that the promises you make to yourself are not grandiose, and that they allow for unexpected interruptions and surprises. Allow yourself opportunities to start again if you fail to keep your promises.

Tell a good friend about your intentions and your promises. Ask him or her to periodically check in with you about your progress. Offer the same service to him or her.

The Meditation:

Here it is Labor Day and I still have my baptismal shell, given to me at a retreat this summer, still unused. The worship leader gave it to us. She wanted me to have a new beginning this fall. I don't seem to be able to find the time or place to make that new beginning, that fall, Labor Day promise. I have my new notebooks and pencils but not the rebirth from "above."

Where is "above" anyway? Is it that clear, uninterrupted time that I find only on vacation? Or the kind of Celtic time known as "thin" time, when heaven and earth coalesce and kiss each other? Or, is it sleep? Or what some people call peace, as though they knew what they were talking about? I know that I must be reborn from "above," and yet I continue to hope I can manage transformation by myself. Where is Frank Sinatra when I need him, singing "I Did It My Way"? Imagine how intimidated I will be by the end of the fall speed-up!

I really appreciated the retreat leader's words as she gave us the shells. She told us to look for our place of new beginnings. Now where is my place? Probably right after the last chorus of "I Did It My Way." Right there, where I sing my fruitless song one more time and then let go and let God.

There may not be just one time for the shell to open and pour. We may have to be born over and over again. God knows that clarity comes and clarity goes. There is peace, and then there is creative dislocation, and then there is peace again.

Late summer, when the asters are standing on the toes of the grapes that have twisted on to the bittersweet vine, and the dogs have had their day, most of the hope for clarity is lost. We join the dogs and flowers in a haze. Back-to-school sales are gone, and our notebooks are full. These days are anything but the tabula rasa of our early summer hopes. Then we assumed the impatiens would not be invaded by the spearmint. Then we fantasized a life of staying ahead of the weeds. Focus, surely by August, should return. But it rarely does.

E. L. Doctorow said that writing a novel was like driving a car at night. "You can see only as far as your headlights, but you can also make the whole trip that way." Often we want an imperial clarity—one that is impossible on any given day. Clarity for the day, not the season, should be our goal. Such clarity will take us through our days and our seasons and our centuries.

The Song:

I was there to hear your borning cry, I'll be there when you are old.
I rejoiced the day you were baptized to see your life unfold.

(John Ylvisaker, "I Was There to Hear Your Borning Cry")

The Prayer:

Focus us, O God, on what is important. And then let the details have their say. And then let the important things have their say with the details. Give us the Zen of errands, the Hajj of moving cars, the promised land of our own block.

Let us become holy, O God. But if we truly live, we will get bumped and bruised. Let us become holy today in the larger way, holy with blemishes, not holy without blemishes. We will bring our bruises with us to work today. Some will not yet be healed before another comes along. Some of our blemishes have been there for years. Some won't go away. God, hold us nonetheless, blemishes and all. God, hold us nonetheless, empty baptismal shell and all.

Let us be satisfied with the clarity we have, not the clarity we covet. And let us be born, again and again, from above. In the name of Home, Amen. (Donna Schaper)

SEPTEMBER 3, 2000

Twelfth Sunday After Pentecost

Worship Theme: God wants a loving heart revealed in loving actions, not our religious piety and flowery words.

Readings: Song of Solomon 2:8-13; James 1:17-27; Mark 7:1-8, 14-15, 21-23

Call to Worship (Psalm 72:1-8):

Leader: Give the king your justice, O God,

People: **and your righteousness to the royal son!**

Leader: May he judge your people with righteousness,

People: **and your poor with justice!**

Leader: Let the mountains bear prosperity for the people, and the hills, in righteousness!

People: **May he defend the cause of the poor of the people, give deliverance to the needy, and crush the oppressor!**

Leader: May he live while the sun endures, and as long as the moon, throughout all generations!

People: **May he be like rain that falls on the mown grass, like showers that water the earth!**

Leader: In his days may righteousness flourish, and peace abound, till the moon be no more!

People: **May he have dominion from sea to sea, and from the river to the ends of the earth!**

Pastoral Prayer:

O Lord of the cosmos, Master of all, we cannot imagine the immensity of your power or the energy of your love, a love so great that it defeats oppression, loneliness, despair, illness, and even death. It is a love that is creating our world just for the delight and beauty of it all. O thank you, Lord God; we praise holy Christ. Give to us a new heart that is quick to listen, slow to speak, and even slower to anger and rage. Give to us the faith to love boldly, to live boldly, to proclaim your good news boldly in our words and our deeds. Keep us from playing it safe. In the name of the bold One who risked everything, even his life. Amen. (Thomas Gildermeister)

SERMON BRIEFS

THE SONG OF SONGS

SONG OF SOLOMON 2:8-13

Open almost any commentary on the Song of Songs and you will read that it is a love song, and a pretty explicit song at that. One commentator describes it as being filled with "language of sensuality, longing, intimacy, playfulness, and human affection" (*New Interpreter's Bible* [Nashville: Abingdon Press], p. 363). Another calls it an idyll celebrating the love of a shepherd and shepherdess. The literary form of the book is a dialogue between a young woman and her lover, told mainly from the point of view of the young woman. Fifty-six verses are spoken by the woman; thirty-six by her lover.

A major literary form in the Song of Songs is the Arabic poetic device called the wasf. In the wasf, the young woman and her lover use images from nature, the military, and architecture to describe one another's physical attributes. In 5:10-16, the young woman describes her lover; in 4:1-7, 6:1-13, and 7:1-5, the lover describes the young woman. Other poetic forms within the book are poems of encounter, which depict the meetings of the lovers (1:12-14; 2:4-7; and 5:1); poems of seeking, in which the lovers seek one another in pastures and city streets (1:7-8; 3:1-5; and

5:2-8); and poems of beckoning, in which the lovers call to one another, as in our passage, 2:8-13, and in 4:8-11.

God is never mentioned in the Song of Songs, which leads many to wonder how it came to be included in the canon of Old Testament Scripture at all. But as early as the second century C.E., the Jewish rabbis taught the book's great value: "All the [world is] not worth the day [that] the Song of Songs was given to Israel; all the Writings are holy, but the Song of Songs is the holy of holies" (Mishnah Yadaim 3:5).

How do we understand this erotic poem as part of our canon of Scripture? One of the major "findings" of biblical scholarship in the past twenty years is that biblical texts can be "read" in a variety of ways. The Song of Songs can certainly be read as a love poem, but interpreters through the centuries have read it in other ways as well.

The book may be viewed as another attempt to define the mystery of God's love for humankind, using the imagery of bride and bridegroom, of wife and husband, of lover and beloved. This image is somewhat more satisfying than some others that are used in the Old Testament—pot and potter, vineyard and vine-keeper, sovereign and subject—because in such a relationship we have the possibility of true dialogue between the covenanting parties, and also something nearer to a genuine equality. I think the best description of God's love for humanity is "a true passion." God expects us to love the Divine with that same passion.

In the Song of Songs, the young woman and the lover are continually seeking each other. In 2:8 (NASB), the young woman says, "Listen! My beloved! Behold, he is coming." And in 2:9, the lover is "looking through the window / He is peering through the lattice."

"Seeking and finding" is a major theme in the Song of Songs and in the whole Old Testament (and the New). It is a continual element of the story of the ancient Israelites and their God. The Song of Songs plays out this seeking and finding, however, without a single historical reference, no reference to God or to Israel—just beautiful, lyrical poetry. God seeks us, and we are to seek God. We may conclude, then, that the Song of Songs is about love and it is about seeking and finding.

The book is also attributed to Solomon, which explains its name in the NRSV translation of the Bible. Verse 1 of the book identifies it as "The Song of Songs, which is Solomon's." Solomon is remembered in ancient Israel for his great building projects (especially the Temple), for his many wives, and for his wisdom. Solomon sought wisdom and found it (1 Kings 3:3-15). And according to Proverbs, the one who finds wisdom finds life and favor from the Lord (Prov. 2:1-6).

The Song of Songs is a love poem with many layers of possible meaning. It is an erotic love poem. It is a poem about God's love for humankind and God's seeking out of humankind. We may also understand it as a poem about seeking and finding the wisdom to somehow understand the unfathomable love—the passion—of the Lord for humankind. " 'Arise, my darling, my beautiful one. And come along. For behold, the winter is past'. . . " (2:10-11*a*). (Nancy L. deClaisse-Walford)

DOERS OF THE WORD

JAMES 1:17-27

"Be doers of the word." That is the theme of the book of James. This book has the form of a letter, but it may actually be a sermon or a collection of teachings, like the book of Proverbs. It is attributed to James, the brother of Jesus, the leader of the church in Jerusalem. It may, however, have been written in his name by a later church leader. There is evidence that the church had been around long enough to have developed some misunderstandings and distortions of the faith that needed correcting. Some of those will look familiar to us. That is part of the value of this book.

The theme of this book is not "salvation by works," as some think it is. Instead, the main theme is sanctification. James thinks that the Christian faith should make a difference in the lives of believers. James 1:4 speaks of growing toward becoming "mature" (NIV and NRSV) or "perfect" (KJV and RSV). James sees this happening in the lives of people who live daily in openness to the saving work of God and in disciplined response to it. He shows us the relationship between deep spirituality and down-to-earth, "practical" religion.

In the last half of chapter 1, James uses an image familiar to gardeners to show us how to grow toward spiritual maturity.

I. God Wants to Plant the Seed of New Life in Us

James remembers that there is a wisdom that is active in all of God's creative work (Prov. 3:19) and the Word through which all things come into being (John 1:3). Through that same agent, incarnate in Jesus, God performed a new creative act for our salvation. "In fulfillment of his own purpose he gave us birth by the word of truth, so that we would become a kind of first fruits of his creatures" (James 1:18).

Just as the writer of Proverbs urged us to learn wisdom and live according to it, James urges us to receive the good gift of wisdom—and the Word—that God wants to plant in our lives as a gardener plants a seed. Luke Timothy Johnson says that God calls us into a new understanding of reality (*New Interpreter's Bible vol. XII* [Nashville: Abingdon, 1998], p. 190). That must include a new understanding of who God is and what God wills, and who we are.

The source of new life is a gift from God. But we must discipline ourselves to receive it and to allow it to flourish.

II. We Must First Weed the Garden and Prepare the Soil

James speaks of weeding out all of the sordidness and rank growth of wickedness. A person who is serious about letting new life grow will not indulge in the things that could stifle it. Here, he mentions anger. In other parts of the book, he speaks of jealousy, strife, irresponsible talk, violence, and other destructive forces. It is strange how many Christians claim the right to continue in these things. James will not let us get away with it.

Receive into an appreciative heart the gift that God is trying to plant in you. Nurture it and care for it.

III. We Must Nourish the Gift of God by Living According to It

The Christian faith should make a difference in our lives. It is not enough just to hear about it and talk about it. We must intentionally do something about it. Live like the person God is trying to help you to be.

James remembers the relationship between wisdom and law.

313

But the law we are called to obey is not an oppressive formality. It is the royal law of love in which we find real liberty.

Wesleyans will recognize how closely these teachings parallel the "general rules" given to the early Methodist societies by John Wesley, the great advocate of "going on to perfection."

Have you ever planted a garden? Remember what you learned through that experience, and let it help you grow toward fullness of life. (Jim Killen)

THE HEART OF THE MATTER—HOLINESS

MARK 7:1-8, 14-15, 21-23

"Who is a holy person? . . . The answer is in the direction of life: One who moves toward God steadily."—Ladislas Orsy (Albert Wells, *Inspiring Quotations* [Nashville: Thomas Nelson, 1988], p. 88)

The Pharisees and scribes desperately wanted to be holy people. Every action they took symbolized that desire. Somewhere along the way a detour got them off track from a holiness depot to a legalistic depot, and set them at odds with Jesus, the epitome of Jewish holiness. Throughout his life, Jesus would be at odds with these religious leaders because his holiness perception moved his life toward God's will, while the Pharisees' lives steadily moved them away from God's will.

The text helps us obtain a better grip on God's idea of holy living.

I. The Heart of the Matter of Holiness: A Spiritual Principle (vv. 1-8)

At the genesis of the Jewish religion, the law meant the observance of the Ten Commandments and the directions of the Pentateuch, the first five Old Testament books. The Pentateuch carries much detail when it comes to life, many rules. They were written to help, not hinder, the common person. When it comes to moral issues, holiness issues, what God proposes is a progression of moral principles to ponder and apply. In the Old Testament that concept capsulizes the prophets and leaders of Israel.

A detour occurred about four or five centuries before Christ. A group of scholars grew up with a real passion for definition. Every law had to be defined, amplified, and expanded into thousands of minuscule little rules, regulations, and laws governing every possible aspect and action of life.

These laws were not written down until three centuries after Christ. So between seven to eight centuries was what is called "oral law" or "the tradition of the elders." William Barclay points out that the word *elder* in this case means "ancients," not officials of the Synagogue. It was in the third century that these thousands of minute rules and regulations were written in a book called the Mishnah.

The incident of the washing of the hands in Mark 7:1-4 typifies the extent of rules and regulations to which the Pharisees had taken the principle of hygiene for health's sake. There was a lengthy description of how to wash their hands to be ceremonially clean, and the disciples trampled this rule by not observing the exact details of washing.

Barclay correctly observes, "Now, note that to fail to do this was, in Jewish eyes, not to be guilty of bad manners, not to be dirty in the health sense, but to be unclean in the sight of God" (*The Daily Study Bible* [Philadelphia: The Westminster Press, 1954], p. 167).

Holiness is direction of life, moving by principles, cleansed by the Holy Spirit, and the steady following of God's commands and demands of life, not man's.

II. The Heart of the Matter of Holiness: A Spiritual Quality

In the text, Jesus' encounter with the Pharisees becomes a teaching moment as he calls the crowd to him. He uses the simple fact that external things, such as food that's unclean, hands that are unwashed, and dirty bowls and utensils, cannot defile the inner spirit, but it is the heart—the will of a person—that determines cleanness of life.

III. The Heart of the Matter of Holiness: A Spiritual Lifestyle

Though rules and regulations cannot be dictated for every situation, with every person the commands of God are delineated by lifestyle. No one who lives a holy life desires to live with an unholy lifestyle. In verses 20-21, Jesus becomes very specific about what an unholy lifestyle produces. Satan, not God, dominates people who live with filthiness in life. God's folks want to stay away from the things that make them unclean.

In the *Communicator's Commentary* (Dallas: Word Publishing, 1989), David McKenna writes: "The heart has been made the center for a defilement that no outward ritual can cleanse. Jesus has signed his death warrant, but at the same time, positioned himself for the redemptive act which only he can fulfill." (Derl Keefer)

SEPTEMBER 10, 2000

Thirteenth Sunday After Pentecost

Worship Theme: If we are to claim a place with Christ, we must stand humbly with the poor and oppressed children of God.

Readings: Proverbs 22:1-2, 8-9, 22-23; James 2:1-10 (11-13), 14-17; Mark 7:24-37

Call to Worship (Psalm 146:1-10):

Leader: Praise the LORD! Praise the LORD, O my soul!

People: **I will praise the LORD as long as I live; I will sing praises to my God while I have being.**

Leader: Put not your trust in princes, in mortals, in whom there is no help.

People: **Their breath departs, they return to the earth; on that very day their plans perish.**

Leader: Happy are those whose help is in the God of Jacob,

People: **whose hope is in the LORD, their God,**

Leader: who made heaven and earth, the sea, and all that is in them;

People: **who keeps faith for ever; who executes justice for the oppressed; who gives food to the hungry.**

Leader: The LORD sets the prisoners free;

People: **the LORD opens the eyes of the blind.**

317

Leader: The LORD lifts up those who are bowed down;

People: **the LORD loves the righteous.**

Leader: The LORD watches over the sojourners,

People: **and upholds the widow and the orphan; but the LORD brings the way of the wicked to ruin.**

Leader: The LORD will reign for ever, your God, O Zion, from generation to generation.

People: **Praise the LORD!**

Pastoral Prayer:

O Lord, the One who comforts the afflicted and afflicts the comfortable, we praise you for being the Master of us all—rich and poor, well-educated and illiterate, folks like us and folks who couldn't be more different. Help us, dear Jesus, to hear the call to follow you to the poor and oppressed; to offer these sisters and brothers our friendship; and to provide charity, but also to strive for justice. Lord, you have given to us so much privilege. And we have used it for only our gain. Forgive us. Free us so that we can release our hold on the values of greed and embrace the values of the gospel. Open our eyes to see the desperation. Open our ears to hear the cry of the needy. Lord, in your mercy, hear our prayers. Amen. (Thomas Gildermeister)

SERMON BRIEFS

WISDOM SAYINGS

PROVERBS 22:1-2, 8-9, 22-23

Chapter 22 is part of what I like to call the "meat and potatoes" of the book of Proverbs. In chapters 10-22 and 25-29, we encounter those pithy sayings that seem to summarize the essence of wisdom teachings. Wise sayings have been a part of human culture since the first group of our ancestors attempted to live together in community. In the everyday encounters of human existence, lessons were learned and passed along for posterity, and the ancient Israelite culture was no exception. Wise words were passed down from parent to child, from generation to generation, from clan to clan, from wise teacher to student, from wisdom school to wisdom school. And our Old Testament contains much passed-down wisdom material, especially in the book of Proverbs.

We twentieth-century readers tend to think of proverbs as one-line sayings such as "A rolling stone gathers no moss," "A stitch in time saves nine," or "A penny saved is a penny earned." And each of us has our special family (and clan) wisdom sayings. Stop for a moment and recall some of your family's wisdom sayings. In the book of Proverbs, the ancient Israelite family preserved their wisdom in poetry, rather than prose. And Hebrew poetry is a little different from English poetry. Hebrew poetry generally consists of two-line units of expression, which we call "parallel lines." In each two-line expression, the second line in some way adds to the understanding of the first line. And the two lines, read together, give a complete meaning to the expression.

These two-line expressions achieve their meaning in a number of ways. In 22:1, for example ("A good name is to be chosen rather than great riches, and favor is better than silver or gold"), the two lines say essentially the same thing, or are synonymous. In 22:2 ("The rich and the poor have this in common: the LORD is the maker of them all"), the second line gives the reader more information about what the rich and poor have in common. And in 22:12 ("The eyes of the LORD keep watch over knowledge, but he overthrows the words of the faithless"), the meaning is conveyed by the contrast of opposite views between the first and second lines. Therefore we must remember to read the two lines of the Hebrew poetry together, understanding that one line adds to and completes the meaning of the other.

In verses 1-2, 8-9, and 22-23, the writers admonish their hearers to value a good name and favor over riches and silver and gold; to sow justice in order to avoid calamity and the rod of anger; and to not rob the poor or crush the afflicted just because they are poor and afflicted. These verses outline a number of

319

functions of the ideal king in the ancient Near East. The ideal king was to give security and protection for the inhabitants of that king's city and to provide for those who could not adequately provide for themselves—the widows, the orphans, and the poor.

In the book of Proverbs, these community obligations are addressed not to a king, but to all humanity. Recall that Proverbs is a book about everyday human existence, an existence in right relationship with God and with our human companions, not a manual of right conduct for the kings and political leaders of ancient Israel. And so wisdom's admonition to all of humankind is that they acknowledge, consider, and provide for the ones within their communities who cannot provide for themselves.

Chapter 22 of Proverbs, then, is a practical, heart-felt approach to wisdom. It is humanity's responsibility not only to establish and maintain a right relationship with its God, but also to establish and maintain a right relationship with its human companions in this enterprise we call life. (Nancy L. deClaisse-Walford)

THE PURPOSE OF RELIGION

JAMES 2:1-10 (11-13), 14-17

What is the purpose of religion? That is the question James is trying to answer when he speaks about faith and works.

I. There Is Something Wrong When Professed Religion and Way of Life Don't Match

James was troubled by people who were very proud of their religiousness but whose lives were obviously not being shaped by the faith they professed. Specifically, the different ways in which rich people and poor people were being treated in the church was obviously being shaped by the values of the culture rather than by a commitment to God. God loves all people equally and teaches us to love our neighbors as ourselves. James says that a person who is not obedient to the whole law of God is not really obedient to any of it. Disobedience represents a basic departure from the relationship with God that should be shaping life.

II. It Is the Purpose of Religion to Shape Life

It is the purpose of religion, with all of its doctrines and rituals and customs, to lead us into a relationship with God that will shape our lives. Whatever shapes your life is your real religion. If you profess the Christian faith, you should intend to live in the kind of relationship with God which that faith teaches, and to allow that relationship to shape your life.

When Paul spoke of "salvation by faith," he understood the word *faith* to represent a life-shaping relationship with God. To him, faith meant living out of a basic trust in the love of God. Evidently, by the time of James' writings, some people had come to think that the word *faith* referred to formal religion, a profession of faith and all that goes with it. To them, "salvation by faith" meant that a person could be saved by making the right profession of faith and following the right formal religion. Many people still seem to believe that. James rejected that notion, and Paul would certainly have agreed with him. If the Christian faith is your real faith, it will shape your life and your works. Faith (religion) that produces no loving works is dead. James goes on to say, "Show me your faith apart from your works, and I by my works will show you my faith" (2:18).

III. What Does a Life That Is Being Shaped by the Christian Faith Look Like?

James says, "Religion that is pure and undefiled before God, the Father, is this: to care for orphans and widows in their distress, and to keep oneself unstained by the world" (1:27).

Once there was a pastor who had loved and served a community for many years. The people of the community loved and honored him. Then one day the pastor's adult son moved back into his parent's home. He was sick. He had come home so that his parents could care for him. Eventually, the news traveled quietly through the community that the pastor's son had AIDS.

How would the people of the church react? Would they withdraw in fear? Would they stop respecting the pastor, believing that he had been unable to keep his son from slipping into some kind of moral failure? Would they be angry at the son for letting his father and the church down?

They might have done any of those things, and the reactions would have been understandable. But they didn't. Instead, they gathered around the pastor and his son in love. They brought food. They helped with the nursing. They washed the linens. They did all they could to help. And when the pastor's son died, they joined the family in grief. That is the way love behaves.

The real purpose of religion is to lead us into a life-shaping relationship with God. There is something wrong with a "Christian" faith that does not produce loving works. (Jim Killen)

SALVATION FOR ALL

MARK 7:24-37

The story is told about a young bellhop in a Toledo, Ohio, hotel back in the 1930s. After work one day, he returned to his room and laid down to take a nap. Just as he began to doze off, somebody began knocking on his door. Irritated, he yelled out, "Get away from the door and leave me alone!" But the knock persisted. The young man jumped out of bed, ran over and jerked the door open. Two men, attorneys, stood there and asked permission to enter his room. He invited them in and asked them to be seated. Once they were situated, one of them pulled out some papers for the bellhop to review and sign. He explained that a deceased aunt had left the young man $25,000, a large amount of money during the Great Depression.

Today, Jesus seeks entrance into every life to give good news of salvation and to take up living in the heart so that he can continually give an inheritance right now.

Strange, isn't it, that people, like the young bellhop, yell at him to "get away from the door and leave me alone." They reject rather than greet him!

I. Salvation's Message of Love Is for the Jews

From antiquity the Jews anticipated the Messiah to be born a Jew. The prophets heralded it, and the literature declared his coming.

1. Why God would choose a small, rebellious, itinerant band

322

of people to be the nation the Savior would come to is a question only God can answer, but God did.

2. Why God would choose a young teenager, barely out of puberty, to be the avenue of incarnation for the Savior is a question only God can answer, but God did.

3. Why God would choose a small, insignificant, and dirty town like Bethlehem for the birth of the Savior is a question only God can answer, but God did.

Salvation is the offer of God's forgiveness to change a rebellious, unloving, stubborn, and sinful heart to a redeemed, softened heart filled with divine love.

The Jews were always fussing with God, but God loved them unconditionally.

In *Just Like Jesus* ([Dallas: Word Publishing, 1998], p. 3), Max Lucado writes: "If you think his love for you would be stronger if your faith were, you are wrong. If you think his love would be deeper if your thoughts were, wrong again. Don't confuse God's love with the love of people. The love of people often increases with performance and decreases with mistakes. Not so with God. He loves you where you are." That was what the Jewish nation needed to hear. How often they spurned God's love. How often they rejected God's message. How desperately they attempted to earn God's love by making and worshiping the laws of religion, thinking they were worshiping God. The Jews needed John 3:16 as much as anybody.

II. Salvation's Message of Love Is for the Gentiles

The incident with the Syrophoenician woman with a demon-possessed daughter has much more meaning than just a "simple" healing. A missionary melody can be heard loud and clear as Jesus dialogues with her.

Previously Jesus dealt with the distinction between foods that were clean and unclean. Jews would never soil their lives by coming into contact with a Gentile who they knew was ceremonially unclean. William Barclay observes in his *Daily Study Bible* (Philadelphia: The Westminster Press, 1954): "It may well be that here Jesus is saying by implication that the Gentiles are not unclean, but that they too have their place within the kingdom."

Today the church must follow the example of Jesus and reach

out to people of all colors, backgrounds, and idiosyncrasies. If you aren't Jewish, you are a Gentile, and salvation is for you!

III. Salvation's Message of Love Is Complete

Lloyd Ogilvie reminds us that at the center of Christianity is the heart. "The essential purpose of our faith is to bring the heart of God, Christ himself, into touch with the heart of man, his deep inner self—man himself as he is in the inner springs of personality" (*Life Without Limits* [Waco: Word Books, 1975], p. 146).

Jesus himself is the completion of salvation. Nowhere else can salvation be found but in Jesus as he is put on the throne of our heart's life. (Derl Keefer)

SEPTEMBER 17, 2000

Fourteenth Sunday After Pentecost

Worship Theme: What we believe and say about Jesus—who he is and what that means—is vital.

Readings: Proverbs 1:20-33; James 3:1-12; Mark 8:27-38

Call to Worship (Psalm 19:7-10):

Leader: The law of the LORD is perfect, reviving the soul;

People: **the testimony of the LORD is sure, making wise the simple;**

Leader: the precepts of the LORD are right, rejoicing the heart;

People: **the commandment of the LORD is pure, enlightening the eyes;**

Leader: the fear of the LORD is clean, enduring for ever;

People: **the ordinances of the LORD are true, and righteous altogether.**

Leader: More to be desired are they than gold, even much fine gold;

People: **sweeter also than honey and drippings of the honeycomb.**

Pastoral Prayer:
Great God of the universe, how wonderful is your creation! The evidence of your love is everywhere. We praise your name. But no greater praise can we offer than for your Son, Jesus

Christ, the One through whom you created all that is, was, and ever will be; and the One whom you sent to redeem and re-create this world. Lord, forgive us when we are satisfied with our ignorance and unwilling to listen to your wisdom. Forgive us when our words become weapons, and not the vehicles to convey your love. May your mercy extend to us and beyond so that everyone bows and declares that Jesus Christ is Lord. In his blessed name we pray. Amen. (Thomas Gildermeister)

SERMON BRIEFS

A NEW OUTWARD FOCUS

PROVERBS 1:20-33

In Proverbs 1:20-33, we are introduced to the main character in the book of Proverbs—"Woman Wisdom." Woman Wisdom shouts in the streets, lifts her voice in the square, cries out at the head of the noisy streets, and speaks at the gates of the city. Her message to all who will listen is to seek knowledge and to seek the fear of the Lord.

Woman Wisdom is contrasted with Woman Folly, a figure who entices young students of wisdom into her clutches and leads them in destructive ways (Prov. 5:3-14). The sharp contrast between wisdom and folly is outlined in the first nine chapters of Proverbs.

Who is Woman Wisdom? Where does she come from? And what is her role in the life of ancient Israel? Wisdom was an important element of life in the cultures of the ancient Near East, including Egypt, Mesopotamia, Asia Minor, and Palestine. In the Hebrew language, the word *wisdom* is a feminine noun, and the concept "wisdom" became personified as "woman wisdom." This personification allowed the biblical wisdom writers to create vivid and beautiful images of wisdom, and wisdom's role in the life of ancient Israel. And it allowed for the personified contrast between Woman Wisdom and Woman Folly.

But perhaps a better question is, What is wisdom? (and as a corollary, What is folly?). What is the role of that elusive characteristic of ancient Israel's worship system? When one examines carefully the character of wisdom in the literature of the ancient Israelites, it seems that the essence of wisdom is a matter of right relationships with God and with our human companions on earth. Wisdom is about right relationships. And folly is about the distortion of right relationships.

Wisdom is as simple and as complicated as that. Where there is life, there is wisdom. Wisdom is profoundly and simply about life. The book of Proverbs presents us with a God who is concerned with the mundane and the everyday, with our most intimate relationships, and with our most painful emotions. The book of Proverbs is about relationships. It is not about covenant promises, commandments at Sinai, and the stories of the Israelite ancestors. Nowhere in its pages do we read about Abraham and Sarah, about Rachel and Jacob, about David and Jonathan, about Moses and Aaron, about Deborah, or about Samson. The God of creation, the God who made the earth and everything in it "very good" (Gen. 1:31), is the subject and object of wisdom literature. In the book of Proverbs, the name used for God is "Yahweh," translated in our English Bibles as "LORD." Yahweh is God's personal name, which was revealed to Moses and to the ancient Israelites, and it is the very personal nature of the relationship between the Creator and created that the book of Proverbs addresses.

The book of Proverbs is about common, ordinary, everyday human existence that is wrapped up in some mysterious way with the divine. And Woman Wisdom is a common, ordinary, everyday character that calls us beyond and outside our human inward focus to a new outward focus on the will of God.

Chapter 1 of Proverbs invites us as readers to listen carefully and faithfully to the words of Woman Wisdom and the wisdom teachers within the pages of the book of Proverbs. Here the ancient Israelites share their traditional wisdom, their words about right relationships with God and with humans, preserved in a document handed to us Christians two thousand years later as "the Word of God." May we listen carefully as Woman Wisdom cries out in the street and raises her voice in the squares. (Nancy L. deClaisse-Walford)

SPEAKING IS DOING

JAMES 3:1-12

All of us, especially Christians, ought to accept responsibility for what might happen as a result of the things we do or say.

I. Irresponsible Talk and Action Can Be Destructive

Something was evidently going on in the early church that provoked James to launch into a diatribe against destructive talk. We don't know what that was. But we don't need to. We can furnish our own examples of the destructiveness of irresponsible speech. Many people seem to feel that they have the right to say anything that expresses their feelings, regardless of its impact on others, or say anything they think will be useful, regardless of whether or not it is true. Frustrated and unhappy parents may vent their anger in verbal abuse of their children in ways that can permanently damage a child's self-esteem. Marriage partners sometimes dump their hostilities on each other in ways that can destroy their relationships.

Gossip can still destroy reputations and relationships.

The new rules for political rhetoric make it okay to say any vicious thing about an opponent or his or her position whether or not it is true. As a result, important debates on issues that are crucial for public welfare get lost in petty demagoguery.

The leaders of disadvantaged peoples feel that it is necessary for them to verbalize the hostilities of those they hope to lead. Their inflammatory comments reinforce bitterness and hatred, and the attempts to justify angry actions. The results of that can be catastrophic. James speaks of a great forest being set on fire, but we have seen great cities set ablaze in riots that leave the disadvantaged even more disadvantaged and that destroy the mutual respect that is necessary to enable communities to work together to make things better.

II. Christians Must Certainly Be Able to Find a Better Way of Addressing Human Needs

It is true that hurts need to be attended to, differences of opinion need to be worked through, and injustices need to be corrected. But these things can be done best in an atmosphere of mutual respect and constructive action.

The Rotary Club International recommends a four-way test of everything we think, say, or do: Is it the truth? Is it fair to all concerned? Will it build goodwill and better friendships? Will it be beneficial to all concerned? If a civic club can offer that kind of a rule for responsible action, the church must certainly be able to offer more.

People whose lives are being shaped by the Christian faith should experience an affirmation that gives a self-respect that does not have to be defended irrationally. They should also be growing in the kind of love that will generate respect for every person and concern for the well-being of all. They should hold a belief in the active involvement of God in human history that will cause them to believe that things can be made better by constructive action. At the very least, belief in the judgment of God should cause Christians to accept responsibility for the results of the things they say and do.

III. Those Who Are Real Leaders Still Behave Responsibly

The American people have a bad habit of tearing down their public leaders. Once, during a time when the attacks upon the president were especially vicious, a certain elder statesman of the opposing party was interviewed on a television talk show. Everyone knew that he disagreed with the president on many important issues. Finally, the talk show host set up a situation in which the elder statesman could join the multitudes in taking a cheap shot at the president. But he wouldn't do it. He just smiled and said, "I don't want to say anything bad about my president."

What a difference it would make if we could all learn to behave with that kind of respect. (Jim Killen)

EVERYBODY OUGHT TO KNOW

MARK 8:27-38

I. Everybody Ought to Know Who Jesus Is

Jesus was concerned about public opinion. The church continues to be concerned about public opinion. It is important to know what people think about Jesus. But sooner or later the question must come to each person individually and personally.

Who is Jesus?

It is not enough to know what Jesus did. It is not enough to know what Jesus thought. It is not enough to know what Jesus taught about life or death, about sin or righteousness. The central question always deals with his identity. It was upon the basis of a correct understanding of the nature of Jesus that the man from Ethiopia was baptized (Acts 8:37). It was upon the basis of a correct understanding of the nature of Jesus that salvation was promised in Romans 10:9, 10.

Jesus will not accept faint praise. If we only acknowledge that his teaching was good, it is not enough. If we only acknowledge that his influence was great, it is not enough. If we only acknowledge that his power was awesome, it is not enough. Jesus must be confessed as the Christ; that is, the Anointed One, the long-expected Messiah.

Jesus wanted everybody to know this, but he did not want the message to go out prematurely. He wanted the world to be prepared for this message. The same Jesus who on this occasion said not to tell anyone later said to tell everyone.

II. Everybody Ought to Know What Jesus Did

For a long time Jesus had been hinting about his sacrifice, and now he speaks plainly. He foretells that he will be rejected, killed, and raised from the dead. These are the central facts of the gospel in 1 Corinthians 15:1-8. If you study the sermons in the book of Acts, you will find that these three events are prominent in every sermon.

It is natural for Peter to object strongly to these impending events. But Jesus knows they must occur, and he does not want to be tempted to bypass them. So he speaks severely to Peter and to the rest of the Twelve.

We too find it hard to understand the role of suffering. We cannot understand Christ's suffering and we cannot understand our own. But life offers abundant evidence that suffering comes often, and the presence of suffering should not shake our faith. Augustine said, "God had one son without sin. He had none without suffering." So, from his own suffering, Jesus goes on to tell them frankly what they will face if they follow him.

III. Everybody Ought to Know What Jesus Requires

No believer should be embarrassed at the cross of Christ. No believer should be ashamed of a suffering Savior. And no believer should be surprised if suffering comes his or her way. Certainly, early Christians faced greater suffering than most of us will encounter today. But we need to be prepared to pay whatever price is necessary to remain loyal to Christ.

In recognizing the value of things, we must never underestimate the price of our own souls. Jesus believed that your salvation and mine was worth the price he paid to secure it. We must know that even if we suffer (or die) for our faith, that the price is right. What we gain is worth far more than what we lose. (Robert Shannon)

SEPTEMBER 24, 2000

Fifteenth Sunday After Pentecost

Worship Theme: An authentic follower of Christ must be willing to live the life of the Suffering Servant.

Readings: Proverbs 31:10-31; James 3:13–4:3, 7-8*a*; Mark 9:30-37

Call to Worship (Psalm 1:1-3):

> *Leader:*   Blessed are those who do not walk in the counsel of the wicked;
>
> *People:*   **or stand in the way of sinners, or sit in the seat of scoffers;**
>
> *Leader:*   but their delight is in the law of the LORD,
>
> *People:*   **and on God's law they meditate day and night.**
>
> *Leader:*   They are like trees planted by streams of water that yield their fruit in season, and their leaves do not wither.
>
> *People:*   **In all that they do, they prosper.**

Pastoral Prayer:

Long-suffering and all-loving God, we worship you in awe and humility. No greater way do you love us than through our families. Those of us gathered here who have been blessed with marriages grounded in your love offer a special praise for our spouses. What a source of holy support and comfort and wisdom has come through our wives and husbands. We ask that you heal marriages that are broken, that you restore the love that initially brought these people together. O heavenly Redeemer, help us to recognize that the least and last in our world shall be first in your kingdom. Give us the courage to live in the shadow of your suffering Son, willing to be last in the world's race, but one of the first in your kingdom of servant-love. Amen. (Thomas Gildermeister)

SERMON BRIEFS

A WOMAN OF STRENGTH

PROVERBS 31:10-31

Proverbs 31:10-31 is the last poem in the book of Proverbs. Its twenty-two verses summarize the characteristics of what is called "a capable wife" in the NRSV; "a wife of noble character" in the NIV; "an excellent wife" in the NASB; "a virtuous woman" in the KJV; "a good wife" in the RSV; and "a truly good wife" in TLB.

Proverbs 31 is about a woman who does good, works with her hands, rises while it is still night, considers and buys a field, extends her hand to the poor, makes linen garments, opens her mouth in wisdom, and looks well to the ways of her household. It is a favorite text for Mother's Day. But what more can we discover about this unusual and beautiful text in our Old Testament?

First, Proverbs 31:10-31 is the climax of the book of Proverbs, a book that is, in some sense, a summary of the collected wisdom of ancient Israel. Proverbs opens with an introduction to the reader of the character of woman wisdom (1:20-33). Why woman wisdom? Because the Hebrew word for wisdom is *hokmah*, which is a feminine-gender word. "Wisdom shouts in the street, she lifts her voice in the square" (1:20 NASB). The book continues with page after page of instruction to the young student about right conduct toward God and right conduct toward other human beings.

Second, Proverbs 31:10-31 is an acrostic; each line of the poem begins with a successive letter of the Hebrew alphabet. The acrostic was a favorite wisdom literary form, and I suspect quite fun for the scribe who composed it. Acrostics forced the scribe to be succinct and disciplined, and signaled to the reader that the writer had summarized the topic from aleph to tav (from A to Z). No more needed to be said. Acrostics also provided readers with a handy memory device and were popular for common wisdom sayings because they were more easily memorized than other poems.

Third, the Hebrew words that are translated in the NRSV as "a capable wife" are *eshet hayil*, literally "a woman (or wife, since the Hebrew word for *woman* can also mean "wife," just as the Hebrew word for *man* also means "husband") of power, strength, valor, military force, army, virtue, honesty." *Hayil* is a very interesting word in the context of Proverbs 31. It is used two hundred and forty times in the Old Testament, primarily in accounts of battles and military encounters. Perhaps the best translation in Proverbs 31:10 may be "a woman of strength."

Fourth, in the Hebrew Bible some of the books appear in a different order than in our Old Testament. In the Hebrew Bible, for instance, the book of Proverbs comes right after the book of Psalms, as it does in our Old Testament, but just before the book of Ruth. And in the book of Ruth, Ruth is referred to as an *eshet hayil*, which the NRSV translates as "a worthy woman" (3:11).

And so, who is this "woman of strength" whose characteristics conclude the book of Proverbs, the quintessential wisdom book of the Old Testament? Based on its position within the book of Proverbs and in the Hebrew Bible, on its acrostic character, and on its use of *eshet hayil* to begin the description of the woman, do we have here a description of woman wisdom in the book of Proverbs (see 1:20ff)? Of the ideal woman in the Old Testament (see Ruth 3:11)? Of an ideal woman in the ancient Near East (the acrostic poem)? Or, a concrete description of the embodiment of wisdom in the human realm, female *or* male? Interesting. (Nancy L. deClaisse-Walford)

GROWING IN GRACE

JAMES 3:13–4:3, 7-8*a*

Sanctification and *holiness* have become two of the most unattractive words in the Christian vocabulary. But when the process they represent takes place "for real" in the life of a person, it produces the most genuinely attractive form of the Christian life. Sanctification is the Christian faith working to reshape a person's life from the inside out until it produces a Christian life that is the real thing.

I. Our Religious Experience Should Not Be Allowed to Stop with That First Experience of God's Grace, Which We Often Call "Being Saved"

The first experience of grace, through which we come to know ourselves as beloved children of God, is called "justification." It is a wonderful thing. But it ought to be regarded as the beginning of our experience of the saving work of God, not the end of it. God wants to take us on beyond that experience and enable us to actually live like children of God.

This process of growing in grace is called "sanctification." It is spoken of often in the New Testament (see Matt. 5:43-48, Rom. 8:18-25, and 1 John 3:2-3). James tells us that he is writing about this same subject when, in 1:4, he expresses the hope that we may be "perfect and entire, wanting nothing" (KJV), or "mature and complete, lacking in nothing" (NRSV).

II. James Tells Us About the Nitty Gritty of Sanctification

For James, sanctification is not something that comes in the euphoria of a "mountaintop" religious experience. It comes as people live their lives in this world of stress and ambiguity and frequent disappointments, not as others live them, but in openness and responsiveness and disciplined submissiveness to both the demanding grace and the enabling grace of God. It comes through the experience of relying on God through the tough times (1:2-4). It comes from wrestling with temptations and resisting them (1:12-16, 4:1-3). It comes from living in obedience to what we know is God's purpose for us (2:8-12). But it is not a matter of "pulling ourselves up by our own bootstraps." These endeavors only give us the opportunity to experience the living God working to make a difference in our lives.

James is realistic. He knows that we will have to cope with bitter envy, selfish ambitions, and other such bondages of our hearts. Those things do not just evaporate the moment we make our profession of faith in Christ. They keep on working in our lives, and they can lead us to disorder, wickedness of every kind, and destructive conflicts.

But God is working in our lives to lead us into something better. "The wisdom from above is first pure, then peaceable, gentle, willing to yield, full of mercy and good fruits, without a trace of partiality or hypocrisy" (3:17). And those who take that wisdom into themselves and allow it to shape their lives will experience a changed life. "A harvest of righteousness is sown in peace for those who make peace"(3:18).

III. People Who Really Take the Christian Faith Seriously Will Live Different Lives

The differences that the Christian faith makes will not necessarily take the shape of conspicuous religiousness. It certainly will not take the shape of the condescending piety that most people associate with the words *sanctification* or *holiness*. It will rather be the subtle differences that appear and make us know that a person is marching to the beat of a different drummer.

When a young couple adopts an orphaned baby of another race; when a person practices a "secular" profession as if it were a calling from God; when someone prays his or her way through to serenity while coping with a terminal illness; when a group of retired men make a second profession of repairing the homes of the needy, then all who see will know that there is something different about them, and the difference will be attractive. They themselves will experience the difference, not in pride, but in gratitude.

God can make your life better. "Draw near to God, and he will draw near to you" (4:8). (Jim Killen)

ON GETTING A NEW PERSPECTIVE

MARK 9:30-37

Perspective enables us to tell how far or how near an object is from us, and how large or how small it is. Perspective is further defined as "referring to the proper evaluation of the importance of things." In this text, we learn what is important and what is insignificant.

I. A Disturbing Review (vv. 30-32)

While this is a preview of things to come, it is also a review of what Jesus has already taught the disciples (Mark 8:31). He kept coming back to the predictions of his sufferings because the Twelve found it very difficult to understand or accept it. In the previous chapter, there were four elements: his suffering, his rejection, his death, and his resurrection. In this chapter, there are three—his betrayal, his death, and his resurrection. As they could not accept the fact that Jesus must die, they could not accept the fact that one of their own would betray him.

II. Surprising Refusal (vv. 33-34)

This text surprises us in three ways. First, it surprises us that the disciples could argue about such little things when Jesus had just predicted such enormous things. In the light of his betrayal, death, and resurrection, how important could it be to decide which of the twelve was the greatest?

Second, it surprises us that they felt there were things they couldn't tell Jesus. Did they think he would not understand? Were they embarrassed that they had talked of such things? Surely believers today feel that they can bring anything to God in prayer. In fact, they feel they must bring everything to God in prayer. We even have a song, "I Must Tell Jesus."

Third, it surprises us that they did not understand that Jesus knew their thoughts. Certainly the verses that follow show how clearly he read their minds.

III. A Memorable Riddle (v. 35)

Jesus often spoke in riddles (see John 4:13-14; 6:27, 35). This one is memorable: If you want to be in first place, take the last place. Jesus said a similar thing in Matthew 20:26. It fits in with the beatitude from the Sermon on the Mount: "The meek shall inherit the earth." Such an idea runs contrary to all that we are taught. We think that we must look out for number one, that it is the go-getter who rises to the top. We would find this text hard to believe if we did not see in the life of Jesus what was taught by the mouth of Jesus. But "gentle Jesus meek and mild" has become the Lord of all. Just as Columbus went west to go east, so we need sometimes to go in the opposite direction to achieve our goals.

IV. A Chain Reaction (vv. 36-37)

If we welcome the child, we welcome the Christ; and if we welcome the Christ, we welcome God. The reverse of that must also be true. If we reject the child, we reject the Christ; and if we reject the Christ, we reject God. We are commanded to love God, but the only way we can really do that is to love the people created in God's image. We are told to serve God, but the only way we can do that is to serve people in the name of God. We are told to lay our treasures in heaven, but the only way we know to do that is to invest our treasure in people who are going that way. (Robert Shannon)

DOORS AND WINDOWS

OCTOBER

Reflection Verse: "I am the gate. Whoever enters by me will be saved . . ." (John 10:9).

The Discipline:
Think deeply this month about someone who is not you. Let the stranger come into your heart. Make a place for difference there. Don't just say "I love difference." Learn to actually love it.

"Heaven is not a gated community," said a cartoon in the December 9, 1996, issue of *The New Yorker*. The twentieth century may have been the century of the refugee. People mixed themselves up in many different ways. Ethnic blending took a giant leap forward. More people closed the door on their homeland and opened the door on a new frontier than at any other point in human history. The strong likelihood is that these blending trends will continue into the future.

In its statement on "uprooted people," the World Council of Churches challenges "churches worldwide to rediscover their identity, their integrity, and their vocation as the church of the stranger." The year 1997 was designated as the Year of Uprooted People. More than one in every fifty human beings is now a refugee or international migrant.

The uprooted face often finds closed borders, closed hearts, and closed minds. The WCC document states, "As churches, we lift up all these who are compelled by severe political, economic, and social conditions to leave their land and their culture. . . . Uprooted people are those forced to leave their community, those who flee because of persecution and war, those who are forcibly displaced because of environmental devastation, and those who are compelled to seek sustenance in a city or abroad because they cannot survive at home."

Pick a person with a name that is unusual, and who is a

stranger to you. Think about him or her all month. Bring that person into your heart.

As the century ends, we have only to remember our own families of origins to understand what all this uprooting has meant. My great-grandparents came from Scotland and Germany to America in the early 1900s. Who knows where my children will go in the next century? My son swears he is going to outer space, and maybe he will.

When we open doors, we risk ethnic blending. We risk uprooting. We also risk becoming, finally, the church of the stranger—the whole people of God.

The Meditation:

Jesus meant it when he said that his door was open to any and every man.

Did you know that the top wealthiest 10 percent of the population controls 70 percent of the national wealth? Did you know that the average CEO earns 179 times more than the lowest-paid worker in America? In Germany, the ratio is 20 to 1; in Japan, 11 to 1. Many wonder why these distorted differences occur. A big reason is the type of doors that Americans open and that Americans close. We opened the ethical door on private initiative; yet the Japanese found it somewhat shameful for one person to gain at the expense of another. Germans placed more value on the social compact than on the private wealth of individuals. In both the Japanese and German example, the economy manages, but the door is closed on individuals being the engine.

As the church, we are in charge of opening and closing ethical doors. We exist to applaud what God applauds and to demean what God demeans. God through Jesus Christ has a strange attitude about wealth—less is more! We could learn to believe what Jesus said about doors. He meant it when he said any man, any woman, any person. We need to learn how to mean it, too.

T. S. Eliot said, "You bring me news of a door that opens at the end of a corridor, sunlight and singing, when I had felt sure that every corridor only led to another, or to a blank wall." Those who have made friends with their own trouble know what he means. We have come to know the dark places within us, and we have seen their doors and windows. I have become intimately acquainted with the bottom of my stomach. It opens! But not until it is ready to open. Pain takes its own good time. But God, whom Eliot is addressing here, can be counted on to show up at the bottom of the bottom of the bottom of the trouble—and there to open a door.

The Song:
Come, ye disconsolate, where'er ye languish;
Earth has no sorrow that heaven cannot tame.
("Come, Ye Disconsolate")

The Prayer:
Open our hearts, O God, to all your people, one by one, each by each—and thereby let us open to our true self as your son or daughter. Let us know ourselves in the ones we call others, and let them know themselves by us as well. Amen. (Donna Schaper)

OCTOBER 1, 2000

Sixteenth Sunday After Pentecost

Worship Theme: As we have the Advocate in heaven, so too must we be advocates, and never stumbling blocks, for one another.

Readings: Esther 7:1-6, 9-10; 9:20-22; James 5:13-20; Mark 9:38-50

Call to Worship (Psalm 124:1-8):

> *Leader:* If it had not been the LORD who was on our side—let Israel now say—
>
> *People:* **if it had not been the LORD who was on our side, when foes rose up against us, then they would have swallowed us up alive, when their anger was kindled against us;**
>
> *Leader:* then the flood would have swept us away, the torrent would have gone over us;
>
> *People:* **then the raging waters would have gone over us.**
>
> *Leader:* Blessed be the LORD, who has not given us as prey to their teeth!
>
> *People:* **We have escaped as a bird from the snare of the fowlers;**
>
> *Leader:* the snare is broken, and we have escaped!
>
> *People:* **Our help is in the name of the LORD who made heaven and earth.**

Pastoral Prayer:

O Lord, our God, you have brought sin and death to its knees. You stand with us and on our behalf through your Son, and our Lord Christ Jesus. We praise you and adore your Son. But surely our lives contradict such testimony. Surely we look to this world and its answers to our problem first—sometimes first and last. Surely we stumble, and often we are stumbling blocks for your beloved children. Holy God, we throw ourselves at the feet of Christ and beg for mercy, knowing that your grace always exceeds your judgment. If that was not so, not one of us would have a prayer. But because of Christ, we have the confidence to pray even this prayer. And so, in his name. Amen. (Thomas Gildermeister)

SERMON BRIEFS

DO WHAT YOU HAVE THE POWER TO DO

ESTHER 7:1-6, 9-10; 9:20-22

"Esther . . . was taken into the king's house and put into the custody of Hegai, who was in charge of the women. Now the young woman pleased Hegai and found favor with him. So he quickly provided her with her cosmetics and food, gave her seven choice maids from the king's palace, and transferred her and her maids to the best place in the harem. Esther did not make known her people or her kindred" (Esther 2:8*b*-10*a* paraphrased).

We readers in the late twentieth century aren't quite sure what to make of Esther, the Jew, who manages to get herself wrapped up in the affairs of the Persian court of king Ahasuerus. Why doesn't she refuse Mordecai's counsel? Why does she allow herself to be taken by the Persian king? Why doesn't she stand up for her own rights as a woman and as a human being?

And yet Esther turns out to be the hero of our biblical book. She single-handedly saves the Jews from annihilation at the hands of the Persian government. And her righteousness is recorded for all humanity to read within the canon of our Old Testament. So what do we do with Esther? Do we condemn, or worse, ignore her for violating everything we may believe about self-respect and personhood? Or, might we find a way to praise Esther for her cunning and bravery?

Helen Pearson wrote a book in 1992 titled *Do What You Have the Power to Do* (Nashville: Upper Room, 1992). In the book, Pearson recounts the stories of six seemingly powerless women in the New Testament who, nonetheless, used whatever power was within their means for the furtherance of their God. The woman who anointed Jesus' feet with costly perfume had no power in her society (see Luke 7:36-50). She was, after all, an immoral woman. But she used what she had, the power within her grasp, to anoint Jesus, the ultimate embodiment of God's love for humanity. In the Old Testament, we read about Bathsheba, who appears to be a rather powerless person in the pages of Samuel (2 Sam. 11:1-5; 12:24). But Bathsheba, the betrayed wife of Uriah, uses the power she does have to assure the succession of her son Solomon to the throne of ancient Israel (1 Kings 1:11-31).

I have an aunt who has been like a mother to me, especially since my own mother died thirteen years ago. My aunt, a second-generation German immigrant to America, contracted polio when she was two years old. The effects of the disease are prominent, but she never allowed her "disability" to interfere with her life. She graduated from high school, helped my grandparents on their farm, worked a full-time job, married, and has spent the majority of her adult life helping the elderly relatives within the close-knit German farming community in which she grew up. She took care of my grandparents until their deaths, cared for my grandfather's widowed sister-in-law, and made regular trips to another town to visit and care for relatives. She has always been available to take anyone who asks into town to go to the doctor, the pharmacy, the bank, or the grocery store. And she calls me every weekend to see how I'm doing.

To the outsider, my aunt may seem insignificant. But she is to me a wonderful example of an ordinary person using the power she has to make a difference, perhaps—yes, I am sure—an eternal difference.

May we learn from Esther that our circumstances and our situations are not as important as our willingness, first, to believe that we can make a difference; second, to speak and act honestly (from our hearts); and third, to always strive to do what we have the power to do. (Nancy L. deClaisse-Walford)

GROWING TOGETHER

JAMES 5:13-20

A special kind of community often develops among people who meet periodically in the waiting room of the offices of oncologists. These are the patients and family members of patients who are going through chemotherapy as part of their treatment for cancer. No one asks them to form a fellowship. They are there to meet their individual needs. But they are drawn to each other because they are going through a frightening experience, and they need the emotional support of others who are sharing a similar experience.

They learn to care deeply about each other because they identify with each other. They know that some of them will not survive the illness, and that grief will be part of the cost of their caring. Yet they do dare to care. Those who are religious pray for each other. They do it spontaneously, though probably privately, because it just makes sense to do that. When they can do anything helpful for each other, they do it. But the most valuable thing they do for each other is to care—and listen, and talk, and share one of the most important experiences of their lives.

A similar kind of community can and should develop in the church among people who are serious about growing in their Christian faith and living it out in an unfriendly or indifferent world. After helping us to get realistic about what it means to live the Christian life and to grow in it, James tells us some helpful things about how serious Christians can share their faith journey in the fellowship of the church.

I. Share All of Life with Your Friends in Faith

Suffering and joy, sickness and health, defeat and victory are all parts of the experience of anyone who has the courage to venture out into life and live it fully. The Christian faith is about that adventure into life. God cares about every aspect of it. Every aspect of it is an occasion for an interaction with God.

Tevye, the Jewish milkman in *Fiddler on the Roof*, seems to know that and to carry on a running dialogue with God about whatever is happening in his life at any given time. Every aspect of life's adventure can and should be lifted up to God in prayer and worship. Every aspect of life can and should be shared with other Christians who care. Doing so will enrich life with meaning. And, sometimes, those who care can help. Church singles groups often serve this function for their members. The fellowship of the church can be important to all who let themselves be drawn into caring relationships.

II. Share Your Struggle with Your Friends

Some will think that is the most ridiculous idea they have ever heard. If anything is going wrong in their lives, they are inclined to hide it from their friends at church. They certainly are not about to talk about their struggles with sin. But sin is not just some little naughtiness that we have to hide to avoid the disapproval of the pious. Sin is a deep, life-distorting force with which we all have to struggle.

Look at the specific examples about which James talks: anger, sordidness, wickedness, discrimination, irresponsibility, selfish ambition, greedy cravings, arrogance and others. These things are at work in our lives, and they will mess our lives up if we let them. Other people are struggling with the same problems. If we can move into an open and honest, and caring relationship with others, we can help each other along the way.

Alcoholics Anonymous probably does the best job of sharing the struggle with destructive forces. It takes a very special relationship to allow people to talk openly about their deepest problems. But it may not be necessary to talk about specific problems. It can help just to be part of a fellowship of people who are honest with themselves and others about the real shape of life, and who care enough about each other to believe in each other and to be there to help if they can.

III. The Life You Share Together Is Important

It is sad to see church members treating their involvement in the church as a thing of little importance, a mere propriety that they observe. When the sharing of life in the church means what it can to church members, it will make the difference between fullness of life and a living death. Such a relationship should be celebrated and renewed regularly. (Jim Killen)

OCTOBER 1, 2000

TWO SIDES TO ONE COIN

MARK 9:38-50

Harry Truman used to say that he would like to find a one-armed economist so the man couldn't say, "But on the other hand. . . ." In this passage, Jesus gives us some reassuring words about service and then seems to add, "but on the other hand. . . ."

I. The Positive Side (vv. 38-41)

Like the Twelve, we often want to call a halt to some Christian project or some deed of kindness because the person or persons involved are not "one of us." We are here warned against such action. It is just possible that somebody in another group would like to stop us. We are not sure what Jesus meant when he said he had other sheep "not of this fold" (John 10:16 KJV), but his words should make us hesitate before we judge other believers, and it should make us hesitate before we try to put a stop to somebody's Christian service.

It is reassuring to know that the smallest deed of service does not go unnoticed by our Lord. If many people have secret sins, there are also many people who have secret virtues. They prefer to do their work quietly behind the scenes. They prefer to give their gifts anonymously. They know that Christ will not fail to reward all who serve him and all who serve their fellow human beings in his name. They would prefer that reward to the praise of men. In Matthew 6:1, Jesus seems to suggest that we have a choice. We can have an earthly reward or a heavenly reward, but we cannot have both. If that's a correct interpretation, we all should opt for the heavenly reward.

II. The Negative Side

Now we are ready for those disturbing words, *on the other hand*. Jesus says we must be very careful about our example. Even people who have no children are still role models for others. It may be a little one in the chronological sense, or it may be a little one in some other sense. We must never cause others to stumble.

347

Jesus says we must be very stern with ourselves and take our temptations very seriously. Of course Jesus did not mean to be taken literally when he said to cut off your hand or pluck out your eyes. If these verses were taken literally, all believers would be without limps and eyesight, since none of us is immune from temptation. Jesus chose these words to get our attention. He wanted us to know that we must be very strict with ourselves, even while we are being very charitable with others. Usually we reverse the process. We allow ourselves a lot of leeway, while allowing little for others. We've gotten it backward.

So serious is Jesus about our resisting temptation, he gives us a vivid picture of the punishment that awaits many. As surely as Jesus rewards the good, he will punish the evil. It is instructive that both reward and punishment are discussed in this little conversation Jesus had with his followers. The discussion ends with Jesus saying that we are the salt of the earth. There is no real substitute for salt, as those of us who have had to restrict it in our diets know. Neither is there any way to salt the salt. While recognizing how important our work, example, and holiness are to others, we are also to live peaceably with others. Pride is not to be mixed with our holiness. We are to be peacemakers, example setters, and water carriers, all the while being lenient with others and strict with ourselves. (Robert Shannon)

OCTOBER 8, 2000

Seventeenth Sunday After Pentecost

Worship Theme: In Christ, our suffering can have meaning, bringing to us a gift of childlike dependence on God.

Readings: Job 1:1; 2:1-10; Hebrews 1:1-4; 2:5-12; Mark 10:2-16

Call to Worship (Psalm 26:1-4):

Leader: Vindicate me, O LORD, for I have walked in my integrity, and I have trusted in the LORD without wavering.

People: **Prove me, O LORD, and try me; test my heart and mind.**

Leader: For your steadfast love is before my eyes, and I walk in faithfulness to you.

People: **I do not sit with the worthless, nor do I consort with hypocrites.**

Pastoral Prayer:

Gracious God, our source of all life and love, though we have strayed so far since the very beginning of our human race, still you sent your Son. Still, you send your Holy Spirit. But our childlike wonder of and reliance on you fades so quickly. Especially when suffering arrives, as we know it arrives in every life, we turn and seek the shabby lifeless-life of our "grown-up" world. By your grace, restore in us the mind of a child that knows the visitation of hurt and longs to depend only on you. Give to each of us a humility that comes from the universal experience of soulful pain so that our only goal is to know your Son, Jesus Christ, more fully. Amen. (Thomas Gildermeister)

349

SERMON BRIEFS

WHY BOTHER TO DO GOOD?

JOB 1:1; 2:1-10

Saint Teresa of Avila was traveling and got caught in a violent thunderstorm. She prayed an earnest prayer to God, saying, "It's no wonder you have so few friends, if this is the way you treat them." Perhaps all of us have felt that way at one time or another. Certainly Job must have felt that way. The book of Job does not give us final answers on why the righteous suffer. It does, however, encourage us by saying that suffering does not mean that God is angry with us. It also encourages us with promises that there are blessings for those who are faithful.

I. God's Commendations

The introduction of the book of Job describes him as a man who was "blameless and upright; he feared God and shunned evil" (1:1 NIV). What higher praise can there be for a man than that? While Job was not perfect, this analysis suggests he was the very epitome of faith and integrity. In chapter 2, after Job has already experienced the loss of family, God says of him, "There is no one in earth like him; he is blameless and upright, a man who fears God and shuns evil" (v. 3 NIV). All those things were said about Job before he went through persecution, and he still had those character qualities after persecution. God took note of Job, and Job's character pleased God.

II. Satan's Accusations

Satan makes his indictment based on the prosperity of Job. He suggests that Job is a good and righteousness man because God has allowed only good things into his life. It is interesting, from a theological standpoint, to note that Job's trials did not come directly from the hand of God. They came from the hand of Satan. This doesn't eliminate all of our dilemmas. Job's suffering was at least part of God's permissive will, but it was not part of God's prescriptive will. In other words, Satan does the oppressing, and God does not prevent it. Satan moves his attack from Job's family to Job himself. He probably did not realize he had already given Job the greatest pain through the loss of his family. Satan vainly thought that if Job was attacked personally with illness, that he would curse God. So Job is afflicted with painful sores. Satan had already done his worst when he afflicted Job's family. That being said, the additional pain of personal affliction is still significant.

III. Job's Conclusion

In the midst of Job's adversity, his own wife asks, "Are you still holding on to your integrity" (2:9 NIV)? Then she says to him, "Curse God and die!"

Even in this moment Job does not give up his faith in God. He ponders, "Shall we accept good from God, and not trouble?" Job did not believe that he had been promised a trouble-free life. He did not hold God to promises that had not been made.

The summary of Job's character is seen in this statement: "In all this, Job did not sin in what he said" (v. 10 NIV). Job, in fact, records for us that he became even stronger in faith as a result of all of his trials. That phenomenon is very puzzling to unbelievers, but people of faith will affirm it.

A young boy and his sister were climbing up a rugged hill together. The girl said, "I can't keep going. There are too many bumps." The brother replied, "Don't you know the bumps are what you climb on?" While Job's character and goodness did not prevent him from suffering, it did bring him to an even closer fellowship to God in spite of the external circumstances. (Michael Shannon)

THE WORD BECAME FLESH

HEBREWS 1:1-4; 2:5-12

Someone said the book of Hebrews begins like an essay, proceeds like a sermon, and ends like a letter. And indeed, it may be all three. The author is unknown, and we may speak of Paul, Barnabas, Luke, Silas, Priscilla, or Apollos as possible authors, along with some unknown person. In any event, the writer of Hebrews stresses some wonderful spiritual truths.

I. God Spoke (vv. 1-4)

God spoke to mankind. Not using fairy tales, not blowing smoke, and not encouraging us to just whistle in the dark, God spoke a strong word of commitment and hope through the prophets. God spoke in various times and ways; the message often seemed only partial, but it always rang true. And what was said always pointed to the coming of the True Light that enlightens every man. The prophets over the years pointed to Jesus, the coming of the Word of God in human flesh.

The description of Jesus, the son of God, is seven-fold. The writer wants us to know that Jesus is more than mere man, though he is surely a man. He is heir to all the wealth and glory and knowledge and immortality possessed by God. And we who believe in Jesus are fellow heirs (see Rom. 8:17; Gal. 4:7; Titus 3:7; James 2:5). It was through Jesus that all the worlds that are and may be throughout this cosmos were made. What a stirring thought, that the same Jesus who walked along the Sea of Galilee also created the stars and the constellations and the worlds at the edge of space.

This same Jesus carries the glow of God's glory, and reflects the reality of God, as the sunshine reflects the reality and warmth of the sun. He exhibits the character, the essence of God, as a coin bears the stamp of the king or emperor. And the purpose of this God-man, this demonstration of God in the flesh, is to move all creation along toward the goal of God, a re-creation, a putting right of the ravages of sin. And so Jesus made the cosmic sacrifice, the ultimate sacrifice and purification for sin, and sat down at the right hand of God on high.

II. A Son, Not Angels (vv. 5-12)

In this passage, the writer stresses the superiority of the Son over the angels. Perhaps there was a problem of angel worship in the community to which the writer wrote. Certainly we are not strangers to the various New Age themes, which include a strong emphasis on angels, and even worship of them. But we see here that God chose to become a man, a little weaker, a little lower than the angels, to do something angels could not do—redeem mankind. And so the angels worship the Son, and all creation is subject to the Son. So the writer would turn our thoughts from angels to the Son of God, Jesus of Nazareth. The Son came to die on the cross, to taste of death for all men, that he might set those free who would hear his message of salvation. "This is my beloved son, hear him," says God through these verses.

And how difficult it is to focus on the Word-become-flesh in the form of a carpenter of Nazareth. Amid all the clamor of the world and the allurements of false religion, we may fail to hear the good news of Jesus, who is "crowned with glory and hour because of the suffering of death, so that by the grace of God he might taste death for everyone" (v. 9).

I remember a few years ago traveling the Romantic Road of Germany. My wife and I were staying that night in Nordlingen. Next to the hotel was the famous old church of the town. Beginning at seven o'clock or so in the evening, upon the striking of the hour by the church tower bell, the sexton of the church would appear in a window high up in the tower and would shout out the hour and the news that all was well. Having a romantic streak, I wanted to hear his announcement, and joined a small crowd on the sidewalk gazing up to the tower window. The time arrived, the window opened, we craned our necks and strained to hear, and just as he began to speak, a group of motorcycles roared down the narrow little street. We heard nothing but their noise. We could see the crier's mouth moving, but we couldn't hear him. Let us hear clearly God's message of sending his son to dwell a little lower than angels, and to die for us.

III. A Son and Many Sons (vv. 11-12)

Let us mark that the object of the suffering of the Son was to bring many other sons and daughters to glory. It is a wonderful affirmation—what we cannot do in our wrestling with sin and Satan, and what angels cannot do—Jesus, the Son of God, accomplished through his death. The one Son suffering for the many sons. And here we see in these and the following verses a beautiful variation of the older-brother theme. Jesus is our older brother who comes from heaven to us prodigal brothers and sisters, we who are the "many sons and daughters," and sanctifies us and calls us and sets us apart through his blood.

And in coming to earth in flesh, God identified with our

humanity. In verses 14 and 15 is a wonderful statement of the Easter faith. God, in Jesus Christ, took upon himself human flesh and blood to destroy the one who had the power of death, the devil. Because of the work of the one Son, all of us prodigal sons and daughters can come home, can live free of the fear of death, and can know our sins are forgiven. (Earl C. Davis)

A LOADED QUESTION

MARK 10:2-16

A paradox is a statement that seems to contradict itself, and yet expresses a valid principle or truth. For example, the apostle Paul used a paradox when he wrote, "Whenever I am weak, then I am strong" (2 Cor. 12:10). There are times when the best way to state a truth is by means of a paradox. Jesus did precisely that in the tenth chapter of Mark. He gave us five important lessons that were expressed in five succinct, paradoxical statements. The first of these five statements is this: "Two shall become one" (v. 8).

I. A Loaded Question

Jesus is rapidly moving toward Jerusalem. He resumes his public ministry, and the Pharisees reinstate their public attack. While Jesus is teaching the people, the Pharisees approach Jesus with another one of their loaded questions: "Is it lawful for a man to divorce his wife?"

Theirs is a trick question. It is aimed at Jesus to find the spot where he will either sin against God or give his enemies a reason for putting him to death. If he opposes divorce on legal grounds, he contradicts the Law of Moses. If he makes divorce a moral issue, he exposes himself to the same fate as John the Baptist at the hands of an adulterous monarch. At the same time, if he accepts divorce on legal grounds, he subjects himself to the Law of Moses and the interpretation of the Pharisees. And if he refuses to accept divorce on moral grounds, he chooses to side with the Shammai faction of the rabbinical school in their heated debate with the students of Hillel.

(The Shammai faction contended that divorce could be

granted only for unfaithfulness on the part of the husband, while the more liberal faction, students of Hillel, interpreted the Law of Moses to permit a man to divorce his wife for any reason of dissatisfaction, including burnt toast.)

II. Jesus' Counter Question

Jesus knew better than to give a direct response to their loaded question. Choosing his words very carefully, he tosses the question back to them, "What did Moses command you?"

Feeling secure in their knowledge of Mosaic law, they recite the provision for divorce that Moses permitted. They do not say "commanded." Jesus takes advantage of their choice of words to address the question of divorce from God's perspective.

Jesus acknowledges that Moses' provision for a certificate of divorce was predicated on humankind's unwillingness to forgive: "And Jesus answered and said to them, 'Because of the hardness of your heart he wrote you this precept' " (v. 5 NKJV). Divorce is not something God intended. It is proof of humankind's sinfulness.

Jesus does not launch into a fiery sermon on divorce as evidence of the hardness of humankind's hearts. Instead of dignifying divorce, he chooses to elevate the sacredness of marriage.

God's purpose for marriage has not changed. God's intention for marriage is revealed in the very beginning. A man breaks away from his parents and is joined to his wife so that two persons will become one.

III. Clarification for Confused Disciples

Later, when Jesus and his disciples are alone in the house, the conversation continues. Confusion still exists in the disciples' minds. If Jesus' public statement is taken literally, divorce is not permissible under any circumstances.

Jesus' response is difficult to interpret. Some take it to mean that divorce and remarriage on the part of either husband or wife is adultery. Others refer to Matthew's account of the same conversation in which Jesus makes sexual immorality a legitimate exception for divorce and remarriage (see Matt. 19:9). Others believe Jesus was correcting the antifeminism of Jewish law, which let a man divorce his wife for any reason but left not recourse for the wife, even if her husband were guilty of adultery.

Perhaps Jesus wants the disciples to consider the spirit of the law rather than the letter of the law. Jesus does not introduce a new legalism, nor does he back away from the truth that divorce is a symptom of humankind's sin and that permanent marriage is God's intention.

While divorce may be a tragic reality in our society, we do not have to condone it as God's original purpose. Divorce falls short of God's original purpose, but it is not the unforgivable sin. In the midst of our own confusion, may we not only ask, Is it legally permissible? but also, Is it God's intention? (Bob Buchanan)

OCTOBER 15, 2000

Eighteenth Sunday After Pentecost

Worship Theme: Christ Jesus has opened the possibility for an entirely new relationship with God, one that is honest and bold but always humble at the same time.

Readings: Job 23:1-9, 16-17; Hebrews 4:12-16; Mark 10:17-31

Call to Worship (Psalm 22:25-27):

Leader: From you comes my praise in the great congregation;

People: **my vows I will pay before those who worship the LORD.**

Leader: The poor shall eat and be satisfied;

People: **those who seek the LORD shall praise the LORD! May your hearts live for ever!**

Leader: All the ends of the earth shall remember and turn to the LORD;

People: **and all the families of the nations shall worship before the LORD.**

Pastoral Prayer:

Great God of power and light, we praise you for your Son and our Lord Jesus Christ. He is our bridge from our broken-down lives to your perfect life and love. Can we be as bold as our brother Job? Can we follow the guidance of that ancient letter to the Hebrews? Can we drink from the cup of Christ, the cup of servanthood, even painful sacrifice? O Lord, give us strength. O precious Redeemer, give us mercy. We faint at the mention of surrendering our piety and our tidy lives wholly to your Son. We withhold much of ourselves with the hollow claim that Jesus was perfect, never tempted, not really human. But he is fully one of us as he is fully at one with you. Help us to see him more clearly, follow him more nearly, and love him more dearly. Amen. (Thomas Gildermeister)

SERMON BRIEF

WHERE IS GOD?

JOB 23:1-9, 16-17

Many of today's problems are actually indications of a thirst for God. There are people who thirst for God who don't even know that's what their longing is. They try to satisfy that longing in various ways, only to come up dry. Even those who believe in God sometimes doubt their ability to reach God. One of H.G. Wells' characters was told that his problem was that he needed closer fellowship with God. He replied, "That up there have fellowship with me? I'd sooner think of drinking from the Milky Way or shaking hands with the stars."

In Chapter 23 of Job, we see Job thirsting for fellowship with God. His concerns are expressed frankly and passionately. But we see that his thirst finally ends in fulfillment.

I. A Complaint

It is amazing at times how brutally honest the people of faith can be. Biblical characters often pray with the same boldness as Tevye in *Fiddler on the Roof*, who said, "I know we are the chosen people, but, Lord, can't you sometimes choose someone else?"

Job admits that he is in pain. He admits that he feels far from God. He desires to take his case before God, to talk with God about his problems, to try to come to some kind of understanding about his suffering. Job says, "I would [state] my case before him and fill my mouth with arguments. I would [find out] what he would answer me, and [consider] what he would say to me" (vv.4-5). Job's boldness is not a hindrance to his relationship with God. God has always delighted in bold faith.

II. A Search

Job describes his longing as a search for God. He looks to the east and west but doesn't find God. He looks to the north and south but cannot find God. Maybe the problem is that Job is looking too far away. God may be a lot closer than he thinks.

In the book of Acts where Paul is before the scholars at the Areopagus, he tells them that God is not far from any of us: "For 'In him we live and move and have our being' " (Acts 17:28). So Job has his eyes trained in the wrong direction. The evidence of God is all around him; he just has a hard time seeing that through tear-stained eyes.

III. A Confidence

Even in the midst of this gut-wrenching search, Job believes that all things will eventually come out all right. He says with confidence, "He knows the way that I take" (v. 10). Without arrogance, Job says, "When he has tested me, I shall come out like gold" (v. 10). That is not an arrogant assumption; it was Job's own personal experience that in relationship with God he found his highest potential. God says, in the words of an old hymn, "The flame shall not hurt thee; I only design / Thy dross to consume and thy gold to refine."

Job thought he couldn't find God, but God was very near him. A skeptical professor once wrote on the blackboard the statement, "God Is Nowhere." During the break between lectures, a student rearranged the spaces until the statement read, "God Is Now Here." When we face struggles and that lead to feelings of separation from God, we are prone to conclude that God is nowhere. We may find that right in the midst of the struggle God "is now here." (Michael Shannon)

THE POWER OF THE WORD

HEBREWS 4:12-16

In the middle of the admonitions and warnings, the writer of the Book of Hebrews speaks of the nature and power of God's Word. Now, the author of Hebrews did not know he or she was penning Scripture, and the Bible the writer knew was the Old Testament. Here in verses 12 and 13 we see that the writer has a very high view of Scripture. Notice that he or she says the Bible is living—alive, active, reaching out, and judging the reader as well as presenting information. The writer says the Bible is nothing to play with; it is sharper than any double-edged sword and slices right down to the bone. He or she indicates the Bible is the tool of the Creator, before whom nothing is hidden.

We are accustomed to thinking of the Word of God in terms of its unity, written over a thousand years by perhaps more than one hundred people, and yet all through the Bible runs the theme of the plight of man and the love of God. We tout the durability of the Bible: "The grass withers, the flower fades, but the word of our God will stand forever" (Isa. 40:8). Sometimes we get carried away in a superstitious vein about the durability of the Bible.

I remember years ago when a relative's automobile caught on fire. All the insides were burned and melted. But the Bible, laying in the back window, was still intact. An aunt was mightily impressed with the "eternal nature" of the Word of God. Even as a child, however, I had enough sense to notice that a Sears & Roebuck catalog laying beside the Bible in the back window also came through unscathed. The power of the Bible is deeper than superstition, and for it to have its edifying power in the Christian's life and its spiritually surgical power in the life of the unbeliever, the Bible must be seen as more than a part of our custom and tradition, laying on the coffee table.

I. The Power Is in Its Purpose

I once had a retired physician as a church member who wrote a book about how he came from the Nolichucky River area in East Tennessee to Memphis to enter medical school, and stayed in Memphis the rest of his career. He wanted his grandchildren to know the story of their grandfather; of his beginnings, his struggles, his joys. I don't know about the grandchildren, but the book sure worked on me.

The Bible has as its purpose to help us understand who God is and what God is doing in this world. The purpose of the Bible is to lead you and me to a personal relationship to God through his son, Jesus Christ. When we assign other purposes to the Bible, whether it be of science, history, geology, and so forth, we obscure its real purpose. The Bible cannot be alive and active and sharper than a double-edged sword, cutting down to the spiritual bone and judging the thoughts and the intents of the heart if we seek to harness it to all the latest thinking of science or psychology.

II. The Power Is in Its Inspiration

The inspiration of the Bible has to do with both the writing and the reading of the Bible. The Bible, speaking for itself, says it is God-breathed. That means it is filled with the very breath, heart, and thoughts of God toward us. It is God's book; it is the only one God wrote.

I stood at the window in the home of Sir Walter Scott, in the same room where he died. He was taken there so he could look out over the vast lawn during his illness. As I too looked out over the lawn, I remembered the story of Sir Walter Scott in those last days turning to his son-in-law and asking him to "bring me the book." His son-in-law replied that Scott had written many books; of which one did he speak? And Scott replied, "There is but one book."

There is, indeed, but one book, which is authored by God. There is but one book that has the power to change lives. Many manmade books come with all sorts of helps, but only the Bible comes with its "built-in interpreter, the Holy Spirit."

We must always define the inspiration of the Bible not by the method—verbal plenary, dictation, illumination, dynamic, and so forth—but by the result. The Bible is, in its aliveness and its ability to cut to the heart of man's sin and man's conscience, the only book intended through the Holy Spirit to bring every man to a saving relationship to God through Christ. And though all the Bible is equally inspired, not all the Bible is equally useful in the conviction and the conversion of the lost, or the daily walk of the saved. Every Christian has his or her Bible within the Bible,

361

those sections most loved and most used, under the guidance of the Spirit.

III. The Power Is in Its Infallibility

In some circles much emphasis is placed on the infallibility of the Bible. And, indeed, it is infallible in terms of the purpose for which it was written. Infallibility must be related to purpose.

My wristwatch keeps wonderful time, but it isn't worth a hoot for cooking supper. I can lay it on the kitchen counter and command it to cook supper from now to Christmas, but it will not do my bidding. That is not its purpose.

The Bible is infallible in terms of its purpose. God wrote the Bible to lead sinful men and women to find salvation. Period. It is designed, as someone used to say, to tell us how to go to heaven, not how the heavens go. And the Bible fulfills its purpose of drawing men to God, not as a club over them, but by confronting men with the love of God and the salvation God offers. And this wonderful work of the Bible is done by the guiding presence of the Holy Spirit. The Bible speaks not just to Adam when it says "Where art thou?" in Genesis 3; it is asking the question of us all. It is not just Abraham to whom the promise and the covenant is made, but to all of us who are the sons and daughters of Abraham through the blood of Christ.

The terms used in this passage in Hebrews to describe the nature and the work of the Bible take on their full meaning when we read the Bible and are confronted, through the Holy Spirit, with promises we need to claim, with attitudes we need to change, with examples we need to follow, with sins we need to confess, with errors we need to avoid, with action we need to take. It's God's book, and it has a happy ending that includes you and me if we will allow it. (Earl C. Davis)

WHEN YOU LACK JUST ONE THING

MARK 10:17-31

A few years ago I was putting together a white, laminated bookshelf for my daughter. The piece of furniture was simple, so

I tossed the directions aside. After placing all the pieces on the floor exactly as they should be assembled, I proceeded to attach the horizontal boards to one of the vertical boards, using the supplied bag of wooden dowels, screws, and locking inserts. As soon as I finished one side, I immediately started on the other side. Starting at the top of the bookshelf, one by one I locked the shelves into place. Only the bottom shelf remained. I reached into the plastic bag to grab the last screw, but the bag was empty. Thinking the screw must have fallen out of the bag, I searched the box that the pieces came in as well as the room. The only thing that I found was the directions that I had laid aside earlier.

I glanced at the directions, hoping to discover that somehow I had made a mistake and put a screw where it didn't belong. The very first statement on the directions was in bold print and surrounded by a border: "Before you begin, please read the entire instructions and make sure you have all the necessary parts and tools required."

Determined to make it work, I tried improvising. Every time I failed I became madder and madder. When I finally called the store and informed them of the problem, the manager said he was sorry and that he would be happy to give me another bookshelf, if I returned the other. I protested, saying, "You mean, I have to disassemble this bookshelf and return it for an unassembled bookshelf just because one screw was lacking?"

Sometimes, lacking just one thing can be terribly frustrating.

Of all the people who ever came to Jesus, the rich young ruler is one of the few who went away worse off than when he arrived. Yet he had so much in his favor. He was a young man with tremendous potential (see Matt. 19:22). He was respected by others and held some ruling office (Luke 18:18). He had high morals and a sincere desire for spiritual things. In many ways, he was an ideal young man and a high achiever.

Kneeling before Jesus, the young man asked, "Good Teacher, what must I do to inherit eternal life?" His question was right, but his assumptions were wrong. His question was based on at least three false assumptions. His first assumption was that *goodness could be achieved*. His second assumption was that *eternal life could be earned*. His third assumption was that *everything could be bought for a price, including eternal life*.

Jesus shatters all three false assumptions. Jesus reminded him that "no one is good but God" (v. 18). While the young man was faithful in some things (vv. 19-20), he still lacked one thing. Jesus identified the one thing that stood between the rich young ruler and God when he said, "Go, sell what you own, and give the money to the poor." That was more than the young man was willing to do. The rich young man was so close, but yet so far way. He "went away grieving, for he had many possessions" (v. 22).

Jesus shatters the last false assumption by reminding the disciples that the kingdom of God is not for sale. The kingdom of God does not come as a result of our own effort and achievements; it is the result of God's initiative and grace. When the disciples asked, "[If the rich man can't be saved], then who can be saved?" (v. 26), Jesus answered, "For mortals it is impossible, but not for God; for God all things are possible" (v. 27).

Barbara Brown Taylor captures the essence of the encounter: "[It] is not a story about money, because, if it were, we could buy our way into heaven by cashing in our chips right now, and you know that is not so. None of us earns eternal life, no matter what we do. We can keep the Commandments until we are blue in the face; we can sign our paychecks over to Mother Teresa and rattle tin cups for our supper without ever earning a place at the banquet table of God. The kingdom of God is not for sale. It never has been; it never will be. The poor cannot buy it with their poverty, and the rich cannot buy it with their riches. The kingdom of God is a consummate gift" (*The Preaching Life* [Boston: Cowley, 1993], p. 122).

Grace, the unmerited favor of God, is the one thing that you and I cannot lack if we wish to enter the kingdom of God. (Bob Buchanan)

OCTOBER 22, 2000

Ninteenth Sunday After Pentecost

Worship Theme: The Almighty God who came to us in Jesus Christ displayed the power of love and humility.

Readings: Job 38:1-7 (34-41); Hebrews 5:1-10; Mark 10:35-45

Call to Worship (Psalm 104:1-4, 24-25, 35*b*):

Leader: Bless the LORD, O my soul!

People: **O LORD my God, you are very great!**

Leader: You are clothed with honor and majesty, and cover yourself with light as with a garment;

People: **you have stretched out the heavens like a tent, and have laid the beams of your chambers on the waters;**

Leader: you make the clouds your chariot, and ride on the wings of the wind;

People: **you make the winds your messengers, fire and flame your ministers.**

Leader: O LORD, how manifold you are works!

People: **wisdom you have made them all; the earth is full of your creatures.**

Leader: Yonder is the sea, great and wide,

People: **creeping things innumerable are there, living things both small and great.**

Leader: Bless the LORD, O my soul!

People: **Praise the LORD!**

Pastoral Prayer:

Holy and Almighty God, what surprises you have for us! We are mute with our gratitude, for we hardly can believe the words we read in our Scriptures. Your very Son, our Savior, was not first, but last? He was our servant, a ransom for us who hear and obey him? But you are God. You created the heavens and the earth. We cannot imagine your power and might. But you allowed your Son to die that miserable death? For me? For all of us? O God, it is too wonderful or too horrible to believe. But we stand before you this day with all of our sin, and declare boldly that we believe. Amen. (Thomas Gildermeister)

SERMON BRIEFS

I'M NOT GOD

JOB 38:1-7 (34-41)

Two men were seated in a fast-food restaurant. One was clean-shaven, the other bearded. A young child came up to the bearded man and asked, "Mister, are you Jesus?" The bearded man, who was a devout Christian, blushed and said, "No I'm not, but I do believe in him and love him."

It was not difficult for that man to admit he was not Jesus. There are, however, some people in this world who persist in playing God.

A wise man once said, "The two greatest thoughts that changed my life were (1) that there is a God, and (2) that I am not [God]." That is really the answer God gives Job for all of Job's questions. There is not a final explanation to the mystery of suffering. It is not a cruel answer, but an honest one that is given to Job. The answer is basically this: The mystery of suffering is beyond human understanding. Even though Job did not get a final explanation, he did get his audience with God. He came out of it a greater and stronger man.

I. God's Appearance

God does honor Job with a personal appearance. That in itself testifies to God's personal concern for Job. Notice that a great storm arose. Our text says, "Then the LORD answered Job out of the whirlwind." This is very appropriate because often it is in the storms of life where we do meet God.

In words that sound a little stern to modern ears, God asks, "Who is this that darkens counsel by words without knowledge?" God is simply saying that there are things God understands that we can never understand. At first that might not seem to be a comforting answer. But the longer we ponder it, the more we understand that there is a liberation that comes to us that can free us from trying to understand everything. Some examination of tough questions is useful and needful. This is not an admonition for people of faith to quit thinking. We must simply accept the limitation of our human brain.

II. God's Creative Power

God begins the explanation to Job by asking where Job was when the earth was formed. It is obvious we were not there. In a beautiful poetic fashion, God describes the creation of this earth. The implication is that we should not question God, since we are not in the position to do the mighty acts that God performs. We human beings think we are quite clever in the world of science and technology. We are nowhere near the abilities of God. We think we are great artists, but God has created far more beauty that we will ever be able to comprehend.

III. God's Sustaining Power

Throughout the remainder of chapter 38, God talks not only about his creative power, but the fact that he continuously sustains life on this planet. God talks about the cycles of nature, the mysteries of the human mind, the food chain. While sometimes there are anomalies in nature (floods, hurricanes, droughts, and famines), most of the time this earth produces enough for human beings to eat. It is safe enough that most human beings survive. While the earth is not a perfect place, it is a place filled with indications of creative design and sustenance.

In one of Gary Larson's *Far Side* cartoons, a character seated in the classroom raises his hand and says to the teacher, "Teacher, may I leave now? My brain is full." That is the way Job must have felt, and that's the way we feel. There are things beyond our human understanding. But as the old song says, "We will understand it better by and by." (Michael Shannon)

VICTORY IN LIFE'S MOST COMMON BATTLE

HEBREWS 5:1-10

One day I climbed into a taxi and struck up a conversation with the driver, who discovered that I was a minister and soon blurted out that he planned to start going to church.

"It's a jungle out here," he said, waving his hand toward the city skyline. He went on with his story, and it was obvious that he had been fighting a hard battle, and losing, against the world, the flesh, and the devil.

The most common battle in life is with temptation. No person, including Jesus, has ever managed to escape being tempted. In verses 15 and 16 of chapter 4 of Hebrews, the writer announces the good news, the gospel, that our High Priest knows our struggles with temptation, has been where we are, and has struggled with temptation and won. The admonition is to draw near, then, to the throne of Jesus, that we may receive both mercy—like cool water to the beaten-down sinner—and also grace to help us in our struggle. We can be victorious. This theme is further laid out in this passage.

I. Know the Source

If we are to rise above our temptations, we must know the source of our temptations. We usually know better, but go ahead and fall in the hour of temptation because the source of temptation is not just in our heads, but in our hearts. And the heart, says the Bible, is deceitful above all things.

For instance, sometimes when visiting folks in the hospital, I will see people standing outside the "smoke-free environment" of the hospital, puffing away. I say to myself, "Don't they know better? Haven't all of us seen friends die a slow and terrible death from lung cancer as a result of smoking?" And then I may notice a doctor, or a group of doctors, puffing away, having untied their surgical masks so they can get a cigarette to their mouths. And I say to myself, "Of all people, these folks ought to know most clearly the danger of smoking." But you see, it is more than just a head decision. It is a matter of the heart and habit. The head knows all the reasons, but the heart doesn't believe them.

And even beyond the source of temptation in our lusts and desires (James 4:1-5), there is the ultimate source of temptation in the devil. Here again, even Christians read the biblical warnings about the wiles of the devil, but we really don't believe them. Jesus took the devil seriously, the early Christians took him seriously, but we laugh about him. We need to see ourselves in William Blake's painting Adam Naming the Beasts. We see Adam from the waist up, caressing a serpent. That's us.

II. Draw Near to God (Heb. 4:16)

In Paul's writings (a beautiful description is found in Ephesians 6), we have the emphasis upon standing firm and resisting the devil. Peter, too, stresses this aspect in 1 Peter 5. James also urges us to resist the devil.

When urged by a Bible study leader to resist the devil and told that the devil would flee, the members, fresh from the struggle with the world, told the teacher that the order was all mixed up in their lives: "The devil doesn't flee, and we don't resist him." Before we can effectively resist the devil, we must submit ourselves to God; we must draw nigh to God.

By submission to God, we are not speaking of a surface commitment, or of merely joining the church or being baptized. There is a depth of commitment that includes being controlled by the Holy Spirit, and allowing the Spirit to have access to all our life. Only when we draw near to God in commitment and submission to God's will can we resist the devil.

III. The Sympathy of Christ (Heb. 5:1-10)

For victory in the most common battle of life, we need to lay hold on another spiritual reality—the sympathy of Christ.

Because Christ has been in the eye of the storm of temptation and was not destroyed, we have a resource of strength in his encouragement.

A Bible study group was asked, "Could Jesus have sinned?" The group answered a resounding "Yes!" Verses 1-5 point out that the human priest, being a sinner, can deal gently with the ignorant and misguided. How much more can Jesus understand our temptations. The Bible says he was tempted as we are, yet without sin. And because he did not fall to temptation, we know he understands our struggle. And more than that, we know he wants to strengthen us in the battle.

In verses 8 and 9, we read that Jesus, as one of us, learned obedience through his suffering, and having become perfect, is able to strengthen those who come in obedience and faith to him. And even further, we know that he can bring forth good from the very presence of temptation and evil. This entire passage, Hebrews 4:14–5:10, tells us we are invited to go boldly in our time of temptation and find mercy at the throne of Jesus. Whether we survive our temptations depends upon whether we draw near with confidence to his throne. For if we do, we will find mercy and, even more, grace to stand firm in the hour of temptation. (Earl C. Davis)

SERVANTS, NOT CELEBRITIES

MARK 10:35-45

When I was growing up, my family didn't make a big deal about birthdays. However, I married someone who gives a lot of attention to birthdays.

A few years ago my wife really surprised me on my thirty-ninth birthday. She gave me a gift certificate for a tennis racket of my choice and four private tennis lessons with a local pro. Not that I haven't needed one, but I've never paid for a professional lesson for anything in my life.

I was excited about my first lesson. I showed up several minutes early. When the club pro asked what I wanted to learn, the answer was easy. I needed a backhand stroke and a good second serve. Without a doubt, those two things were the weakest part of my game.

I still don't have a great backhand, but I have a better second serve. The local pro taught me a couple of key things about a second serve. He taught me to slightly close the face of the racket when hitting a second serve and to hit the ball at a two-o'clock position instead of a twelve-o'clock position. Those two adjustments will put a spin on the ball and keep it lower as it crosses the net.

Unfortunately, we live in a society that either doesn't know how to serve or doesn't want to serve. Many don't even know how to spell the word. Instead of spelling it S-E-R-V-I-C-E, they spell it S-E-R-V-E U-S.

In Mark 10:35-45, we discover that our primary calling as disciples, or followers, of Jesus Christ is to be servants and not celebrities. That was a difficult lesson for the early disciples to learn, and it is a difficult lesson for us to learn, too.

Jesus was marching toward Jerusalem while the disciples were lagging behind (v. 32). In a short while he would be handed over to the authorities, condemned to death, and crucified upon a cross. James and John, two brothers nicknamed "the sons of thunder," make an unusual request to Jesus: "Grant us to sit, one at your right hand and one at your left, in your glory" (v. 37). These two disciples had no idea what they were asking.

Jesus asks them, "Are you able to drink the cup that I drink, or be baptized with the baptism that I am baptized with?" Still unable to comprehend that Jesus was speaking about his fast-approaching death, they answer quickly, "We are able." In spite of their enthusiasm, Jesus declines their request saying, "The cup that I drink you will drink; and with the baptism with which I am baptized, you will be baptized; but to sit at my right hand or at my left is not mine to grant, but it is for those for whom it has been prepared" (vv. 39-40).

When the other ten disciples heard of James and John's request, they became angry. They were angry because James and John had beaten them to the punch. They were ticked off because the "sons of thunder" might get the glory they wanted. There was no way they were going to give up those top spots without a fight.

Jesus calls the disciples together and points out the sharp contrast between his philosophy and the philosophy of the world. There may be distinct levels of authority and privilege in the secular world, but when it comes to the kingdom of God, Jesus emphatically says, "It is not so among you." In God's family, there is to be one great body of people, and we are all servants. The only way up is the way down: "Whoever wishes to become great among you must be your servant."

Albert Schweitzer said, "One thing I know: the only ones who will be really happy are those who will have sought and found how to serve."

How well do you serve? Charles Swindoll, in *Improving Your Serve* (Dallas: Word Publishing, 1997), identifies the ingredients of authentic servanthood. Authentic servants give anonymously, generously, voluntarily, and personally. Authentic servants freely forgive others. Authentic servants forget about their past failures and move on with a renewed determination. (Bob Buchanan)

OCTOBER 29, 2000

Twentieth Sunday After Pentecost

Worship Theme: In faithful humility, shout your needs to the Lord. God will respond.

Readings: Job 42:1-6, 10-17; Hebrews 7:23-28; Mark 10:46-52

Call to Worship (Psalm 34:1-8):

Leader: I will bless the LORD at all times; God's praise shall continually be in my mouth.

People: **My soul makes its boast in the LORD; let the afflicted hear and be glad.**

Leader: O magnify the LORD with me, and let us exalt God's name together!

People: **I sought the LORD, who answered me, and delivered me from all my fears.**

Leader: Look to God and be radiant, so your faces shall never be ashamed.

People: **The poor cried out, and the LORD heard, and saved them out of all their troubles.**

Leader: The angel of the LORD encamps around those who fear God, and delivers them.

People: **O taste and see that the LORD is good! Happy are those who take refuge in God!**

Pastoral Prayer:
　　Dearest Lord, Infinite Love, Eternal and Perfect Life, we ask so many questions of you, make so many demands. We cry

aloud in the night and all day long. We know what we want. But our needs? Only you know our needs; here and now, there and then. Our deepest longing is for the love of Christ Jesus, and we know in our minds that this longing has been fulfilled. By your mercy and grace, may these convictions in our heads become passions in our souls. And may this passion mature into a faith that can ask the right questions, a faith that might even move mountains. In the name of the One who makes such faith possible, Jesus Christ. Amen. (Thomas Gildermeister)

SERMON BRIEFS

SURRENDER

JOB 42:1-6, 10-17

When children are wrestling, one will sometimes pin the other and call out, "Say uncle." To "say uncle" is to give up—to surrender. We are very unwilling to make that statement. But it is not always wrong to surrender. Particularly when it comes to our relationship with God. There is survival in surrender, if we surrender to the will of God.

In chapter 42, Job finally gives up. He gives up trying to understand all the ways of God and the universe. He gives up thinking that he could understand what only God could understand.

I. Recognition

Job finally admits to God that he cannot answer all of God's questions. But Job is not completely discouraged by this. Even though he hasn't had all of his questions answered, he has been in the presence of God. He says, "My ears had heard of you, but now my eyes have seen you" (v. 5 paraphrased).

In times of trial, what we are most afraid of is that somehow God's relationship with us will have been damaged or severed. Not only is that not the case, but oftentimes God is revealed to us in special ways, precisely in the time of greatest distress. Anything that drives us closer to God cannot be all bad.

II. Repentance

Job says, "Therefore I despise myself, and repent in dust and ashes" (v. 6). Of what did Job have to repent? He was a righteous man before his illness and was a righteous man in the midst of his illness. He must have believed that he needed to repent of something. I expect it was pride he was repenting of. He was confident of his own righteousness. He was confident that if he could have an audience with God he could make his case by his own cleverness. But he realized that there is always going to be a huge chasm between what we can understand and what God can understand. Therefore, Job says, "I despise myself, and repent in dust and ashes." Job was a good man in nearly every respect, but pride is a serious problem because it can lead to other sins.

Job was rewarded for his faithfulness. The Bible says that the Lord made Job prosperous again, giving him twice as much as he had before. Certainly Job did not disappoint God. Not only was Job prosperous, but he once again enjoyed great fellowship with his family. The Bible says, "The LORD blessed the latter days of Job more than his beginning" (v. 12). Job even had more children, and his daughters were described as the most beautiful women in all the land. I believe God rewards those who have faced great suffering. Sometimes we will receive our rewards in this life, but not always. Sometimes we will have to wait until heaven for that. That is where God has chosen to balance the scales, and that is where God has chosen to reward the faithful. The old hymn is on target when it says,

God hath not promised skies always blue,
Flower-strewn pathways all our lives through; . . .

But God hath promised strength for the day,
Rest for the labor, light for the way,
Grace for the trials, help from above,
Unfailing sympathy, undying love.
("What God Hath Promised")

(Michael Shannon)

THIS PRIEST NAMED JESUS

HEBREWS 7:23-28

"Hail Him! Hail Him! Jesus the crucified:
Crown Him! Crown Him! Prophet and Priest and King!"
("Praise Him! Praise Him!")

So the hymn writer speaks of Jesus, the embodiment of the perfect prophet, priest, and king. In this passage in Hebrews 7, look more closely at the description of Jesus as priest. As Moffatt says, it is generally misleading to parse a rhapsody, speaking of verse 26. But in that verse and the surrounding statements, we have a striking description of our holy high priest.

I. The Everlasting Priest

Jesus is the priest eternal, making intercession for us in heaven. He will never die, nor will anyone else ever take his place.

I remember the serious-on-the-surface remark of a delightful lady in my church a couple of years ago in this respect. We had just finished a course on spiritual gifts, stretching over several evenings of study and discussion. The folks evaluated their spiritual gifts and discussed them in small groups. This lady came up to me after the session on the closing night and said, with a twinkle in her eye, "Pastor, I'm sorry to tell you this, but I've got to have your job. It's my spiritual gift." Well, nobody will ever take the place of Jesus as our high priest. He is priest forever, failing never for us all to intercede.

II. The Priest Who Saves to the Uttermost

This phrase in verse 25 has been interpreted several ways, most frequently as meaning either "saving us forever" in terms of time, or "saving us completely" in terms of sanctification or security of the believer. We do not have to choose between these options; both are true to the uttermost. The resurrection power of Jesus saves us forever, as long as time shall stand. The hymn writer says it this way: "When we've been there ten thousand years . . . we've no less days to sing God's praise than when we'd first begun" ("Amazing Grace"). The blood of Jesus saves us from the depth of our deepest sin and makes us white as snow.

III. The Holy Priest

Jesus is the holy priest, a claim that no priest of Aaron's line could make. Never needing to make a sacrifice on his own behalf, he offered himself as the unblemished lamb needed for our redemption. As the passover lambs, symbols of a temporal redemption from Egypt, were being slain on one hill in Jerusalem that day by frail and sinful priests, the Holy Priest was giving his life as a sacrifice for the sins of many on another hill.

"Holy, holy, holy, Lord God Almighty!" What a title for the whipped man who hung beneath the scornful placard that read, "Jesus of Nazareth, King of the Jews"—holy as we cannot be, but holy as we needed him to be.

IV. The Harmless Priest

This is the priest who stood before the high priest of the Jews, and when reviled did not revile in return. This is the priest who was without guile, who when smitten did not smite back. This is the priest who was without evil; against whom even the bribed false witnesses could not agree in their slander. This is the priest who is harmless, not spineless; who for us and our sins endured the cross, not with cursing, but with forgiveness for his enemies. A priest truly without an evil bone in him. A priest not of this world. His name is Jesus.

V. The Undefiled Priest

Is it possible to walk through this world undefiled? To live unspotted in the midst of a mud-slinging, character-destroying world? To live unstained, embodying true ethical purity, undefiled by the things this world upholds? Jesus did. Temptation could not make a beachhead for the devil; grief and sorrow could not soil his soul nor break his spirit. Evil, while it recognized him, could not cling to his clothes or to his heart. Friend of sinners, yet without sin. Encourager of the broken-hearted sinner, yet not partaking of sin. Only Jesus could do this; only our High Priest forever.

VI. "Separated from Sinners"

The phrase "separated from sinners" in verse 26 has led many simple saints to see and feel Jesus as being distant from them. When the writer speaks of Jesus, our high priest, as separated from us sinners, he is no doubt speaking of the exaltation of Jesus to the right hand of God. For Jesus was certainly not separate from sinners in this world. He moved easily among them, giving hope and help. He died between two sinners, thieves who deserved the cruel death of the cross. He was buried and his grave marked as a sinner. But they were wrong.

In all things helpful to us and leading to our salvation, he was like us and near us. But in his essential nature, he is indeed exalted, high and lifted up. Jesus, our high priest—separate from us sinners, making intercession for us, yet coming to join us soon; then we shall be together eternally. (Earl C. Davis)

WHEN BLIND MEN SEE

MARK 10:46-52

The healing of Bartimaeus, the final miracle performed by Jesus that Mark reports in his Gospel, is very significant. It interrupts the events leading to Jesus' Passion. The setting of the miracle occurs just when Jesus leaves Jericho and begins the last leg of his journey to Jerusalem.

Passover is approaching fast, and the road between Jericho and Jerusalem is packed with pilgrims chanting and celebrating on their way to the Holy City. Curiosity seekers have gathered to watch the parade. Others are too poor, sinful, diseased, or handicapped to make the fifteen-mile journey. The size of the crowd has grown to a great multitude (v. 46).

Jesus' eyes are fixed upon Jerusalem. Nothing would get in the way of his mission now. Above the shouts and cheers of a hysteric crowd, Jesus hears the desperate cry of an unfamiliar voice: "Jesus, Son of David, have mercy on me!" Others in the crowd tell the man to be quiet, but he persists: "Son of David, have mercy on me!"

Jesus stops suddenly. For the first time, Jesus is publicly called "the Son of David." Whether Bartimaeus knows what he said or not, he introduces Jesus to Jerusalem and strikes the keynote for the triumphal entry. Bartimaeus, the blind man, sees more than everyone else sees. Bartimaeus sees Jesus as God meant for him to be seen—as the Messiah.

I. A Call to Faith

Jesus silences the crowd and instructs someone to call the man. A nameless messenger delivers the good news to Bartimaeus: "Cheer up; rise, he is calling you" (v. 49 paraphrased). Bartimaeus has heard "Cheer up" before, but never before has he heard those words alongside the command "Rise." It was a serious call to faith, and it tested his level of trust. Bartimaeus wonders if someone might be playing a cruel joke on him.

II. A Show of Faith

As a blind beggar, Bartimaeus has no place to go but up. Throwing aside the ragged garment that served to catch coins, he enthusiastically demonstrates faith. He bounces up and he goes to stand face-to-face before Jesus.

III. The Result of Faith

It seemed a strange question to ask a blind man, "What do you want me to do for you?" Just a short time earlier, the "sons of thunder" had asked Jesus to grant them one wish. The difference between Bartimaeus' answer and the disciples' request is the difference between faith and ambition. Faith asks for needs. Ambition begs for wants. Bartimaeus needed his sight. James and John wanted places of honor. Jesus refused to give the disciples their wants, but he wasted no time in meeting Bartimaeus' need. Jesus gave instant sight to the blind man. Bartimaeus is pronounced "well." Mark illustrates the total healing of Bartimaeus: "And immediately he received his sight and followed Jesus on the road" (v. 52 NKJV).

The story is filled with irony. A beggar becomes a disciple and a squatter becomes a pilgrim, living, seeing, walking, and singing proof that Jesus is the Messiah.

Amazing grace! How sweet the sound
That saved a wretch like me!
I once was lost, but now am found;
Was blind, but now I see.

Tragically, the rest of the story recorded by Mark is about see-ing people who remained blind and who refused to see what God was doing through Jesus Christ.

Cheer up, friend. God is calling, and God wants to restore your sight, too. (Bob Buchanan)

DOORS AND WINDOWS

NOVEMBER

Reflection Verse: "So that I might live to God" (Gal. 2:19*b*).

The Discipline:

Evaluate your personal or familial budget to find God's place in it. Become a leader of your church's stewardship campaign from a full and knowledgeable heart. Next, empty your wallet and enjoy your credentials. Look through your "black box" of special documents. Then consider this story.

A well-placed church official was traveling through O'Hare Airport. When she went to pick up her purse after going through security, her purse was gone. The police helped search all the trash cans in the hopes that her empty wallet might have been tossed there. No such luck. The purse and everything in it was gone. And thus it was that a woman was in a strange city with no identification, no money, no ticket, no identity. She happened upon one of her former church members while standing around looking dumbfounded. The man was not only a banker, but also the kind of person who carried wads of money with him.

Not all people are so lucky. Consider the experiences of aliens or immigrants or refugees who are new to a country. They are paperless people.

Let stewardship this fall be a matter of the paperless people first—and the full-walleted next. Both are God's people, and both need pastors who are capable of asking for money from a deep and smart and well-considered place within themselves. Both need a pastor who is well acquainted with his or her own wallet—and with how far it will and won't get them in life.

The Meditation:

The most marvelous thing about being saved by grace is how full we become. We give out of a sense of deep abundance. Living to God is not like giving up or giving away, but more like bubbling over. We still have too much left after we've given it away! Tithing is my favorite response to salvation by grace. I also tithe out of a kind of greed for a different kind of wealth than the kind I have. I don't want the poor to continue to embarrass me with their generosity!

Someone once accused Gabriel Garcia Marquez of being rich. He countered that he was not rich but rather "a poor man with money; there is a difference." My family tithes because we want the possibility of being rich. Fat things, like my income, are treasured by the Bible. I can't imagine that God wants everybody living on rice and beans in a world where artichokes were also created.

The absolutely predictable generosity of the poor confirms my response. Sometimes people who live in housing projects take what they don't have down the hall when a mother loses a son to a gang fight. Low-income elderly people will sometimes "pay the church first" before the pharmacist and spread their pills over five hours instead of the recommended four. Poor congregations continue to pay ministers who are HIV-positive, even after the ministers are unable to work. They find a way when there is no way.

I want to be as rich as these people are, with always enough to give something away. I am greedy for the joy of living to God. What may I hope for in the coming century? To be able to give away more and more of what I have.

The Song:

Take my life, God, let it be consecrated faithfully.
Take my moments and my days, let them flow in ceaseless praise.

Take my goods, and let them be always only, all for thee.
Take my money, and give it wings, let me live beyond my things.

Take my hope, my Lord, I pour into thy great treasure store.
Take my confidence, I pray, may there come from it new day.

(first stanza from *New Century Hymnal*)

The Prayer:

Holy Spirit, who makes all things new, you of the Internet and the airport, the pocketbook and the passport, the refugee's courage and the foreigner's safety, break through nooks and crannies, webs and nets. Get where you want to go. Enliven my quick words on rapidly moving filaments. Let them be beautiful. Let them be a sign of you. Open my purse and my heart that all of me may learn to live to you. Amen. (Donna Schaper)

NOVEMBER 5, 2000

Twenty-first Sunday After Pentecost

Worship Theme: Loving God and loving neighbor is simple but never easy.

Readings: Ruth 1:1-18; Hebrews 9:11-14; Mark 12:28-34

Call to Worship (Psalm 146:1-6, 10):

Leader: Praise the LORD! Praise the LORD, O my soul!

People: **I will praise the LORD as long as I live; I will sing praises to my God while I have being.**

Leader: Put not your trust in princes, in mortals, in whom there is no help.

People: **Their breath departs, they return to the earth; on that very day their plans perish.**

Leader: Happy are those whose help is in the God of Jacob,

People: **whose hope is in the LORD, their God,**

Leader: who made heaven and earth, the sea, and all that is in them;

People: **who keeps faith for ever;**

Leader: The LORD will reign for ever, your God, O Zion, from generation to generation.

People: **Praise the LORD!**

Pastoral Prayer:

O God of power and light, of love and life, how grateful we are for the simplicity of your call upon our lives. Loving you seems easy, but we know it is not. Forgive us for turning to you only in troubled times. Help us to show our love in the good times as well. Loving our neighbor seems easy, but we know it is not. Forgive us for turning our backs on the neighbors who are different than us; whose color or language or culture seems odd. Help us to remember that, in your Son, Jesus Christ, we are all one. We are all members of your family. Everyone is our neighbor. By your grace, give us eyes to see the pain of our brothers and sisters. Give us ears to hear their cries. And give us, dear God, the hearts to love them and love you with every ounce of our being. In the name of the One who loved himself onto the cross. Amen. (Thomas Gildermeister)

SERMON BRIEFS

NAOMI AND RUTH

RUTH 1:1-18

The book of Ruth, tucked in the midst of the books chronicling Hebrew history, provides a reminder of the identity and mission of God's people.

First, we find an illustration of the meaning of mentoring in the faith journey, as Naomi clearly does for Ruth. The mentor as the model of faith, the caring friend who listens as well as directs and who is honestly present to the seeker, is seen in a remarkable way in Naomi. She is not a person of power. She is not well-educated or trained to be a mentor. She is not a giant among teachers of faith. She is simply living a very difficult life by trusting in God. She is open to sharing her family life with a woman who is not related by blood nor even by culture or faith tradition.

To understand Naomi we need to know of her experience in her homeland, where faith is shared as community. The life-and-death trust in God that leads Naomi to head back home, unaccompanied by the protection of males, and to lovingly *detach* from these younger women who could certainly have been of assistance in this risky journey back home, lays the groundwork to the faith that Naomi models.

The commitment of Ruth to follow Naomi is a testimony of her conversion to Naomi's faith. It is not just devotion to a mother-in-law, but a longing to know this God who empowers Naomi. The mutual fulfillment of the experience of mentoring that is elaborated in this story is a contrast to the perception that the one who mentors does all the giving and the one who is mentored does all the changing. It happens both ways, and we as baptized Christians must recognize our calling to be in a mentoring relationship with other believers.

Secondly, we must refocus our attention away from the rosy glow usually associated with the famous words in verse 16 and portray the experience of despair and death in the context of their original expression. The words "whither thou goest" (KJV), used to voice the bride's feelings in the formal setting of wedding lights and music, are quite a contrast to the abandonment, fear, and poverty these women experience on a dusty road home after death has visited them all.

The despair of Naomi in urging her daughters-in-law to go back to their people is transformed by Ruth's response. Naomi's perspective is one of hopelessness out of logic; the only hope for Ruth would be remarriage to another offspring of Naomi, and Naomi certainly cannot provide that possibility. Ruth, however, sees hope in the God Naomi serves. And God does not disappoint them, because they *do* make it back home. The decision to stay together and to return to Naomi's people is a profound witness to God's strength in dark days. One does not have to have wedding music to journey down an aisle of a new kind of marriage—one of humans with a Lover God.

Might this experience of Naomi and Ruth—returning, managing on their own—demonstrate that (1) despite the terrible events of Naomi's life, God still took care of her, and (2) God's care extends beyond the Israelites to include all people? Yes, I believe it does. (Kay Gray)

LIVING "ALL OUT" FOR GOD

HEBREWS 9:11-14

Do you remember that scene in *Forrest Gump* when young Forrest is being chased by a group of older bullies down the long road to his house? He has been ridiculed because of his slow speech and the leg braces worn on each leg. In fear, he runs down the road as fast as his brace-encumbered legs will carry him. As he runs, his leg braces begin to break and fall away. To his amazement, Forrest discovers that he can run without them; in fact, he can run very quickly without them. He keeps running and running, which later becomes one of the major themes of the movie.

There is a lesson there: The fewer things that hinder our spiritual walk, the quicker our pace and the more efficient our steps become. When we live life with an unhindered spirit, we are free to serve God in a greater way.

When I was a child, my brother and I owned an old two-seat go-cart. My father bought it from a neighbor up the street for $10. We took an engine from a lawn mower, bought a new fan belt and pulley, and quickly made it into a racing machine of pure wonder and endless joy. Top speed: 22 miles per hour. We discovered years later that our father had placed a small device on the engine, near the carburetor, called simply a "governor." This little device kept the engine from running at too great a speed and in the process probably saved us a lot of scrapes and bruises from driving too quickly, which we are still too prone to do.

Sadly, most of us have "governors" on our lives that keep us from reaching our full potential in Christ. We allow sin, guilt, poorly made decisions, and broken relationships to keep us from living "all out" for Christ. What if we learned to live our Christian lives in an unhindered way? What if there were no encumbrances to hold us back? What if we could live life to its fullest potential and serve God with all of our strength and energy? The good news is that we can. In fact, God has provided a way for that to happen.

The writer of Hebrews describes the sacrifice of Christ, being careful to point out that Christ's sacrifice is both superior and lasting. Christ's sacrifice is superior to that of the high priest system of his day because Christ offers his own blood rather than the blood of goats and calves. His is a perfect sacrifice that is offered for our sins. It is lasting. The author is careful to point out that "[Christ] entered the holy place once for all" (v. 12 NASB). His sacrifice does not have to be repeated, ever. One treatment was all that was needed. And so for all of time, for those of us who are the faithful in Christ, we have been cleansed from sin to serve the living God.

I. Our Cleansing in Christ Frees Us

The blood of Jesus Christ cleanses us, liberates us, and forgives us from our past and from our future. All of us have struggled with past sin. We know what it is like to "miss the mark," to fail, to make our mistakes. And given our past record, we also know that the future will bring with it more of the same. Ideally, we strive each day to live more like Christ. And we hope that we will not continue to make many of the same mistakes ever again. To repeat the same sins can be an abuse of God's grace. But how reassuring it is to know that as we do sin, God *will* be faithful to forgive us and to cleanse us from all unrighteousness as quickly as we confess those transgressions (1 John 1:9). In Christ we are free from our past and our future.

II. Our Cleansing in Christ Motivates Us

It's been said that we have "been saved to serve." Our freedom in Christ offers us the ability to serve God in an unhindered way. With sin removed, and grace abundantly given, we are free to preach, teach, and live out the gospel of our Lord. Our cleansing motivates us to build the Kingdom.

A deacon in our church recently won a battle with stomach cancer. The illness was life-threatening. Surgery was needed along with several months of experimental treatments. He is now alive and well and has been given a clean slate. He is forever changed. He now views life as a precious gift and counts the blessing of each day. He's a modern-day zealot of the best kind. He shares, he loves, he forgives. His life-changing experience has motivated him to live life to the fullest. So it is in Christ. When we feel the embrace of his grace, our lives are changed and motivated to serve God with all our energy and strength. I challenge you to live "all out" for Christ. (Jon R. Roebuck)

THE BASIC ISSUE OF LIFE

MARK 12:28-34

Throughout history, people have attempted to summarize their philosophical and theological commitments or principles of life in pithy statements or maxims. The people of Israel were no different. In their case, the principles of life were expressed in the Torah, or the so-called law books of Moses.

In the time of Jesus, the rabbis debated about what laws were central to the faith of Israel. Because people who live by law are usually casuistic in their reasoning, it is imperative to them to know what laws take precedence over other laws. Jesus' answer to the scribal debater's question of the ultimate law was not only relevant to his context, but is also of great significance for the world of the new millennium.

I. Love of God

In the first segment of his response (v. 30), Jesus reminds his questioner that he should know the answer to the debate. The foundational statement of Israel's faith was contained in the Shema Israel ("Hear, Oh Israel") of Deuteronomy 6:4, recited by pious Jews twice daily. The "religious" scribe knew well that this verse was among the texts contained in the phylacteries (hand and head tefillin) worn by Jewish males, particularly at morning prayers (Exod. 13:1-10, 11-16; Deut. 6:4-9; 11:13-21). It was also in the mezuzah, the little box on the doorpost of Jewish homes (cf. Deut. 6:8-9).

The faith of Israel could be summed up in the Shema, the expectation to love God with one's whole being—heart, soul, and strength. Mark's version of the Shema adds *mind*, which intensifies the completeness of one's being. While we may try to dissect the human in sermonizing, it is important to remember that Semites had a holistic view of personhood. The stress of texts in both testaments is not upon the parts of the person, but upon a total love for God. Moreover, when one's heart loves God (Deut. 6:6), then one should model such love before one's children morning, noon, and night (cf. Deut. 6:7).

II. Love of Neighbor

Jesus also knew that God was concerned about all people. Throughout the Old Testament, the lovingkindness, or tender mercy (*hesed*), of God is a familiar theme. The so-called Golden Rule of treating others just as you would expect to be treated (Matt. 7:12) is set in Luke in the context of love even for those who despise you (Luke 6:31-33). While the reverse or negative golden rule concerning not hating or doing ill to others is known earlier (e.g., Lev. 19:17), this positive action toward one's neighbor in the face of hostile treatment seems unique to Jesus, the one who gave himself for sinners. Such is the self-giving love Christians are instructed by Paul to emulate (cf. Phil. 2:1-7). It is the identifying mark of followers of Jesus (cf. John 13:34-35).

While psychologists understand that it is difficult for some to love others because those persons have not been loved and therefore do not love themselves, the assumption of Mark 12:31 is that people naturally love themselves. Indeed, many regard themselves as the center of their universe. Jesus' twist is that one's neighbor belongs within one's inner circle of direct concern. Indeed, in the parallel text, Luke 10:29, the unsatisfied lawyer who asked the initial question continues the argument by pushing for a definition of "neighbor." By doing so, he reveals the shallowness of his concept of love. In replying, Jesus tells a story that turns the spotlight on racial self-centeredness and identifies the good neighborly one as a despised Samaritan.

III. The Inseparability of the Two Loves

The climax of the Marcan text comes in the fact that love of God and love of neighbor cannot be separated. As John stated, if someone says he loves God and hates his brother, such a person is a liar (1 John 4:20). In the Marcan story, the scribe finally catches on to what Jesus is teaching when the scribe realizes that love of God and love of neighbor are more significant than all the Temple sacrifices and offerings (v. 33). Active love is far more meaningful to God than purchased worship practices. That is what Amos meant when he called for justice rather than feasts, offerings, and irrelevant worship (Amos 5:18-24).

Jesus concludes this encounter by telling the enlightened scribe that he was "not far from the kingdom of God" (v. 34). What about us? (Gerald L. Borchert)

NOVEMBER 12, 2000

Twenty-second Sunday After Pentecost

Worship Theme: Christ has redeemed us once and for all so that we can love freely and completely, not so that we can be respectable in the eyes of the world.

Readings: Ruth 3:1-5; 4:13-17; Hebrews 9:24-28; Mark 12:38-44

Call to Worship (Psalm 42:1-6):

Leader: As a deer longs for flowing streams, so longs my soul for you, O God.

People: **My soul thirsts for God, for the living God. When shall I come and behold the face of God?**

Leader: My tears have been my food day and night, while people say to me continually, "Where is your God?"

People: **These things I remember as I pour out my soul: how I went with the throng, and led them in procession to the house of God, with glad shouts and songs of thanksgiving, a multitude keeping festival.**

Leader: Why are you cast down, O my soul, and why are you disquieted within me?

People: **Hope in God whom again I shall praise, my help and my God.**

Pastoral Prayer:
Great God, Master of the cosmos and lover of my soul, we are thankful for your patient, faithful love—a love that seems only to

grow with our waywardness. O Lord, we hold back so much from you. We hoard our possessions and our love. And we are humbled by the widow whose small gifts represent everything in her life. She truly understands your Son, and we do not. Could it be that we find your unconditional grace too good to be true? Is that why some of us withhold our love from our neighbors and from your Son, Christ Jesus? O God, forgive us. Help us to really believe the story of the cross and empty tomb of our beloved Lord. Help us to realize that you don't want more religion from us, or more respectability. What you want is a love like that of Jesus. And so we pray in his name. Amen. (Thomas Gildermeister)

SERMON BRIEFS

TURNING MOURNING INTO JOY

RUTH 3:1-5; 4:13-17

This story that seems so familiar has in fact several layers.

Consider the amazing turn of events in God's plan for the Chosen People: The line of the Israelites that eventually produces the Messiah is dependent on the intermarriage of Boaz and this Moabite woman, Ruth. A long series of events brought Ruth to this tribe of Israel. Although the origin of the Moabite people is thought to have been through Abraham's nephew, Lot, intermarriage was thought to be prohibited for the Israelites because it was too dangerous to become involved intimately with those who worshiped other gods. Yet it is in fact the God of Naomi who has lured Ruth to follow her mother-in-law back to Naomi's people.

The story of Ruth's involvement with Boaz reflects the faith and tribal responsibility for carrying on the line of a deceased male. Boaz's attempt to offer the hand of Ruth to a relative closer in kinship than he further demonstrates how the decision to marry is integral with the relationship of the believer and God. Rather than prohibiting Boaz from the union, faith explains why the two come together at all. Naomi is thrilled that God has provided for them by the happenstance of Ruth's choosing Boaz's field for her gleaning. Without understanding the exclusiveness of the Hebrew people as a way of protecting the purity of their faith, we cannot comprehend how amazing it is that Boaz and Ruth get together at all!

All this indicates that the story of Ruth is meant to be a corrective to the lost sense of mission that the Israelites are chosen not for maintaining the purity of the faith, but for taking God's love to all of God's creation. As Christians, we wrestle to appreciate our Jewish heritage, but must value even more the good news of Christ, who came for the whole world, and who came from this line of Ruth and Boaz.

Next, we could examine the interrelationships in this story as a mirror for the way our lives intersect, and the choices we make in response to our interdependence. One familiar with the family systems theory could easily find application of that theory in this story.

After Ruth has met Boaz, and Naomi has realized the possibilities for a future after all, the behavior might be characterized as scheming. However, we should also consider the place of women, the powerlessness of widows, and the voicelessness of the poor in Hebrew culture. Naomi's plan for Ruth to go to the threshing room, wait for the right time, search out and mark in her mind where Boaz goes to lay, and then move to his place and under his cover is not from a simple motive; like all of us, she has a mixture of intentions. She cares for Ruth, and once again has hope that Ruth may have a future. She and Ruth have survived day by day on what Ruth could glean; with a commitment from Boaz, they would have security beyond such fitful survival. However, she cares also for Boaz and does not include trickery in her plans for this encounter.

Finally, we can look at the wonder of "mourning into joy," or second and third chances. To consider all the tragedy and loss in the lives of these two women is to portray the kind of tragedy that happens in the lives of us every week and every day. From famine to travel in faraway places, from weddings in a foreign land to one funeral right after another, Naomi, a good Hebrew woman, tries to make the most of a very difficult life. We are called to do the same.

Consider Naomi's decisions, which are not made easily and without revision. Review the risks she has taken and the confusion she endures; but every time a "just when you think . . ." happens, God steps in and provides in the most amazing way. It is certainly a foreshadowing of the "Easter experience," and it will bless the lives of every believer if he or she, like Naomi, is willing to be open to new ways of coping. (Kay Gray)

RIGHT PLACE, RIGHT PERSON, RIGHT TIME

HEBREWS 9:24-28

A lot of churches have sound system problems, usually the source of which is the personnel that operates the equipment. How many times have you attended a service in which a sudden feedback "squeal" nearly scared the congregation to death? Or, how often have you heard only bits and pieces of a sermon or prayer because the sound system was not being properly monitored? Most sound equipment operators do their best, yet some are just a little overmatched by the equipment. Thankfully, our church is not like that. We very seldom have any sound equipment problems. The sound is always clear, crisp, and properly balanced. All the credit goes to one man who knows the system extremely well and who is faithful to be present each time we worship. He is the right person, at the right time, in the right place.

The writer of Hebrews describes the role of Christ as our Savior, Redeemer, and Lord. In his writings, there are many wonderful descriptions of the way in which Christ gives himself on our behalf. This passage includes three descriptions that illustrate how Christ is for us the right person, at the right time, in the right place. Let's outline it this way: Christ enters the dwelling place of God, he appears on our behalf, and his death is sufficient for us.

I. Christ Enters the Dwelling Place of God (v. 24)

On our behalf Christ goes to where God is, to intercede for us. God's dwelling place is heaven itself. In the Old Testament, the presence of God was thought to dwell in the holy of holies in the Temple. It was there, in the presence of God, where the high priest would enter each year on the day of atonement to offer sacrifices for the sins of the people. While the people were wandering in the wilderness en route to the promised land, the presence of God was thought to dwell in the tabernacle. The tabernacle was a temporary tentlike structure. It is interesting that the word *tabernacle* means "tent." When the Scriptures speak of the tabernacle of God, it literally means that God pitches a tent with God's people. Hebrews 9, however, teaches that the eternal God is in God's eternal dwelling place and it is our Lord and Savior who goes there to be where God is.

Over the course of my ministry, I have had the opportunity to visit a number of homes. They vary in shape, size, and color. I've been welcomed into apartments, travel trailers, mansions, and log cabins. Homes are not defined by the materials that make up the construction. They are defined by the families that dwell in them. I have discovered that there is something very important that happens when, as a pastor, I visit the homes or dwelling places of families. For us, Christ enters the dwelling place of God.

II. Christ Appears on Our Behalf

Make the connection with the text. Christ enters the dwelling place of God, so that in a very direct way he can speak to God on our behalf. There is no greater ambassador. In the very presence of God, Jesus mentions our names, he talks of our needs, he offers his life for our mistakes.

I got a call one afternoon; it was a friend from another state. His voice indicated that something was very wrong. I discovered that his mother and father had been vacationing in our area. His father had suffered a massive heart attack and had died as a result. The hospital had just called to tell him the news. He called to ask if I could go to the hospital, find his mother, and offer her words of comfort and support. I was glad to do so. He was frustrated that he could not be with his mother at that moment. I was glad to go on his behalf and remind her of his love for her.

Christ goes to the dwelling place of God, and there he intercedes on our behalf.

III. Christ's Death Is Sufficient (v. 28)

"Having been offered once. . . ." With those words, the writer of Hebrews affirms that the death of Christ was both a perfect and final sacrifice. The giving of Christ's life was a one-time event. It is not necessary for Christ to die over and over again. Once was enough. His grace was, is, and will continue to be sufficient for our sins. Some events do not need to be repeated.

This past summer, our family journeyed to Disney World. We carefully planned our trip to make the best use of our time. On day one in the park, we arrived early and rushed into the park to be the first ones in line for Space Mountain. (Space Mountain is a high-speed roller coaster that travels its path in complete darkness.) Our youngest daughter, who was six at the time, had no idea what she was about to experience as she cheerfully boarded the ride. When it was over, she declared, "Not again!" For her, once was enough, and we retreated to the slower, safer rides of Fantasy Land. Some events do not have to happen more than once. Christ's death is sufficient for our sins. He was the right person, at the right place, at the right time. (Jon R. Roebuck)

JUDGING TRUE RELIGION

MARK 12:38-44

People are inherently religious, whether they are devotees of Islam, Buddhism, New Age perspectives, traditional tribal religions, secularist worship of possessions and power, and, of course, Christianity. As Luther said, people will have "entweder Gott oder abgott" (either God or an idol). Moreover, generally people's actions are a better test of their god than their words.

The Gospel writers have no difficulty in identifying the actual commitments of people. By means of linking the stories of Jesus, the evangelists often shrewdly illustrate their messages in an unmistakable manner. This passage provides an excellent example of such a story link.

I. Inconsistent Scribal Religion

The first story focuses on the human desire for recognition. Religious institutions are often the means by which people seek to gain status in the eyes of others. Special clothing or badges are used to signify one's station in the institution. Titles are likewise employed as identifying marks (v. 38). The point is that status ought to bring privileges, such as special seats of honor at important functions (v. 39). What a contrast the pursuit of privilege is to the model of servanthood, which Jesus displayed in washing the feet of the disciples (John 13:3-17).

But using the example of dispossessing widows, the text indicates that religious status is no test of Godlikeness in human affairs. Scribes and religious authorities, such as priests, pastors, elders, deacons, professors, and presidents, are fully capable of lying to and cheating others (v. 40). They can even do so in the name of Jesus. Integrity is not guaranteed by status.

II. An Example of True Piety

Using the word-link principle, Mark chose Jesus' evaluation of a very poor widow as a contrast to the fake piety of the religious leaders. Her piety was very costly because her giving of two small coins to the temple directly affected her ability to sustain her life (v. 44). Her gift to the Temple would, according to her standards, hardly be noted on a donor's list, and her name would never be inscribed on a bronze memorial plaque like those who would be recognized for their significant gifts. Yet Jesus, in his typical pattern of human reversals, categorizes the widow's gift as the most significant of all the donations received (v. 43).

III. The Point of the Passage

Does this story not sound like a fairytale in which the poor little cinder girl becomes the queen? The answer is no. The widow does not become rich because she gave all she had. She does not get the hen that lays the golden eggs. She is still a very poor widow. But God knows her heart, that her piety is not fake. God also knows the scribes' piety. They may be unjustly rich and receive the accolades of the world, but their praise is just transient (v. 40). They are hollow men. Their piety is public, and they already have their reward (cf. Matt. 6:1-2).

Like the widow, the Son of God gave his all for us. He knows how to judge the integrity of a person's piety. What kind of piety are you choosing in this new millennium? (Gerald L. Borchert)

NOVEMBER 19, 2000

Twenty-third Sunday After Pentecost

Worship Theme: Christ calls us to live each day not as though it may be our last day only, but as though it may be the last day in the history of the world.

Readings: 1 Samuel 1:4-20; Hebrews 10:11-14 (15-16), 19-25; Mark 13:1-8

Call to Worship (Psalm 16:5-11):

Leader: The LORD is my chosen portion and my cup; you hold my lot.

People: **The lines have fallen for me in pleasant places; I have a glorious heritage.**

Leader: I bless the LORD who gives me counsel; even at night my heart instructs me.

People: **I have set the LORD always before me; the LORD is at my right hand; I shall not be moved.**

Leader: Therefore my heart is glad, and my soul rejoices; my body also dwells secure.

People: **For you do not give me up to Sheol, or let your godly one see the pit.**

Leader: You show me the path of life;

People: **in your presence there is fullness of joy, in your right hand are pleasures for evermore.**

Pastoral Prayer:

Merciful God, Redeemer of our souls, we offer our praise this day for bearing good news and blessing to one and all. We know that through your Son, Jesus Christ, you do not promise to keep us forever from troubles. But, O Lord, we give thanks to you and your beloved Son for making good the promise to meet us, and to be with us in the midst of our trials and fear and heartache. Great God of mercy, we are urgent; but so often our urgency and frantic lives result from our unholy pursuit of the values of this broken-down world. Forgive us, and give us an urgency only for the values of the gospel of Christ. Give us only an urgency to build your project—your kingdom of love and justice. Make us ready for the coming of your Son. In his blessed name we pray. Amen. (Thomas Gildermeister)

SERMON BRIEFS

HANNAH THE HERO

1 SAMUEL 1:4-20

In 1998, my brother and I traveled to Kenya with my father for his sixty-fifth birthday. One of our morning outings took us to a Samburu village. It was quite a surprise to learn that even at the close of the twentieth century, polygamy was still honored as a way of life. Our young guide explained that this has always been their way. A man might have as many as four wives, and all of them got along. For instance, if one wife had a baby, the others would pitch in to take care of the new mother as well as the daily chores. No rivalry existed among them.

In this story, however, we are witnesses to the expression of utter degradation of Hannah's ego. But this is not necessarily negative. It is not for our sympathy. Rather, Hannah's life story is for us to interact and empathize with Hannah, as we would whenever shame and degradation are inflicted by one person upon another. She is a woman at the end of her rope. Certainly she is loved by her husband, but his love seems somehow as impotent as she is barren. She must endure the false shaming from Peninnah, who makes her feel inferior and ashamed of herself. It became psychosomatic: She stopped eating; the least upset started a deluge of tears.

A public school teacher had a challenging student in her combined third- and fourth-grade classroom. The youngster had progressed quickly in school, yet was physically inferior to his classmates. An inquisitive lad, he asked many questions. Unable to handle his insatiable curiosity, as she had so many children to deal with, the teacher cued the other students to laugh at him whenever he raised his hand. False shame is devastating to a child and is difficult to overcome. In Hannah's case, though, a positive result is that room was made for God to act. And, by the same token, there is room for Hannah to grow and individuate; that is, she can become whole in the living, moving, and being of the Lord of hosts.

Hannah's resolve is transformation in process. As the epitome of the suffering servant, Hannah takes her stance before Yahweh in the midst of adversity: Peninnah's humiliation, Elkanah's helpless distress, Eli's mistaken interpretation of her prayer activity, not to mention that it was abominable then for a mere woman to address the Lord of hosts. Talk about protofeminism! Hannah is, for all intents and purposes, a hero—not like Xena the Warrior Princess, or Boadicea, the tribal queen of the Britons who fought the Romans on the island nation. Instead, Hannah has embarked on the traditional hero's quest. She expands our sense of the possible, and yet reminds us of the necessary boundaries of the human condition. Hannah, along with others who suffer needlessly like her, embodies the redeeming nature of the awareness of wholeness. It is a vision of fulfillment she expresses. This is not wishful thinking, but the desire for completeness. She is answering her call.

In her confrontation with Eli, she is thought to be drunk with wine (shades of Pentecost). Actually, Hannah demonstrates she is capable of handling and enduring the power principle represented by the priestly Eli, and its abuse, practiced by Phinehas and Hophni, his eager and lusty sons. Hannah endures neither with violence nor by succumbing to despair. Rather, she maintains her resolve. And she is blessed with a son, whom she names Samuel, which means "I have asked God." Samuel is heroically sacrificed (*sacer* + *facere* = "to make sacred") by a mother's love into the hands of the Almighty. Love endures all things. (Eric Killinger)

THE DANGER OF ROUTINE

HEBREWS 10:11-14 (15-18), 19-25

One of the things that I enjoy about my work is the diversity of schedule that it affords. Although I might complain at times about the hectic pace and the overworked calendar, still I enjoy the fact that each day is different, that there is no such thing as a "typical" day. I feel for those who work in very routine occupations. I am sure that at times the monotony can be overwhelming. In fact, several years ago I had the opportunity to tour a Ford truck plant in Louisville, Kentucky. It was a fascinating process to watch. Very quickly, the raw materials were assembled into a finished product. Hundreds of employees worked at the plant, each doing his or her job day in, day out. Each doing the same job over and over again.

That kind of routine is described by the writer of Hebrews as he writes about the work of the priest in the Temple of the first century. Each day the priest goes to work, making the same sacrifices, for the same sins, while offering the same prayers. It is a tedious task that accomplishes nothing. That continual ritual never makes a dent in the problem of sin for those who continue to fail in their relationship to God. Though the worshiper may find a temporary sense of relief from guilt, the overwhelming need for grace, forgiveness, and change never can be accomplished.

Contrast the role of the priest with that of Christ. Christ has offered a one-time sacrifice for sins (v. 12). By his offering, he has "perfected for all time those who are sanctified" (v. 14 NASB). Translation: Christ makes a lasting difference in our lives. We are not the same ever again after we find salvation in him. In Christ, we gain the courage to live as faithful Christians. Our lives can no longer follow the same patterns of continual sin and failure. There is to be a change of routine. We are no longer chained to our guilt, we are free to live and serve God's kingdom. In this passage, four imperatives are given of things that Christians should be doing. Let's explore each one.

I. Hold Fast the Confession of Our Hope (v. 23)

Our call in Christ is to a consistent, continual walk of faith. We are to "hold fast" to our faith. That means with each new day we tighten our grip, and we cling more closely to the essentials of our faith that draw us close to God. I recently heard a heartbreaking story from a friend about an event that happened in his hometown. During a school field trip, a young student fell into a creek that was swollen with flood water. A schoolmate reached out and grabbed the fellow student by the hand. Holding as tightly as he could, he called for others to come and help. Just moments before help arrived, a sudden swell in the fast-flowing water caused the grip between the boys' hands to slip and the young student was washed away to his death. As my friend told me the story, I was reminded of how important it is to "hold fast" to those things in our lives that give us life. As Christians called to new life, we must cling to our faith in Christ Jesus.

II. Stimulate One Another to Love (v. 24)

One of the distinguishing marks of a Christian should be authentic, unselfish love. Loving our enemies, loving those who have hurt us, loving the unlovable is a very demanding challenge of the gospel. In fact, it is a challenge that we rarely meet without the help of others who remind us to live as Christ would live. Christian love has two primary motivations. We are motivated by the love of Christ. Because he loves us, we are able to love each other. We are also motivated by the love of others. When we feel the love of Christian friends, praying for us, sharing with us, forgiving us, we are able to offer love to others.

I have a close friend who is notorious for running out of gas in his vehicle. I really don't understand why it happens. He is smart, well-educated, and has been driving for years, and yet nearly once a month he runs out of gas. How silly. Anyone with good sense knows that when the tank gets low, it must be refilled. The same is true of Christian love. Without the continual filling of love in our lives, we will be unable to extend love to others. Christians are to stimulate one another to love.

III. Do Good Deeds (v. 24)

James makes this argument in his book. It's the old question of faith and works. James goes so far as to say that faith without works is useless. As Christians, our faith must find practical expression. It is not enough to pray, to study, and to claim a Christian faith. We must do more. The world will never be impressed by our private devotions. It will be touched by our acts of human compassion. Just ask the injured man who waits for the Good Samaritan. Let us hear the challenge to do good deeds that are the result of a living faith within us.

IV. Encourage Each Other (v. 25)

Perhaps the greatest ministry needed within the walls of our congregations is the ministry of encouragement. No one survives for very long without the support of others who nurture and care. Encouragement is a vital ministry, one which is easily given. Encouragement comes through a friendly smile, a pat on the back, a well-timed phone call, a word of praise, or through a promise of prayer. We desperately need others who will cheer us on to victory.

Here in East Tennessee, college football reigns supreme. Saturday afternoons throughout the fall season, the faithful supporters of the Tennessee Volunteers jam Neyland Stadium in Knoxville to cheer on the "Big Orange." The stadium seats one hundred and seven thousand fans. It is a place where "home advantage" makes a difference. The cheer of the crowd allows each player to do his best and reach for his potential. Christians need that kind of ministry in their own lives. We must encourage others to be their best in Christ, to reach their highest potential.

May it never be said of us that we are "routine" Christians. Let's reach for more. Let's grow in our faith and in our ministry to each other. (Jon R. Roebuck)

SECURITY AND THE QUESTION "WHEN?"

MARK 13:1-8

Human beings are enamored with great buildings. The rebuilding of the Second Temple in Jerusalem was one of the highlights of the Herodian period. The Jewish records indicate that it was begun in approximately 20-19 B.C. John indicates, unlike our quick building schedules, that during the ministry of Jesus it had already been in the construction process for forty-six years (John 2:20). It was not completed until 64 A.D., more than three-quarters of a century after it began. It was destroyed soon thereafter in 70 A.D.

I. The Disciples' Perspective and Jesus' Shocking Words

Like most people, the disciples were awestruck by the magnificence of their great temple (v. 1). For the Jews, it was a symbol of God's presence in their nation and of the stability of Israel in the midst of a hostile Roman world. They were sure that Jesus would be likewise impressed. Even God must have been impressed.

Scarcely did they expect Jesus' shocking reply that their great monument would be destroyed (v. 2). Their symbol of stability would be removed.

II. The Disciples' Anxiety

Among the first responses of humans to a prediction of disaster is the question "When?" (v. 4). Accompanying the "When?" question is the human desire to cope with the unknown by seeking to prepare or avoid the consequences of such a disaster. But knowing when may not really alter the coming of tragedy. We may dike rivers and build earthquake-resistant buildings, but we cannot stop all death and destruction. The disciples fail to grasp that Jesus is in fact calling them to consider the more serious question of ultimate reality. They are mired in earthly means of security. The world, however, cannot provide ultimate stability and security.

III. The Warnings of Jesus

Instead of providing an easy response to the question, Jesus instructs his disciples not to be led astray by simplistic answers to ultimate questions. Human predictors and saviors will only give people a false sense of security and knowledge (v. 6). Human conflicts (wars) and natural disasters (earthquakes and famines) may seem to be signs of a final cataclysm, but they are merely earthly phenomena (v. 7-8). They are only a clue to ultimate tragedy (v. 8). The answers to ultimate hope do not lie in work-oriented signs anymore than stability lies in human edifices.

IV. The Unanswered Answer

Since the unanswered question of "When?" cannot be answered by the world, indeed it will not even be answered by Jesus (v. 32), the question points beyond itself to the only reality that can supply both the answer and the hope of stability and security. The answer is only to be found in God. It is not an answer which permits us to control destruction or tragedy in our lives. It is an answer that points us beyond tragedy to the God who can and will save us in the midst of tragedy. Here then is not only a warning against accepting false answers to ultimate questions, but a call for endurance in the walk with Christ (v. 13; also see Luke 21:19; Heb. 10:36; Rev. 14:12). (Gerald L. Borchert)

NOVEMBER 26, 2000

Christ the King Sunday

Worship Theme: The kingdom over which Christ Jesus reigns is like no other kingdom on earth today or throughout all time.

Readings: 2 Samuel 23:1-7; Revelations 1:4*b*-8; John 18:33-37

Call to Worship (Psalm 135:1-7, 13-14):

Leader: Praise the LORD! Praise the name of the LORD!

People: **Give praise, O servants of the LORD, you that stand in the house of the LORD, in the courts of the house of our God!**

Leader: Praise the LORD, for the LORD is good; sing to the LORD's name, for the LORD is gracious!

People: **For the LORD has chosen Jacob as God's own, Israel as God's own possession.**

Leader: For I know that the LORD is great,

People: **and that our LORD is above all gods.**

Leader: Whatever the LORD pleases, the LORD does, in heaven and on earth, in the seas and all deeps.

People: **It is the LORD who makes the clouds rise at the end of the earth, makes lightnings for the rain and brings wind from the storehouse of God.**

Leader: Your name, O LORD, endures for ever, your renown, O LORD, throughout all ages.

People: For the LORD will vindicate his people, and
             have compassion on his servants.

Pastoral Prayer:

Holy God, Christ the king, Lord of lords, the world may think
we're crazy, but we believe, dear Savior, that you reign over this
world. We believe that in you, your kingdom has come. Hallelujah, it has begun! But great God of the Universe, we also know
that your kingdom has not yet been fulfilled on earth as it is in
heaven. We see children dying by the thousands from wars,
famines, and worst of all, from our own indifference. O Lord,
come quickly. We can look beyond the horizon by faith and in
hope, knowing that all will be well. But right now, Jesus, this
world is a mess. Violence, addiction, neglect, and greed seem to
have their way in our lives and the lives of millions more. We can
never make it on our own. Without your grace working through
your Holy Spirit, all of our efforts to bring about your kingdom of
perfect peace will be futile. And so, Lord, we beg you to come
quickly. The anticipation is killing us. Amen. (Thomas Gildermeister)

SERMON BRIEFS

FOCUS OF A SPIRITUAL LEADER: DAVID

2 SAMUEL 23:1-7

David, the king, the patriarchal leader of the nation of Israel,
comes to the end of his reign. Like Jacob, Moses, and others
before him, he gathers his people around him to share his last
words and to give them a blessing.

I. The Development of Leadership (v. 1)

David reminded his people about his humble beginnings. He
wasn't born in the palace, but in the home of a sheepherder who
passed along his trade to his younger son. David was tending
sheep when God called him by way of the prophet Samuel. Noth-

ing spectacular stood out in this potential leader's life that would draw people to him, but God saw the potential. God divinely appointed David to organize the government, lead the people in worship, and envision a nation devoted to God. He was developing his skills as God led. You too can be leaders despite your humble beginnings.

II. The Inspirational Motivation of Leadership (v. 2-5)

True leaders inspire people through words and actions. They speak words of justice, hope, and guidance.

A wall of obstacles faced Fred Smith, founder of Federal Express, in the early days of the company's existence. The obstacles for Smith included a $30 million debt. He was indicted for defrauding a bank, he was sued by members of his own family, and he narrowly escaped a takeover of the company. Through all the difficult days, Smith still inspired his employees to unbelievable commitment. Some of the van drivers pawned their watches to buy gasoline so that they could get their packages to the airport on time.

Herb Miller said that effective leaders have "inspirational qualities that motivate common people to do uncommon things."

III. The Goal of Leadership (v. 6-7)

The goal of leadership detours people from the wrong to the right. We must never lose focus of the good.

A lighthouse keeper along a bleak coastline was given a sufficient amount of oil by his supervisor to last one month. The lighthouse keeper was instructed to keep the light burning every night. One day a neighbor down the coast stopped by to ask for help. Her oil supply had dwindled, and she didn't have enough to heat her home for the rest of the week. He supplied her with oil. A little later a farmer's son needed oil for his lamp in order to do homework. The compliant lighthouse keeper gave it. Someone else needed some of the precious oil for an engine. Before the month's end, the lighthouse keeper's oil tank was dry as a bone, and the warning signal died out.

One stormy night three ships crashed on the rocks. More than one hundred passengers and crewmen drowned. A government investigation was dispatched to discover the reason for the crashes. Upon interrogation of the lighthouse keeper, he revealed what he had done with the oil and why. The investigator sternly stated, "You had one task only—to keep the light burning. Everything else was secondary. There is no defense for what you have done. Lives were lost because you lost sight of what you were to do."

Our focus must be on the task God has shown to us to do. Spiritual lives, including our own, are at stake. (Derl Keefer)

WAITING FOR FULL VICTORY

REVELATIONS 1:4*b*-8

A major challenge for Christians is maintaining the Easter reality into the weeks following the day of Resurrection. Obviously the new reality we proclaim is not here in its fullness. The starkness of this fact sets in quickly. The federal office building bombing in Oklahoma City came between Easter and the second Sunday of Easter.

The Revelation to John presents challenges. It has been so mishandled by so many, that a failure of nerve, driving one to other texts, is understandable. Not infrequently do preachers find themselves repeating Martin Luther's reaction: The Spirit is unable to accommodate itself to the book. Yet, there is material in these words of introduction that can help sustain us into the coming weeks.

I. A Bridge from the Present to the Future

The Revelation, being an instance of apocalyptic writing, "unveils" (the meaning of *apocalypse*) the destiny of the cosmos within the sovereign design of God. These verses herald the perspective from which this may be discerned. But apocalyptic literature is often described as writing for hard times. It comes from reality that appears to fall short of God's intent. This is literature forged in the crucible of persecution.

Such is the case of this book, coming from the persecution in the Roman province of Asia during the reign of Domitian (92-96

C.E.). Apocalyptic literature is intended to convey assurance of God's ultimate and certain triumph in such times. As such, Revelation builds a bridge from the present time, in which Christian communities long for the fullness of what is glimpsed in Easter, to the eschatological future. It interprets the former in light of the latter.

II. Time, Priesthood, Victory

In reading today's text, three themes capture our attention. The first is time. The twofold designation of God as the One "who is and who was and who is to come" declares that time is subject to God, and not vice versa. Jesus loves us (v. 5). He has freed us from sin (v. 6). The clouds with which Jesus is coming (v. 7) recall the clouds of theophany in which he ascended, the cloud at the Transfiguration, the cloud at Sinai and in the exodus from Egypt. In the Christian faith, there is neither "Once upon a time" nor "Happily ever after." These imply some timelessness that bracket the story. Christians confess that all time is determined by the saving work of the Alpha and the Omega. Such declaration speaks comfort to persons who are victims of their historical circumstances.

The second theme is priesthood. The persecuted community is given a role in the ministry of Christ to the world. Christ's ministry meant suffering. The saints' suffering is interpreted in light of his suffering, which cannot be thought apart from his victory. The suffering of the community makes it a participant in Christ.

Worthy of note is the way in which this does not confirm individualistic notions of "the priesthood of the believer." There is nothing here of priesthood granting a right of direct access to God. While the individual Christian's approach to God ought not be rejected, the emphasis here is upon service to God in the pattern of Christ.

The third theme is victory. As the faithful witness, the firstborn from the dead (v. 5), and the ruler of the kings of the earth, the risen Lord is the preeminent declaration of God's victory. He witnesses to the eternal purpose of God. In his resurrection he is the dawning of the fulfillment of this purpose. As ruler, he is now bringing all lesser powers under the rule of God. It has been said that the word of this victory has not yet reached the enemy all along the front. The enemy still attacks and does great damage. But the matter is settled. The descriptive terms of this verse identify who Jesus presently is. Thus we continue to sing: "The strife is o'er, the battle done; the victory of life is won; the song of triumph has begun: Alleluia!" ("The Strife Is O'er"). (Philip E. Thompson)

ENCOUNTER WITH THE KING

JOHN 18:33-37

When the twelve apostles are depicted in stained-glass windows or in other artwork, by symbols or themes incorporated in the depiction, a viewer can often tell who's who without reading a label. Peter is usually shown holding keys. Andrew has an X-shaped cross, signifying the manner in which he was crucified. The four Gospel writers, too, have their symbols. But if we were to differentiate them by the Passion narratives alone, John's Gospel could be symbolized by a crown, for John is the writer who goes into the most detail about the kingship of Jesus Christ. It is true that the phrase "king of the Jews" appears in all four accounts of Jesus' suffering and death. But for John, the meaning of that kingship is central to understanding who the Messiah was, is, and shall be.

In this text, Pilate's first question to Jesus is, "Are you the King of the Jews?" The discussion that follows reveals both Pilate's confusion and how Jesus understood his nature and mission. He tells Pilate that his kingship is not of this world, that he has come to bear witness to the truth, and that Pilate would have no power unless it had been given to him from above. In other words, Jesus identifies himself with the One who allowed Pilate power. The angry mob is presented as taking issue primarily against the kingship of Jesus. They prefer the reign of Caesar, and their chief priests complain against the "King of the Jews" inscription at the top of the cross.

But the sovereignty of Jesus Christ is suggested in another way in this chapter. When the soldiers and officers from the chief priests came to arrest Jesus at Gethsemane, they said they were seeking Jesus of Nazareth. Jesus responded, "I am he," and they drew back and fell to the ground. Jesus actually spoke the divine name "I AM," the same formulation used in Exodus 3:14 when the Lord spoke to Moses from the burning bush. Elsewhere in Scripture, falling down is a reaction to divine revelation (see Dan. 2:46; 8:18; Rev. 1:17). It can also be a sign of devotion and adoration (see Phil. 2:10-11 and Rev. 4:9-11).

We live in a culture that is hostile to the idea of kingship. Public opinion polls tend to measure the popularity of elected officials, not assess how worthy they are to hold an office, or whether their works match their rhetoric. Kingship, which is hierarchical in nature, is antithetical to relativism and egalitarian values. Our bias against it is seen in some translations of the Bible where the word *sovereign* has been substituted for *king*, and *realm of God* for *kingdom of God*. Christ the King Sunday (or Judgment Sunday, as it is known in some traditions) is countercultural, but Christians may also see it as a gift. It reminds us of who Jesus Christ is, and, by God's mercy, who we may be in relationship to him.

Those who shouted "We have no king but Caesar" not only separated themselves from those who are subjects of Christ the King, but they also cut themselves off from the power of that king to save. They did not see him resurrected and ascended, and will not see the King enthroned in glory. In our own time, it is by confessing that Jesus is one with the "I AM" revealed in the Old Testament, God's ultimate revelation to humanity, that we gain the privilege of standing in his holy presence.

A British friend of mine was known for his vociferously anti-royalist views, so when his name appeared on the Queen's honors list, I wondered what he would do. To receive his award, he would have to participate in a presentation ceremony at Buckingham Palace. I was relieved and pleased when he did make the trip to London and bowed to the queen at the appropriate moment. All doubts and cynicism were put aside, and in meeting and acknowledging her as sovereign, he received the award that only she could give.

So it is with us. Christ is king no matter what we think about it or how we respond to him. But this king came and dwelt among us, offering eternal life. And whosoever will may come, worship, and obtain the award offered by his grace. (Carol M. Noren)

DOORS AND WINDOWS

DECEMBER

Reflection Verse: I was glad when they said to me, "Let us go to the house of the LORD" (Ps. 122:1).

The Discipline:

Book yourselves and your loved ones, in full nonclerical regalia, into a local Christmas or Advent vesper service that you do not conduct or prepare.

The worst thing about clergy is the way we make Sabbath for others but not for ourselves. We "do" Christmas, but we don't make it to the house of God for Christmas. This Advent and Christmas be different—worship with someone else as the leader.

You might even want to schedule Christmas Eve and gift-giving with your family at an earlier or later date than Christmas itself. Why not? That way you might not fall asleep during the pudding. You might want to use a family devotional as a way to make sure the Christmas full-tilt boogie at church doesn't get in your way of rehearsing the story at home. Whatever you do, be glad at the invitation to go into the house of the Lord.

The Meditation:

No matter how booked or exhausted I am, I make a pilgrimage to New York City every Christmas to see the big tree at Rockefeller Center. One year, as I was leaving the city, I realized that Grand Central Station was filled with song. Lo and behold, there was music in the station—and it was the entire Yale University Glee Club singing a concert for the homeless. Often I miss the music, so grim to the grindstone is my nose! That night I got lucky. I left my bustling discipline and was able to join the song.

Ears are underused. They are too full of the Muzak of the move, move, move, move of our days, too empty to join the singing. Fatigue lifts when we listen for the music. All we have to do is pause, like the rest between notes that makes the rest of the sound good. Caesura is the name for creative rest. Sometimes that rest takes just a second.

Once I was on a big ferry boat, speeding across the Long Island Sound, rushing to my next destination, and barely noticing the splendor of my voyage. A group of teens who were terribly pale-skinned for August caught my eye. They turned out to be the Welsh National Choir on tour. When the music rose from the boat, and I looked up from my calendar, while dropping my pen, the sound of "Oh, Shenandoah" rose in rehearsal.

The music is always there. Maybe it is not a grand or youthful choir, but the music is there. Sometimes a little button will provide it. More often, though, there is the slight gesture of hope that puts our ears just right on the "grindstone," making us listen deeply to hear what is already going on.

The Song:

With joy draw water from the spring; salvation's living well.
The Holy One is in your midst; glad praises sing and tell!
("With Joy Draw Water," *New Century Hymnal*)

The Advent Prayer:

Come, thou long-expected Jesus, come as footprints in the snow and show us your way. Thou who brings the scattered home, thou who heals the abandoned senses, thou who brings streams to the desert, come softly to us in this Advent season. Bring us home by your path. Open our eyes and ears. Revive the desert places in us that we may yet blossom. Don't let the world be cold. Don't let the world be dry. But bring your promises close to it. Freshen it. And let us stand on tiptoes of expectation daily through Advent, convinced that we will find your footprints on our paths, and that one day soon we will see the new heavens and the new earth as well. With gratitude for your promises.

The Christmas Prayer:

Holy Spirit, thou who broods over all the space where silence reigns, hear us when we find no words, no justifications, no excuses, only the thud of fact and memory, only the knowledge that too many tables are too thinly laid, that too many fathers drive their children on tires too bald, that even we are poor in ways that frighten us. Come, as you have promised, to the place in us that cannot speak, and stir us up. Stir us up to memory and to hope. Restore our voice to us. Remind us that you have regarded the low estate of many handmaidens. Remind us that you do not put down the poor or the little but rather exalt us. Break through the drumbeat of violence and poverty and show us ways to raise our small voices to large hopes. Bring Bethlehem deep in our hearts, let God be human and close, let heaven descend to earth, and eternity touch time: Incarnate in us the full Spirit of God's Son. Overcome in us the fear of the Christmas message and its power, and let us willingly make the case for the handmaiden, with the handmaiden, that we may in our time know the exaltation of those of low estate. Through Jesus Christ our Lord, Amen. (Donna Schaper)

DECEMBER 3, 2000

First Sunday of Advent

Worship Theme: We must stay alert for the coming of the Messiah and the kingdom of justice and righteousness.

Readings: Jeremiah 33:14-16; 1 Thessalonians 3:9-13; Luke 21:25-36

Call to Worship (Psalm 25:1-5):

Leader:	To you, O LORD, I lift up my soul.
People:	**O my God, in you I trust, let me not be put to shame; let not my enemies exult over me.**
Leader:	Let none that wait for you be put to shame;
People:	**let them be ashamed who are clothed with treachery.**
Leader:	Make me to know your ways, O LORD;
People:	**teach me your paths.**
Leader:	Lead me in your truth, and teach me,
People:	**for you are the God of my salvation; for you I wait all the day long.**

Pastoral Prayer:

O Lord, our God, and our hope, we know that the coming of your kingdom in glory, in all its wondrous fulfillment, can never be predicted. Forgive us when we use the blessed truth found in Scripture like tea leaves to satisfy our curiosity. But gracious Christ, how grateful we are to know that you give us signs of warning, signs to keep us faithful and alert. Help us to stay awake. So often we sleep-walk through our days—maybe some through their whole lives. We need you, Lord. We cannot make it through this life of joy and sorrow without you. And so we wait, Lord. And so we wait. Amen. (Thomas Gildermeister)

SERMON BRIEFS

TWO WORDS IN ONE

JEREMIAH 33:14-16

Advent can be jarring after the themes of growth and discipleship in "ordinary time." The operative words become "longing," "expectation," "judgment," and "hope." Advent takes us into the company of all who have lived in expectancy of the fullness of salvation. Given human fallibility, however, expectation is often misplaced.

I. Jeremiah's Promise

An interesting thing about this passage is that it occurs not once but twice in Jeremiah. Already, in 23:5-6, almost identical words have appeared. Although there are specific reasons why this is so, our interest is the contexts of both occurrences, for they work together to speak of Advent expectation.

Scholars divide Jeremiah's ministry into four periods. Chapter 23 comes from the period between 609 and 605 B.C.E., the four years of Jehoiakim's reign before the Babylonian conquest in 605. Popular opinion was optimistic. Clearly, YHWH had overthrown the dreaded Assyrians (in 622). Surely, YHWH would deal with others who threatened his people. Jehoiakim was the son of good king Josiah, but was not the king his father was. He was one of the bad shepherds of whom Jeremiah spoke (23:1-4). Against him, and the optimism of the time, Jeremiah foretold a Branch from David's line who would be righteous where the present king was corrupt. The One to come would make the people righteous in truth, not merely their own opinion.

As found in today's scripture text, the words function differently. This chapter is located in a period dating from the fourth year of the reign of Zedekiah, Jehoiakim's successor, to the fall of Jerusalem in 587-586 B.C.E. Zedekiah tried political and military gambits to throw off Babylonian rule. He failed. The popular opinion was that the nation faced doom. Here Jeremiah's words bear hope. A future beyond the destruction was promised to the people. "Judah will be saved and Jerusalem will live in safety" (v. 16).

II. Justice and Righteousness

Jeremiah was indebted to his prophetic predecessors. The words *mishpat* and *tzedakah*, familiar from Amos, stand out here. Unlike the English terms of translation, "justice" and "righteousness," these are not abstract concepts used to define the quality of human action. They are rather spheres of influence and power that go before, make possible, and influence human behavior. They provide the arena in which life in accord with YHWH's purposes may be lived.

In Hebrew thought, social order was dependent upon the king. Kingship had a sacral quality. The king was an intermediary between God's mishpat and tzedakah and the life of the people. Both Jehoiakim and Zedekiah had failed to serve this role in the right way. Neither was righteous. Neither made life in YHWH's righteousness possible for YHWH's people. In light of each, Jeremiah promised that YHWH would raise up one who would rightly establish this possibility for the life of YHWH's people, bringing salvation and shalom. The execution of judgment, then, is not active punishment. It is the establishment of a quality of existence that counters human arrogance and human hopelessness.

III. Adjusting Our Eyes to God's Vision

The Word of Advent is two words in one, set against both false hope and premature despair. It looks to God as the One who is active in history to bring about salvation through the One who gives life and life abundant, who makes possible the life of salvation. Advent gives us time to correct the false hopes and despairs of our age, and to adjust our eyes to God's vision seen in Jesus Christ, the righteous Branch. (Philip E. Thompson)

ADVENT WISHES

1 THESSALONIANS 3:9-13

In his commentary, F. F. Bruce described this passage as a "wish-prayer" because it is in the optative rather than the imperative mood. In this passage, Paul describes his wishes for the believers in the church at Thessalonica. By extension, this passage allows the preacher to share with his or her congregation his or her Advent wishes for them.

I. An Advent of Healing

I am glad that Advent follows Thanksgiving, for I identify with Paul's rhetorical question in verse 9: How can Thanksgiving ever be enough in return for the advent of Christ? Thanksgiving is appropriate for us, but only worship can express our joy at the presence of Christ's incarnation at Christmas.

Paul's prayer, composed of compounded phrases of earnest concern for his readers, is appropriate for today's preacher. The phrase "supply what is lacking" (NIV) describes the first-century activity of mending one's fishing nets. What greater wish can any minister have than that of praying for the healing of a person's or a congregation's faith?

II. An Advent Presence

There are two ways of helping a lost person find his or her way—by giving directions to the desired location or by taking the lost person where he or she needs to go. The divine means of direction, Paul says, is the latter. God and the Lord Jesus Christ will lead you to your destination as surely as Jesus led Paul to his. No obstacle will stand before the might of God and God's Son. Just as the star will lead the wise men, and the angel will direct the shepherds, so Jesus will lead you on a journey into the presence of God.

III. An Advent Preparation

By the time we reach the first Sunday in Advent, many of us are already spiritually and physically tired. Preparing for Advent is no small feat for the faithful. Yet here Paul prays for the Thessalonians that their love might increase and overflow, that they might experience the high tide of God's love. The journey toward Christmas will be arduous at times, but we will not have the selfish luxury of deciding when we will stop or where our destination will be, for God wills us to mature and grow as God's disciples even at this busy time of year. Our task will take us beyond the confines of our comfortable Christian compounds, for we are to grow in love even for everyone else. Advent is a rare opportunity to plant seeds of faith in our friends and relatives, for the love taught and shown at Advent is attractive to all.

IV. An Advent Purpose

Verse 13 is the key to this passage and to our Advent this year: "May he strengthen your hearts so that you will be blameless and holy in the presence of our God and Father when our Lord Jesus comes with all his holy ones" (NIV). The purpose of this Advent is to prepare us for the Second Advent. Our Advent prayers, presence, and preparation are our practice for that great and unknowable day when Jesus will once again reveal himself to us, and our lives will be revealed to him in the presence of God. Our lives then will be the answer to the psalmist's question: "How can I repay the Lord for all his goodness to me?" (Ps. 116:12 NIV). (Mickey Kirkindoll)

WATCH AND PRAY

LUKE 21:25-36

Jesus reminds us that the One who has come is indeed coming again. As we celebrate the first Advent, we are reminded there will be a second. The signs of the times help us to stay prepared.

I. Disciples Who Persevere

The context of Jesus' words focus on two important themes: being prepared for times of persecution (Luke 21:12-24), and being prepared for the coming of the Son of Man (vv. 25-36). Our text focuses on this second theme, exhorting us to preparation and perseverance.

This section echoes important themes pronounced earlier in the Gospel, particularly Luke 14:25-35. Jesus invites all to come (14:23) while discouraging hasty enthusiasm. True followship involves counting the cost before embarking on the way. Perseverance is essential for true Christ-followers. If Luke 14:25-35 speaks to would-be followers, then Luke 21:25-36 addresses those who are already followers. The emphasis on perseverance is clear in both passages.

II. Disciples Who Prepare

Using apocalyptic language, our text describes the "last times," the meaning of which was most likely clearer to the original hearers than to us. This symbolic language identifies the signs that call for Christ-followers to wake up, that Christ's coming is near. As is sometimes the case in Luke's writing, the words of judgment may include the destruction of Jerusalem in A.D. 70 but point ultimately to the Coming Day of the Lord. When these things are fulfilled, the Son of Man will come "in a cloud with power and great glory." When they begin to take place, Christ-followers should "stand up" and lift their heads, because "redemption is drawing near."

To emphasize his point, Jesus tells a parable. He notes how one can tell the time of year by noting the condition of a fig tree. Summer is near when the tree sprouts leaves. So likewise, when we begin to observe the signs in Luke 21:25-36 taking place, we can know that the kingdom of God is drawing near. Jerusalem's fall points to the next matter on God's timetable. The variety of cosmic signs point to the coming of Christ. The parable in verses 29-31 calls for us at this season to look around and see what God is doing. Are we ready? The return of the Son of Man means that God's people will see victory, God's powerfully manifested presence in rule and judgment.

III. Disciples Who Pray and Watch

In the meantime we must be ready. Jesus calls for us to watch and pray so that that day will not close in on us unexpectedly. Some will be surprised. Those who watch and pray—the characteristic signs of perseverance—will, however, be ready.

Watchfulness suggests a preparedness in order to avoid being taken unaware. Vigilant watchfulness demands alertness and detachment from earthly pleasure and activities. This spirit of preparedness enables true disciples to battle temptation. In many ways, Jesus' struggles in Gethsemane serve as an adumbration of the disciples' struggle at the end of time. Christ-followers must watch lest savage wolves, influenced by the evil one, overtake them in temptation (Eph. 6:10-17; 1 Pet. 5:8).

We must watch and pray with unfailing faithfulness. The actions of watchfulness and prayer are indissolubly united. Prayer is an act of vigilance, and vigilance a consequence of prayer. Intense watchfulness is a manifestation of genuine spiritual life. It keeps disciples faithful in avoiding being lulled into false security. The cares of this life will not distract those who watch and pray.

Therefore persevere. Be prepared. Let us watch and pray, for we all must render an account to the Cosmic Judge. (David S. Dockery)

DECEMBER 10, 2000

Second Sunday of Advent

Worship Theme: As we await and prepare for the Lord's coming, we must have a new mind, changing from our wayward path and onto the straight path of a right relationship with God in Christ.

Readings: Malachi 3:1-4; Luke 3:1-6; Philippians 1:3-11

Call to Worship (Luke 1:68-79):

> *Leader:* Blessed be the LORD, the God of Israel, who has come to set the chosen people free.
>
> **People: The LORD has raised up for us a mighty Savior from the house of David.**
>
> *Leader:* Through the holy prophets, God promised of old to save us from our enemies, from the hands of all who hate us;
>
> **People: to show mercy to our forebears and to remember the holy covenant.**
>
> *Leader:* This was the oath God swore to our father, Abraham:
>
> **People: to set us free from the hands of our enemies, free to worship without fear, holy and righteous in the LORD's sight, all the days of our life.**
>
> *Leader:* And you, child, shall be called the prophet of the Most High, for you will go before the LORD to prepare the way,

People: **to give God's people knowledge of salvation by the forgiveness of their sins.**

Leader: In the tender compassion of our God the dawn from on high shall break upon us,

People: **to shine on those who dwell in darkness and the shadow of death, and to guide our feet into the way of peace.**

Pastoral Prayer:

All-loving and forgiving God, how long will you remain patient with us? How long will you wait for us to turn from our broken and sinful lives and take upon ourselves the mind of your Son, Christ Jesus? All you ask is for us to accept your love, accept your grace, accept your forgiveness, and fall into your arms. But we hold back. We're too busy right now, or we're this or that. God, forgive us. O Lord, have mercy. We confuse the shabby rewards of this world with the perfect and eternal rewards of Jesus Christ. We cling to our possessions as if our life depends on them. And all the while, you lovingly whisper that our lives depend on letting this stuff go. We do not wait on your Son very faithfully at all, but we wait and we believe. Give us the faith to persist. In his holy name. Amen. (Thomas Gildermeister)

SERMON BRIEFS

THE JUDGMENT OF DESPAIR

MALACHI 3:1-4

Advent lections, speaking at once of the first and final comings of Christ, bring themes of judgment. "Prepare!" "Repent!" These are Advent themes. With them comes the temptation to try simply to "afflict the comfortable," to subvert complacency in our hearers (and perhaps ourselves). Yet Advent gives judgment and hope together, "no" and "yes" together. The former is for the sake of the latter. Difficulties arise from this odd pairing. There are words of judgment in this scripture text, yet for the sake of restoring hope.

I. The Rise of Despair

We can only infer the context in and for which these words were written. Even the name of this prophet, which means "my messenger," seems to be a title rather than a name. The community had long since returned from exile. The Temple and walls of Jerusalem were likely rebuilt. There was slackness of spirit and slackness in worship. The cause was not corruption (as in, for example, Amos), but profound despair born of life falling short of divine promises. The age of God's final triumph and reign had been expected to begin when the Temple was consecrated. One hundred years had passed since the consecration, and the community were still waiting. Their city was still small and rather insignificant. The Temple did not compare favorably to the one of former days. Enthusiasm had all but evaporated. The community had deep doubts about the worth of their faith.

The prophet shows profound pastoral concern, and works diligently to connect with the spiritual needs of the people. Our passage is found in the fourth of six oracles which compose the book of Malachi. The oracle deals with the problems stemming from the delay in God enacting universal justice that had been promised long before by Isaiah (Isa. 11:1-5).

II. Malachi's Word to the Despairing

God will indeed appear! Yet intervention will not be direct. It will come through the work of a messenger who will prepare God's way. This preparation will be judgment; hard judgment, like refining fire or fuller's soap. It will be comprehensive. "Who can endure it? Who can stand it?" the prophet asks rhetorically while knowing the answer is "No one can" (v. 2 adapted). None can escape, all are subject to the judging work of the One to come. Yet, the judgment that prepares God's way will bring purification, the elimination of human guilt, the restoration of right relation with God in which salvation may be known. Rather than causing further despair, this judgment is for the sake of hope. Judgment and hope go together.

III. The Lesson

As preparations for Christmas begin to shift into high gear, Advent reminds the church of the need for spiritual preparation for Christ's coming. This lesson offers the opportunity to address the deeper aspects of preparation, to speak of the renewal of the community of faith. The realities of preparation may be harder as well as deeper. Festive seasons can heighten despair. We as Christians would do well to wrestle with the relations of judgment, hope, and concern. We must explore the tension, taking care not to resolve it too easily, passing too quickly from judgment to hope. An example of letting this tension stand comes from Flannery O'Connor's "Why Do the Heathen Rage?" A woman, whose life falls short and seems to be falling apart, reads in Jerome's letter to Heliodorus, "[S]ee how our General marches fully armed. . . . Out of the mouth of the King emerges a double-edged sword that cuts down everything in the way." The story ends, "Then it came to her, with an unpleasant little jolt, that the General with the sword in his mouth, marching to do violence, was Jesus" (Flannery O'Connor, *The Complete Stories* [New York: The Noonday Press, 1992], pp. 486-87). (Philip E. Thompson)

AND YOU CALL THIS GOOD NEWS?

LUKE 3:1-6

John's announcement of the Messiah's coming fell softly on no one's ears. He certainly didn't try to lull his audience into believing that they could welcome the Savior with an unreflective enthusiasm like that of a child who looks forward to Santa Claus coming to town. John the Baptist's words were troubling. Almost everything he said seemed to be calculated to provoke his hearers. He did not adorn his speech with compliments or consolations which might have made his message more readily acceptable. The harshness of the tone made it evident that he had no patience with those who would require coaxing or cajoling before they would be receptive to his message. John spoke with brutal frankness.

The great church reformer Martin Luther once stated that the most consistent outcome of the Word of God is that on its account the world is put into an uproar, for the sermon of God comes to change and revive the whole earth insofar as it really gets through to it. John no doubt put things into an uproar. Personally, I would not have wanted to bear the brunt of his preaching. He spoke of mountains being ripped down and valleys being filled up to prepare the way for the Lord. That's radical disruption.

The Christ that John the Baptist announced is certainly a threat to anyone who has become complacent and overly comfortable with their lives, values, and opinions. The Christ that John called people to prepare for was One who came to interrupt the normal course of life in order to introduce the way of God. Jesus is that Christ, and Jesus came to disturb us. William K. McElvaney wrote a challenging little book a few years ago, entitled *Good News Is Bad News Is Good News* (Maryknoll, N.Y.: Orbis Books, 1980), in which he said, "All my life, from time to time, I've sung 'Blessed Assurance, Jesus Is Mine.' These words can become little more than a sentimental exercise in reducing Jesus to our own size unless accompanied by the theme 'Blessed disturbance, I am Christ's!' Not that I welcome God's disturbance when it occurs in the midst of my life. At least, though, I've learned from past experience that sometimes the news I thought was bad news turned out to be some of the best news I'd ever heard."

The preaching of John the Baptist, upon first hearing, was as disconcerting as a clanging burglar alarm that shatters the sleepy silence of the night. His message sounded quite distinctly like bad news. But in fact it was wonderful news. The Christ was coming and the people needed to be prepared to meet him, even though the preparation was going to disrupt their lives. His coming is disruptive to our lives as well. If not, then we have created a *Christ* after our own image, an idol that satisfies our desires and warms our hearts but does not move us beyond our self-centeredness.

The most crucial preparation was, and is, not ritual but ethical—not entirely internal and individualistic but external and social. Devotion to God, and compassion toward those in need are indispensable if we are to prepare the way of the Lord.

Hugh Kerr, past president of Princeton Theological Seminary, once observed, "We live in a world that answers back to us. It says yes to our yes, and no to our no. The sailor must hoist his sail if he is to catch the wind. The miner must sink his shaft if he is to discover the gold. The engineer must swing his bridge if he is to harness the river. The aviator must spread his wings if he is to search the sky. The financier must make his investment if he is to find his fortune. The Christian must prepare the way if the living God is to appear."

Let us prepare ourselves for the celebration of the coming of Jesus Christ by working for a world in which no one is ill-clad while others of us have closets filled with clothes which we throw out and replace as styles change. Let us work for a world in which no one goes to bed hungry while so many of us are thoughtlessly wasteful and self-indulgent. If we are ever to have a just and fair world, the adjustments that will be required of us privileged folks may be painful. But these are labor pains that precede a new birth of joy. There is no better way to prepare for the Lord. (Craig M. Watts)

TAKING THE BEDLAM OUT OF BETHLEHEM

PHILIPPIANS 1:3-11

"Bedlam: A scene of uproar and confusion." Webster's definition of *bedlam* is also a description of our lives during the Advent season. There are now only fourteen shopping days till Christmas, and every evening, it seems, already requires our presence at a Christmas party. The word *bedlam* came from the pronunciation by the inhabitants of southeast London of the word *Bethlehem*, as in the title of the Hospital of St. Mary of Bethlehem, an insane asylum.

In this scripture passage, Paul offers to the church at Philippi, and to us, the secret of focusing our attention on Christ and taking the bedlam out of Bethlehem.

I. Pray with Joy

Paul was thankful for his relationship with the Philippian believers. They had been his partners in the ministry, they were continuing to learn and to live in Christ more each day, and Paul was justifiably proud of them. He held them all in his heart (v. 7). Isn't this the formula for recentering our Advent? Each present we must buy, each card we must address, and each home we must visit gives us an opportunity to thank God for another person or family. Like Mary, we can ponder God's miraculous gift of each friend in our hearts.

II. Act with Confidence

Paul's confidence was in Christ, not in his friends. God initiated the good work (*ergon*) in their lives, and God would complete it. As Luther described it, God's "left-handed" power of love will lead each believer to completion in faith at the convergence point of Christ's return. This eschatological note is our pivot point in using this scripture during Advent: We will finally encounter peace on earth and good will among believers when the kingdom of God is finally realized in the Second Coming of Christ. In the meantime, we can relax; the outcome of our lives and ministries is in the hands of our Creator.

III. Accept Your Circumstances

In verse 8, Paul calls God to witness with what intensity he wishes to see his friends. Paul's circumstances left much to be desired, and much to his regret he could not be with them. The Advent season comes with the anticipation of Christ's birth, but it intensifies our regrets—broken relationships, bereavements, and separation from loved ones. Paul's message in this letter is one for our times: Joy and fulfillment come from our relationship to God, and not from our circumstances.

I cannot listen to "I'll Be Home for Christmas" without hearing through the ears of my friend Albert, who first heard this song as a soldier in the Ardennes during World War II. Separated from his family, under attack and in peril of death, and trying to survive the worst winter storm in years, Albert found that his greatest consolation was that the Christ who looked after his family in Georgia was also the Christ who protected him. Advent reminds us to trust God in spite of the bedlam around us.

IV. Love Appropriately

Use this Advent season to practice discernment in your relationships. Emphasize the building of strong relationships rather than building a mound of presents. Allow the "tender compassion of Christ" (NLT) to flow through you and into those most tested by the bedlam of Christmas—the salesperson, the overworked assistant, the harried mother, the exhausted child. "You need to use your head and test your feelings so that your love is sincere and intelligent, not sentimental gush" (vv. 9b-10a, The Message). Whether in ignorance or by intention, Christ is at the center of the Advent season, and your love for others, which is a gift of the Holy Spirit, will witness to the love that God has for each person, personified in the birth of his Son, Jesus.

V. Focus on What Really Matters

"For I want you to understand what really matters, so that you may live pure and blameless lives until Christ returns" (v. 10, NLT). This can be our challenge this Advent, to live so that our lives are a witness to the glory of God's love for us. When this is our priority, peace will reign in our hearts and we will live not in bedlam, but in the peace of the miracle at Bethlehem. (Mickey Kirkindoll)

DECEMBER 17, 2000

Third Sunday of Advent

Worship Theme: As we await our liberation in Christ, our relationship with the poor indicates the authenticity of our repentance and faith.

Readings: Zephaniah 3:14-20; Philippians 4:4-7; Luke 3:7-18

Call to Worship (Advent):

Merciful God, you sent your messengers the prophets to preach repentance and prepare the way for our salvation.

Give us grace to heed their warnings and forsake our sins, that we may celebrate aright the commemoration of the nativity, and may await with joy the coming in glory of Jesus Christ our Redeemer, who lives and reigns with you and the Holy Spirit, One God, for ever and ever. Amen.

Pastoral Prayer:

Holy God, long-expected Christ, have mercy on us. We desire to turn from our old lives of broken values and actions that have only served to separate us from the freedom of your Son and our Lord, Jesus. But we cannot. We do not have the strength or the courage. We do not have the discipline or the focus. We do not have the faith. Be gracious to us, your wayward, prodigal children. Help us to turn, to change. Help us to abide in our Redeemer so that he might transform us. We can see beyond the horizon, if only for a moment. We can imagine and claim forgiveness. O Lord, we do rejoice. And we do wrap our arms around the Promise, the New Covenant. Come quickly, and please be merciful when you arrive. Amen. (Thomas Gildermeister)

SERMON BRIEFS

A VISION FOR THE OUTSIDE

ZEPHANIAH 3:14-20

Christmas is like a rose: full of beauty, color, and luxurious fragrance. In both cases there is a sting. Roses have thorns. Christmas has a way of turning against us, a hollowness that proves our friendly smiles and cheerful greetings false. For some this is a time for fun, family, and reveling in prosperity. Most of us, though, do not get through the holidays without feeling the sting. I use the phrase "get through the holidays" intentionally, for that is exactly what many hope to do, just get through. Those who work in counseling and pastoral care see more people with depression around this time of year. Those who have lost family members often feel their loss most acutely at Christmas. Tradition sets us up for disappointment, building for us an ideal that never materializes in real life. Do not forget physical needs. There is no worse time to lose a job. And, of course, family is not always an unqualified good. You probably see some relatives at Christmas that you have not seen in twelve months, many of whom are not easy to get along with. I remember my mother's annual mission to "keep peace in the family."

For so many reasons, people struggle through the holiday season. Christmas can make you feel as if you are on the outside, missing something wonderful that everyone else gets to enjoy. The truth is, more people are outside than inside. The good news is, something wonderful is available even, and especially, to those outside.

I. Enter Zephaniah

Zephaniah is just the sort of prophet to bring good news to those on the outside. Today among the more obscure minor prophets, Zephaniah was God's mouthpiece in Judah during the reign of King Josiah. Zephaniah highlighted the need for the religious reforms that made Josiah a hero to those who wrote much of our Old Testament.

If you only read the passage you heard a moment ago, you

might think Zephaniah a positive, upbeat kind of guy. Not so. The book begins, "I will utterly sweep away everything from the face of the earth, says the LORD." And it goes downhill from there. God promises destruction for Judah and Jerusalem, then for all the nations around them. Idolatry and wickedness abound. Justice and mercy are conspicuously absent. God vows punishment.

Then a startling reverse occurs between verses 8 and 9 of chapter 3: "In the fire of my passion all the earth will be consumed" shifts without a clutch into "At that time I will change the speech of the peoples to a pure speech, that all of them may call on the name of the LORD."

II. Zephaniah's Gift

I love to say that God's wrath is redemptive in purpose. In its own way, this prophetic book says the same thing. Notice too that once the tide turns from destruction to healing, the water rises to a new level. The prophet promises suffering, then restoration, and then a mighty work of God that will right all wrongs. As so many writings in Scripture do, this one looks beyond the suffering, and even beyond the healing, to a glorious future that God has prepared. This prophetic vision continues in Jesus' preaching about the kingdom of God and our hope of resurrection and eternal life.

Zephaniah proclaims this as a vision for those on the outside. To the oppressed and outcast, God promises, "I will change their shame into praise . . . I will bring you home. . . ."

We who are on the outside have learned to suffer. Let us also learn what it is to hope. (David Mauldin)

BE HAPPY OR ELSE!

PHILIPPIANS 4:4-7

Rejoice always, and oh, by the way, don't worry about anything. Christmas is the time of year when we feel pressured to be cheerful even—and especially—if we don't feel that way. Maybe that is why so many people struggle through the holidays. The difference between what we are supposed to feel and reality makes our hearts grow heavier, not lighter.

This passage belongs to the category I call "scripture I understand perfectly but still have trouble living." At times this encouragement may seem to taunt us: We want to rejoice always and exchange our anxiety for thankfulness, but we just don't feel it in our hearts. Hearing it read from the pulpit may only make things worse. How can we discern here a healing word?

I. Whistling Through Hell

The difference between rejoicing always and feeling peppy exceeds the difference between the deep meaning of Advent worship and the shallow commercialism of secular Christmas. Paul has not coined a slogan or a bumper sticker or a buzzword. From confinement in prison he encourages his friends in Philippi to discover not a quick-fix but a quality of life. This is not about feeling good; it's about receiving from God the strength and poise to persevere. As Paul writes a few lines later, neither suffering nor prosperity disrupts his spiritual equilibrium. The peace and joy that come with mature Christian faith serve as ballasts.

The holiday spirit says "happy." The holiday spirit says "now." We seek something more real. This peace that so entices us grows in time. We believe and we trust. From this grows hope. Living in hope gives rise to joy and peace.

Is anyone else a fan of "The Far Side"? For those who are not, Gary Larson used to draw a wonderful comic by that name. One of my favorites is set, oddly enough, in hell. The picture shows the souls of the damned laboring in agony while two demonic figures look on. But something is amiss, for along comes a man pushing a wheelbarrow and whistling happily to himself. The demonic figure with a pitchfork turns to his companion and says, "You know, we're just not reaching that guy."

I clipped that comic and posted it in my office as an example to emulate. I want to be that guy. The torments of hell were not enough to bring him down. Apparently he is just too clueless to be miserable. That is not the approach I would want to take, but I do believe that in Christ we find the poise and the courage and the peace to go on—regardless of our circumstances. In fact, not only can we go on, but we need not be miserable.

II. The Lord Is Near

Paul offers a theological basis for rejoicing always: The Lord is near. We may remember how Peter walked out to Jesus on the lake. The wind and waves scared Peter, and he began to sink. Jesus, however, was near and reached out to hold Peter and save him. Yet Paul has more in mind, I suspect, than Jesus is always with us. "The Lord is near" sounds the Advent theme of the coming of Christ. "The Lord is near" means God is about to act. Our hope as Christians is that God is not yet finished. What began with the Resurrection will finally be completed, and thanks be to God we have a share in it! Here is the fountainhead of the joy and peace we seek. The Christian life is oriented toward the future God has prepared for us, a future that is closer than we often realize.

As we live toward this future, we discover a balance that the vicissitudes of existence, including Christmas cheer, cannot shake. We rejoice in the Lord—and maybe, just maybe, we do so always. (David Mauldin)

PREPARING FOR CHRIST'S COMING

LUKE 3:7-18

Preparation for the coming of the Messiah was carried forth by John the Baptizer. Just as a king traveling to a new country would have his way prepared to ensure safe arrival, so John, in a spiritual way, prepared for the coming of Jesus Christ.

I. Courageous Proclamation

John employed the language of the prophet Isaiah to herald the coming Messiah. In doing so, John took on the role of the last of the Old Testament prophets, with the accompanying fierceness, as well as the first of the New Testament evangelists. Borrowing a figure of speech in reference to the scrub fire of the Jordan wilderness, from where the hidden vipers of the undergrowth darted to safety, John confronted the crowds coming out to be baptized by him: "You brood of vipers! Who warned you to flee from the wrath to come?" (v. 7). With these words, John thrashed the national pride on which many of the hearers placed their hope for salvation.

The reference to the coming wrath points not only to the forthcoming destruction of Jerusalem in A.D. 70, but also to the Day of the Lord. Thus, in the spirit of Elijah, who is the epitome of the Spirit-enabled prophet, John's proclamation is courageous in every respect. The prophets were those on whom the Spirit came, giving them insight into the secrets of human hearts.

Based on that insight, John proclaims, "Produce fruit in keeping with repentance" (v. 8 paraphrased). This prophetic preaching calls for an ethical lifestyle from the hearers. His words again reflect the surrounding countryside. Israel's largest forest, the Jordan jungle, provided him with the image of the ax, which he indicates "is already at the root of the trees, and every tree that does not produce good fruit will be cut down and thrown into the fire" (v. 9 paraphrased). These haunting words symbolize the reality that, in the coming of Christ, judgment is near for those who give no evidence of repentance. "The fire" is a symbol of judgment throughout the New Testament.

Today's hearers, like those who first heard the prophet, must recognize that national identity, ancestry, or heritage will not commend one before God. Salvation comes not by family inheritance, but through repentance and faith, turning to Christ to follow after him.

II. Call to Change

The listeners raise the question, "What then should we do?" John turns the message in a more horizontal direction, indicating that true repentance is evidenced by ethical activity in relationship to others. The crowd, in hearing John's forceful message, recognizes that the important issue is not just baptism, but also a right response to God, followed by a change in heart and life.

John tells the crowd to be generous; he tells the tax collectors to operate aboveboard by collecting only what is required; and he tells the soldiers not to use force to extort money, for they are to be content with their earnings.

III. Coming of Christ

While John preaches personal preparation, the heart of his message points to Jesus Christ, who will baptize "with the Holy Spirit and fire" (v. 16). The difference between John and Jesus is great. John's message and role are most significant; but compared to the Messiah, John is not even worthy to untie Jesus Christ's sandals. Jesus, not John, is the true Messiah, and would by his coming reveal God fully and eventually separate the evil from the righteous. Ultimate judgment does not belong in the hands of John. He prepared the way for the One who would use the ax and the winnowing fork to clear his threshing floor.

During this Advent season, let us remember that everything true about his arrival in the first century is true today. What kind of heart response will we have? We too come to Christ only by repentance and faith. That is true forgiveness of sins. That is the message for us even as we celebrate his coming this Advent season. (David S. Dockery)

DECEMBER 24, 2000

Fourth Sunday of Advent

Worship Theme: God's kingdom of peace and justice seems remote, but we are blessed in our belief that someday the Kingdom will be fulfilled.

Readings: Micah 5:2-5*a*; Luke 1:39-45 (46-55); Hebrews 10:5-10

Call to Worship (Canticle of Mary):

Leader: My soul proclaims the greatness of the LORD,

People: **my spirit rejoices in God my Savior, who has looked with favor on me, a lowly servant.**

Leader: From this day all generations shall call me blessed:

People: **the Almighty has done great things for me and holy is the name of the LORD, whose mercy is on those who fear God from generation to generation.**

Leader: The arm of the LORD is strong, and has scattered the proud in their conceit.

People: **God has cast down the mighty from their thrones and lifted up the lowly.**

Leader: God has filled the hungry with good things and sent the rich empty away.

People: **God has come to the aid of Israel, the chosen servant, remembering the promise of mercy, the promise made to our forebears, to Abraham and his children for ever.**

Pastoral Prayer:

The eve of Emmanuel! O dear God, precious Savior, we fidget and fret with impatience. We want peace in our world dropped in our laps. We want justice for all to fall out of the sky. And we aren't willing to do your legwork. We act as though either you haven't called us to love our neighbors or we don't *really* believe that you are coming again. We punch our tickets with an embarrassed response to an altar call, and then sit on our hands. God, forgive our need for lazy, simplistic answers to the world's woes. Give us the heart of Christmas, not only during this season of pomp and celebration, but every day of the dreary winter, the hopeful spring, the doldrums of summer, and the musty autumn. Give us a new heart, sweet Jesus. Amen. (Thomas Gildermeister)

SERMON BRIEFS

WAITING AND HOPING

MICAH 5:2-5*a*

Micah 1:1 tells us that he was a prophet during the reign of Jotham, Ahaz, and Hezekiah in Judah, dates somewhere around 742-687 B.C.E. Micah was a contemporary of Isaiah and Hosea. He came from Moresheth, a small village outside Jerusalem. He was from among the common folk. Micah was an advocate of the pure worship of God and for social justice. Within his prophecy, there are words of judgment and promised hope of restoration.

I. Micah's Message

It may be helpful, in studying this passage, to look at the complete pronouncement from Micah 4:6–5:9. Prior to verse 5:2 in the pronouncement, there is a siege (5:1). The people of God are walled in; they are surrounded. There is an urgent need for help. Someone must come to the rescue. In the midst of the siege, the prophet speaks a word of hope, though the hearers probably did not see it that way.

In verse 2, the prophet reclaims the promises of the past by proclaiming that a shepherd king will come from Bethlehem to rule Israel, just like David. Matthew 2:6 quotes this verse to show Jesus as the fulfillment of the prophecy.

Verse 3 is not a happy verse to hear under siege. It refers to the time of exile. God will give up God's people until this new ruler comes. Examine Micah 4:10: "Writhe and groan, O daughter of Zion, like a woman in labor; . . . you shall go to Babylon. There you will be rescued. . . ." The image of labor is the suffering pains the people must go through until the coming of the new ruler.

In 5:4 the prophet uses the shepherd imagery. The new ruler will protect and provide for God's people. None of the messianic prophecies speak of the Messiah to come as the incarnation of God. This prophecy comes close, however, declaring that he will care for the people in God's strength and majesty.

Verse 5 gives a unique characteristic of the ruler to come as one of peace. This is contrary to the expected military messiah of the Old Testament and even during the time of Jesus.

II. Waiting Then and Now

It may be tempting to look at the Micah passage simply as a prophecy that was fulfilled in Jesus' coming. The New Testament confirms this interpretation. However, do not miss out on the original historical context. If we use the imagery of the "woman in labor," then we see that the exiles had a time of waiting ahead of them. This would have been a time of waiting and suffering like a woman in travail. Think of the great anticipation and joy that occurs once labor is over and she has delivered. Hearing these words under siege, the hearers were probably not very happy or hopeful. "How long?" was probably the question in their minds. They must have thought this prophet Micah had a great imagination to dream of such a messiah coming and restoring them. No Davidic king had saved them from such great powers before. What a wonderful, unbelievable dream this was. The prophet had no way of knowing it would be another seven hundred years before it came to be. How wonderful that the dream came true in Jesus.

God's people still find themselves waiting. We are in the "between time." The Messiah has come and reigns as our Savior,

Jesus Christ. In the present time there is suffering and sin, but the shepherd king Jesus has redeemed his people and brings wholeness and renewal in the midst of pain and struggle. In Jesus we find hope, for the final fulfillment of God's promise is anticipated as we wait for the Second Coming. (Marcia T. Thompson)

BLESSED BELIEF IN PROMISES

LUKE 1:39-45 (46-55)

A prominent nineteenth-century French author was asked by the wife of an undistinguished writer to support her husband's bid for a place in the prestigious French Academy.

"I beg you, vote for my husband," she implored. "If he's not elected, he'll die."

The noted author pledged his support. Nevertheless the woman's husband failed to be elected. Several months later, another seat in the French Academy became vacant, and again the woman called upon her prominent friend to solicit his vote for her husband. This time, however, he reminded her of their previous conversation and replied, "I kept my promise, but he did not keep his."

Even the best of people occasionally fail to keep their promises. It is not just deliberate liars who don't fulfill their word. All of us have shared in this shortcoming at some time or another. In our enthusiasm we may promise more than we can or even should perform. At other times, circumstances overwhelm our good intentions. Factors we can't control get in the way. In our desire to offer comfort, we promise our children that "Grandpa will get better, don't worry." But he doesn't. We promise a friend, "I'll play tennis with you at 5:30." But then we have to work late. We promise ourselves, "This year I'm going to start exercising regularly." But a legion of obstacles rise up before us.

Promises are certainly easier to make than they are to keep. But we can't get along very well without promises. So many of the basic structures and institutions of our society depend upon the reliability of promises.

Believing in a great promise transforms life. For one thing, it fills life with joyful anticipation. When we genuinely believe some wonderful event is coming, we are given a foretaste of the happiness of the future. The event that has not yet arrived becomes real in the emotions of the present moment. We see this truth as we look at the children who eagerly anticipate Christmas. Their beaming smiles and gleeful chattering tell the story. Their belief in a promise has permeated their present with excitement.

Belief in a great promise also empowers us so that we can endure an unfortunate or unfulfilling present. In Psalms 119, there is a passage that states, "This is my comfort in my distress, that your promise gives me life" (v. 50). Belief in God's promise enables us to continue despite the perplexing brokenness of the present, for we trust that God will fill every emptiness and mend every broken aspect of life.

Belief in a great promise does something more: It motivates us to ready ourselves for what is coming. When we accept a promise, we begin living in the light of the coming reality. When a woman and a man get engaged, they don't wait until they are married before they start being faithful to each other. The promises have an impact upon their present. It changes them. It obligates them to live a special kind of life even before they say that decisive, "I do." So it is when we believe in the promise of God. We put our life in order so that we can be truly receptive to what lies before us.

But promises often heard grow stale, even divine promises. It is easy to start treating our God-words as no more than just words, mere sounds that appease our anxieties and evoke fond feelings; holy-toned utterances that are useful as psychological tools to comfort us when we feel threatened and to reassure us when we feel unsettled. In a world where generations have come and gone without seeing mighty acts of God, it is easy to assume that any talk about divine promises is little more than whistling in the dark, albeit to a religious melody. Mary was not exempt from this inclination. But in her life it was overcome. And so she sang, "My soul magnifies the LORD, and my spirit rejoices in God my Savior" (Luke 1:47). With blessed belief may we sing such promise-filled songs. Amen. (Craig M. Watts)

THE MYSTERY AHEAD

HEBREWS 10:5-10

As we come to the final Sunday in Advent, the anticipation of welcoming anew the Christ child reaches its zenith. As we prepare to give in to the great joy of the celebration, this scripture passage surprises us. It reminds us that the mystery of the incarnation makes sense only in light of the paschal mystery. We celebrate the birth of Jesus only because of the death and resurrection of Jesus. Advent and Christmas point ahead to the cross. This text is a pointer.

I. Remaining in Christ

The anonymous writer of Hebrews seeks to sustain persons, predominantly Jewish Christians, who are wavering and in danger of abandoning their faith. The writer seeks to persuade them to remain in Christ by assuring them that God has acted decisively and finally in history to make them acceptable before God. Redemption and sanctification by the work of Christ are spoken of in the perfect tense. The work is complete. There is no need for remediation or repetition. By means of interpretation of all three portions of the Jewish Scriptures, Jesus is shown to be superior to the angels, to Moses, to the Levitical priesthood, and, in this biblical passage, to the sacrificial system.

II. Why Read This at Advent?

On first consideration, this lection seems out of place in this season of the liturgical year. Familiar Advent themes such as preparation, expectation, and hope are absent. Yet it may correct the way in which we focus upon Christ's coming, especially if we are prone to being too sentimental over the baby Jesus. Hebrews is identified by many commentators as a sermon from the early Apostolic Age (as early as 52-54 C.E.) celebrating the significance of Christ. As such, it reminds us that the early church found Jesus' significance not in his birth, miraculous though it may be, but in his obedience unto death. This drove their interpretation of him. What is more needed at Advent?

III. Be Careful!

A great temptation to which Christians have fallen repeatedly, with disastrous consequences, is the idea that Christianity has superseded the Jewish faith. Hebrews, with its language of Christ's superiority to key aspects of the Jewish religion, is especially liable to be interpreted in this way. Indeed, Hebrews has been used to underwrite much supersessionist theology. We need to take care to avoid this.

Sensitivity to such issues may lead some to question Hebrews. Does it somehow disqualify itself? The use of the Jewish Scriptures to interpret Jesus, such as in Psalm 40, affirms his continuity with the Jewish faith. Indeed, it places Jesus the Jew, who is the same "yesterday and today and forever" (Heb. 13:8), within the Jewish context for all time.

However, understanding Hebrews involves working within yet another Advent tension. This time the tension is that of the real and proper joy over the birth of Jesus, and the realization of what lies ahead.

The dual themes of welcoming the baby Jesus in knowledge of what awaits him was expressed in stunning fashion by W. H. Auden in his Christmas oratorio, "For the Time Being" (which is excellent spiritual reading for Advent). Auden lets us hear Mary's anxieties in the words she speaks to her newborn son:

> In your first few hours of life here, O have you
> Chosen already what death must be your own?
> How soon will you start on the Sorrowful Way?
> Dream while you may.

(W. H. Auden, *Collected Longer Poems* [New York: Random House, 1969], p. 171)

Such is an appropriate Advent word for we who in baptism receive new life by being united with him in death. (Philip E. Thompson)

DECEMBER 31, 2000

First Sunday After Christmas

Worship Theme: Faith and wisdom grow over time when we spend time in God's house.

Readings: 1 Samuel 2:18-20, 26; Colossians 3:12-17; Luke 2:41-52

Call to Worship (Psalm 148:1-14):

Leader: Praise the LORD! Praise the LORD from the heavens, praise the LORD, in the heights!

People: **Praise the LORD, all his angels, praise the LORD, all his hosts!**

Leader: Praise the LORD, sun and moon, praise the LORD, all shining stars!

People: **Praise the LORD, highest heavens, and all waters above the heavens!**

Leader: Let them praise the name of the LORD, who commanded and they were created,

People: **who established them for ever and ever, and fixed their bounds which cannot be passed.**

Leader: Praise the LORD from the earth, sea monsters and all deeps,

People: **fire and hail, snow and smoke, stormy wind fulfilling God's command!**

Leader: Mountains and all hills, fruit trees and all cedars!

People: **Beasts and all cattle, creeping things and flying birds!**

Leader: Kings of the earth and all peoples, princes and all rulers of the earth!

People: **Young men and maidens together, old men and children!**

Leader: Let them praise the name of the LORD, whose name alone is exalted, whose glory is above earth and heaven.

People: **God has raised up a horn for his people, praise for all his faithful ones, for the people of Israel who are near their God. Praise the LORD!**

Pastoral Prayer:

How surprising is your wisdom, Holy Christ! We praise you for turning the tables and keeping us a little off balance, but we plant ourselves too firmly in our ways of living. We rarely can hear the faithful and wise words of the children. Too often we find reasons to stay away from this community of faith. Some here today are reluctant to become a part of any church. Too many "good reasons" not to commit. O Lord, open our eyes and ears so that the joy of church is evident; so that the blessing of study is clear; so that the songs and Scriptures of old brim with newness and meaning. Dear God, many resolutions will be made in the next twenty-four hours. By your grace, may we all resolve to follow Christ into your House and out into the world to love you, know you, and serve you in all that we do. In the name of the Messiah, the Christ Jesus. Amen. (Thomas Gildermeister)

SERMON BRIEFS

FOLLOWING SAMUEL'S EXAMPLE

1 SAMUEL 2:18-20, 26

In an interview, renowned West Coast furniture maker Sam Maloof told how a young man came to him seeking an apprenticeship. Unfortunately, there was no room for another up-and-coming woodworker to study with this master, so Sam called his friend George, who works in Pennsylvania. The young man and George spoke over the phone. Sadly, the interview went poorly. The young man reported that George wouldn't take him.

"Why not?" asked Sam.

"He said, 'I could not teach you to sweep my floor in three months.' I told him already knew how to sweep floors. And then he just hung up on me."

Sam said the young man should have said, "If it takes a year, I want to learn how to do it."

Samuel was in Yahweh's service. There was never any question of "How long?," unlike the cries of the psalmist. Samuel did what was required of him. He didn't live at home with his brothers, sisters, mother, and father. And yet, he was at home. His mother continued the family ties, making him coats and taking them to him on the annual excursion to the temple at Shiloh. It's like sending homemade cookies to a child in college or at seminary.

Whenever anyone asks me how I came to enter the ministry, I invariably tell a little story: When I was five years old, I was playing on the front porch at my maternal grandmother's house. She and Mom were talking about this and that. At some point, Grandma placed her pudgy little hand on top of my head and said to my mother, "Eric is going to be a minister when he grows up."

"Over my dead body!" retorted Mom, who knew from past experience what a difficult task lies ahead for ministers and their families. Even I couldn't see myself preparing a sermon a week, much less getting up in the pulpit on Sunday morning and preaching. I was going to be a musician, or a psychologist, or an English teacher, not a preacher.

The first day of seminary classes, the professor asked us to introduce ourselves and to say why we came to seminary. Everyone had something nice to say. Finally, it was my turn. I told the class where I'd gone to school, and made the usual introductions. The professor asked me why I had come to seminary. "To spite my mother," I replied. Needless to say, she wouldn't have me doing anything else.

Here is Samuel, growing in stature and favor. As Samuel increases, not only does Eli begin to decrease in importance, but so do Eli's sons, Phinehas and Hophni. They lose face before God as Samuel surpasses them, standing in stark contrast with his mentor's children. He practices what they in their greed and lust for power had long since forgotten, that silence isn't really silent, and even darkness has bold luminosity for those who wait on it. The window of opportunity is flung open for God to sweep in and call out to young Samuel, who is something of an essentialist. That is, he is gripped by the realization that there is a given nature from which many of us have become estranged—God. Hophni and Phinehas have become separated from God, and God's fury is expressed in willful destruction of these two failed servants. (Eric Killinger)

BE-ATTITUDES FOR A NEW MILLENNIUM

COLOSSIANS 3:12-17

Today is the day. At 11:59 this evening, I, like many of my friends who were into science fiction during the 1960s and 1970s, will hear the strains of Strauss's *Also Sprach Zarathustra* as I await the coming of the year 2001. The end of the twentieth century brought with it "the cultural equivalent of an earthquake," as one scholar put it. Now we face the rebuilding of the predominant Western civilization into a new global civilization, with new sensitivities and emphases. How will we, the church of the living God, speak to these realities? The scripture for today speaks to this question.

I. Be Positive

In the preceding verses, Paul describes what must be "taken off" and rejected by the Christian. Most non-Christians and many Christians regard faith as primarily negative in content, like the boy Stephen in Clyde Edgerton's *Where Trouble Sleeps* (Chapel Hill, N.C.: Algonquin Books, 1997): "A lot of it—getting saved—had to do with visiting old people and going to church every time you were supposed to . . . and not drinking beer and whiskey. And it had to do with not saying ugly words, not running away from your mama . . . and not playing in the mud."

In verses 12-13, Paul turns to a positive note, providing the runway commentary for a Christian fashion show. The "laundry list" of virtues that a Christian wears is lovely, and any decent commentary will help you to explicate the textures of these virtues. The primary emphasis here is that God chose us to go into his own closet to choose our wardrobe!

II. Be Perfect

The difference between a nice wardrobe and a stylish look is the "tied-together" style of the accessories. In the case of the Christian, love is the attitude that brings the parts of our characters into a single whole. Love, in the words of one writer, is "not an emotion but a policy." Just as wood putty fills cracks and defects in wood so that the wood might be useful, so love covers the individual defects and idiosyncrasies in our faith so that we can be useful to God. As described in The Message translation, love is our "basic, all-purpose garment" (v. 14).

III. Be Peaceful and Thankful

Living at peace with other Christians is sometimes difficult. Noah had as much to fear from the woodpecker inside the ark as he did the storm outside. Our "umpire of conduct," paraphrasing the Greek, is the rule of peace. "Will my action promote peace in the church?" is an excellent guide to contributing to the progress of each church. The corollary to this question is that of thankfulness: Will I, will God, be thankful for how I conducted myself toward fellow believers? The refusal to behave in a peaceful manner toward others, coming out of gratitude toward God, results in a loss of harmony in our own hearts.

IV. Be Praise-Full

The "culture wars" of the 1990s invaded the church, so much so that division rather than diversity characterized the dispute over the proper style of worship. In this scripture, Paul proposes a basis for unity in this endless debate: If it is in harmony with the Word, it is appropriate for worship. If the word of Christ dwells in you, then whether you sing psalms or gospel songs, praise choruses or anthems, have a praise team or a robed choir, is of little importance. If the word of Christ is not in you or your praise, your praise is hollow anyway. Worship is the only remedy to the irrelevance of the twenty-first century church, for only God is the only constant priority in the history of the church.

IV. Be Purposeful

The name of Jesus Christ is the center of our Christian living. His name provides both our identity ("I am a Christian") and our authority ("I do this in Jesus' name") for our conduct. As a Christian acting in his name, I need not cower nor bully, neither whine nor despair as I hear the theme from "2001" this evening. I am adequately prepared for the new millennium. (Mickey Kirkindoll)

NOT HOME ALONE

LUKE 2:41-52

I can't help but think of the movie *Home Alone* when I read Luke 2:41-52. Of course the star of the story is not Kevin, the little boy left behind when his family left on vacation, but Jesus. In the bustle and confusion of getting ready for a trip, he gets left behind in Jerusalem. Jesus' mother, Mary, was even slower than Kevin's mother to realize the child was missing. Instead of a few hours, it took a whole day for Jesus' parents to notice that his passenger seat was empty.

The family had been in Jerusalem for the Passover, the most important religious holiday of the year for Israel. After the festivities, they packed to head back home to Nazareth, their hometown. Jesus' family was traveling with a group of others. Apparently his parents thought he was with some other people. I can imagine the shock they must have felt when they realized they left him alone in the big city.

It took Mary and Joseph three days to find Jesus. Three days of anxiety, tears, and guilt, I imagine. I can hear it all now: "We should have been paying more attention. We should have been absolutely certain he was with us. How could we have left him there? What rotten parents we are."

But after three days of frantic searching, they neared the great Temple. They turned a corner and there he was. He wasn't crying and worried. He didn't blame his parents for neglecting him. No, instead Jesus was sitting with the teachers, the religious experts, asking questions and listening to their answers. It seems that the people who had heard Jesus had been pretty impressed with what he had to say.

His parents were more appalled than impressed. When they saw that Jesus was not frightened or in any kind of danger, they got upset in a different way. Parents are like that, kids. Sometimes if they think you're lost or in trouble, and when they find out that you're all right, they don't know what to do first, hug you or spank you for not listening to them in the first place. It seems that's the way it was with Mary and Joseph. When they found Jesus, his mother said, "Child, why have you treated us like this? Look, your father and I have been searching for you in great anxiety." In other words, "Jesus, we've worried ourselves to death because we thought you were lost. You should be ashamed of yourself for making us feel so terrible." Have your parents ever talked to you like that, kids?

Well, what did Jesus say? "Mom, Dad, I'm sorry. I'll never do something like that again." Is that what he said? No, what he said was, "Why were you searching for me? Did you not know that I must be [about] my Father's [business]?" Jesus' earthly father, Joseph, was a carpenter. Jesus wasn't sitting there with a saw and hammer. He wasn't talking about his earthly father's business, but that of his heavenly father, God. Jesus had left his parents and caused them a lot of worry by going to the Temple to get involved in divine business.

What do you think about that? Those of you who are parents, I know what you think. You'd go wild if your child tried a stunt like that. So would I. Most of you who are still living with your parents probably wouldn't want to be left in a big city without your folks. But if you did ever take off on your own without permission for a little unsupervised adventure, chances are you know you'd face a lot of love but also plenty of trouble when you got back home. Let's be clear about this: The lesson we can learn from this episode in Jesus' life is not that it's all right to take off on your own without your parents' permission. There are some lessons that this story about Jesus does suggest.

First, there is something more important than parents and families. Jesus realized this early in his life, and he taught it later as an adult. He said, "Whoever loves father or mother more than me is not worthy of me; and whoever loves son or daughter more than me is not worthy of me" (Matt. 10:37). God is first.

One time when Jesus was preaching in front of a crowd, Mary got concerned. She came with some of Jesus' brothers to get him. Some of the people told Jesus his family was looking for him. What did Jesus say? He said that his mother and brothers are those who hear the Word of God and do it (see Matt. 12:46-50). Jesus loved his family, but he knew that doing what God wanted him to do was the most important thing ever. Kids and parents need to know this as well.

Second, kids, you need to be patient with your parents. Someone once said that a child becomes an adult three years before his parents think he does, and about two years after he thinks he does. Some parents really don't know how to let their children grow up. Not long ago I heard a fifty-year-old woman say, "My mom is still trying to tell me how to live my life." It happens.

Third, listen to your parents. Even though Jesus did fine in Jerusalem all on his own, when his parents told him how upset they were, he paid attention. The Scriptures tell us that when he went back home with his folks, he "was obedient to them." It's tempting to close your ears to your parents when they say things you don't want to hear.

Maybe you feel that you know more than your parents. Sometimes you might be right. Jesus certainly knew more than his parents. Can you imagine raising the son of God? Still, he listened to his earthly parents. (Craig M. Watts)

BENEDICTIONS

Advent Season

We have heard the prophet's words of consolation for the humble, and we have heard the Baptist's words of judgment for the haughty.

As with these ancient worthies we anticipate the Coming One, let us prepare for Christ's table-turning presence, as he comes to redeem the shame of the lowly and to reveal the sham of the lofty. Let us receive his righteous judgment, that we might bestow his gentle consolation.

Send us home, O God, in the assurance that the power of the Most High will overshadow us as it did Mary. Then, when your surprises burst upon us, we shall greet them as Mary did hers, in the spirit of faithful surrender, saying, "Behold, we are the servants of the Lord; let it be to us according to your will" (Luke 1:38 adapted).

Christmas Season

L: Servants of God, depart now in peace; prophets, go in power—
P: For we have seen salvation prepared by the merciful hand of God.
L: With Mary and Joseph ponder these things; with Anna and Simeon praise the Lord.
P: Let us grow and be strong, that we may find wisdom.
A: May God's hand and ours hold the hands of earth's children.

Someday soon we will be standing by the side of the road when someone walks by. And behold, we will recognize in that person the presence of Christ. When we are asked to "come and see" where Christ is staying, let us go. Let us not hesitate, for there we are needed; let us not hesitate, for we too have need. Let us make haste to the God who dwells with our neighbor, and together we will discover what once was hidden.

Season After Epiphany

Arrest us, O God. The time of preparation is now past. The time of expectation is now fulfilled. As the new world rides into our midst like a child on the shoulder of Christ, let us stop—and look—and listen. For the form of our old world shall pass away, and the newly born shall lead us.

Go now in the knowledge that you are known by God and that you may know God. Go in the assurance that what is known is not as important as *who* is known. And go in the confidence that *whoever* is known will be loved.

Lenten Season

As we go forth into the world, let our worship be to us as the rainbow was to Noah: a reminder of your covenant with us, that we might be instruments of your blessing.

The journey of Jesus took him into a world of suffering, rejection, and death. As we go into this same world, embolden us, O God, that we too might take up our cross and follow you. Teach us to ask not that you shield us from temptation, but that you keep us from evil in temptation's midst.

Go forth among your neighbors as ambassadors of the Lord, your eyes enlightened with God's commandments, your minds quickened with God's testimonies, your hearts rejoicing in God's law, and your souls aflame with God's love.

Easter Season

O God, as you have brought us together to think the thoughts of Christ, send us forth to do the deeds of Christ. Let the affections of our hearts and the deeds of our hands proclaim our devotion to you and our love for one another.

O God, who takes no pleasure in creeds unmatched by deeds, let the works of our hands confirm the words of our lips. Curb our impulse to proclaim our faith apart from works, that by our works we may proclaim our faith (see James 2:18).

No one has ever seen God. But, if an angel appears and tells you to rise and go down a desert road, do not be afraid. Though barren, the desert is the place of revelation. As you pass through, someone will draw near. It may be the risen Christ, disguised as a weary stranger. Behold the face of your God, and offer the stranger your water.

Season After Pentecost

L: Spirit, steer us from our path of destruction into the way of life.
P: Sustain us as we go with the bread and the wine of the new world.
L: Guide us to your beacon,
P: Endowing our ability and inspiring our will.
L: Be our bridge over troubled waters and the step that moves our feet;
A: And be ahead of us, among us, and behind us until our journey's end.

The love of Christ constrains us. In the staying power of the Lord, we find the courage to dream. Therefore, let us dream passionately. In the abiding will of the Lord, we find the determination to act. Therefore, let us act resolutely. In the enduring spirit of the Lord, we find the grace to persevere. Therefore, let us persevere boldly.

Go to the world in confidence, for there the table of the Lord is spread. Draw near; drink from its cup, and receive the mercy of God. Draw near; partake of its bread and find the grace of God. Go, and the feast shall be to you as you shall be to your neighbor: a very present help in time of trouble.

Special Occasions

O God of beginnings, encourage our hearts as we greet this new hour, this new day, this new year! Knit us gently together in love, so that when we go apart in body, we shall be one in spirit.

We sang your praises, Lord, and as our voices mingled, our elders became youths, and our youths became elders. You are the One who embraces all generations, who makes of us together more than we can make of ourselves alone. Every day we will bless you for this, O God, that the world may witness the faithfulness of your word and the graciousness of your work.

Eternal God, you have made us co-laborers with you in a good but imperfect world, in a formed but changing universe, in a healthy but precarious environment, and in a growing but dangerous society. As you send us forth to do your work, make us aware of the dangers and the opportunities of our task. Give us the patience of those who, without your blessing, would undertake nothing, and the impatience of those who, with your blessing, would undertake anything.

O God, look with compassion upon the city; wipe away every tear from its eyes, and banish death; exile its grief and pain to the desert, to perish there of thirst. O Lord, we cry out! Visit us! Let your new Jerusalem come, that you might look upon us without weeping and enter a city where every foot is leaping with joy on golden streets.

TEXT GUIDE°

THE REVISED COMMON LECTIONARY (2000)

Sunday	First Lesson	Second Lesson	Gospel Lesson	Psalm
1/2/00	Isa. 60:1-6	Eph. 3:1-12	Matt. 2:1-12	Ps. 72:1-7, 10-14
1/9/00	Gen. 1:1-5	Acts 19:1-7	Mark 1:4-11	Ps. 29
1/16/00	1 Sam. 3:1-10 (11-20)	1 Cor. 6:12-20	John 1:43-51	Ps. 139:1-6, 13-18
1/23/00	Jon. 3:1-5, 10	1 Cor. 7:29-31	Mark 1:14-20	Ps. 62:5-12
1/30/00	Deut. 18:15-20	1 Cor. 8:1-13	Mark 1:21-28	Ps. 111
2/6/00	Isa. 40:21-31	1 Cor. 9:16-23	Mark 1:29-39	Ps. 147:1-11, 20c
2/13/00	2 Kings 5:1-14	1 Cor. 9:24-27	Mark 1:40-45	Ps. 30
2/20/00	Isa. 43:18-25	2 Cor. 1:18-22	Mark 2:1-12	Ps. 41
2/27/00	Hos. 2:14-20	2 Cor. 3:1-6	Mark 2:13-22	Ps. 103:1-13, 22
3/5/00	2 Kings 2:1-12	2 Cor. 4:3-6	Mark 9:2-9	Ps. 50:1-6
3/12/00	Gen 9:8-17	1 Pet. 3:18-22	Mark 1:9-15	Ps. 25:1-10
3/19/00	Gen 17:1-7, 15-16	Rom. 4:13-25	Mark 8:31-38	Ps. 22:23-31
3/26/00	Ex. 20:1-17	1 Cor. 1:18-25	John 2:13-22	Ps. 19
4/2/00	Num 21:4-9	Eph. 2:1-10	John 3:14-21	Ps. 107:1-3, 17-22
4/9/00	Jer. 31:31-34	Heb. 5:5-10	John 12:20-33	Ps. 51:1-12
4/16/00	Isa. 50:4-9a	Phil. 2:5-11	Mark 14:1–15:47	Ps. 31:9-16
4/21/00	Isa. 52:13–53:12	Heb. 10:16-25	John 18:1–19:42	Ps. 22

°This guide represents one possible selection of lessons and psalms from the lectionary. For a complete listing see *The Revised Common Lectionary.*

Sunday	First Lesson	Second Lesson	Gospel Lesson	Psalm
4/23/00	Acts 10:34-43	1 Cor. 15:1-11	John 20:1-18	Ps. 118:1-2, 14-24
4/30/00	Acts 4:32-35	1 John 1:1–2:2	John 20:19-31	Ps. 133
5/7/00	Acts 3:12-19	1 John 3:1-7	Luke 24:36b-48	Ps. 4
5/14/00	Acts 4:5-12	1 John 3:16-24	John 10:11-18	Ps. 23
5/21/00	Acts 8:26-40	1 John 4:7-21	John 15:1-8	Ps. 22:25-31
5/28/00	Acts 10:44-48	1 John 5:1-6	John 15:9-17	Ps. 98
6/4/00	Acts 1:15-17, 21-26	1 John 5:9-13	John 17:6-19	Ps. 1
6/11/00	Acts 2:1-21	Rom. 8:22-27	John 15:26-27; 16:4b-15	Ps. 104:24-34, 35b
6/18/00	Isa. 6:1-8	Rom. 8:12-17	John 3:1-17	Ps. 29
6/25/00	1 Sam. 17:(1a, 4-11, 19-23) 32-49	2 Cor. 6:1-13	Mark 4:35-41	Ps. 9:9-20
7/2/00	2 Sam. 1:1, 17-27	2 Cor. 8:7-15	Mark 5:21-43	Ps. 130
7/9/00	2 Sam. 5:1-5, 9-10	2 Cor. 12:2-10	Mark 6:1-13	Ps. 48
7/16/00	2 Sam. 6:1-5, 12b-19	Eph. 1:3-14	Mark 6:14-29	Ps. 24
7/23/00	2 Sam. 7:1-14a	Eph. 2:11-22	Mark 6:30-34, 53-56	Ps. 89:20-37
7/30/00	2 Sam. 11:1-15	Eph. 3:14-21	John 6:1-21	Ps. 14
8/6/00	2 Sam. 11:26–12:13a	Eph. 4:1-16	John 6:24-35	Ps. 51:1-12
8/13/00	2 Sam. 18:5-9, 15, 31-33	Eph. 4:25–5:2	John 6:35, 41-51	Ps. 130
8/20/00	1 Kings 2:10-12; 3:3-14	Eph. 5:15-20	John 6:51-58	Ps. 111

*This guide represents one possible selection of lessons and psalms from the lectionary. For a complete listing see *The Revised Common Lectionary*.

Sunday	First Lesson	Second Lesson	Gospel Lesson	Psalm
8/27/00	1 Kings 8:(1, 6, 10-11) 22-30, 41-43	Eph. 6:10-20	John 6:56-69	Ps. 84
9/3/00	Song of Sol. 2:8-13	James 1:17-27	Mark 7:1-8, 14-15, 21-23	Ps. 45:1-2, 6-9
9/10/00	Prov. 22:1-2, 8-9, 22-23	James 2:1-10 (11-13), 14-17	Mark 7:24-37	Ps. 125
9/17/00	Prov. 1:20-33	James 3:1-12	Mark 8:27-38	Ps. 19
9/24/00	Prov. 31:10-31	James 3:13–4:3, 7-8a	Mark 9:30-37	Ps. 1
10/1/00	Esther 7:1-6, 9-10; 9:20-22	James 5:13-20	Mark 9:38-50	Ps. 124
10/8/00	Job 1:1; 2:1-10	Heb. 1:1-4; 2:5-12	Mark 10:2-16	Ps. 26
10/15/00	Job 23:1-9, 16-17	Heb. 4:12-16	Mark 10:17-31	Ps. 22:1-15
10/22/00	Job 38:1-7 (34-41)	Heb. 5:1-10	Mark 10:35-45	Ps. 104:1-9, 24, 35c
10/29/00	Job 42:1-6, 10-17	Heb. 7:23-28	Mark 10:46-52	Ps. 34:1-8, (19-22)
11/5/00	Ruth 1:1-18	Heb. 9:11-14	Mark 12:28-34	Ps. 146
11/12/00	Ruth 3:1-5; 4:13-17	Heb. 9:24-28	Mark 12:38-44	Ps. 127
11/19/00	1 Sam. 1:4-20	Heb. 10:11-14 (15-18), 19-25	Mark 13:1-18	Ps. 16
11/26/00	2 Sam. 23:1-7	Rev. 1:4b-8	John 18:33-37	Ps. 135:1-12, (13-18)
12/3/00	Jer. 33:14-16	1 Thess. 3:9-13	Luke 21:25-36	Ps. 25:1-10
12/10/00	Mal. 3:1-4	Luke 3:1-6	Phil. 1:3-11	Luke 1:68-79
12/17/00	Zeph. 3:14-20	Phil. 4:4-7	Luke 3:7-18	Isa. 12:2-6
12/24/00	Mic. 5:2-5a	Luke 1:39-45, (46-55)	Heb. 10:5-10	Luke 1:47-55
12/31/00	1 Sam. 2:18-20, 26	Col. 3:12-17	Luke 2:41-52	Ps. 148

*This guide represents one possible selection of lessons and psalms from the lectionary. For a complete listing see *The Revised Common Lectionary.*

CONTRIBUTORS

Don Aycock
McLean Baptist Church
4794 N. Milnor
Memphis, TN 38128

Gerald Borchert
Northern Baptist Theological
    Seminary
660 E. Butlerfield Rd.
Lombard, IL 60148-5698

Linda McKinnish Bridges
Baptist Theological Seminary
    at Richmond
P. O. Box 9157
Richmond, VA 23227

Michael B. Brown
Centenary United Methodist
    Church
P. O. Box 658
Winston-Salem, NC 27102

Bob Buchanan
Parkway Baptist Church
5975 State Bridge Road
Duluth, GA 30155

Joseph Byrd
Senior Pastor
Stewart Road Church of God
1199 Stewart Road
Monroe, MI 48162

Carol Cavin
Brentwood United Methodist
    Church
309 Franklin Road
Brentwood, TN 37027

Jim Clardy
Grace United Methodist
    Church
2905 N. Mt. Juliet Road
Mt. Juliet, TN 37122

Earl C. Davis
Trinity Baptist Church
8899 Trinity Road
Cordova, TN 38018

Nancy L. deClaisse-Walford
McAfee School of Theology
Mercer University
3001 Mercer University Drive
Atlanta, GA 30341

David S. Dockery
Union University
1050 University Drive
Jackson, TN 38305

Thomas Gildermeister
Cook's United Methodist
    Church
7919 Lebanon Road
Mt. Juliet, TN 37122

Kay Gray
Hamilton United Methodist
  Church
3105 Hamilton Church Road
Antioch, TN 37013

Mark D. Haines
City Road Chapel United
  Methodist Church
701 S. Gallatin Road
Madison, TN 37115-4054

Scott Hudgins
Wake Forest University
The Divinity School
Winston Salem, NC 27709

Derl Keefer
Three Rivers Church of the
  Nazarene
15770 Coon Hollow Road
Three Rivers, MI 49093

Jim Killen
Trinity United Methodist
  Church
P. O. Box 5247
Beaumont, TX 77726-5247

Eric Killinger
408 E. Boyd Road
Hogansville, GA 30230

John Killinger
127 Yorkshire Drive
Williamsburg, VA 23185

Gary G. Kindley
First United Methodist Church
508 N. Gray Street
Killeen, TX 76541

Mickey Kirkindoll
First Baptist Church
P. O. Box 395
Jefferson, GA 30549

Harold L. Martin
Grace United Methodist
  Church
2905 N. Mt. Juliet Road
Mt. Juliet, TN 37122

David Mauldin
Brentwood Cumberland
  Presbyterian Church
516 Franklin Road
Brentwood, TN 37027

Carol M. Noren
North Park Theological
  Seminary
3225 W. Foster Ave.
Chicago, IL 60625

Sam Parkes
First United Methodist
  Church
P. O. Box 512
Tullahoma, TN 37388

Kathleen Peterson
Palos United Methodist
  Church
P. O. Box 398
Palos Heights, IL 60463

Jon R. Roebuck
First Baptist Church
P. O. Box 347
Gatlinburg, TN 37738

Vance P. Ross
First United Methodist
  Church of Hyattsville
6804 Calverton Drive
Hyattsville, MD 20782

Donna Schaper
165 West Street
Amherst, MA 01002

Michael Shannon
First Christian Church
200 Mountcastle Drive
Johnson City, TN 37615

Robert Shannon
P. O. Box 716
Valle Crucis, NC 28691

Thomas R. Steagald
P. O. Box 427
Marshville, NC 28103

Marcia Thompson
Pendleton Baptist Church
P. O. Box 128
Pendleton, NC 27862

Philip E. Thompson
Pendleton Baptist Church
P. O. Box 128
Pendleton, NC 27862

Timothy Warren
Dallas Theological Seminary
3909 Swiss Avenue
Dallas, TX 75204

Craig M. Watts
First Christian Church
7700 U.S. 42
Louisville, KY 40241

INDEX

OLD TESTAMENT

NEW TESTAMENT